The Complete Book of Aussie Yarns

The Complete Book of Aussie Yarns

Mike Hayes

ABC
BOOKS

Published by ABC Books for the
AUSTRALIAN BROADCASTING CORPORATION
GPO Box 9994 Sydney NSW 2001

First published in one volume in 1998
Reprinted September 1999
Reprinted October 2000

National Library of Australia
Cataloguing-in-Publication entry
  Hayes, Mike.
  The complete book of Aussie yarns.

  ISBN 0 7333 0709 4.

  1. Country life – Australia – Humour. 2. Farm life –
  Australia – Humour. 3. Australian wit and humour.
  I. Australian Broadcasting Corporation. II. Title.

A823.3

Cover design Toni Hope-Caten
Colour separations by Finsbury, Adelaide
Printed and bound in Australia by
Australian Print Group, Maryborough, Victoria

Yarns from all round Australia
Copyright © Mike Hayes 1993
First published 1993. Reprinted 1994, 1995, 1996, 1997 twice
Illustrated by Colin Cameron
Designed by Tony Denny
Set in 10/11pt Garamond Book by Midland Typesetters

Tell us anotheree!
Copyright © Mike Hayes 1994
First published 1994. Reprinted 1997
Illustrated by Colin Cameron
Designed by Kaye Binns-McDonald
Set in 10/12¹/₂pt Cambridge by Midland Typesetters

Didja hear about ...?
Copyright © Mike Hayes 1996
First published 1996
Illustrated by Colin Cameron
Designed by Kaye Binns-McDonald
Set in 10/12¹/₂pt Cambridge by Midland Typesetters

5 4 3

CONTENTS

Yarns!

From all round Australia

'DID I TELL YER ABOUT THE LAST TIME THIS 'APPENED TER ME?'

WARNING!

If you're the sort of person who believes

    a. Aussie yarns are all about colourful old bushmen who wear corks around their hats and drive bullock teams;

    b. There are certain things that just *shouldn't* be discussed in public;

    c. No decent yarns need to be dirty to be funny;

    d. Swearing is totally unnecessary, and only proves that people who do so are inarticulate;

    e. Any attempt at humour involving women, non-WASPs, members of the cloth, farmers or the government, is either sexist, racist, sacrilege, un-Australian, ideologically unsound . . . or all of the above,

then you might be better served going over to the Mills and Boon counter. On the other hand, these yarns might give you something new to whinge about, and thereby broaden your narrow little horizons.

WHAT'S THE DIFFERENCE BETWEEN...?

yarn: *noun.* **1.** nylon, cotton or wool thread used for knitting and weaving. **2.** a long story, especially one about unlikely happenings.

The Macquarie Junior Dictionary

In a world of fast food, instant everything and quick fixes, it's only natural that short-form humour has become the go. The quick one-liners epitomised in blonde jokes and riddles about New Zealand animal husbandry practices are a sure sign of a world rapidly denying the need to take the time for a good laugh—as typified in a good old Australian yarn. Despite the trend, there are still enough Australian yarn spinners around to remind us that we don't *have* to be in a hurry to get to a punchline. In fact, we don't *have* to get to a punchline at all. It's not as though yarn spinning and joke telling are one and the same thing, anyway.

The question 'What's the difference between a yarn and a joke?' is a common enough one, which seems to arise whenever people make the unforgivable mistake of starting to discuss yarns seriously. To do that is in itself a bit of a joke (rather than a yarn).

It's a bugger to answer succinctly, and, invariably, the sort of atmosphere you're in when confronted with it is often sullied somewhat by the presence of a strong drink. As a result, whenever I'm asked that bugger of a question, I invariably waffle. Now, because there are undoubtedly hard-nosed folklorists out there who take all this sort of stuff seriously, this is the time for me to translate such waffle into . . . umm, well, something. So, to keep academia and the folkies happy . . . both yarns and jokes have a common goal—to amuse. They both have other common elements, too—they improve with the individual's telling; they grow in stature with the use of such clever tricks as exaggeration and lies; and a teller can justifiably claim authorship simply by adding a few of his or her own personal touches.

7

Where jokes and yarns differ is in the *psychology* motivating them. A joke is a more selfish creation. The teller is really saying 'Look how funny I am. Laugh at me.' Yarn spinners are more sharing. They want you to be part of their story. They want you to know the people involved, like (they claim) they do. They're saying 'Look how funny old so-and-so was.' While yarn spinners inject part of themselves into their tales, they rarely play the hero. Their subject does that. Good yarns tend to have a punchline—an outcome or some point—but, because the tellers aren't trying to prove how hilarious they are, it's not so important. Therefore, yarns can be sad, emotional and self-deprecating and still amuse and entertain, because 'amuse' doesn't necessarily mean leaving your audience in stitches. A stand-up comedian without a punchline or without laughs is a disaster. A yarn spinner can get away with it . . . at least for a while.

A yarn, which I've heard described as *the* quintessential one, is typical of this.

ROLL YOUR OWN

Dawn rises quickly in the bush, and it certainly came up like thunder in the backblocks of VRD. Two ringers rose slowly from their swags, placed, as they always were, just within the range of the warmth from the camp fire. One of them scuttled over to the embers and gave them a poke. A wisp of smoke curled encouragingly in the thin, cool light. He bunged on a few extra pieces of wood and new flames suddenly crackled into life. His mate stretched and strolled slowly to where the scrub started. He undid the fly of his grubby moleskins and, as he relieved the heavy ache in his bladder, he reached into his waistcoat pocket and drew out an almost grey tin of Champion Ruby and a packet of Boomerang papers. He quietly rolled a smoke and his mate heard the sharp scrape of a match in the gloom. Eventually, the smoker strolled back to the fire, which was now showing a fair bit of promise.

'Hey Curly,' he muttered quietly.

'Yeah, mate.'

'Ever smoked a rollie you've just pissed on?'

'No mate.'

'Well, you haven't missed much.'

It says it all and it says nothing.

In selecting these yarns, I was tempted to make it a big wank and merely give you some of the millions I've collected over the millennia. But that would have reduced me to the level of a mere joke teller—'Look how funny I am.'

I thought it far preferable to go back to my primary sources—
some of the funniest bastards I've ever met. While some people
may claim that true Australian yarn spinning is dying, I hope this
book will prove that it's only resting between engagements. I've
tried to present Yarn Spinning as Alive and Well in 1994—rather
than elements of a dying tradition. I've also tried to go beyond
the bush yarn—although that's where yarn spinning is at its
strongest.

My own apprenticeship in yarn spinning was completed in the
grimy inner-city pubs of Melbourne. Some of the best yarn spinners
are Victorians. In 1991 I took the World Yarn Spinning Title off
Frank Hardy (he was a Victorian from around Bacchus Marsh, the
same district where I almost grew up). Pete Steel, who came third,
was also a Victorian. My own personal belief is that the strength
of yarn spinning in Victoria is a spin-off from drinking 7 ounce
glasses of beer (or whatever their metric equivalent is these days).
After a hard day's yakka, the average Victorian worker can sink
half-a-dozen beers, spin a few yarns and still remain reasonably
decorous. In Sydney, by the time the average bloke knocks off and
sinks half-a-dozen schooners, he's lucky if he can engage in any
conversation at all, let alone remember and credibly spin a yarn.
On the other hand, as you'll find, this book contains some excellent
yarns from all over Australia.

Some people will probably also notice that yarn spinning, as
covered here, tends to be predominantly a male activity. They're
not wrong, although there are some great yarns here told by woman
and about women. Look, folks, there are some areas of sexism
that are best left alone. Women have their own version of yarn
spinning, which has its own set of rules, its wonderful peculiarities
and its own hidebound traditions. It's called gossip, and there's
no way in the world that I'd venture into its inner sanctums. As
a mate's old mum used to say, 'If you can't say anything nice about
someone . . . come over and sit next to me.'

There *will* be yarns here that those obsessed with political
correctness may regard as sexist, or maybe even racist. I've gone
out of my way to avoid the sort of bigoted rubbish that you still
see photocopied off and stuck on pub noticeboards, but there have
been times when I've decided that the yarn's worth risking being
declared ideologically unsound by some pedantic funamentalist.
If it offends anyone, stiff cheddar!

Our yarns reflect our times, and we all know we've lived through
times that have been sexist and racist. Let's just mark those yarns
down as historic records of what Australia really is like, warts and
all. Crikey, if future archaeologists happen to be lucky enough to
dig up this book, we don't want them to think all we did was
sit around, yarning and laughing and being perfect. Far more

important are the yarns that, through their humour and character, indicate some of the better sides of the Australian character which, hopefully, we won't lose.

Just an additional observation . . . In writing this book, I've had to commit the ultimate sin of editing yarns—not censoring them, mind you, but cutting out the 'ums', 'errs' and 'y'knows' that make the Australian spoken language the colourful tongue that it is, but which also make it resemble one of my thirteen-year-old son's poorer school essays when put in print. I hope I haven't affected the character of the stories by doing so. Some of the yarns are almost directly transcribed from 'how they was spoke'. Others were always in written form. A few of the spoken items were more in the way of carefully rehearsed performances than off-the-cuff yarns. It doesn't matter. They're all authentic examples of Aussie yarns.

Wherever possible, I've tried to stick to the original teller's style of telling yarns—especially with the extremely personal ones, or where the teller has crafted something highly original.

Many of the yarns appear as a result of a competition trying to track down the Great Australian Yarn, run on ABC Regional Radio in August 1993. Others have been tossed off by their tellers with a cheerful, 'Yeah, go ahead, use whatever you like.'

The rest are often yarns I've shamelessly stolen, given my own personal facelift to, and claimed as my own for so long that they've taken on a life of their own. Wherever possible, I've honourably mentioned where I think I first heard them. But if the originators of these yarns can't quite recognise them as theirs, I'm sorry. They've become my Frankensteins.

SIGNS OF
A MISSPENT YOUTH

Tom Barry, an inveterate yarn spinner, gave me a bell from his home at Grosse's Plains, near Jindabyne, NSW, some time back.

'Jesus, Haysie, the bush is changing,' he observed sorrowfully. 'I was talking to the new preschool teacher in Jindabyne the other day. She reckoned kids just aren't the same any more—even country kids. She'd overheard two of her four year olds talking. One of them said: 'I found a condom on the patio this morning.' His little mate replied, 'What's a patio?'

I reckon Tom was over-reacting a bit. Kids in the bush aren't all that different these days—or they wouldn't be, given half the chance. Those little Jindabyne four year olds were cast in the same mould as the bush kid Gordon Slack, of Gayndah, Queensland, told us about in his entry in ABC Regional Radio's yarn competition.

THE GREAT CREATOR

A minister was driving along one of the lonely bush roads in his parish, when he noticed a small boy standing beside a bullock dray. The minister, seeing a chance to sample the level of religious knowledge in the district, stopped to chat with the lad.

'Who does the team belong to?' he asked.

'Me farver,' said the boy.

'Do you know who made them?' the minister asked.

'Yes. Me farver,' replied the lad.

'Oh, dear me, no!' the minister admonished. 'God made them.'

The boy gave the minister a withering look. 'God made 'em *bulls*, Mister,' he said. 'Me farver made 'em *bullicks*.'

The Jindabyne and Gayndah kids were all part of a truly Australian tradition. Everything has to start somewhere. Even gnarled, untruthful yarn spinners begin life as rug rats and ankle-biters. I've scoured the grimy recesses of my own memory to try to pinpoint exactly *where* I may have developed the need and/or talent, to lie, exaggerate, plagiarise, titillate and bore. Little kids mightn't tell yarns as such, but they spin fairly good whoppers. Although most of them grow up to be liars (to some degree) or politicians, they don't all end up propped on one elbow in a boozer regaling all and sundry with as much of their repertoire as they can remember before interest flags or they go face down on the counter.

The Child Bride blames my dear old mum for most of my personal failures, so I suppose there must be something in it. She was a great storyteller. In the days before television, when kids' radio serials such as *The Air Adventures of Hop Harrigan* and *Captain Silver and the Seahound* ended at half-past seven every night, and we still had half an hour or so of summer daylight left before we could reasonably be packed off the bed, she'd read to us from classic (but non-Australian) books, such as *Children of the New Forest* or *The Yearling*. And she'd also tell us whispered stories of her own wild youth and many husbands in Ceylon, England and all points west, north, south and east.

Our favourite was about husband number two, who disgraced himself in some English stately home by coming home 'quite tight' and cleaning his teeth with the ashes of the dear departed father of the house.

The kids I grew up with were all English. My dear old mum was a cottage mother at a place called Northcote Farm, near Bacchus Marsh, in Victoria—about 50 kilometres west of Melbourne. There were fourteen boys in our cottage at Northcote—all except my brother and I—transported from the United Kingdom under what was called the Lady Northcote Scheme, to be lightly educated and then turned out as farm labourers or domestic servants. Their yarns are the ones I first remember. They're the sort of things small kids used to giggle over, crouched in exciting grass and corrugated iron cubbies built around the twisted trunks of old wattle trees.

No, they're not especially brilliant, but I pass on a couple for the record. Dedicated academics are quite welcome to take notes. I heard the first one from a little snub-nosed girl called Gwen Chatham. The other one was told to me by Alec Towerzy. They were about seven and nine, respectively, at the time. Alec later became a copper. I wonder what they're doing now.

THE GOLDEN TRAIL

This man had constipation. He went to the doctor. The doctor gave him some tablets. 'Here, take a quarter of a tablet every eight hours and you'll be fine.'

But the man with constipation was a bit stupid. He decided to take his first dose just outside the surgery door, but he couldn't recall what the doctor had told him. He tried to remember but he couldn't get it right. Was it a quarter of a tablet every eight hours or eight tablets every quarter of an hour?

'Oh well,' he told himself, 'I'd better play it safe.' So he took eight tablets straightaway and started to walk home. He lived about an hour's walk from the doctor's, so he made sure he took his tablets as he went.

Just near his home, another man stopped him. 'Excuse me,' said the stranger, 'could you tell me the way to the doctor's?'

'Sure,' said the man. 'Just follow the golden trail.'

God, we used to get hysterical over that one . . . Now, here's Alec's yarn.

TITSWOBBLE

There was this lady, and she had a little dog called Titswobble. She was very fond of Titswobble, but one day he got lost. So the lady walked up and down the street looking for him. She couldn't find him at all and she started to cry. Then she saw a policeman on his beat. She ran up to him.

'Oh, officer,' she said, 'Have you seen my Titswobble?'

'No,' he replied. 'But I'd like to.'

There were cruder variations of that yarn, but they were no funnier. God knows why those two are the only ones I can remember from my very earliest days. Maybe they *were* the only two we knew. So much for the incredibly high standard of yarns we told each other as kids. Of course, the main source of supply was adults— and not just parents. There's many a good yarn that starts out with 'There was this old mate of my father's . . .'

But, really, a yarn-spinning dad was probably the greatest bad influence any impressionable ankle-biters could have, as Keiran East, of Carrara, Queensland, indicated in his fine entry in the ABC's search for the Great Australian Yarn.

CYCLING THE WIND

My father, who was a shearer in the early 1900s, passed this tale on to me and swore as to the authenticity of it.

He often spoke of riding his pushbike from shed to shed during the shearing season. As you may imagine, he would have encountered all types of weather. On one particular journey; he was forced to race thunderstorms from Ipswich to Toowoomba, where the shearing was due to start next day.

Needless to say, he swore that he beat that storm, but only just. When he finally arrived at his destination, they found a thick coating of mud on the back wheel . . . and a fine layer of dust on the front!

And what about Stephen Leuckel, of Fernleigh, New South Wales? Look at the bad company *he* fell in with when he was a boy. As he explained, the story was told to him and his mates by a next-door neighbour in the early 1950s. He described the originator of this yarn as a quiet man, whose only vices were yarn spinning and his garden.

WATSON'S WATCH

It was one of those hot, airless, Sydney January afternoons. My mates and I were swinging on the front gate and hanging off the fence, when I saw Mr Watson, from next door, resting in the cool shade of his veranda.

'G'day, Mr Watson,' I called, and the other boys joined in. He smiled and gave a friendly wave. He soon left his easy chair and came to the dividing fence.

'G'day boys. I've been away, y'know.' We had gathered at the fence and immediately wanted to know where he'd been. He eyed us over the top of his horn-rimmed glasses and began.

'Went back to the old home town for a bit of a look around. Hadn't been there since I went off to the Great War. It hasn't changed much, except the trees. They've all grown a lot.'

We were all settled comfortably on the grass and we waited while he rolled his cigarette. He lit it and took a deep puff.

'Drake's a nice little place . . . up north, y'know . . . good climate and the people are all right, too.'

He leaned closer. 'A funny thing happened while I was visiting the old farm . . . very strange.' His voice trailed off and he gazed out over the freshly mown lawn. He drew on his cigarette.

'Y'see, when I left the farm for the last time, to go off to the war, my dad gave me a silver pocket watch to remind me of home. It was a beautiful afternoon and I decided on one last ride over the old place so I could fix it in my mind. When I came back from the ride, I couldn't find the pocket watch. We searched everywhere, without luck. The light was fading. I had to catch the Sydney train—so I left.'

He tipped the ash off his cigarette and continued. 'My dad never found the watch and I'd forgotten clean about it until the other day, when I was walking in the bottom paddock.

'There was a stand of gums there that I couldn't remember. They must've grown since I left. I was looking up, trying to guess their height, when I noticed, about 20 feet up, something glinting in the sunlight. I climbed up the tree, and way out on one of the long branches I could see something caught in a fork of the branch.'

He bent down, pushed his cigarette butt deep into the garden compost, straightened up and adjusted his stance against the big corner post of the fence.

'I got a ladder from the farmhouse and guess what I found in the tree?'

Our eyes widened in anticipation as he reached into his waist-coat pocket and drew out, very slowly, the most beautifully carved silver pocket watch I'd ever seen. He held it low so we could all inspect it. When he pressed the large knurled winder with his thumb, the lid sprang open to reveal a fine porcelain dial, with delicate gold numbers and hands. We could hear the robust tick, tick, tick, as the finely sprung escapement wheel whirred back and forth.

'The strangest thing was, though,' he said, 'the watch was ticking when I found it and it was keeping perfect time. Then I noticed a small branch, which rubbed against the winder and turned it a little, every time the breeze moved the tree.'

He carefully closed the lid of the watch and slipped it back into his pocket.

'You wouldn't credit it, would you?' he said with a twinkle in his eye. 'After being regularly wound for all those years—still running perfectly.'

It's like my next offering, which was perhaps the first real yarn I ever learned. It came from a bloke called Roy McLean, who, of all things, was one of many city Scout leaders who used to come up to Northcote and try to teach us feral bush kids about survival in the wild.

AT LEAST HE HAD GUTS

There was this bloke in Melbourne who had dreadful wind. He just couldn't help himself. It didn't matter if he was at work or at some high society function, he kept letting fly with enormous belches and farts.

Even at his own wedding, he couldn't maintain decorum. Right in the middle of his very sacred vows, he kept exploding like a hand grenade. His poor wife put up with it for years. In fact, she was the only person who did. As time went by, everyone else kept giving him the body swerve. They were never invited to parties. He lost his job. His wife took him to doctors. She tried adjusting his diet. But still the Human Cannon kept up his fusillades.

Eventually, one doctor gave her some hope. 'Look,' he told her. 'There's no longer any medical reason for his condition. By adjusting his diet, you've eliminated the natural cause of his wind. The only reason he's still doing what he does is force of habit. I'd suggest you take him to a psychiatrist.'

The psychiatrist was pretty sympathetic, but threw the ball right back in her court.

'Look, your Medicare doesn't cover his condition,' he told her. 'And it's too late to try private health insurance. It's essential you get on top of the problem straightaway. I suggest you try aversion therapy. Try shocking him out of his condition—a bit like giving someone a fright when they've got hiccups. That'll be $200, thanks very much.'

As you can imagine, the poor woman was almost at the end of her tether, but she applied herself to trying to find a way of shocking the bugger out of his nasty habits. As he burbled away in front of the telly in the living room, she sat alone at the kitchen table and formulated a grand plan.

Next morning, before going off to work, she told him, 'Look, I read an article in the *Women's Weekly* the other day that said that people with bad wind often bring up their own entrails if they don't find a cure.'

Her old man just shrugged and kept watching *Agro's Cartoon Connection*.

That evening, on her way home from work, his wife called in at the local butcher's and, for a couple of bucks, bought a large plastic bucket full of assorted sheep, cow and pig guts.

When she got up for work next morning, her old man was still out like a light, having had a long hard night of windswept adventuring.

Being careful not to wake him, she dragged the plastic bucket out of the garage and draped the festoons of offal over him. Then she quietly crept out of the house and went to work.

That night, as she returned, she tried to act as nonchalantly as possible. She was rather surprised to find her husband at his old familiar spot in front of *Ducktales*, apparently unconcerned at what he'd experienced. An uneasy silence reigned for about half an hour. Then, during a commercial break, her old man called from the lounge, 'Oh, darls.'

'Yes, love.'

'Remember what you told me (burp), about bringing me innards up if I kept on belching and that?'

'Yes, love.'

'Well (pfffft!), you were right. It happened this morning.'

'Did it, love?'

'Too right (Blaaarp!). It give me quite a turn, but it worked out all right.'

'Did it, love?'

'Yeah (burp!). It took a couple of goes, but I managed to get 'em back down again with the help of a big glass of water.'

Perhaps the first yarn that really gave me a chance to embellish and improvise also came from a most unlikely source. Dick Ross was our fourth grade teacher at Glenmore State School, about 2 kilometres from where we lived. He wasn't really your typical yarn-spinning type, although he certainly taught us to be proud of our bush heritage. He'd taught at Jeparit, in the mallee, and introduced all of us little Poms to Aboriginal Australia. We learned about the explorers. He made us research local history—virtually unheard of in the puritanical fifties. And often, he'd come out with little surprises, like this yarn. God knows why he told us. He built up to it all morning, promising us that he had a special surprise for us after lunch. If I remember rightly, most of the other kids didn't 'get' the joke. But I salted it away, added a bit of myself to it (to give it greater credibility, of course) and have used it occasionally . . . very occasionally.

MONKEY BUSINESS

Back then in the fifties, the biggest town in our area was Ballarat. Actually, Melbourne was closer, but it represented decadent city living. Ballarat was nice and comfortable and rural. And it looked suitably English—with parks full of big old elms and oaks. That was important in the fifties. We all still wanted to be seen as British. We kids only got to go to Ballarat a couple of times. Once was when the Queen was there in 1954 and once to visit the zoo. That old zoo was obviously suffering hard times. Even when I was only seven or eight, I could sense it. Towards the end, there wasn't much there—just a camel and a couple of ponies and a cocky or two. It isn't there at all now—I don't think you can even see the marks where it once was.

But back in the old days, before it really started going down the gurgler, the Ballarat zoo management was still fighting to keep it going. Anyway, this bloke breezed into Ballarat after doing a bit of shed work further out west in the Wimmera. In better times, he'd been a fairly well-known Shakespearian actor, but the theatre game was fickle and, down on his luck, he'd been forced to take

whatever he could find. The shed work hadn't exactly been to his liking and he'd bailed out, supposing that Ballarat, being a largish sort of genteel place, might be able to provide something suitable for a classical thespian. But Ballarat wasn't exactly booming at the time—theatrically or otherwise. Realising he'd have to accept anything that came up again, he spent a miserable night sleeping on a bench under the old elms in the park. All night, strange animal noises kept him awake. He had a bit of a look around at first light and discovered the zoo.

'Egad,' he thought, 'I've had experience with animals. Maybe I'll get a guernsey in here.'

He waited until the gates opened about 9 o'clock, then went straight up to the office.

'Any chance of some work?' he asked the little sheila behind the counter.

'Hang on, I'll go and see,' she replied and vanished out the back. She returned about five minutes later. 'You're in luck,' she told him. 'The head keeper reckons he's been looking for someone.'

She led him into a big wood-panelled office, where the head keeper was sitting behind a desk looking pretty worried. 'Are you looking for work?' he asked the actor.

'Too right.'

'Are you willing to do almost anything?'

'Too right.'

The head keeper breathed a big sigh and leaned back. 'I don't suppose you have any acting experience?'

The old actor's heart skipped a beat. 'I, sir, have played King Lear in *Hamlet*, and the title role of Les in *Les Miserables*.'

The head keeper seemed less than impressed. 'Well, I've got a rather unusual role for you. You see, last night we lost our main attraction.'

'Indeed?'

'Yes. For years we've been slowly going broke. People just haven't been coming. They wanted to see more than a few motheaten lions and a couple of daggy cockatoos. So we took the plunge. We went across to Adelaide Zoo and bought their orangoutang. It cost a mint, but it's been worth it. People have been coming all the way across from South Australia and even Gippsland to see it. It's the best investment we ever made. Why, with the weekend starting tomorrow, we're expecting nearly one hundred bus loads of visitors paying a pound a head just to see our orangoutang.'

'By the living Henry, that's pretty good.'

'Bloody oath. There's only one problem.'

'What's that?'

'Last night the bloody orang-outang died.'

The head keeper put his head in his hands and looked like he was about to cry. 'And that's where you come in.'

'What?'

'We've got a bloke up from the butcher's shop in the main street and he's out the back skinning the ourang-outang. Later a bloke's coming in from the tannery and he's going to do a quick tanning job on the skin.'

'So?'

'What we thought was that you could put the skin on, get into the cage and pretend you're the orang-outang.'

'Come off it.'

'No. It'll only be for the weekend. All you'd have to do is swing about the cage a bit, eat a few bananas and pull faces. It'll keep the visitors happy and, providing no word gets out, we should make enough to buy a replacement for next weekend.'

'I'm not sure . . .'

'It's worth ten quid and all the bananas you can eat. But remember, if anyone twigs what's going on, you won't get a cracker.'

'It's a deal,' said the actor, who remembered that he hadn't had a feed since the previous lunchtime.

He even helped finish the skinning and the bloke from the tannery. Although it took all night to dry out in front of the big fire in the head keeper's office, the orang-outang skin was finally fit for use. The head keeper's wife put a big zip in the back just in time for the actor to strip to his undies and put it on. The first crowds arrived an hour later. By then he was well and truly into the role of the orang-outang. He swung from the dead trees in the cage. He ate more than his fair share of bananas. In the afternoon he had a brainwave and started pelting the crowd with banana skins. The visitors, especially the little kids, loved it. They clapped and cheered.

'Egad, there's nothing to this role,' thought the actor to himself.

By next morning, word had quickly spread about the Ballarat zoo's fabulous orang-outang. More buses than ever started heading west from Melbourne, south from Bendigo and east from the little wheat towns across the South Australian border.

The Victorian Railways even put on two special trains. By mid-morning, hundreds of enthralled people were clapping the orang-outang's antics.

To say the acclaim went to the actor's head would be understating the case. Naturally, the more applause he got, the more he tried to please. His swings became higher. His faces funnier. He even performed some bodily functions that one would normally expect from an ape, but never from a human (apart from a wool classer).

To thunderous applause, the actor in the orang-outang suit climbed to the very top of one of the dead trees. Perched precariously on the end of a thin branch, he stood on one leg thumping his chest and yodelling like Tarzan. The crowd gasped in amazement as he stood on his head, then grabbed the branch and started to swing. Round and round he went. Higher and higher. Just when he seemed nothing more than a hairy blur, he let go of the branch, intending to fly across the cage and grab the topmost branch of the next tree. Unfortunately, fatigue must have set in. Instead of heading towards the next tree, he went the other way— right across the cage and, to the horror of the crowd, straight over the high wall, over their heads, across the path and . . . right into the lion's enclosure across the way. The impact of his fall knocked the actor out for a few seconds. When he came to, he found he was looking straight into the face of a large lion.

He tried to stay calm, but the lion leaned over to him, growling menacingly. Finally, the actor cracked—and who wouldn't? He didn't want to be torn apart by a lion.

'Help! For God's sake, help!' he screamed. The lion leaned closer.

'God! I don't want to die! Please help me!' bellowed the actor. No one in the crowd moved. Finally, with his gaping jaws only an inch in front of the orang-outang's face, the lion stopped.

'Shut up, you silly bastard,' a voice muttered from somewhere under the mane. 'Do you want us all to get the sack?'

I'll introduce you to the unique modern style of yarn spinning of Pete Steel later. His yarns are very much of today. And one of the best of them is about his childhood.

MOVING OUT

Now, my father and I, we've got a great relationship. We've always been able to talk about anything. So I approached him one day with a big problem. It was in my heart to talk to him about it. I said, 'Dad, I've got to move out from home. I've had enough, Dad, I just can't live here any more. I can't take the stress and the strain. It's too much for me, I'm a growing boy.'

He looked at me and said, 'It's something that happens in every man's life. Sooner or later he wants to move out. Bit early for you at five years old, sport, but what do you want to do?'

As I said, I'd always been able to talk to him, so I told him, 'Dad, I've decided to run away.'

'Where would you like to go?'

'What do you mean?' You see, we lived at Glen Waverley and I didn't know any other places.

'I tell you want, I'll go and get an atlas of the world. You pick where you'd like to go, we'll buy you an air ticket in the morning and you can go there.'

So we had a bit of a talk and a think about it and I told him I really wasn't ready to go overseas at that stage of my running away.

Dad observed wisely, 'You're not all that prepared son, so why don't you have a bit of a practice at running away? We'll set up the tent in the backyard, see, and you can pretend you're running away into there. When you're quite happy with looking after yourself for the rest of your life, you let us know and we'll put you on the train to wherever your heart desires.'

So there we were—you know what it's like—two men toiling hard under the midday sun, working up a sweat—the brotherhood of common labour binding us together. We got the tent up and we put the camp stretcher in there, and the sleeping-bag and the light. By then the sun was going down. I had a look around. My dad wasn't around. I went to the back door of the house and knocked. I heard a voice. Phew! He *was* there.

'Can I get some tea?'

'Sorry, mate, we didn't cook you any. Your mother thought you'd run away. Hadn't you planned what you were going to eat for tea? Now that's a shame, because we've put it all away and we're going to bed.'

So I tramped back to my tent and . . . well, I didn't give up really. It's not like I caved in really quickly, because I made it until about half past eight. Then I headed round to the front of the house and knocked on the lounge-room window. I knew Dad would be in there, sitting by the fire.

He said, 'Y . . . yeah . . . y . . . yeah . . . who is it?'

I said, 'Dad, it's me. I want to talk about running away.'

As I said, we've always been able to talk and he pulled me in and sat me on his knee.

'Son, what d'you want to do?'

'Well, I'm not really ready to go.'

So then, we talked about most of the contributing factors making it impossible for me to remain at home any longer, at the age of five. We ironed out some big problems. After we'd done that, I had a glass of water. He had a glass of beer.

Then he said, 'Tell you what, son, let's make ourselves a deal. I can see you've got some major dissatisfaction with the way the house is being run at the moment. Your mother and I will discuss 'em and you and I will make this deal. Any time in the future, if you decide it all gets too much for you, you can go.'

I went back to my bed and went to sleep. About twelve years later, at the age of seventeen, I held him to his promise. Off I went to join the Navy.'

22

Pete Steel in full cry seems young, brash and pretty full of himself—everything a naval officer should be. But at a time when our tradition of yarn spinning is somewhat under threat from cheap imports, he's a breath of fresh air. The thing I like about Pete is that he's not afraid to wear his heart on his sleeve. He's a romantic and he's sentimental. I wish there were more blokes like him. This childhood reminiscence also proves that they don't all have to be hysterically funny to be good yarns.

THE NEW ARRIVAL

The three boys in our family were all born by caesarean section. After that my mother couldn't have any more children, but she and Dad wanted to have a baby girl. I remember Dad coming home from work one day and asking us, 'How would you like a baby sister?'

We all thought it was a great idea. I wasn't particularly sure what a baby sister was, but I wanted one anyway. I was three, my older brother five and the young feller was one.

Anyway, Dad announced, 'If you want a baby sister, we'll go and get one tomorrow.'

The next day we got into the car and off we went, driving into town. Dad asked, 'What would you like to call her?'

Murray was going to Big School at that stage, so he knew a couple of girls' names, like Jane and Debbie, and we all thought they were great. But, then Dad said, 'What about Katherine?'

'Katherine? . . . Katherine? . . . Why don't we call her Katherine?' So we decided on Katherine.

'Are you sure?'

Yeah, I was sure.

We arrived in the middle of Melbourne at a place called the Mission of St James and St John, across the road from the Flagstaff Gardens. It was a huge building and I remember we went up in this big lift. At the top there was this ward full of babies, as far as the eye could see. There were probably twelve, but to my three-year-old eyes it looked like every baby in Australia was in this ward. Dad spoke to the nurse for a little while. Then she came over and said, 'Boys, you can chose whichever baby you want in this ward.'

Off we went. I went across to the first bed and thought, 'We'll have this one . . . We'll have *this* one . . . No, we'll have . . .' But after about five minutes, I noticed my mother standing at the end of one of the beds looking at a little baby. We all went over and there were these beautiful big blue eyes, looking—she's still got them—and we decided we wanted *this* one.

We all wanted *this* one.

Dad said, 'Are you sure this is the baby you want?' We said it was. He picked each of us up and he sat us on the bed where we could see her. 'Remember this day for as long as you live. Remember that you *chose* her. She was never an accident. Of all the babies in Melbourne today, *you* chose her. Of all the babies in the ward, you chose *her*.'

We all know that you don't just adopt a kid—especially in Victoria—especially if you've got three children. But the mother of this girl had said, 'She's to be brought up in a family with boys; she's to have brothers and it's to be a Church of England family.' And that was us.

The whole thing had been organised months ahead, but I didn't know that and I was about thirteen years old before it ever struck me—the trick that my parents had played. I grew up all my life believing that I chose my sister. She always had two birthdays— her real one and, two weeks after that, her Doppy Day. As soon as she could understand, she knew she was ''dopted'. I don't think she knew what ''dopted' meant. I don't think any of us knew what it meant. But we used to say to the kids down the street that we fought with (and we still do, although I'm twenty-five now), 'She's better than *your* sister because we chose her. She didn't just fall down out of the sky and land in our house. We picked her and she's ours and she's better than yours.'

Now I don't know whether you've got an adopted brother or sister, or daughter or son. But one day, they're going to want to meet their mother. It is going to happen.

I guess we knew it. Although we never talked about it, we knew the day was coming. I'll always love Katherine in that she waited until she was eighteen. In Victoria that means that your parents don't have to say yes . . . and also they can't say no. That terrible decision, which weighed on my parents all their lives, they never had to take.

We went into the Mission of St James and St John. She was twenty-one years old, and I clearly remember the day. We were all standing in front of the building. It was a bit smaller now—although the nurse looked about the same. My heart was breaking at that time, like it had never broken before. What about if this lady was something *special*? What if she was something better than us? What if Katherine didn't want *us* any more?

Katherine was taken downstairs by the nurse to meet her mother. When she came back upstairs, you could see that this *was* Katherine's mother. She was her image. Her face, her hands . . . I remember in particular, the hands . . . they were so obviously hers. And I looked across at my mother. She's got a particular way of standing. She stands with her hands just folded and sitting on her hip in a particular way. There we were, just looking and seeing this lady was so obviously Katherine's mother . . . and Katherine was looking as well. She was standing next to my mum, exactly *her* image . . . exactly the same. And while I was seeing that this was her mother, her mother was seeing that we were so obviously Katherine's family.

Katherine hasn't wanted to contact her mother since. She was a stranger. She was just another Australian woman. I don't know any more about her than that, but I do know that for perhaps the first time ever in Katherine's life, she knew who her mother was and she knew the lady who bore her.

And they weren't the same person.

That's probably where Australian kids have changed most in recent years. Their adolescent and teenage years are nowhere near as innocent as they used to be a generation or so back.

Young people are required to be far more serious, far earlier, these days. It's a pity. When I see the teenagers in our home town sitting round the pubs, with nothing more enlightening to discuss than beating the hell out of each other and how they're going to get into the nearest big town to pick up their dole cheque, I get a bit depressed. I remember watching a mob of hoons at the recovery party for our local B and S Ball. They were having a great old time—suitably lubricated, of course—but there didn't seem to be the good-natured wit I claim to remember from my own wasted youth. I might be having myself on, I admit, but I seem to recall that the wags in our day could muster up something a bit cleverer than mass grunting when the police turned up to move us on.

Dawn Murray, of Bunbury, Western Australia, entered this next yarn in the ABC competition. Its innocent, knockabout good humour illustrates the way bush larrikins *used* to be. I hope I'm merely out of touch with what's going on and kids are still coming up with things like this.

AN OFFICER AND A GENTLEMAN

Towards the end of last century and early into this one, Tasmania was a popular choice for retiring British ex-India Army officers. By the 1920s, those officers and their families formed an exclusive clique, which excluded most of the locals from its goings on— not that it usually bothered the locals.

However, one small town on the northwest coast had what it considered a plague of those characters. With their English county names, clipped British accents and martinet army ways, they lorded it over everyone, giving peremptory orders where they had no business giving them, and generally being pains in the rear end. Worst of all, they excluded the locals from shooting and fishing on their properties.

Some of the local lads decided to do something about it. Jimmy Wells, who could assume a posh accent fit to split the sides of his mates, telephoned Colonel Evans.

'Good evening, Colonel,' said Jimmy. 'This is Captain Wells. Some of the lads and I will be in your area this weekend and we were wondering if you would allow us a spot of shooting on your property on Sunday.'

'Delighted, Captain,' the Colonel replied. 'If you and your chaps would care to partake of luncheon with me first, I'll escort you to the back paddocks. Deuced fine sport there at the moment.' Jimmy was nearly floored, but not quite.

'How kind of you, Colonel,' he waffled, thinking fast. 'Regretfully, we are bidden to an early luncheon elsewhere, otherwise we would have been delighted to accept your hospitality. Perhaps another time.'

On Sunday afternoon, half a dozen of the lads loaded themselves and their guns into Jimmy's dad's old truck and rattled up to the Colonel's property. Tooting merrily, they drove past the house and down to the back paddocks, where, as the Colonel had said, the rabbits were plentiful and the sport was good.

As they were leaving, they found the Colonel at his front gate waiting to farewell them. 'Thanks, mate,' said Jimmy, his posh accent slipping.

The Colonel peered suspiciously at Captain Wells and his youthful friends. 'Aren't you rather *young* to be a captain, Wells?'

'Not at all, Colonel,' Jimmy replied, as he drove through the gate. 'I'm Captain of the Under 19 footie team.'

Of course, childhood and adolescent days have to end. Darwin's Kevin Naughton obviously had some memorable ones . . . but, these days, the glinting of the sun on his shiny cranium is more than proof enough that it's all past and gone. That doesn't stop him reminiscing and recording the wistful transition between one's youth and the hard, cruel world of adulthood.

SISTER MARY FRANCESCA

The other night, I thought I'd pop into the pub just to see what was going on. I was walking along Herbert Street and, lo and behold, I came across a woman that I hadn't seen for thirty-five years. She'd taught me in primary school in Adelaide. She saw me coming and

she said, 'Stone the crows! It's Kevin Naughton and you've taken a bit of a shine on in your later years.'

'Sister Mary Francesca, I haven't seen you for so long. I recall falling asleep in your arms in Grade Two in primary school.'

She said, 'What are you doing with yourself these days?'

'Not much. I'm working for the ABC.'

'Where do you think you might be going right now?'

'I'm going into the Green Room to have a few beers and see if I can catch up with Cowboy Bill and Mike Hayes and the Yahoo from the Barcoo.'

'Don't tell me you drink, after all that education I gave you. You don't drink, do you? You took the pledge when you were twelve.'

'I didn't know what I was bloody doing at twelve. Two years later I worked out that a beer wasn't a bad thing.'

'You should never, ever drink, Kevin. It's a thing that you should never do. It addles your mind. It plays tricks with your soul. You could finish up with a strange woman.'

'I did. And I married her. She left me, though—shot through with another bloke. She took the car as well. Gee, I miss that car.'

But Sister Mary Francesca repeated her message. 'You shouldn't drink. It's a thing you shouldn't do.'

I said, 'Sister Mary Francesca, you don't understand. Drinks can lubricate a person socially. They *can* make you a much better person.'

'Do you think so? I'm sixty-eight and I've never had a drink in my life.'

'Sister Mary Francesca, just this once, let me give you a drink so you'll know what you've missed.'

'Well, I don't know what to drink. What sort of drink does a woman drink?'

'Well,' I said, 'I think they have a vodka and orange.'

'Okay I'll have one of those, but I'll wait outside the pub.'

So I walked inside, went up to the barman and said, 'I'll have a Powers light, thanks, and I'll have a vodka and orange.'

He said, 'A vodka and orange? Is that bloody Sister Mary Francesca outside again?'

2

IF MUSIC BE
THE FOOD OF LOVE—
RAVE ON!

In September 1958, my brother Pete and I stepped onto a stage, swallowed hard at the grim faces of the huge audience and launched shakily into the forgettable Everly Brothers hit 'Dream'. The venue was the great hall of the Sunbury Mental Hospital, in Victoria. It was our onstage debut as fledgling rock gods. A lot of guitar strings have flowed under the bridge since then . . . and a lot of grim-faced audiences.

Somewhere in my personal pipeline, there's a book under way of my thousands of fruitless years in the music industry. There's a lot to tell. God knows how many volumes it would fill, had we become the music legends our dear old mum was sure we'd be. But if international fame eluded us, the music game's greatest legacy—the yarns told by, and about, musicians—did not. Who cares if we didn't eclipse Elvis as the King, when we got to know so many great characters and live and hear so many great yarns?

This first one, another entry in the ABC's quest for the Great Aussie Yarn, conjures up the sort of gigs we used to do back when we first started in music. We spent many years as teenage members of concert parties—assortments of sub-mediocre musicians, performing free of charge—inflicting something less than entertainment on unsuspecting audiences (like the one at the Sunbury Mental Hospital) and innocent folk in little bush halls. This yarn was sent in by Ted Ryan, of Benalla, Victoria.

MINDO THE GREAT

It's three months since it happened. Experts from the city reckon it'll take six months or so, and then the aroma should disappear. Locals who are asked what's up with the community hall, say there's a methane gas problem, and refuse to go into any further detail . . . apart from agreeing that it *may* reopen in three months' time.

I personally doubt it. I went near the hall the other night, and it was still pretty high.

The tragedy for this little town happened the night Mindo the Great—an out-of-town magician and hypnotist—booked the hall. About four hundred people packed in to witness the marvel. Mindo put on a brilliant show and at 11 pm, when his performance was due to finish, the crowd was begging for more.

Mindo weakened, and said he would hypnotise the entire audience for his final act.

He walked down each aisle, hypnotising a full row of people at a time. In the last row, a bloke sitting on the aisle seat had his foot sticking out.

Mindo the Great did not see the foot.

He stumbled and nearly fell.

'Shit!' yelled a startled Mindo the Great.

The audience response was breathtaking.

And *that's* the tragedy that's led to the temporary closure of our little community hall.

Like my good self, Leith Ryan is a long-time musician who should have known better. These days he operates as a travelling horse dentist. His postal address is at his mum's place at The Rock, near Wagga. But most of the time, he's zotting around the traps dispensing dental hygiene to the equine set. This is his version of a yarn he swears is true, but it tends to crop up in other forms, elsewhere. On the other hand, Leith is one of those blokes that this sort of thing happens to.

SPEAKING IN TONGUES

I was doing this job the other day in one of those tourist joints. You know the sort of place. They wheel in all these tourists and you sit up one end singing your bloody guts out and no one takes any notice. What makes matters worse is these tourists were all Japanese. It doesn't matter what you do for them, they can't understand what you're singing about. You can't joke with the Japanese. There's no point trying to do so. Anyway, I'd just finished my best Merle Haggard bracket, when this little Japanese bloke came up. He was very polite, very serious.

'You play very nice,' he said.

'Thanks, mate.'

'You play for a long time?'

'About thirty years, mate.'

'What else you play?'

'Well, I play mainly country music, mate, but if you want a song, maybe I can work it out for you.'

'Very good. You play jazz chord?'

I thought, 'Jesus, this bloke doesn't seem to understand that jazz isn't my go.' But seeing he was being so friendly and that, I picked up the old guitar and strummed the nearest thing I knew to a jazz chord . . . a big G-eleventh diminished fourth, or something. He smiled and nodded.

'That very nice. Now you play jazz chord, please.'

Bloody hell. Didn't this bastard listen to anything? But he was still standing there smiling and bowing, so I couldn't be rude. I didn't know any other jazz chords, so I tried one of my best George Golla runs . . . all fiddly, up and down the neck. His smile grew even wider and he actually clapped.

'Oh yes, that very nice. You play very well. Now can you please play jazz chord?'

This wasn't getting us anywhere and I was starting to get a bit shitty. 'Look, mate,' I told him. 'Like I said, I play mainly country music. I've played you the nearest things I know to jazz, but the message just doesn't seem to be getting through to you. Now, if you want a bloody request, I suggest you try to hum or sing me something like what you want to hear and I'll see what I can do for you.'

'Oh yes, yes,' he said. 'Very sorry. I sing. Now, what I like is jazz chord.'

And with that, he threw back his head and started . . . 'I jazz chord to say I love you . . .'

That one is almost identical to another muso's yarn about the drunk who kept pestering the band working at a St Patrick's Day turn to play 'Paddy Me Bhuoy'. When the band leader did his nana, said he'd been playing music for thirty years, had never heard of an Irish song called 'Paddy Me Bhouy' and challenged the drunk to sing a few bars, he was treated to 'Paddy me bhouy, is that the Chattanooga Choo Choo?' . . . Or, same song, only referring to the moggy that monstered Roy Rogers' best cowboy boots— 'Pardon me Roy, is that the cat that chewed your new shoe?' . . . Or the crustacean who'd had too good a time dancing in heaven and 'Left His Harp in Sand Crab Disco'.

But if Leith says his is true . . .

This one *is* true. I first heard it from a Goulburn musician, the late Garth Shelley, but it's been dished up again and again around the district by many others . . . with very little alteration. The bloke it's about is still convinced he's going to make it big in Tamworth

31

one day, so I'd better not give his real name. Let's just call him Tex Tile and imagine Garth's still cutting up rough about him.

A NOSE FOR MUSIC

Bloody Tex Tile. You know, that bludger never has his guitar in tune . . . and you know what sort of guitar he's got, don't you? It's a bloody Gibson Les Paul. In *original* nick. And you know what it's worth? Bloody thousands. There's a lot of musicians round Goulburn who'd kill for a guitar like that. And, like I said, the bastard never keeps it in tune. Well, one night he's playing with his band down the Yass Soldiers Club. Anyway, Tex has this bad back, so he always sits on a stool to ease the pain. This night he was fairly pissed, so he hooked his cowboy boots behind the little rung that goes round the legs of the stool so he wouldn't fall off. And not only does the bugger never tune his guitar . . . that *beautiful* guitar . . . but he can never remember the words to his songs. So he's got this little music stand in front of him so he can get the lyrics right, see?

Anyway, like I said, he was fairly full and, when he leaned over to read the small print in the dim lights, he found he'd gone too far and he started to fall. Now, he couldn't untangle his legs from the stool quick enough and he couldn't risk letting go of the guitar. You see, not only hadn't he tuned it, but he'd left the strap at home. If he'd dropped it, it would've smashed all over the ground. I mean, if the bastard knew anything, he knew how much that guitar was worth. Bloody thousands.

So there he is. He can't move his feet. He can't let go of his guitar to save himself and he's falling slowly forward off his stool.

D'you know what saved him? The little pointy bit on top of the music stand. It went right up his left nostril. So there he hung— claret everywhere—unable to do a bloody thing until the rest of the band finished playing 'Me and Bobby McGee'.

Speaking of 'Me and Bobby McGee', this, also, really happened. And, surprise surprise, it involves the same bunch of musicians.

FREEDOM'S JUST ANOTHER WORD

Personally, I wasn't exactly heartbroken when it became apparent that the legendary Tex Tile wasn't going to call up and offer me some lead guitar work in his band. Let's just say there were one or two artistic differences that remained insurmountable. So I was a bit surprised when one afternoon the phone rang and there was

Tex, offering me a night's work for quite a considerable sum of money. Suddenly, those insurmountable artistic differences just vanished.

It was to be a big country music night for charity at the Goulburn Workers Club. Although my main motivation was purely mercenary, it was somewhat heartening to find, on the night, about fifteen hundred people gathered. It wasn't going to be nearly as boring as I'd convinced myself it would be. And, by crikey, those people had a great time. From the opening chord of Tex's first number (which happened to be 'Me and Bobby McGee'), they were up shaking like billyo all over the dance floor. Even the most cynical musician weakens when confronted with an appreciative audience and this audience was super-appreciative. Old Tex was in his element. He warbled his way through everything from 'Your Cheating Heart' to 'Redback on the Toilet Seat'. And whenever things looked like going a bit slow, he'd launch, yet again, into 'Me and Bobby McGee'.

Just before midnight, it was time for the last bracket. We all mustered on stage for the final fifteen renditions of 'Me and Bobby McGee', when someone noticed that the drummer hadn't returned.

'Last time I saw him, he was pretty full,' observed the pedal steel guitarist. 'Maybe he's gone in the dunny for a chuck.' So much for art. But, with the clock ticking on, old Tex didn't feel like mucking about. 'We'll go on without him or we'll run out of time,' he decided. So we trooped back on stage and into it.

'Busted flat in Baton Rouge. Waiting for a train . . .'

Instantly, the crowd was up on the dance floor. There was still no sign of the drummer, but no one seemed to notice.

'Bobby flagged a diesel down, just before it rained . . .'

In fact, we were three-quarters of the way through the song, when there was a bit of a disturbance out in the wings, and the drummer turned up, very much the worse for wear. He sort of closed one eye, trying to work out how to make it across the stage to the podium on which his drum kit sat, without mishap. After only a few tries, he made it. Admittedly, the last and final attempt was made on his hands and knees, but he got there. To do so, he had to crawl between my legs. I observed, as Tex and the others launched into the chorus, that the drummer was getting decidedly more ashen with each passing second. 'This could be interesting,' I thought. After all my years in music, I'd never played with someone actually chundering on stage. The night was becoming more enthralling all the time.

Out the front, Tex and the troops were totally unaware of the mini-drama unfolding behind them. Thankfully, neither was the dancing audience.

'Freedom's just another word for nothing left to lose . . .'

The drummer concentrated hard. He grabbed the upright bit of his drum stool with both hands and slowly tried to raise himself to his feet. It took an effort, but he made it. Gingerly, he lowered himself onto the padded seat. Phew! That seemed successful, too.

'Feeling good was easy, Lord, when Bobby sang the blues . . .'

Unfortunately, the forces of gravity were a bit stronger than our old mate's. The sheer momentum of manoeuvring himself onto the drum stool got the best of him. He just kept going, falling over backwards with one hell of a crash and sending his hi-hat arcing into the crowd. It could well have decapitated some poor bastard, but it didn't. And, still, no one seemed to notice. The whole audience was singing along with Tex.

'Buddy, that was good enough for me. Good enough for me and Bobby McGee.'

Luckily, 'Me and Bobby McGee' isn't the most demanding song in the world for a guitar player, because, I must admit, I was far more interested in what was going on behind the drums than I was in what we were supposed to be playing. It didn't really matter that the audience and other band members were oblivious to what was going on, they weren't likely to miss any of my tasteful and innovative guitar licks. The old drummer shook his head like a dazed prize-fighter and made another valiant attempt to get behind his instrument. In fact, he made several, all except the last being disastrous. Finally, a shift in the breeze, or some other miracle of nature, proved enough to stop him pitching backwards or forwards off his perch. He then concentrated on trying to pick up his drumsticks, which he'd left resting in a little fork in his snare drum stand. That took a while to resolve, too. Every time he managed a grip on them, they developed a life of their own and skittled onto the floor. That meant he had to get back on his hands and knees and rummage under the kit for them. Still the audience and the rest of the band didn't bat an eye.

'Nah nah nah nah nah nah nee. Good enough for me and Bobby McGee.'

Tex actually had the whole crowd on its feet, clapping its fifteen hundred pairs of hands over its head. And, although 'Me and Bobby McGee' had officially ended, why spoil it when you're on such a good thing? He started the whole song again.

'Busted flat in Baton Rouge . . .'

The drummer overcame his immediate problem by gripping his retrieved drumsticks in his teeth and groping his way back up the drum stool. Now quite an old hand at staying upright for seconds at a time, he managed a reasonably secure position and tried to come in on the beat. Unfortunately, his radical 72/131 timing didn't quite fit the rather conventional four-four rhythm of 'Me and Bobby McGee', but it didn't matter, anyway. About three seconds into the song, the drumsticks flew out of his hands and speared off into the crowd. Again, how he never killed some poor bugger, I'll never know.

'I dragged my old harpoon, out of my dirty red bandana . . .'

That he still hadn't impaled or maimed anybody after six more similar incidents with his drumsticks, was even more remarkable. Eventually, things fell into place slightly and he not only managed to keep a grip on things, but actually rustled up a back beat of sorts. Tex, out the front, gave no indication that he was aware there'd ever been a problem.

'With those windshield wipers beating time, Bobby clapping hands . . .'

It was about then that the drummer's gaze caught mine. It was also the time his next looming personal crisis became blatantly obvious. His face was almost transparent with nausea. Disaster didn't strike, however, until Tex was caterwauling,

'One day outside Salinas, lord, I let her slip away . . .'

Realising doomsday was upon him, the drummer flung his drumsticks aside (again, without causing any major injury) and literally flew past me into the dressing-room just beyond the wings.

But I wasn't giving up that easily. I knew there was some reason I had such a long lead between my guitar and amplifier. Without dropping a bar, I was able to follow him right into the dressing-room. The dressing-rooms on each side of the stage at the Goulburn Workers Club aren't very big. There's room for four or five people in each: a small bench, a sink and a big mirror directly opposite the doors. Our embattled drummer had stopped about an inch in front of the mirror. For a second he gazed morosely at his pathetic reflection—then brought up his last three meals straight into the glass. And what cared the rest of the world for his plight?

'Nothing ain't worth nothing, but it's free . . .'

At this stage, I wasn't the only witness to our percussionist's plight. His girlfriend, who was now sharing the joyous occasion with us, broke into shrieks of hysterical laughter and squealed supportively, 'Jeez Wayne, you're gross.'

Our drummer wasn't a man to be sidetracked by anything. In his befuddled state, the only thing he was aware of was that he couldn't breathe properly—the diced carrot and other hardware having clogged up his 'bronchials' somewhat. But he knew about such things. Being an asthmatic, he had just the gear on hand. Without further ado, he whipped his Ventolin inhaler out of his back pocket and gave himself a massive squirt. Unfortunately, it was a massive overdose. Bang! Down he went, like a bag of spuds.

'Feeling nearly faded as my jeans . . .'

Bloody hell, out the front, on stage, Tex and the boys were so moved by the drummer's plight that they'd started a third rendition of 'Me and Bobby McGee'. The drummer's girlfriend changed her 'Jeez Wayne, you're gross' to some perfectly understandable hysterical screaming. I was so stunned by what was going on, I actually considered putting my guitar down and searching the bloke's wallet for some hint as to what to do in such an emergency. However, while I was wrestling with my conscience, the external fire door suddenly collapsed in and a copper and a couple of paramedics came hurtling in. Some good Samaritan, obviously not mesmerised by the hypnotic beat of Tex's version of 'Me and Bobby McGee', had seen fit to call in professional help.

'Feeling good was easy, Lord . . .'

The paramedics banged away on the poor old drummer's chest, until he brought up his three *previous* meals, made sure he was breathing again, strapped him to a stretcher and rushed outside with him.

Out the front, Tex was bowing graciously to the wildly applauding audience. 'Thank you folks, you've been great. See you again next year.'

I collected my money and went. I heard later the drummer slept the whole incident off without the slightest recollection of what had happened. I haven't seen him or Tex again, to this day.

And I haven't been game to play 'Me and Bobby McGee' again. Maybe it's just guilt, but somehow, to me, it seems to bring out the worst in everyone.

Ted Egan is a unique Australian performer. I first met him just after he'd come to public notice for steering Rolf Harris in the direction of his huge hit 'Two Little Boys'. Over the years, we've crossed paths on several occasions—sometimes over a convivial rum, sometimes in a musical sense. The following yarn dates back to the time when country music festivals were the go all around Australia. Actually, they *had* been the go and were starting to decline in popularity. The festival in this story had lost all the promoters' dough even before the gates opened—but that's another story. Ted was one of the headline acts. I was playing in a Canberra-based country rock band called Cactus Jack.

DRINKING TED'S INSTRUMENT

We should have known it wasn't going to be one of the great music festivals. No sooner had we pulled up in the band truck at the stage entrance, than an anxious-looking bloke with a clipboard came striding up.

'I'm one of the organisers,' he told us, without ceremony. 'We already know the gate's not big enough to pay everybody, so you've got two choices—you can turn your truck around and go back home, or you can come in and do your thing. If you do come in, I must warn you that you probably won't get paid.'

It wasn't much of a choice, but there was only one thing we could do, really—go in and play. That way, the organisers would, at the very least, owe us something. If we bailed out, we'd have fewer grounds on which to claim any money that might be due to us.

'Okay,' said the organiser wearily. 'Drive your truck around the back of the stage and set your gear up. There's a couple of site huts there, with food and beer in them. Just help yourselves.'

In those days, we carted so much equipment around that we had to hire a couple of roadies to set it up for us. All the band members also mucked in and gave a hand. We weren't too big for our cowboy boots, yet. It took forty minutes or so to lug all the amps and instruments onto the stage and set them up. By then it was a bit on the warm side, and concensus was that a cold beer wouldn't go astray. One of our roadies, nicknamed The Animal (like every second roadie in the world), was sent to do a quick recce on the site huts behind the stage.

He came back with a triumphant grin on his face. 'I've found the one with the beer in it,' he announced. Sure enough, on a card table in one of the little sheds was a carton of Fosters. It wasn't much to go around our big contingent of musicians and hangers-on, but it was wet and it was free. That Fosters barely touched the sides and it only took a few seconds to empty the carton. Being diligent lads, we commissioned The Animal to take the carton and put it in a rubbish bin. We couldn't have litter around the place. Then, as we weren't due to go on stage for an hour or so, we split up and wandered around the festival site.

When I came back to the site shed, there was a very agitated Ted Egan pacing up and down, wringing his hands. I hadn't seen him for years and greeted him warmly, but Ted's heart didn't seem to be on social niceties.

'You blokes haven't seen a carton of Fosters around here, have you?' he asked fearfuly. Oh shit. We'd drunk Ted's grog.

'Yeah, well, I have mate. But, you see, like . . . errr . . . ummm . . . We drank it. The bloke at the gate said we could just help ourselves to whatever grog was here and we thought . . .'

'Crikey! I don't mind you drinking the beer—it's the carton I was after. It's my bloody instrument and I'm due on stage in twenty minutes.' He started wringing his hands pathetically again. If you're not a Ted Egan fan, you mightn't be aware that part of Ted's uniqueness in the music world is that he accompanies himself on a Foster-phone, beating out a rhythm on an empty beer carton. We'd misplaced his Stradivarius, as it were.

'Well, no worries. We'll just nick out to the nearest pub and buy you another carton,' we offered.

'But you don't understand,' wailed Ted. 'This is bloody Victoria. They don't have cardboard cartons in Victoria.' And they didn't. In Victoria, all canned beer came in plastic blister packs. Ted had had to cart his precious carton for his festival appearance all the way from Alice Springs.

We tried to set the wrong right. The Animal, full of remorse, raced off to the rubbish bin where he'd stuffed the carton, in the hope of restoring it to stage-suitability with a bit of judicious panel beating—but it wasn't there.'

'Obviously, it's been discovered by some astute music lover,' observed Ted grimly.

There was no way out of the situation. Ted called The Animal aside.

'There it is, son. The stage is that way and the New South Wales-Victorian border is back there. You have less than twenty minutes to make it there and back again before I go on.' And The Animal did. A musically aware New South Wales publican was quite happy to replace Ted's instrument with a slab of equal quality. Ted made it on stage with seconds to spare.

While he tapped out 'There's Lots of Bloody Good Drinkers in the Northern Territory' to the audience, we sat silently in the site hut and looked at the twenty-four cans of Fosters growing warm on the table in front of us. We would have loved to have sampled them—but we didn't dare.

Musicians' yarns can be difficult to do justice to in print. A lot of them are far easier to sing than to write down. Typical of that sort of yarn is the following offering. I'll swear it's true. It's usually told about a prominent artist, who, for various reasons, is often the butt of musical and show biz jokes. It really doesn't matter whom this yarn refers to—it's a good tale, anyway.

BLUE HEAVEN

Without a doubt, one of the greatest live television shows ever to grace Australian screens was the old *In Melbourne Tonight*. It went for years, five nights a week, and broke all sorts of endurance records—for audience and production crew alike. My own associ- ation with it lasted several years in the mid-sixties. Mostly, I would provide guitar backing for various folk artists. Occasionally, I'd help out in the odd comedy sketch. I'd like to think my juvenile strum- mings were of some help to members of the Peter, Paul and Mary set. Singers with a more conventional repertoire weren't necessarily as well served.

In those days, the musical directors of television stations had an unenviable job. Generally, they had to have, within easy reach, suitable scores with every song known to humankind. The go back then, was to have a band call about 7 pm, to which all the night's musical guests would flock. They'd let the long-suffering MD know what they planned to sing. He'd be responsible for whipping out the appropriate sheet music, distributing it to the band members, and providing the backing when the show went to air live at 9 pm. If the singer was really lucky, they'd get a chance for a couple of run throughs with the band—but not always. These days, singers pay big money so they can have their personal repertoires all set and ready for any band they might have to work with. Thirty years ago—especially in Melbourne, where there wasn't a thriving club scene like Sydney's—most people appearing in IMT relied very heavily on the sheer professionalism of the MD and his cohorts.

On this particular night, the star attraction was to be a rather self-indulgent baritone, whose arrogance was legendary among musos. He arrived for the 7 pm band call, with no intention of sticking around for a full rehearsal.

'Look,' he told the MD, 'I've got other more important things to worry about. I haven't time for a rehearsal. If you're any good, you blokes should know what I'm going to do, anyhow.'

'Fine. What are you singing?' asked the MD.

' "Blue Heaven", in G,' replied the baritone. 'Standard tempo. I'll see you just before I go on,' and he swept out of the studio for a quick dinner appointment at the legendary Dick Reardon's pub, not far from the channel.

As was usual in such a situation, the MD repaired to his trusty suitcase, which he'd converted into a sort of portable filing cabinet for the thousands of band arrangements he had on little cards. He just went down the index until he found the M file—M, for 'My Blue Heaven'—riffled through the cards until he found the required music in the key of G, and distributed it to his troops. Then they went about the business of seeing to every other singer's arrangements for that night's show.

A couple of hours later, it was show time and every pair of eyes in Melbourne was glued to the little black and white screens in households around the city. The show churned along at its usual entertaining high standard. Finally, the time came to introduce the well-dined baritone.

'And now, ladies and gentlemen, here's Herc McLerk, with his personal favourite, "Blue Heaven".'

With that, the MD waved the band into a natty little up-tempo version of the old standard 'My Blue Heaven'. It's hard to replicate in print, but if you know the song, it sort of went . . .

'When whippoorwills call . . . bop bop de bop . . . And evening is nigh . . . wah wah . . .'

While our old mate the baritone stepped onto the set, struck an heroic pose and droned, 'Blue Heaven and you and I . . .' from the musical *The Desert Song*.

After winning the World Yarn Spinning Contest in Darwin in 1991, I decided the event needed a bit of an international flavour. When you start trying to translate something as unique as Australian yarns overseas, you can get into strife. I remember, years ago, in Japan, watching replays of the old *Monty Python's Flying Circus* on Japanese TV. Apart from the incongruity of hearing John Cleese, Eric Idle, Michael Palin et al dubbed into Japanese, there was an obvious difference in the way the Japanese and the British lunatic fringe regarded comedy. The Japanese overcame the problem by having an expert panel discuss, gravely analyse and explain each sketch after it ended. Clearly, Japanese and British senses of humour had their differences.

Having worked occasionally overseas and extensively in the local tourist industry, I've fallen foul of that difference fairly often. When considering candidate nations for possible inclusion in the Darwin yarn fest, I rejected the obvious ones out of hand. But I made a real attempt to try to find some American candidates who might be interested in participating.

It wasn't so much pandering to the Americanisation of Australian society, as looking for a chance to beat the bastards at something. But it wasn't as easy as you might think. We're all pretty familiar with American comedy, having it thrust on our senses almost nightly on the box. However, it's not quite the same as ours (although the TV ratings figures would suggest otherwise). Even their yarn-spinning tradition is different. They tend to go for the tall story sort of thing far more than we do. Sure, one or two yarns in this volume might fit that category . . . but our lies tend to be more entertaining than theirs. In their tall story tradition, the lie itself is probably more important than the package in which it's presented.

The search for American yarn spinners to possibly come over here and compete actually took me to some hallowed halls of academia. The Yanks take their traditions very seriously. Finally, through contacts in the folklore game, I tracked down a small publishing house in Arkansas, and, there in their catalogue, was a list of material which seemed to be just what I was looking for. In fact, its books and spoken word cassettes looked very much like American versions of the sort of stuff ABC Marketing offers as Australiana. I selected a couple of names at random— Billy Ed Wheeler and Loyal Jones—and wrote to them, care of the publishing house.

To my joy, they both wrote back. The interesting thing about the whole episode was that although Loyal is a university administrator in Berea, Kentucky, Billy Ed is a musician (among other things). He's worked out of Nashville, Tennessee, and, in fact, is best known here for his hit of a few years ago, 'Coward of the County', recorded very successfully by Kenny Rogers.

In our correspondence, Billy Ed sent me a whole swag of great yarns. Apart from a few geographical differences, and the names of people involved, they could well have been Australian yarns. In fact, he's revealed to me that the commonest tie between our two yarn-spinning nations, seems to be the type of yarns told by musicians. This one's typical. What I've done is scrubbed the American placenames and made it Australian.

RESURRECTION

A group of retirees was on one of those package tours of Central Australia—you know, where they travel by coach all over the outback, camping out at night and living the great Australian dream of seeing the country. On this particular tour, the coach captain had them well trained. They'd been on the road for over three weeks, and the tourists had the camping routine down pat. At lunchtime, they'd help set up the barbie, and take turns cooking, serving and washing up. Every evening, they'd stream out off the coach, drag the tents out of the little trailer up the back, and set them up in neat rows. They slept like soldiers, three to a tent— the women in one row of tents, the blokes in another.

Late one night, just the other side of Ayers Rock, towards the West Australian border, one old feller started nudging his mate, in the sleeping-bag alongside him, in the ribs.

'Hey, Charlie, wake up! Wake up!'

'What's the matter, Fred?'

'Wake up, mate. You wouldn't believe it. I've just woken up with the greatest erection I've had in years. It's a beauty.'

'Yeah. Yeah. Well, turn over and go to sleep.'

'No way, mate. Like I said, I just reached down, and there it was. I haven't had one like this for ages. I reckon I'll just nick over to the ladies' tents across the way and give the missus a bit of a surprise.'

'Well, if you do, you'd better take me with you.'

'Why's that?'

'It's *my* old feller you've got a hold of.'

It's funny, when you lump a whole lot of yarns together like this, you get definite patterns. (Time for some serious analysis, folks—

you've got to pander to academia from time to time.) I hadn't realised, until now, that a lot of musician's stories are about old age. 'Why?' I sometimes ask myself. 'Damned if I know,' I often reply.

On the other hand, to maintain some sort of credibility, I should try to come up with a serious answer. Is it because musicians are more aware of the rigours of growing ancient? Very few of them manage to maintain the physical presence of a Rock God once they pass thirty-five—Mick Jagger and my good self being obvious exceptions.

This next musician's story, then, could well be considered as yet another example of faded old has-beens confronting their own mortality. Or it could just be regarded as a good yarn.

NOT YET PAST IT

The word got around the media that an old bloke in the wilds of Tasmania had just married for the fifth time—to a nineteen-year-old girl. And he was ninety-five.

The press went down there in force. When they arrived, they were a bit put out to find that the old feller was asleep and they had to talk to a contingent of his strapping sons.

'I'm sorry,' the oldest one said, 'but Dad *is* ninety-five and he needs his sleep. On top of that, he's almost blind. He's deaf . . . and he can't walk.'

'But, is it true he's just married a nineteen-year-old girl?' one of the reporters asked.

'It sure is. That's why he needs his sleep.'

The media contingent resigned itself to the fact that, at least for the time being, it would have to make do with talking to the old bloke's immediate family.

'Can we speak to his wife, then?' someone asked.

'No, well, she needs her sleep, too—to match his odd hours.'

'Well, could you give our readers some idea of his routine? I mean, if he's ninety-five, how does he cope with a young wife?'

'Well, every day, as soon as he wakes up, three of us sons carry him down the hallway of the house to his wife's bedroom. We leave him there for four hours, then six of us go down and carry him back to his own room.'

The reporters took copious notes.

'Hang on,' one of them called. 'How come only three of you carry him *down* to his wife's bedroom, but it takes six of you to bring him back?'

'The old bastard always puts up a hell of a fight.'

I've been looking for a vehicle for this next yarn for decades. It *is* true. Some people may question the taste of the story (when compared with the other tasteful and sensitive ones in this collection), but I have no qualms about it. The problem it concerns is one which my own family has to deal with on a daily basis, and I have no personal hesitation about inflicting it on you. If ever there was a high point in my own musical career, this was probably it.

LOVE'S RADIO AUDITIONS

For aspiring musicians in the late 1950s, breaks were hard to come by. For a start, the whole entertainment world was in turmoil. Television had just come on the scene—so had rock'n'roll. Radio stations had lost their monopolistic grip on the entertainment industry and were trying to fight back with such unconventional moves as broadcasting a weekly Top 40—instead of the old Top 10. Established artists such as Sinatra, Frankie Laine, Jo Stafford and Doris Day, were being eclipsed by such luminaries as Little Richard, Elvis and local heroes Johnnie O'Keefe and Col Joye.

The dream of anyone who owned a guitar was to graduate to shows like *Bandstand* or *Six O'Clock Rock*. To kids from the suburbs, such a dream seemed purely out of reach. But there were little glimmers of light at the end of that long tunnel. One of them was *Love's Radio Auditions*.

Love's was a furniture store in Bourke Street, Melbourne. It sponsored its weekly talent quest on the most popular, hit-minded radio station in that fair southern city, 3UZ. The talent quest was broadcast live from the Oliver J. Neilson auditorium, above an electrical store at the top end of Bourke Street, from about 7 o'clock every Saturday morning. All anyone had to do was front up, put their name on the list, and they could go to air. There was even an accompanist to back them, if required—the wonderful Margot Sheridan. The compere was an old radio star of yesteryear, Tiny Snell—a giant of a man with a head as bald as a billiard ball. Tiny was a real trouper. He could handle anything from news reading to advice for the lovelorn. The third member of the production team was a fledgling announcer, whose task it was to judge the talent quest. He was stashed away somewhere in the bowels of the radio complex, with a set of headphones and a Phantom comic, to decide the fate of the contestants.

That one person had sole control over some truly glittering prizes. With a flick of his wrist, he could wave a little hammer and gong each contestant's score accordingly. One gong scored you a prize of ten bob. Two gongs entitled you to a copy of any record off the 3UZ Top 40. Three gongs and you netted a quid and a promise that you'd be brought to the attention of someone at Channel Nine. Wow!

Is it any wonder we turned up in droves to compete? My brother Pete and I were aged about fourteen and sixteen, respectively. We put in at least twenty minutes intensive practice in preparation for our turn on *Love's Radio Auditions*. Our choice for the occasion was 'What Do You Want to Make Those Eyes At Me For?', a hit at the time for the totally forgotten Emile Ford and the Checkmates.

We caught a very early tram with our mum on that fateful Saturday morning, to make sure we arrived in time to be high up enough on Tiny's list to actually get to air.

Inside the studio, the air was chilly. It was a big auditorium— obviously a relic of better days, when radio stations had the facilities to broadcast big bands live. There were rows of seats and, right up the front under the stage, a deep, dark orchestra pit, which had once played host to some of the big-name combos of the war years, but now was used only to store light aluminium stack-chairs.

We'd made it there in time to be sure of inclusion in the morning's program and stood, along with the other lucky artists, in a line stretching from the back of the stage, waiting to be summoned forth by Tiny. At the appointed time, the theme was played, Tiny welcomed everyone, cajoled some enthusiastic applause for Margot, and started working his way through the list. They'd come from all over, singers, guitarists, yodellers, trumpet players, jugglers, conjurers and mime artists—all of them judged and awarded by the anonymous Mr Somebody out back, gonging his decisions with gusto.

Gradually, Tiny worked his way through the list until he was almost up to us.

'Now let's see who's coming up next on *Love's Radio Auditions*,' he rumbled, one hand over his ear and the script held at arm's length so he could read it without his glasses. 'Why, it's Bruce Twaddle from Highett. Morning, Bruce.'

'Mornin', Tine,' mumbled Bruce in nervous embarrassment.

'Don't be shy there, Bruce. Step right up to the old microphone and speak up. Tell us Bruce, what do you do for a living?'

'Errr. I'm a fitter and turner, Tine, at Orwell Brothers in Cheltenham—if it's all right to give them a bit of a plug . . . her her her.'

'Of course it's all right, Bruce. We're always pleased to send a big cheerio to our friends at Orville Brothers. Now, I see by your card Bruce, that you're a singer.'

'Yeah, Tine, that's right.'

'And where do you sing?'

'Aww, at parties and barbecues and church socials.'

'That's great. And I notice your big ambition is to appear on television.'

'Yeah, Tine, that's right.'

'Well, Bruce, you never know your luck here on *Love's Radio Auditions*. Tell me, what song have you selected for us this morning?'

'Yeah, Tine. Well, it's a lovely number from Rodgers and Hammerstein's immortal *South Pacific*—"Some Enchanted Evening".'

At that point, Margot performed a dazzling arpeggio on the piano and Tiny wrapped it all up with, 'So here we have him, ladies and gentlemen, contestant number four million, eight hundred and seventy-six thousand, nine hundred and forty-three on *Love's Radio Auditions*—Bruce Twaddle of Highett with Margot Sheridan at the piano and "Some Enchanted Evening".'

Margot thumped out the few bars of intro to that grand old song we all knew so well. Bruce cleared his throat, stepped right up to the microphone and sang 'Some . . .' before throwing a full grand mal epileptic fit.

With Margot in full flight in the background, the poor bugger went rigid and sort of hopped backwards, past the rest of us, until he hit the back wall of the stage. Then he tilted forward and precipitated back towards the front, hurtling past Tiny and the microphone, straight off the edge of the stage and into the orchestra pit.

It was only then that the true enormity of the situation sank in. Bruce was down in the pit, still in the grip of his seizure—sending the ultralight stackable chairs zotting several feet into the air. Margot didn't drop a beat, but everyone else did. Quick as a flash, Tiny had leaped onto poor old Bruce's chest. People were rushing in from everywhere to help. 'Make sure he doesn't swallow his tongue,' someone yelled.

'And stick some biros into his mouth to make sure he doesn't bite it,' some other good Samaritan suggested. The additional noise prompted Margot to play even louder. The stackable chairs still crashed out of the orchestra pit. By then, half-a-dozen stalwarts were each giving Bruce their version of what they believed should be done for someone suffering a grand mal fit.

Poor bloody Bruce.

And also, poor bloody judge . . . up there in the Gods somewhere. Imagine, sitting there reading your Phantom comic, waiting for 'Some Enchanted Evening' and hearing only the sounds of what seemed suspiciously like Custer's Last Stand, complete with piano accompaniment. With no idea of what was really going on, the judge did the only thing he could do in the circumstance—he played it right down the middle. He gave poor old Bruce two gongs.

As the metallic echoes rose around us, Tiny realised someone was due an explanation. With one hand deep down Bruce's throat, hanging onto his tongue, and the other neatly arranging pens through the gaps in his teeth, Tiny, still sitting on his patient's chest, bellowed in the general direction of the microphone, 'And that was Bruce Twaddle from Highett, with Margot Sheridan at the piano . . . contestant number six thousand, nine hundred and forty-three, on *Love's Radio Auditions*. And he wins a copy of *any* record off the 3UZ Top 40 for his rendition of the classic "Some Enchanted Evening".'

Almost as a second thought, he rather wisely added, 'And now some messages from our sponsors.'

By the end of the extended commercial break, Bruce had come good and was being escorted to a seat in the auditorium, somewhat confused and clutching the Top 40 record that someone had thoughtfully selected for him.

The story should have ended there, I suppose, but it's important to realise that we went on immediately afterwards. We sang 'What Do You Want to Make Those Eyes At Me For?' as though our little hearts would break, and also only scored two gongs.

There's a message there, somewhere.

HOLD THE PRESSES!
YARNS FROM
THE BIG SMOKE

There's an old journalistic axiom that far too many people, including journalists, seem to take very seriously—Don't let the facts ruin a good story. It's a worry when it's applied to the work journalists are supposed to do. But it's a positive plus when applied to telling their own stories.

I joined the Melbourne *Age* in 1961. I wasn't straight from the bush—I'd done a teenage apprenticeship, of sorts, in city living from the time we left the bush, when I was twelve, to when I started work. I had already been thrown into the insane cauldron of professional music when I was fifteen. While I was never tempted to make it a full-time job, it was scarcely more outrageous than the alleged career I eventually *did* pursue.

It's funny that journalists seldom seem to write their own biographies. We all threaten to, but somehow . . . And anyway, those that are written, tend to be extremely formal, pompous and boring. Journalists' published anecdotes are mere shadows of the ones they recycle in bars and dingy press rooms—at least they were in my time. The seemingly callow youths and Barbie doll girls who pursue journalism these days don't look as though they'd survive an old-fashioned night of true dinginess. I keep telling myself that one day I'll write a real book about my newspaper, radio and television days. In the meantime, this chapter will have to do.

While many of the yarns are about journalists, others are merely the stories we used to tell each other . . . some having nothing to do with journalism at all. What they show is that the bush doesn't have a monopoly on characters or yarns. With most Australians living in our cities, it's only natural that they should have been, and should remain, hotbeds of our finest art form, and should also reflect the multicultural nature of our cities.

ZORBA THE DUCK

A highlight of Melbourne living has always been the Victoria Markets. I used to go there with my mum, who was sure you could score a cheaper bag of spuds, a better line of T-shirt, or a more tasteful line of two-bob jewellery there, every Saturday morning. We'd always leave the markets laden with string bags full of loot. At midday, when the shops closed, all the trams in Elizabeth Street were chock-a-block, after picking up the homeward bound shoppers from outside the Victoria Markets.

One Saturday morning, a little Greek bloke from out Richmond way went to the markets, as he always did, and bought up big. Right on 12 o'clock, as he was rushing for a tram, he passed a poultry stall that was just closing. A big bloke blocked his path.

'There you are, mate. Special closing price. Two bob for a duck.' The stallholder waved a big white Pekin duck at the little Greek bloke. And, by crikey, it wasn't a bad sort of duck.

'Only two bob?' the Greek bloke asked.

'That's right, mate. For you, two bob . . . closing time special.'

The little feller put down his bulging string bag and fossicked through his pockets for some change. They did business, he put the struggling duck into the top of one of his string bags, and continued on to the tram stop.

'Where the hell do you think you're going?' asked a hulking great tram conductor menacingly, as the little bloke laboured aboard.

'Flinders Street Station, please.'

'No way in the world. You're not going anywhere with that bloody duck.'

'But I only wanna go to the station. I catch another tram to Swan Street.'

'Be buggered. Can't you read the sign? No animals on this tram, mate. You'll have to get off.'

By then, the tram was halfway to Flinders Street, anyway, so the little Greek bloke got off. At the corner of Collins Street, he realised there was no way he was going to be able to catch public transport home. With the duck wriggling and quacking, he wasn't likely to be allowed on board a taxi, either. Oh well. Richmond wasn't that far. He'd have to walk. The first few hundred yards were a bit of a bugger . . . all the way up the Collins Street hill towards Russell Street with those big bags. He'd almost got there, when he paused for a spell outside the old Lyceum picture theatre. There, for a limited season that weekend, they were showing *Zorba the Greek*. As the little Greek bloke paused to catch his breath, he had a bit of a look at the stills from the show in the big display cases outside the cinema. Crikey. There were shots of his home island off Greece.

And wasn't that his Uncle Dimitri dancing behind Anthony Quinn? And surely that wasn't little cousin Thula? He became quite excited. He just *had* to see the picture.

But as he approached the ticket box, he noticed the lady looking at his duck wriggling in the top of the string bag. There was no way he'd be able to get in with *that* thing. Quickly nipping around the corner, he grabbed the duck and shoved it inside his shirt. Then, doing the buttons up to the neck, he walked gingerly back to the ticket box and ordered a seat right up the front of the front stalls. The ticket seller didn't even look twice at him.

At the very front of the theatre, there was just one seat remaining. Already, he could hear the distinctive bouzouki music of the soundtrack and was feeling well and truly at home.

And what a film it was. There were great shots of his home village and members of his family kept popping up all over the place. He soon immersed himself in the movie.

On the other hand, the duck wasn't enjoying itself at all. It wriggled, scratched and twisted, trying to extricate itself from the stranglehold of the little Greek bloke's string vest. Finally, it managed to worry its head out through the fly of his trousers and, exhausted after its struggle, rested for a while on his lap.

Of course, the little Greek bloke was so rapt in *Zorba the Greek* that he didn't notice.

But one of the teenage girls sitting next to him did.

'Hey, Cheryl,' she nudged her companion.

'Yeah, Tracy.'

'This Dago bloke next to me's exposing himself.'

'He's just seeking attention. Don't take any notice of him.'

'Yeah, well, I'm trying not to . . . but the bloody thing's eating me Twisties.'

Yes, life in the Big Smoke turned out to be a lot different from the carefree *Smiley Gets A Gun* existence we'd known at Bacchus Marsh. But, back in the fifties, there was a much stronger sense of community in the city than there is now. Terms like 'multiculturalism' hadn't been invented and, although Australia was getting used to the idea of a large non-English speaking influx, bad feeling between races wasn't half the problem it appears to be these days. The cosmopolitan atmosphere in grimy old East Brunswick, where we lived, was very laidback and friendly—a lot like people expect country towns to be. The Hungarian family, the Stotzkas, on one side, were just as friendly as Luigi and Anna on the other. There was no sense of isolation that so many bush people feel today when circumstances force them to move to the city.

ONE POTATO, TWO POTATO . . .

Billy had been forced to move to Sydney from the bush to look for work. There was just nothing available for him round his home town of Crookwell, other than a bit of spud picking and some shearing-shed work. In Sydney, he managed to pick up a job as a storeman in a big warehouse, without much trouble. It wasn't the job he'd set his heart on when he passed his Higher School Certificate, but it was better than nothing. What really got to him though, was the loneliness of the city. After work, there was nothing much to do except go back to his flat and watch television. He'd always imagined that Sydney was full of action, but without any real mates his own age, he found it pretty tough going. It got slightly better in summer, when he could just walk from his flat down to Bondi Beach, but, after a while, he couldn't help but feel depressed at the lack of friends—especially girls.

One day, as he was sitting alone on his towel in the middle of the crowded beach, his mind blank with boredom, he hardly noticed the young bloke who threw his towel on the sand beside his.

'Hey! Don't I know you?'

Billy looked up. The sun was shining in his eyes and he couldn't properly see the newcomer. 'I don't know . . .'

'Hey, aren't you Billy Stephenson from Crookwell? Didn't you go to Crookwell High?'

'Yeah, I did . . . but I don't remember . . .'

'It's me, Craig McCormick. I was in the same class as you.' When Craig moved, Bill got a better look at him. Of course he remembered, he and Craig had been pretty good mates. But they hadn't set eyes on each other for eighteen months or so . . . when they both headed to the city looking for work.

They had a great yarn that afternoon. As they talked, Billy couldn't help but notice the number of spunky sheilas who kept coming and chatting Craig up. His mate exchanged phone numbers with several of them. Poor old Billy wished *he* could have that sort of success with women.

Later, over a beer, he mentioned it to Craig. 'You sure know how to crack onto the birds, mate. I wish I could. How do you do it?'

Craig looked up from his beer in amazement. 'And you call yourself a Crookwell boy? Don't you remember the old potato trick?'

'Potato trick?'

'Yeah. It always worked. My old man told me about it. If you want to attract the women, all you have to do is put a good old Crookwell potato down your bathers. It really does the trick.'

Billy didn't like to admit it, but he'd never ever heard of the old Crookwell potato trick. But if it worked for Craig . . .

'Yeah, of course. I just forgot it for a minute. I must give it a go next time I'm at the beach.'

So, later that night, they parted company. Craig had an assignation with one of the spunks he'd met on the beach. Billy had only his flat and his telly to return to, but, this time, he did it with a spring in his step, safe in the knowledge that tomorrow, weather permitting, he'd be able to pull the old Crookwell Potato Trick before he went to the beach . . . and after that, who knows?

Next day dawned bright and sunny. Billy could hardly wait until he'd finished work. When he did, he nicked back home, did as Craig suggested and whacked a good-sized Crookwell spud into his bathers and headed down to the beach.

The sand was crowded . . . but not for long. Within seconds of his arrival, Billy couldn't help but notice people staring at him. And they weren't the stares he'd been hoping for. All of a sudden, families started packing up their gear and fleeing from the beach. Parents mustered their kids and headed at speed back to the parking area. Within twenty minutes, there wasn't a soul anywhere near him within a radius of about 400 metres. Worse still, no pretty young spunks came within a kilometre of him.

Billy was mystified. As the sun set, he pulled his tracksuit on and headed to the pub, where he'd arranged to meet Craig. He explained to his old school mate what had happened.

'I don't understand,' Craig admitted. 'Look, come with me into the Gents and show me exactly what you did.' Making sure that no one followed them, Craig and Billy snuck into the toilet.

'Now, show me what you did,' demanded Craig.

Billy whipped off his tracksuit pants and demonstrated to his mate how he'd slipped that big old Crookwell spud into his bathers.

'You silly bugger,' Craig muttered. 'You're supposed to put the spud down the *front* of your bathers.'

A large part of my work as a city journalist was spent as a crime reporter. They were exciting times—a lot different from today's coverage of crime, where true investigative reporting has been replaced by monosyllabic police spokespeople and earnest, humourless reporters frowning their way through intros to re-enactments of dreadful events (which today's coppers can't solve by themselves) in the hope that unsuspecting members of the general public will do their work for them.

I suppose, to some extent, we sometimes did the wallopers' work for them, but it was more in the way of competition than anything else. Crash-hot reporters, such as Geoff 'Clanger' Clancy and Bruce 'Knobby' Turner, often got to witnesses and victims of crimes before the police. Heck, I pulled off a couple of scoops like that myself. Most cops hated us. Others enjoyed our boozy carefree lifestyle, and put up with us. Like the police themselves, and like the crims, we were at the fringes of Melbourne society.

I suppose that partly explains why so many of *my* city yarns involve the constabulary. Maybe it's just a sign of a troubled youth.

SUNDAY AT STUDLEY PARK

Most great cities of the world contain oases of one sort or another. Here in Australia, especially, little sanctuaries of green are to be found everywhere, sometimes in the most unlikely places. For those of us who lived in the dreary industrial slums of Melbourne, Studley Park, beside the Yarra River at Kew, was just such a haven.

One sunny Sunday morning, Trevor rose early. Being careful not to wake his old mum, he tiptoed into the kitchen and fixed her a special breakfast. It wasn't Mother's Day, or anything special like that, but Trevor had big plans for that particular Sunday. When he carried the tray in to his mum's room, she woke with surprise.

'Oh, Trevor. How nice!' she said, as he arranged the toast and tea in front of her.

'You just take your time, Mum. After I've done the washing up, I reckon I'll get the Vanguard Spacemaster out of the garage and we'll go for a bit of a spin.'

'Oh, that would be *lovely*, Trevor.'

Mum had a big feed and, while she was enjoying her shower, Trevor tidied up the kitchen. True to his promise, he carefully backed the Spacemaster down to the front door. It didn't take Mum long to get ready.

'Where are we going, Trevor?' she asked as she settled herself in the front passenger seat.

'Well, Mum, I thought, seeing it's such a lovely day, we'd drive out along the Yarra to Studley Park and enjoy a bit of a stroll along the river.'

'Oh Trevor, that *would* be lovely.'

And off they went.

Fifteen minutes later, Trev pulled up in the car park near the Kane Street Bridge. 'There y'are, Mum. All safe and sound. And the perfect day for a little stroll.'

'Oh Trevor, it's *wonderful.*'

Mum fossicked in the boot for the little thermos they'd packed. They headed across the freshly mown lawn to the banks of the Yarra, which flowed deep and cool between willow-covered banks. They didn't say anything—just listened to the carolling of the magpies against the backdrop of the traffic's mumble from the Boulevard.

Soon they found themselves to be alone. Although there'd been a number of cars parked in the car park, there wasn't a soul to be seen. It was as if they were the only two people left on Earth.

Trevor's mum walked right to the water's edge and threw a stick out into the sluggish flow.

All of a sudden, Trevor decked her.

With a heavy push, he sent her flat on her face in the mud. Before she could work out what was going on, he picked her up by the ankles—one in each hand—walked over to the river and started ducking her into it, headfirst. Naturally, every time he pulled her out of the water by her ankles, Trevor's mum let out one hell of a scream.

'Eeeek! Eeeek! Help! Help! Eeeek! Trevor, what are you doing? Eeeek!'

But Trevor didn't reply, he just kept lowering her back into the water, leaving her for a few seconds and pulling her out again.

Luckily, over on the Kane Street footbridge, a young constable on his way home heard Trevor's mum's pitiful shrieks. He ran across the bridge and down the river bank until he'd reached the scene of this particular little domestic drama.

As Trevor lowered his mum yet again into the Yarra, the young copper grabbed him by the shoulder and yelled, 'Hey, you! What the hell do you think you're doing?'

Trevor didn't reply. He merely dropped his mum headfirst into the shallows, turned around and king-hit the copper. The policeman went over backwards and Trevor started running as fast as he could back towards the car park.

It was then his dear old mum sat up in the shallows and screamed at him, 'Trevor, you're nothing but a mother-ducking cop-socker!'

This next yarn comes from a copper cum musician, the wonderful Russ Hawking, older half of the legendary Hawking Brothers. He could deliver a yarn completely deadpan. Among other things, he was the Victoria Police wresting champion. His untimely death in 1977 meant the loss not only of a great country singer, but a beaut yarn spinner.

COURTING DISASTER

There isn't a theatre in the world that can match the drama or comedy of an Aussie Court of Petty Sessions. Every weekday, somewhere in every major Australian city, the players gather to act out their roles. They come from all walks of life—the drunks, the perverts, the loonies, the professional victims and the parking infringers. Their masters of ceremonies are the police prosecutors; the stage hands are lawyers; their expert critics, closely monitoring every performance, are the magistrates. In the sixties, there were some great old stagers on the bench, meting out their own form of summary justice. One of the most colourful of these was the stipendiary magistrate dispensing justice at Moonee Ponds Court every Wednesday. He enjoyed being the villain of the piece. With a dry wit and a voice that sounded like false teeth being scraped down a blackboard, he was often as hard on victims, police and members of the public gallery as he was on malefactors—and he showed *them* no mercy at all. He had no compunction in fining an old lady who had dropped her crutches one morning while trying to creep out of the court to answer a call of nature. 'Contempt of this court' was how the magistrate described it, ordering her to the front of the court and imposing a two pound fine.

One morning, when Moonee Ponds court was going full bore, there was a bit of a shemozzle up the back. The magistrate had been having a field day—sentencing speeding motorists to death, transporting illegal parkers to Devil's Island for life and ordering the lash for sundry passersby for anything that smacked of contempt of his domain.

As soon as the disturbance erupted, the magistrate actually stopped a witness in mid-sentence and waited to see who dared challenge the smooth running of his court. Eventually, an extremely drunk bloke shook himself out of the hands of the horrified young coppers trying to restrain him and staggered to the front of the court. The magistrate grinned his most devilish grin. He could smell blood.

'Just what is the meaning of this interruption?' he asked the drunk, hissing with malevolence.

'Interruption be buggered,' slurred the drunk. 'Are you the judge, or what?' The magistrate's beady little eyes glittered.

'I happen to be the stipendiary magistrate here and this is my jurisdiction,' he purred. 'And it's a jurisdiction which passes grave penalties on those who don t pay it due respect.'

'In your boot,' mumbled the drunk. 'I pay me taxes and I want justice. And I want it *now*!'

The magistrate seemed content to play with him like a cat toying with a mouse.

'Before I come down on you with the full weight of the law, I'll give you one last chance to explain your disrespectful behaviour.'

'Bite your bum,' ordered the drunk. 'I'm here to get justice and I'm going to bloody well get it.'

For a second, the magistrate actually showed some puzzlement at what was going on. 'What do you mean, justice?' he asked, as though he'd never considered the term before.

'I want a divorce from my wife. And I want it now. She's a rotten bitch.' The gallery gasped at such provocative language.

'I should warn you that this is not a divorce court, it's the Court of . . .'

'Be blowed. I pay me taxes. I demand justice. I want to divorce my wife. She's done me wrong. She's given me a Venetian disease.'

'A what?' The whole court hummed with puzzlement until the magistrate banged down his gavel and demanded order.

'Your wife's given you what?' he asked again.

'A Venetian disease.'

The magistrate turned in frustration to the big fat old police prosecutor, who lurched to his feet. 'What's this man talking about sergeant . . . a Venetian disease?'

The sergeant took a deep breath.

'I think he means Gondolier, your worship.'

While we're on magistrates . . . This next yarn concerns the same beak and the same court. It's really a desperate attempt by my good self to avoid offending the judiciary too much. You never know when you might need them. Besides, give or take the odd embellishment, it's true. I wrote the original story myself for *The Age*, but they were too chicken to run it.

A ROSE BY ANY OTHER NAME

Another busy Wednesday in Moonee Ponds court . . . The large number of defendants watching the old beak in action grew increasingly alarmed at what fate might befall their not so good selves.

Not having a registration sticker on the ute? Bang! Twenty years in the salt mines.

Crossing double lines in your ambulance? Bang! Three thousand strokes with a rattan cane.

Urinating in a public place (to whit, a toilet)? Bang! Public disembowelment.

The old beak worked his way through the long list, until he came to case number several thousand and something.

'Call Warren Tremble,' chortled the clerk.

'Call Warren Tremble,' echoed the copper on the door.

'Call Warren Tremble!' The cry continued to be taken up by coppers and court attendants in the corridor outside. Eventually, a skinny little cove crept to the front of the court.

'Are you Warren Tremble?' asked the clerk.

'Y . . . yes, sir.'

'You are hereby charged with being drunk and disorderly in Alexander Road, Moonee Ponds, on 16 October 1963. You are further charged with drinking a poison, to whit, methylated spirits and also charged . . .'

At this point, the scrawny little defendant started to butt in. It wasn't the right thing to do in *this* court.

'That's not me,' he kept repeating. 'That wasn't me.'

The magistrate had had enough. 'Look, accused. You're in strife enough already. One more interruption and I'll add contempt of court to your charges.'

'But it wasn't me . . .'

'Silence. You'll get a chance to say your piece at the appropriate time. Pray continue,' he told the clerk.

That good officer of the court continued to read a whole list of charges, including indecent exposure, obscene behaviour and assaulting police with a deadly weapon—to whit, one stomach full of vomit. The defendant tried unsuccessfully to state his case, but was continually threatened by the magistrate.

Finally, a twelve-year-old copper was called to the witness box to give his evidence. After mumbling through the oath, he told the enthralled court that the previous evening, he'd been on patrol with Constable Evans in Divvy Van 14, when he espied the defendant passed out on the nature strip in the middle of Mt Alexander Road.

'His trousers were around his ankles, Your Worship. Closer examination revealed that he'd wet himself. There were several women and children in the area obviously distressed by his condition . . .'

At this stage of the evidence, the defendant was sobbing hysterically, all the time moaning, 'It wasn't me. It wasn't me.' The constable went on to describe how he and Constable Evans had tried to load Warren Tremble into the van, and had been decorated with liquid embroidery.

'I was shocked and appalled by his actions and had to take the rest of the shift off to recover,' he swore. Still, the accused kept wailing that it wasn't him.

Enough was enough. The old magistrate had had it. Finally, he spat at the police witness, 'Look constable. Let's settle this once and for all. Is this the man?'

For the first time, the copper looked down at the defendant. 'Oh, shit. No.'

An uneasy silence filled the court. The magistrate looked at the sobbing defendant.

'But you said you were Warren Tremble,' he snarled, accusingly.

'I am. I am. But that wasn't me.'

'Sergeant, could you straighten this out?' the magistrate asked the prosecutor, a little wearily.

'As Your Worship pleases.' And the big feller went down into the cells to see what the hell was going on.

You guessed it. There *were* two Warren Trembles. The poor bugger in the dock had merely been summonsed for not having a red reflector on the rear mudguard of his bike. The *other* Warren

Tremble, Master Criminal Extraordinaire, was still sleeping off the effects of his eventful evening in the comfort of the cells. The old magistrate was in a bit of a cleft stick. Finally, he reached his decision.

'It's a fair cop,' he announced. 'In the interests of justice, I think the charges against both Warren Trembles can be dismissed.'

So one Warren Tremble went home that afternoon, mighty relieved, indeed. The other had no idea of the drama he'd featured in, and was no doubt before the court on similar charges the following Wednesday.

Of course, city life isn't all courts and magistrates. Nor is Melbourne the only city on this continent (even if the best yarns *do* seem to come from there.) This next entrant could be regarded as a musician's yarn—I first heard it from a great bass player called Pieter De Vries. The names in it may be a bit dated, but that's part of its charm. Yes, I know, it *has* a legal slant to it. I'm just trying to gently wean you off magistrates and policemen.

JUST A FEW DETAILS, SIR!

Three blokes decided to head home one night after a heavy session on the turps. It was about three in the morning, and although none of them was in a position to drive, one bloke was adamant that he'd be okay. There's one in every crowd, eh?

Once behind the wheel, he realised that, while they'd been drinking, a major earthquake must have struck. Crikey! The buildings were still shaking, and the road was so wrecked that the car was veering all over the place. To make sure they weren't a danger to themselves or anyone else, the driver decided the best strategy would be to stick to the footpath—especially through the heart of Sydney.

'No worries. The front of the shops'll stop us swerving too far to the left, and the parking meters'll tell us if we're going too far right,' he told his mates. Because he was a particularly responsible driver, he elected to travel at a stately five kilometres an hour, so as not to endanger anyone.

His two mates weren't too happy with the arrangement. 'What if the coppers come along?' they kept asking.

'No worries. We'll be driving too slow to attract any attention. Besides, it's three in the morning, so there won't be anyone around, anyway.'

And off they went—at a painful crawl right through the darkened heart of Sydney's CBD.

By keeping well over to the left and using the shopfronts as a guide, they were able to maintain a surprisingly straight course. But the inevitable happened. A motorbike cop observed their dignified course along the footpath and decided something was definitely up. He stuck on his blue light and siren, drew up alongside the drunks and signalled them to pull over. Parking his bike twenty metres or so in front of them, he walked towards them, pulling his little black book out of his tunic pocket. In the offending vehicle, all hell had broken loose. Panic had set in.

'Jesus, Charlie. Look what's happened now. The coppers have nabbed us.'

'Don't worry. It'll be all right. Just do what I do.'

'What d'yer mean?'

'Well, if we give this bastard the wrong name, they won't be able to track us down afterwards, will they? I mean, I don't have a licence he can check with, so he'll never twig, eh?' A brilliant strategy.

'You're right, Charlie. You're dead right. But hang on, I can't think of a bloody name.'

'Me neither,' piped the third bloke from the back seat. By now, the policeman was pretty close.

'Don't worry about it. Just think of any name. Have a look around you—get a name off a road sign, or a building, or something.'

By now, the constable was well and truly on them. Leaning down, he opened his notebook, winced through the grog fumes, and rumbled, 'Orright, youse blokes, what's your names?'

The driver looked blearily about for a few seconds, then slurred. 'My name's David Jones, constable.'

The copper licked the end of his pencil and laboriously wrote it down. 'Okay, you,' he said to the bloke in the front passenger seat. 'Who are you?'

Again a slight pause as the drunk cast his optics over the street scape. 'Why, I'm his brother, Fletcher.'

'Right.' To the bloke in the back seat, 'And what's your name?'

The drunk looked around in a flat panic. Then it struck him. 'St George and Cronulla Permanent Building Society.'

It's sometimes little appreciated that a lot of Henry Lawson's finest stories were about city life. While Henry is generally associated with the legends of the Aussie bush, he was really a city bloke at heart. The bush frightened and disappointed him. Frank Hardy carries on that tradition. Although Frank grew up at Bacchus Marsh, near where I spent my own childhood, he's very much an urban yarn spinner.

THE DEATH OF DOOLEY FRANKS

I was very pleased to read in the papers recently, about the ninety-two-year-old bloke who'd fathered a child, otherwise, I couldn't have told you about the death of Dooley Franks, because you wouldn't have believed it. Dooley, you see, died at ninety-two, the same age as that old feller—*and* in the field of battle. In fact, he died the night before they were going to let him out of hospital.

The chief doctor arrives on the morning after Dooley Franks had passed away. When he arrives in the ward, there's four or five nurses crying. One of them's in really deep distress, saying 'Oh, sad, sad, day. Dooley Franks is dead. It's terrible. Dooley Franks is dead.'

So the doctor asks, 'What's all this business going on here? What's wrong with these nurses. Get them to work. I've got to do my rounds. There's people here sick and dying all over the place.'

'Well,' the head sister said, 'Mr Franks passed away during the night.'

'But wasn't he fit and well and going to be signed out today?'

And she said, 'Yes, he was . . . Perhaps if I show you something . . . Come here, Doctor.' And she opens the door of the private ward and, there inside, is a tent. It's really a bed with a sheet on it, but it *looks* like a tent.

'Have a look under the sheet, Doctor. That'll explain everything.' So he has a peek and there's Dooley Franks' body and, growing on it, the biggest donger ever seen in history. The doctor looks at it in absolute astonishment. When the sister goes out and shuts the door, he opens his surgery bag, gets out his little sharp saw and says to himself, 'Oh, I must take this home and show it to my colleagues. No one will ever believe it. I want this as evidence.' And he saws it off.

Well, he gets a copy of *The Telegraph* out of the cupboard and tries to wrap it up. But it won't fit. It won't cover it. So he gets a copy of the *Sydney Morning Herald*, with all the classified ads and things, wraps it up and hides it in a drawer.

When his rounds are over, he puts it in the boot of his car and he goes home. When he gets home, the phone rings. He puts the parcel on the bench in the kitchen and picks up the phone. When he gets off the phone, his wife's crying. So he says, 'What's the matter, darling?'

'Nothing.'

'It must be something. I haven't seen you cry in ten years.'

'It's something I can't tell you.'

'But you've got to tell me. I'm a doctor and I'm your husband. What's the matter?'

'Well,' she says, 'Dooley Franks is dead.'

He said, 'How do *you* know Dooley Franks is dead?'
And she said, 'I saw it in *The Herald*.'

Kev Naughton—the Gnorthern Ghone, aka the Mouth from the North—was the bloke who took the World Yarn Spinning Title from my good self. He did so with style and humour. Although he's a long-time Territory identity, Kev is not your stereotypical bush storyteller. A lot of his stuff's as urban as Frank's, or Henry's, with just that dash of Top End cheek. Ken's skill at alliteration is a feature of a lot of traditional Aussie yarn spinning. I don't think anyone does it better than he does. Of course, it's nigh to impossible to judge the effect of this yarn in print. Try it standing in the shower with a mouth full of macadamia nuts.

SCINTILLATING SAM

You've heard of Bond, and you've heard of Elliott and you've heard of Skase. But, by gee, there's a character from the eighties that you've never heard of—and he's one of the unsung tragedies of that decade of greed. Scintillating Sam Smith, the Sensational Super Chamois Salesman sold super chamois on the sales circuit for sixteen years and made squillions. So good was Scintillating Sam's show circuit sales spiel, that nobody could resist. He could talk anybody into buying the super chamois, because, although they sold in shops for $16.60, from Sam, just $6.00.

And *that* wasn't all.

For every super chamois you bought, he threw in a bonus—a second super chamois, and there was more. With the second super chamois, you also got a second semi chamois for use in the sink.

Now Sam used his spiel all over the countryside and made a fortune. He even sold super chamois to his family. Over one Christmas lunch, he sold his sister six super chamois for $6.00 each, then slipped his mother a single, tossing in a super chamois for free.

So good was his spiel that when the cops pulled him over for speeding, he drove off with a driving commendation. When he went to confession, he walked out with a sainthood—and the priest did his penance for him.

Sam made a bloody fortune. In that decade of greed, he plunged all his money into the same place as others did. But then came that dark day—19 October 1987. The stockmarket crashed. Scintillating Sam Smith, the Sensational Super Chamois Salesman, had stuck all his squillions into stocks and shares and the whole lot went down the tube.

Well, Sam Smith was a proud and confident man. He didn't like to lose all his dollars and cents. He was broke, and overcome with grief and depression. I shall never forget that night on Sydney Harbour Bridge, watching the silhouette of Scintillating Sam Smith against the sunset of Sydney—suicide written all over his face. As he prepared to jump a divine moment came upon us all. Mother Teresa was driving past in a silver sedan and she stopped to check out Scintillating Sam.

Mother Teresa walked over to the forlorn figure and started to talk to him. After a while, from a distance, I noticed Sam's confidence was coming back. His chest was puffed out and his face was joyous. Yes, Scintillating Sam was giving a spiel to Mother Teresa.

And together, they jumped off the bridge.

'The ultimate "two for the price of one",' yelled Sam, as they plunged towards Sydney Harbour's murky depths.

And when Mother Teresa was inches from the water, death just a split second away, Sam felt the tug of the bungee rope attached to his ankle.

'Only jokin', Mother Teresa,' he said. 'Only joking.' But, too late, she was gone.

On the other hand, Scintillating Sam was back at his best. He went back into Sydney to sell super chamois. But there were no sales, because there was no money. Day after day, Sam started to feel guilty. He had killed Mother Teresa—all in the name of super chamois and practical jokes. Eventually, it was too much for Sam. He decided to leave Sydney and look for another job.

Scintillating Sam, Sensational Super Chamois Salesman, went surveying in the sandy Simpson Desert for six months. After six months in the Simpson Desert surveying, your mind can play a few tricks, especially if you've recently killed Mother Teresa. Sam became a born-again Christian and decided to return to Sydney. But one problem . . . on his way back to Sydney, he noticed that things weren't the same as in the scintillating sales days. Although the shops and restaurants were open and the lights were on, no one was home. Not a single person was to be seen in all of Sydney.

'You beauty!' said Scintillating Sam, and he went into the shops and got the finest food. He wandered into restaurants—there was no one to stop him—and he drank the finest wine. He lived the life of Riley.

Well, it was all okay for a few weeks or so, but you need a partner to really enjoy the good things in life. Sam searched. There *had* to be another human being left in the world. Sydney offered up nothing. Eventually, it was too much for Sam. Lonely and sodden with guilt, he climbed to the top of Australia Square—this time, no bungee rope attached to his ankles. Scintillating Sam stood there and yelled at God.

'You bastard,' he said. 'And Mother Teresa, too. This is your retribution on me.' He looked at the streets below and jumped into space—free.

And as he passed the twenty-third floor, through an open window, he heard the telephone ring . . .

There can be no more deserving individual to have a final say on the subject of urban yarns than the legendary Harry the Horse. Harry George Lovett was without peer among the journalists of Melbourne in the 1960s. Yarns about him are still told today. The Horse was a big man—not only in stature (he sometimes topped 18 stone), but in character and humanity. But there was always about him an air of tragedy—a feeling that somehow this great individual was going to waste. By crikey, the Horse could drink. And despite all the hilarious yarns that resulted from his drinking, it was grog alone which killed him in the end. And the Horse died hard. The grog doesn't do things by half measures. All the stories, good times and booze aside, I'll treasure the memory of Horse just as a mate. On the other hand, I couldn't resist recording what I'm assured were the last words of a great character.

REQUIEM FOR A HORSE

The word had got around the traps that the Horse was on his last legs. A lot of people had been expecting it. Cirrhosis of the liver doesn't give you a second chance. The Horse had been crook for some time. At first, he took it all fairly philosophically. 'There's three pubs between the city and Brighton that have gone on the market since the quack put me off the grog,' he once announced.

But now, the end was nigh.

When he was admitted to hospital that last time, the Horse was Chief of Staff for the ABC Newsroom in Melbourne. When the word came through that there wasn't a lot of time left, one of his senior colleagues clocked off early and dropped in to see the big feller, possibly for the last time.

The Horse was just an inert form on a bed—a pathetic, inert form, joined up to all sorts of tubes and gauges and wired up to machines which beeped and monitored his fading vital signs.

His workmate tiptoed in and approached the bed. There was a small flicker of recognition from the Horse. He signalled for his mate to come closer and indicated that he wanted to say something. Despite the sadness of the occasion, Horse's visitor was also aware, at the back of his mind, that there was liable to be something special about the Last Words of Harry the Horse. So he moved in really close.

'Hey, see that poor old bugger over there?' the Horse croaked feebly, waving a limp hand at another pathetic, inert form, in a bed over the other side of the room, also wired up to all sorts of gauges and gadgets.

'Yeah, Harry. What about him?'

'The bastard's eighty-three years old, and never had a drink. Now look where it's got him.'

I know most of these big city yarns have a certain common element running through them—mainly petty crime and drink. Is it any wonder I turned out the way I did? The thing is, matters didn't improve much when I went back out bush.

4

THE TERRITORY CONNECTION

When I first walked into the old Vic Hotel in Smith Street, Darwin, on 20 December 1969, I knew I was somewhere different from where I'd ever been before. It was the start of the wet season, and all sorts of characters were wandering out of the bush to weather out the rainy months before the country became passable again.

'Crikey,' I thought. 'What a colourful mob.'

There was the Coddlin' Moth, who used to borrow people's motorbike helmets, draw faces on them with a felt pen and talk to them for hours. He reckoned he got a more intellectual line in conversation like that.

And there were blokes such as the one Paul Greene of Kiunga, Papua New Guinea, wrote about in the search for the Great Aussie Yarn. Paul had met an old character in the Animal Bar of the Karumba Hotel, in Queensland. The bloke he called the Karumba Old Man, to distinguish him from the Darwin Old Man in the yarn, provided Paul with this gem.

OLD HATREDS DIE HARD

He'd been drinking in a pub in Darwin. After a couple of jugs, he noticed an old man come into the pub. The Darwin Old Man looked broke and alone, so the Karumba Old Man invited him across for a beer.

It turned out that the Darwin Old Man lived alone in the bush around the top of Australia, and came out when he desperately needed the essentials of life.

After a while, the Darwin Old Man asked the Karumba Old Man, 'The war son, is it over?'

'Been over for years. How long have you been in the bush?' said the Karumba Old Man.

69

'Did we win?'

'Yeah. We won.'

'Good. Never did like them Boers, anyway!'

That was, indeed, the Darwin I walked full tilt into in 1969. Sadly, five years later, in the very same bar of the very same pub, tourists were coming in and taking photographs of *me*. And I hadn't changed at all. It was an indication of what the Territory was becoming—a less colourful place. A couple of weeks later, Cyclone Tracy blew me out for good. There was a period where I became like every other ex-Territorian and wandered about whingeing how it wasn't half as good as it had been in my time. I don't do that any more.

The Northern Territory still casts its spell on thousands of people who go up there to experience its magic. Sure, it's not *my* magic, but it's theirs and neither me nor anyone else has the right to try to talk them out of it. It's truly appropriate that the Territory has once again become the setting for the World Yarn Spinning Championships. Not long after I arrived there in 1969, I heard stories about Frank Hardy taking the title from Tex Tyrell, who, in those days, ran an auction room and second-hand shop in Bennett Street, Darwin.

I always fancied having a go at the title, but didn't get a chance until 1991, when Frank went back up there to put his crown on the line. To take it off the old bugger was a great thrill. It wasn't quite so thrilling to lose it in 1992 to Kevin Naughton, the Gnorthern Gnome . . . but what the hell? After all's said and done, it's the yarns that are important, not who tells them.

Funnily enough, my first Territory yarn came not from the horse's mouth, as it were, but from a wheat cocky called Miles Bourke, who was very big in wheat-grower politics in western Victoria in the 1960s. Miles is dead now, but his yarns, like this one, live on.

A TOUCH OF THE SPANISH FLY

This mate of mine had a big station just out of Katherine. He was one of those hard men who expected big things from everyone who worked for him, but who always believed in rewarding people who did just that little extra.

He had a head stockman working for him who'd been toiling away for months without the slightest complaint. One day, the boss called him in and said, 'Look, Jacky, you've been working bloody hard for the last few weeks. The long weekend's coming up, why don't you take it off and go into Katherine for the races? I'll bung a little extra in your pay pocket so you won't be short of cash . . . And I might even give you a bit extra to put on them horses for me.'

The head stockman was deeply touched. 'Bloody beauty, boss. I been hoping for a weekend off, ever since that Afghan hawker come around and sold me some of that stuff.'

'What stuff?'

'That Spanish fly, boss. You know, that stuff you take to make you all sexy. I reckon I'll take it with me to Katherine, give myself a bit of a snort and then whip it into some of them young gals there.'

'Jesus, Jacky. You want to watch that stuff,' warned the boss. 'I've heard it can be pretty strong.'

'No worries, boss. I reckon there'll be enough of them young gals in Katherine to take care of me and the Spanish fly real good.'

The boss thought no more about it all until Monday morning, when, uncharacteristically, the head stockman didn't show up on time to start mustering the hill country up the back. The boss was quite concerned—in fact, concerned enough to walk down to the camp to see if something unforseen had befallen the poor old bloke. He found Jack still in his swag, dead to the world.

'Hey, old man, jack your arse into gear. It's nearly eight o'clock. What'd you think you're doing, eh?'

The older feller blinked up at him, realised what was going on and crawled out of the blankets. 'Crikey, boss, I'm sorry. I never slept in this late before, eh?'

'Yeah, well, that's okay now, Jacky. What happened to you? You overdo that Spanish fly like I warned you?'

The head stockman grinned. 'Big mobs, I reckon, boss.'

'Are you sure you're okay?'

'I dunno, boss. Maybe I need some Deep Heat or something. Cop a load of this.' And, with that, he dropped his strides, standing there shamefacedly revealing a battered and worn very personal piece of his anatomy.

The boss was horrified. 'Bloody hell, Jack, you're not going to put Deep Heat on *that*?'

'No boss—on my wrist. No other bugger turned up.'

Sometimes, with Territory yarns, it's difficult to find stories about Aboriginal people that aren't downright racist. On the other hand, you can go overboard in avoiding stories which include Aboriginal characters, simply because you're frightened they might be deemed racist.

The old days in the Territory were tough ones. The place was full of white people who considered the original residents inferior. But there were others just as hard, just as tough, who worked hand in fist with the Aboriginal people. They relied on each other to get by and, wherever it was due, there was always mutual respect.

In those circumstances, it's hard to bypass yarns where one race, or the other, becomes the butt of the joke.

Reg Harris is a long-time Centralian identity. He's lived there since 1946. He submitted quite a sampling of his reminiscences to the search for the Great Aussie Yarn. They included some yarns about the legendary Jimmy Hereen—sometime jockey, prospector and publican.

JIMMY HEREEN

Things began to get a bit too hot for Jimmy in the racing game, so he moved to the Northern Territory and began mining wolfram in the Hatches Creek area, north of Alice Springs. Wolfram is a very hard and heavy black mineral, used in the hardening of steel. It's found in rock, so mining it was quite difficult.

Jimmy operated his mine with the help of an Aboriginal bloke called Fridee. They'd sunk quite a deep shaft and then a drive, to locate the deposits. The procedure was to bore a number of holes in the face of the drive, tap in plugs of gelignite and fix the detonators with fuses. The fuses were cut to various lengths to allow for the elapsed time between the lighting of the first fuse and the last. The trick was to ensure all the plugs exploded simultaneously.

During a rainy period, Jimmy had a lot of problems with wet fuses. Then he read in a mining magazine about a new electric detonator system which, it was claimed, made the messy fuse system obsolete. Jimmy placed an order and the equipment duly arrived.

Jimmy and Fridee drilled all the holes in the drive face and Jimmy extolled the virtues of the new system to his mate. He attached the electric detonators and carefully connected all the wires. Then he ran the cable along the drive, up the shaft and connected it to the plunger at the top.

'You watch this closely, Fridee,' he called. 'No more do we have to light them fuses—just press this handle and up she goes.'

He pressed. Nothing happened. He pressed again. Still nothing.

'God damn,' he said. 'I must have a bad connection. You wait up here, Fridee, and I'll go check.'

So down went Jimmy and checked all the connections—then back along the drive and up the shaft. With just his head and shoulders showing above ground, he said, 'Fridee, I've checked all the joints. Give him a press now.'

Fridee did, but still no action.

A frustrated Jimmy said, 'It looks like the bloody thing's no good.'

'I could have told you that before, boss, because I had him pressed down all the time you bin down there!'

Jimmy screamed at Fridee and threatened to cut his head off with an axe.

Fridee shot through, never to return to the mining industry. Shock had started to take control of Jimmy, so he thought the best way to control it was a trip to the nearest pub—Barrow Creek.

It took a fortnight of steady drinking for Jimmy to recover. By that time, he decided mining was a fool's game and there were better ways to earn a living. So he bought the Barrow Creek pub which, with his brother Bluey, he operated for nine years.

On the Stuart Highway, close to the pub, he had a sign 'Barrow Creek Hotel—Open 25 hours a day'.

The sign attracted a lot of people to the hotel to ask. 'How can you claim to be open twenty-five hours a day?'

Jimmy's reply? 'We don't close for an hour for lunch.'

Peter Knudsen was the ABC's rural bloke in Darwin when I first set foot up there. Knudsen is one of the world's best yarn spinners himself—as a colleague once described him, 'The second funniest man in the world'—and a great appreciator of a tale well told. Not long after I got there, he organised a yarn-spinning contest via the airwaves, and people came up with some beauties. I'm still trying to track Knudsen down to find out what became of them. In the meantime, here's one that I can recount fairly accurately.

WHEN YOU KNOW YOU AIN'T GOT IT ANY MORE

For some time, the members of a well-known Centralian family had been growing a little worried about Dad. After years of battling the vast red inland, his eyes were starting to give out. Not that the old bloke would admit it. 'There's nothing wrong with my eyes. I can still see as clear as when I was twenty,' he'd roar at the nearest hatstand whenever a member of the family brought up the subject of his sight. He kept up his protests for years. The slightest suggestion that he needed glasses would just throw the old bugger into a rage. 'Glasses? You'll never catch me wearing them bloody things. They'd be a bloody danger in the stockyards—falling off and all that. Don't ever mention bloody glasses to me again. There's nothing wrong with my sight.' And he'd storm off and pretend to read the Bible, which he'd invariably hold upside down.

There came a time, though, when the old bloke's near-blindness was anything but funny. He was always getting things mixed up— putting the wrong thing in the wrong place. He was a positive menace with things like medicines and instructions. And no one dared let him anywhere near a gun.

It called for desperate measures. One day, the flying doctor dropped in to check on the old bloke's latest grandkid. While Dad was out of earshot, the eldest son explained the problem to him.

'No worries,' the flying doctor assured him. 'I'll pretend I'm giving him an all-over checkup or something, test his eyes while he's not quite sure what's going on and send the prescription off to Adelaide. They'll post the glasses back to you and after that . . . well, all you have to do is convince him to wear the damn things.'

The ruse proved easier to pull off than everyone thought. Because the old bloke's seventieth birthday was coming up, he admitted that a full medical check was a pretty sensible idea. By the time the quack had checked his heart, his lungs and everything else, he hardly noticed the eye test. The doctor found, as expected, that the old fool *was* nearly blind, but it wasn't so bad that a good pair of bifocals wouldn't help. Without saying a word to Dad, but with a big wink to the other members of the family, he nutted out a prescription for glasses, put it in his shirt pocket and took his leave.

It took a while for Dad's mail-order glasses to arrive from Adelaide. But the big day came. The mail plane only called in once a week and there was the innocuous little parcel, addressed to Dad, along with the bills, threatening letters and R. M. Williams catalogues.

'What's this?' muttered the old feller, as he unwrapped the paper. Everyone held their breath. There, in a nifty little case, was a pair of wire-framed specs. Well, the old bloke went off his head.

'Bloody glasses. Who sent me these? What do I need glasses for, anyway?' Anyone brave enough to try to answer wouldn't have had a hope in hell. The old cove went on and on.

'Bleeding bloody glasses. I don't need them. My eyes are as good as they've ever been.' He carried on so much that he must have worn himself out, because he actually ran out of breath and stood for a moment in silence.

Then the voice of sanity came from the back of the room from one of his little grandkids. 'Well Grandpa, why at least don't you try them on?'

And bugger me dead, he did just that. Still muttering under his breath about not needing the things, he took the glasses out of their case, looped the little curly bits over his ears and, for the first time in God knows how long, peered around the room with twenty-twenty vision.

Everyone held their breath as he turned around and blinked at his wife.

'Jesus, Mum, you've gone orf.'

He's something less than a household name down south, but undoubtedly Cowboy Bill is Darwin's most beloved yarn spinner. I always felt that Bill was the one to beat when I first had the temerity to contest the World Yarn Spinning Championships in 1991. I still think I was lucky that Bill fell at the jumps early in the semifinals. He's a beauty, but not the sort of bloke to put too much effort into competitions.

Bill has spent the last few years winning beers off tourists in the Green Room of the fabulous old Hotel Darwin by spinning yarns, reciting bush poetry, or just shooting the breeze. I remember way back in the seventies, the Darwin branch of the AHA got together to discuss its financial relationship with Bill. Publican after publican got up to complain about how much Bill was into them for. Finally, sanity prevailed. Someone up the back stood up and pointed out: 'Look, this man is the Territory's greatest tourist attraction after Ayers Rock. We shouldn't be here whingeing about how much he owes us. We should be *paying* him for the great job he does entertaining tourists.'

Bill's wide-ranging slate was scrubbed clean.

NOT A BAD SORT OF A DOG, EH?

I came on this old man's camp one night, set on a billabong. I hallooed the camp and he said, 'Come in, mate. Let's have a look at you.'

I rode in and there he was with this old gidgee fire, and sitting on the edge of the gidgee fire was this beautiful old blue dog.

So I said, 'Is he a smart dog?'

And he said, 'Oh yes, mate. He's one of the best blue dogs that ever was.'

I said, 'Show me how smart he is.'

He said, 'No, in the morning. At piccaninny dawn, I'll show you how smart he is.'

So at piccaninny dawn, we rolled out of our swags and he said to me, 'What would you like for breakfast?'

'I'm very partial to boiled eggs.'

'Me too.'

Then he says to the blue dog, 'Come in, Blue.' And he asks me, 'How many can you eat?'

'Two.'

'Me too.'

So he says to the blue dog, 'Boiled eggs, Blue,' and the old blue dog picks up the quart pot, runs down to the billabong and fills it up. While he's gone, the old man builds up a bully fire.

The old blue dog comes back with the quart pot, right? Sits it on the fire and the bloke says, 'Four eggs, Blue.' So the old dog goes to the pack bag, gets four eggs out, sets 'em in the quart pot and sits there, banging his tail in the bulldust.

Next, the old man says, 'You know what he's doing, boy?'

'No, sir, I don't.'

And he said, 'He's timing the eggs—four-minute eggs.'

So the eggs is almost ready and this old dog rushes down to the billabong, puts his nose in the icy cold water, sets himself down in the billabong—freezing cold—comes back and with his cold nose, he pushes the quart pot off the fire, looks up, puts his nose on each egg and then stands on his head.

The bloke says again, 'You know what he's doing that for, boy?'

'No, sir, I don't.'

'Because he knows we don't have any eggcups in the camp.'

JUST HELPING OUT

This man was shooting ducks at Fogg Dam one day.

'Boom!' And he shot this duck and it come tumbling down. He's standing there plucking it—feathers all over his boots, see? Anyway, he looked up the road and he seen this cloud of dust. He said to himself, 'By the sweet powers of piss, it could be a ranger.' And as it got closer, he seen the whisker aerial and the boat and top and he said, 'Jesus, it *is* a ranger.'

So he pulled the last pin feather and threw the duck into the billabong.

The ranger came up and said, 'Have you been shooting ducks, Ace?'

'No way in the world. It's out of season.'

The ranger looked down at the feathers all over the bloke's boots and he said, 'Have you seen a duck at all today?'

The bloke said, 'Just one.'

'I thought so. Where is he?'

'He's over there in the billabong having a swim. I'm looking after his clothes.'

Of course, a bloke like Bill generates a few yarns about himself. One of the best concerns the Queen's visit to Darwin a few years ago. As she was perambulating along what's now the Smith Street Mall, Bill managed to slip through security. The consensus is that he was so well known to the local security blokes that they didn't even think to stop him. Another theory is that they knew he wouldn't hurt a fly and were secretly intrigued to see what would happen when Darwin Royalty met British Royalty.

Anyway, they needn't have worried. It's alleged that Bill strode straight up to Prince Philip, grabbed his hand and told him, 'Look after the little woman, mate. You've got a good one there.'

Whatever the truth of it, there's no doubt about the veracity of Bill's yarns. This one's another one about a dog—so why shouldn't it be fair dinkum? No one ever tells lies about their dogs, eh?

CHECKING THE CREDENTIALS

Many, many years ago, when I was a young man, I used to sit under a peppercorn tree outside the Stuart Arms Hotel in Alice Springs and listen to two old men, by the names of Bob Buck and Vince Shand, telling atrocious lies. And they were good at it. One day Bob said, 'Vince, have you ever had a dog that was worth his salt?'

Vince said, 'Yes, I have. Allow me to elucidate.

'I attended this crown muster and we must have had at least eight thousand head mustered there. We cut 'em out, poddies and cleanskins—the whole lot. I was pushing my little mob back to Erldunda station. There was only me and Curlew, a very old horse, and old Johnny Cake, a very intelligent dog.

'As I was pushing them back, we run into a mob of stranger bullocks just this side of a granite outcrop and they mixed up with my little mob.'

'What did you do?'

'What could I do? I'm an old man, Curlew's an old horse and there was only this good old dog. So I sat under a mulga tree to nut out what I'm going to do about this situation. I saw the old dog was missing. I looked about but he was nowhere to be seen. But all of a sudden, I heard this "Yap! Yap! Yap!", and I saw the dust rising from the other side of this granite outcrop.

'I climbed on Curlew and I rode over. I'll tell you no lies, Bob. There was that old dog, sitting on a burned-out stump, with all these bullies going past in single file. And each time a beast went past, that old dog would spit on his paw and wipe his hide to see what the brand was.'

Old Bill was always the one to beat in the recently revamped World Yarn Spinning Championships. But he just never regarded it as important enough to compete in. He's a national treasure.

When the competition was revived in 1991, it brought all sorts of people out of the woodwork. Stan Gibson was a bloke I'd met briefly when I lived in the Territory, and I bumped into him again on the night of the finals in 1991. He asked me if I was interested in seeing some of his work. It's a favour I'm often asked. Quite honestly, it's something I'm more than happy to comply with. I really am interested in other people's work. But over the years, Stan's about the only person to bother following the matter up. I had returned home only few days with my nice new championship golden shovel, when a thick wad of papers arrived in the post.

Until now, I hadn't any idea what to do with Stan's yarns—and he'd assured me I could do what I liked with them. So here they are, mate—just a couple to tickle people's fancy.

THE RACING GOANNAS

We were once again blowing the froth off a cold one at Frank's Bar and Grill at Wave Hill, when Tosh arrived.

'Here, Tosh, tell the boys about your trip to Sydney,' said Frank.

'Yeah,' said Tosh. 'Well, it *is* a bit involved. It sort of started when the old man and Carruthers and I landed a job as caretakers on one of those mine leases over near Borroloola. You know the score. The mining company takes out a lease, builds a bit of a donga on it and then sits on it for ten years or so. It's just to keep the battlers out of the area. Anyway, they have to have employees on the place to fulfil the lease covenant.

'We were between contracts and reckoned that three months of sitting around doing nothing but answer the radio schedule every day, would be okay at $400 a week and tucker. Well, within a couple of weeks, we had read every book in the place and were getting pretty bored, when the old man suggested that we catch a bull ant each and starve them for a few days, then throw them in a billy can and bet on whose ant was the survivor.

'Well, as you can imagine, with nothing much else to do, we soon progressed to fighting spiders against ants . . . and soon got bored again.

'We were starting to go bush happy and were at each other's throats, when Carruthers came up with an idea. "Look," he says. "These little critters only keep us interested for a few days at a time. Now, if we're going to be stuck here in a dry camp for three months, why don't we catch a mob of goannas? We could train them and put them in the goanna races at the Daly Waters Rodeo. Them blokes in the stock camps catch their goannas on the way to the rodeo and none of them are trained. They just hope for the best. Now, if *we* do it the same as horse trainers do, we can have dead certs and, by the time we leave here, a good bank to back them with. The ringers'll be cashed up and I reckon we could get at least even money . . . maybe two to one or better."

'Well, by dark time next day, we had five young goannas in an old spud bag. Me and the old man weren't too sure where to go from there, but Carruthers reckoned that he had trained goannas for the Wyndham goanna races a few years earlier and he could handle it.

'We had to give him his due. Within a week, he had broken them in and really tamed them . . . made mates of them, more or less. He'd done it just the same as a horse—bagged 'em, lunged 'em . . . but only taking 'em to the long rein stage.

'Meanwhile, me and the old man had knocked together a training track and a stable. Every morning at sunrise, we would all go down to the track and put the reins on them and jog behind them for the hundred metre course.

'It only took a few more days until Carruthers had them doing the training without the reins. Me and the old man were pretty impressed, but Carruthers wasn't content. He introduced them to his two heeler/bully crosses, Knackers and Arsehole.

'The time just slipped past and before we knew it, the contract was over and the rodeo only a few days away. Mate, I can tell you, Carruthers had done his job well. The goannas were knocking over the hundred metres in 4.3 seconds—in a straight line, too—and, at the finish line, Knackers and Arsehole would be waiting to lead them back to their stables.

'We reckoned we'd be on a winner at Daly Waters.

'Mate, we were. We backed them mainly at five or six to one in the first three races, and cleaned up. By the second last race, we were flat out getting odds-on, so we nobbled Tanami with a can of grog, so he ran dead last, and then cleaned up on the final race with Sandy Hollow. Mind you, we had shopped around a bit to get our bets on and had risked two and a half grand each, to pick up a fair swag of money—Biggest Mobs, actually.

'Well, we reckoned we might as well take the goannas to Darwin for the races up there. We thought we'd be on easy street from there on.

'Anyway, we got to Darwin and although they let us nominate, our fame from Daly Waters had beaten us up there. We couldn't get a bet on at all. All the bookies bushgated us and the ringers weren't real happy, as the best they could get was five bucks to fifty—on. Me and the old man reckoned we should take the goannas down to Bagot, give them to the blacks and just get on the piss for a few months. Then, bless his little black socks, Carruthers comes up with a top idea.

' "Listen in," he says. "It's the bloody Bi-centennial. I'll bet you my dillybag to a bucket of stew that those city people in Sydney will be doing their best to be real Australians. You know all the stuff they go on with—billy boiling contests, walking around in Akubra hats, yelling cooees—all that rubbish. They're bound to have a bloody goanna race. They won't have heard of us. If we can turn seven thousand into fifty grand at Daly Waters, just think what Sydney would be like."

'Well, me and the old man were starting to get that capitalistic feeling and reckoned a piss-up's a piss-up, whether it's in Darwin *or* Sydney. So, if not, why not?

'Being cashed-up as we were, we all headed out to the airport, intending to fly down. We reckoned it'd be cheaper, for one thing, and less stressful on our champions.

'That was when things started to go wrong.

'There was no worries about getting us blokes on the plane . . . or Knackers and Arsehole, for that matter. But you blokes know the poofy sort of fellers that work at airports. Well, they jacked up on us taking the goannas. We reckoned it wasn't much point going without them so *we* jacked up. Mind you, by this time, we were all a bit red-eyed and rowdy . . . and next thing you know, we're surrounded by fair dinkum Territory cops, as well as those plastic ones that hang around airports.

'We all looked like being yarded, but Carruthers just apologised to the fair dinkum ones, ignored the plastics and we just sort of jumped in the Toyota—dogs, goannas and all—and hit the road to Sydney.

'We failed at most of the roadhouses until we got to Queensland . . . and the fear of *their* cops kept us pretty straight—so we started making miles.

'Once we hit Boggabilla, in New South Wales, we started flat stick training for the goannas. Every sunrise, lunchtime and sunset, we gave them two solid hours. They were really looking good.

'Sure enough, when we hit Sydney, there it was in the afternoon papers—all the Bicentennial hoo-hah, including a goanna race in the Domain on Oz Day.

'Now, Carruthers had a fair bit of experience with city slickers and he reckoned that we would have to watch ourselves in case we got ripped off. He reckoned that, with so many goannas around on the big day, it'd be hard to pick one from the other, so, just to stop someone stealing one of ours and bringing in a plodder, we should paint ours in the colours of the Territory flag.

'Me and the old man just reckoned we would have to listen to Carruthers, as he knew what he was about. Carruthers knew a bloke who worked at Randwick, so we ended up camping at the racecourse, getting ready for the big day.

'We trained the goannas three times a day and kept them on a high protein diet.

'Mate, they were world beaters. They didn't walk . . . they just sort of pranced, like top thoroughbred horses.

'Knackers and Arsehole were in training, too. They would do a hundred metre gallop with the goannas, then lead them back to their boxes. I tell you blokes, to watch those goannas running in their Territory colours, would bring a lump to your throat.

'Me and the old man started skipping around the inner city pubs and a few bookies, laying a few quiet bets here and there.

'Well, anyway, the big day comes, so we all jump in the old Toyota with the dogs and goannas and head for the Domain. The old man's driving, as Carruthers reckoned that he should empty his mind before the start. Well, you blokes know what the old man'd be like in Sydney traffic. Bugger me dead if he doesn't get lost. And next thing, we're fair in the middle of Kings Cross.

'I see a signpost saying "Domain", and yell at the old man to throw a left. He does . . . and some clown hits us fair in the guts. The two dogs, who'd never seen a city before and were nervous enough without being in a prang, bail out and bolt. I jump out and start calling them.

' "Knackers . . . Arsehole!" I scream. The bloke who hit us reckons I'm talking to him, so he gets raggy and next thing, him and the old man are fairly punching on. I didn't notice all that, as I'm still yelling at the dogs—which in turn attracts the attention of a bloody copper.

'Carruthers sizes up what's going on and tries to calm the cop down. Realising he's not getting through, Carruthers melts into the crowd and leaves the old man just holding his own and me, fair in the middle of the Cross, screaming "Knackers! Arsehole! You bastards!"

'The cop forms the opinion that I'm talking to him and handcuffs me to the bullbar, separates the old man and the other driver and then, bugger me dead, if he doesn't decide to check out the back of the ute.

' "What's in the box?" he growls.

'I say, "Five goannas wearing NT colours.'

'He gives me a belt in the gob for being a smart arse and opens the box.

'If the dogs were a big highly strung, you can imagine how the goannas were feeling. Straight out of the box, up his arms, over his head, down his back . . . and gone!

'I get a glimpse of the dogs through the crowd and yell, "Knackers! Arsehole!"

'The copper puts my bloody lights out.

'Anyway, me and the old man end up doing a month in Long Bay. You wouldn't bloody believe it. They get us out there the same afternoon . . . and there, on the TV they've got there, on the six o'clock news, bugger me dead, if there's not Prince Chuck and his missus in an open carriage, with Carruthers driving a team of five bloody goannas—all wearing Territory colours.

'And that's as true as I stand here. I'll have another green can, thanks Frank.'

THE DRUM RUN

We were having a few beers at Heartbreak Hotel, about 110 kilometres west of Borroloola, when Tosh spoke up.

'Youse blokes talk about the old days on the track with bullocks. Well, I can remember when I was a kid and we were living on a run west of Pine Creek. The old man was having a really bad trot with a late Wet, fires and all the stockmen going walkabout right on mustering time.

'We decided to have a lap at droving. By pure luck, Carruthers happened to be staying at our place at the time.

'The old man lands a contract to overland five hundred head of 44-gallon drums from Pine Creek, down to Longreach on the Queensland side. They took me along to give them a bit of a hand. None of us had ever driven drums before, but Carruthers said that he had worked for a bloke over in the west who had a small herd of domesticated ones, so he reckoned he knew enough about them.

'We were going to head down to Borroloola and follow the Gulf but the bloody stock inspectors got wind of the trip and made us go down to Elliott to dip them. That was a fair way out of our way but the old man reckoned it had to be done.

'We made our first mistake by following the Stuart Highway. We hadn't even got to the Katherine, when three road trains roared past and the herd scattered. We lost the rest of the day rounding them up and then travelled parallel to the road.

'The Katherine was running a banker when we got there, so we had to use the high-level bridge, which meant taking the drums through the centre of town. The cops got a bit stroppy about that, but there was no way around it. So they blocked off the street to traffic and helped us through.

'The mob settled down after a couple of days and we made it to Elliott in a bit over a week. Struth! Do you reckon we had trouble dipping them? They'd swim okay, but you want to try making them go under. The old man did the nana and spat the dummy properly. He ended up shooting three of the beggars before Carruthers showed him that the best way is to tie their legs and drag them through with the Toyota. Three bloody days it took.

'Anyway, the stockies gave us a nod and we headed off. That's when our troubles *really* started. We were east of Renner Springs in the semidesert country, when a big electrical storm blew up. You guessed it. The bastards bolted.

'Now, I ask you, have you ever heard the sound of five hundred empty drums stampeding? It's a terrifying sound. Luckily, Carruthers turned them and settled them down by playing and singing "Moon River" on his accordion.

'Next thing you know, we hit real bad country. Mate, it was

so rough that we lost another half day shoeing the dogs. Then the bloody drums started calving. You reckon bloody rabbits breed? Well, mate, you have never seen anything like these bloody drums. Within days, there were little one-pint tins and quart bottles all over the flat.

'Carruthers, who knew about these things, reckoned that the only thing to do was to camp until they all grew into 5-gallon drums and we could walk 'em!'

'It took a week . . . and it was a bloody hard one. We had to handfeed over two hundred of them, twice a day. And then, when they were big enough to travel, we had to shoe them. We used bully beef tins, cut in half.

'We headed off again, but the young ones were slowing us down, so Carruthers reckoned he'd go ahead with the main herd. Me and the old man could follow on with the poddies. It was slow going for a while, but they grow pretty quick and soon reached 12-gallon size and started making up a bit of time.

'Actually, they grew *too* bloody fast and next thing, they started breeding all over again. Anyway, we lost *another* couple of weeks, waiting for the weaners to grow.

'Then, you wouldn't believe it, but a big mob of wartime bitumen drums joined the herd. And they were wild scrubbers, too. We tried to chase them off so they wouldn't crossbreed with the bloodstock. But it was no use.

'By this time, we had over a thousand drums spread over 5 kilometres. It was bad enough for the old man—at least he had me to help him with the feeding. I found out later that Carruthers was having the same trouble—and he was by himself.

'We made it to the dip at Soudan and the copper, Dick, from Avon Downs, told us that Carruthers was only three days ahead of us. Luckily, Carruthers had shown the old man how to dip 'em and we ran them all through in a couple of days. We still had a couple of hundred head of 5-gallon drums, so it was slow going to Camooweal. You wouldn't believe the scene as we came into town. That bloody Carruthers had got on the rum for nearly a week and his mob had been breeding like mad. Our mob rushed to join them and all you could see from horizon to horizon was a seething mass of drums.

'The Queensland cops were ropeable . . . and the NT stockies weren't too impressed, either. Carruthers had got the message that things weren't too flash and had hitched a ride to Julia Creek.

'The old man reckoned the best thing to do was to cut our losses and head back to Katherine before anyone spotted us. Anyway, that's why, when you're driving through the Territory, you'll see mobs of scrubber drums beside the road.

'I'll have another green can, thanks.'

Stan adds as a footnote that some of Tosh's drums actually made it down as far as Queensland, where they got jobs as mailboxes around Longreach. A few even made it as far as Brisbane, where they're working with local councils directing traffic around suburban earthworks.

Tex Tyrell is a Territory and yarn-spinning legend. When I first lived in Darwin, he ran a knockabout second-hand shop in Bennett Street. He'd been up there since 1954. Tex's story on how he rode his motorbike up there from Sydney, with fellow ratbag yarn-spinner, John Davies, on the pillion seat behind him, is a yarn in itself.

'I had this bloody great Davy Crockett hat. I reckon it was the first Davy Crockett hat in Australia. It had a big black fox head up the front, and a huge tail out the back. Because we were on a motorbike, I wore the hat all the way up. Every time we stopped, I found the tail had grown shorter. By the time we reached Darwin, there was hardly anything left. I found out bloody John had been eating it because it kept flapping in his face.'

John has the last say on the matter. 'Eating it, be buggered. I was biting bits off and stuffing them in my ears so I couldn't hear the bastard talking.'

Because, by crikey, Tex can talk. Frank Hardy claims that when Tex originally beat Walkie-talkie Nelson, in Alice Springs, for the first-ever yarn-spinning titles, he did so by sheer endurance. 'Nelson was carried off crying "Please, please, I can't stand the sound of his voice. Stop him from talking. Please." '

Even in the highly respectable business of second-hand dealing, Tex was able to use his yarn-spinning talents for fun and profit. He tells with relish of the occasion he found an old wartime bomb dumped on his lawn. Sensing a publicity opportunity, he carted it into his shop in Darwin, where he knew the effect would be greater, and immediately rang the authorities to report an unexploded device. The police cordoned off the area, the fire brigade stood by. The *Northern Territory News* sent along a most welcome reporter and photographer. The army sent along a demolition team. The officer in charge wasn't too fussed.

'It's only a dud,' he diagnosed from a safe distance.

Tex took him to one side. 'Look, old mate, a dud bomb's no good to me. If I slip you blokes twenty bucks, would you declare it unsafe and take it out somewhere and blow it up?' A wink was as good as a nod to the officer. He was quite happy to agree that his team could probably do with the practice.

So, of course, the bomb was given the kid gloves treatment, carted out bush and blown up with great ceremony for the newspaper photographer. No one ever questioned why anyone would want to bomb Tex, and the publicity probably put a bit of extra business his way in the long run. If not, well, it was a bit of a laugh on an otherwise dull morning.

In the cut-throat world of yarn-spinning contests, Tex held off Frank Hardy's first challenge, then relinquished the title to him in 1967. They both came back for a rematch in 1991, which some black horse from the south ended up winning.

These days, Tex lives in Beenleigh, Queensland, but he still comes back for the Darwin contest and he'll still regale you with yarns non stop—whether you want him to or not.

PULLING UP FAST

This young bloke in Darwin bought a second-hand Cadillac with his first pay. He took it down the road for a bit of a run. He was pretty proud of this car. As far as he was concerned, it was the best car in the world. He tootled along the highway round about the Berrimah area, dying to show someone else what it could do. He hadn't gone far, when he came across an old swaggie, wandering down the road with a dog.

He said, 'D'you want a lift, mate?'

'Sure.'

The young bloke opened up the back door and the dog jumped in, followed by the old swaggie. Once the door slammed shut, the young feller noticed an incredible pong. Gasping for breath, he turned to the swaggie.

'Crikey, mate. I can't stand the stink. This is a new car. You'll have to get out.'

'Well, it's not me,' maintained the swaggie. And, to the young bloke's surprise, without waiting for the car to slow down or stop, he opened the back door and booted the dog out.

'Don't worry,' he told the driver, 'he's a good runner. That's the fastest dog in the world. He'll keep up with us.'

The young bloke was instantly aware that it wasn't the dog who'd been causing the problem, but he didn't say anything. He was too intrigued by the idea of the dog being able to keep up with a speeding car.

'How fast d'you reckon he can go?' he asked.

'As fast as you like. You just try him out.' So the young bloke put his foot on the accelerator and away they went—about 80 kilometres an hour.

'Is he keeping up with us?' he asked the swaggie. The old bloke looked out the back window.

'Christ, yes. He's still got his nose pressed fair up against the bumper bar,' he reported.

The young feller put the foot flat to the floor.

'How's he going now?'

'No worries. He's scratching on the back window here asking to be let in.' That did it for the young bloke. The honour of his brand-new car was at stake, so he worked on nursing a few more kilometres an hour out of the old Cadillac. They were flying along at about 120 and still the swaggie reckoned the dog was keeping up. Of course, driving like that and not paying any attention to the road, they soon came to grief. In no time flat, they failed to make it round a bend. The car ran off the road, still travelling at full bore, and went slap bang into a tree.

The young bloke was a thrown from the wreckage of his brand-new car and knocked out. When he came to, the swaggie was just getting to his feet, too.

'Where's your dog?' he asked the swaggie. 'Is he still with us?'

'Bloody oath. He's over there,' reported the old bloke, pointing to a dog wandering around sniffing at the wreckage.

'That's not the same dog,' complained the young bloke. 'This one's got a red collar. Your dog never had no collar.'

'That's not a collar,' returned the swaggie. 'That's his arsehole. He's not used to pulling up so fast.'

You're right. There's a certain basic earthiness to Tex's yarns, but he never lets up with them.

A SURE CURE

Back in the old days in Darwin, just after the war, there was this doctor who went into business out at Parap. But he wasn't getting many patients. So he came up with this great idea. He put an advertisement in the *Northern Territory News* guaranteeing to pay fifty quid to any patient who came to him with an illness he couldn't cure. It worked pretty well, too, for a while. People came to his surgery at Fannie Bay with all sorts of ailments—real and imagined—and he managed to diagnose them and cure them without any trouble at all.

Then this smart-arse bloke turned up. He'd just come out to Fannie Bay and felt he could do with fifty quid.

'Well, doc,' he moaned, 'I don't know what's wrong with me. I'm a compulsive liar. I've lost my sense of taste and my memory's gone. D'you reckon you can cure me?'

Bloody hell. Three in one. The poor old doctor had never struck a case like this before, and he knew the bloke was only fishing for that fifty quid. He couldn't afford fifty quid. He didn't *have* fifty quid. For the life of him, he couldn't think of what to do.

He needed some time to think it out, so he said to the bloke,

'Look, I'll need to ponder a bit longer on this. You wait here and I'll go out the back and have a bit of a think. If I'm not back in ten minutes, I'll have to give you the fifty quid.'

So the bloke settled down in the surgery and the doctor went out into the backyard to try to figure a way out of his predicament. All of a sudden it came to him. Out in the backyard he had a dog kennel. The dog was long gone, but there was all this mess about the place. The doctor went over and gathered up some of the dog's poop. With only minutes to spare, he raced into the kitchen, dipped the poop in egg and breadcrumbs and fried it up over the stove like Burdekin duck. Then he took it back into the surgery.

'Here,' he said to the grinning patient. 'Try some of this.' The unsuspecting patient eagerly grabbed one of the breadcrumbed thingummybobs and bit into it.

'Urrrggh!' he choked. 'That's dog shit.'

'And you're cured,' crowed the victorious doctor. 'There's nothing wrong with your sense of taste, because you identified it as dog shit easy enough. You're definitely not a liar, because you said it was dog shit and not any other sort of shit. And your memory's back. Because once you've eaten dog shit, you'll never forget it.'

Darwin these days is a far more respectable city than it was pre-cyclone. A lot of former residents still have a bit of trouble coming to terms with the Smith Street Mall. It used to be the main drag in the heart of the city. These days, it's closed off to traffic and lined with all sorts of shops and arcades that Territorians only read about in the old days. Back before the blow, typically, the main intersection, at Smith and Knuckey Street, was graced on one corner by a car yard. Could you imagine Pitt Street, Collins Street or Rundle Street inviting buyers to come on down?

OH WHAT A FEELING!

A ringer had been working down the track all season, saving up to buy a vehicle. He'd managed to mass together about $2000, feeling that's all he'd need to get something half decent. Even back in the 1970s, prices in Darwin tended to be sky-high compared with other cities, but he didn't expect the situation to be quite as bad as it turned out to be.

He strolled through the cars on offer at City Motors, in the heart of Darwin, for a few minutes, before a salesman came up and put the hard word on him.

'Can I show you anything?'

'Yeah, mate. I'm after a cheap, reliable vehicle.'

The salesman quickly adopted the caring, professional mode of his calling. 'How much money have you got?'

'Two thousand bucks.'

The salesman became hysterical. 'Two thousand bucks? That won't even give you a down payment on a hubcap for a 1960 VW beetle.'

The ringer was mortified. 'But I've been saving all season,' he muttered. 'Surely you've got *something* that'll do.'

He must have been coming down with something, but the salesman had a pang of compassion for the poor young ringer.

'I'll tell you what. As a personal favour, I may just be able to help out,' he told him. 'Come round here.' He led the ringer around the back of the office and there, leisurely pecking at grains of something in the guttering of the building, was a twelve foot high chook. The ringer reeled back in amazement.

'Crikey! I'm not riding *that* thing!'

'Don't be ridiculous. Of course you're not riding it,' scolded the salesman. 'For two thousand dollars, you get the chook, two free bags of feed and this . . .' With that, he wheeled out a dinky little cart, like a pony cart, complete with harness and whip.

At first the ringer was a bit dubious, but the silver-tongued salesman managed to convince him that with his knowledge of animals and his riding prowess, he'd have no trouble driving around in the sulky. 'Anyway, it's all we've got for two thousand bucks,' he reminded him.

The ringer agreed to buy the chook and sulky. The salesman even helped him manoeuvre the rig out into Smith Street and harness the chook up to it. All the car yard staff came out to wave the ringer goodbye as he cracked the whip and the chook started heading off slowly along Smith Street towards Bennett Street. A slight tug at the reins, and the chook did a creditable left-hand turn into Bennett Street.

'Crikey!' thought the ringer. 'It responds better than a horse.' In those days, traffic lights were few and far between in Darwin, and the chook sailed across Cavanagh Street without any trouble. After that, the road dropped a bit down the hill and the chook managed to gather a bit of speed as it continued on past the Chung Wah hall and the Chinese temple. On the approach to McMinn Street, they were going so fast the ringer had to take off his hat and jam it under the seat. At McMinn Street, the right-hand wheels actually lifted off the ground as the chook took the corner at speed.

'What a ripper,' yelled the ringer to no one in particular. 'This is a racing chook.'

In McMinn Street, he took an extra tight hold of the reins, actually stood in the sulky and cracked the whip violently over the chook's head. It dropped its neck and started to lope at full speed.

Have you ever seen a twelve foot Rhode Island Red in full flight? It's a magnificent sight—the sort of thing a film-maker like David Attenborough loves to capture in slow motion—every muscle rippling . . . the huge yellow feet reaching out to gain purchase of the bitumen . . . the comb dragged back by the phenomenal slip stream . . . the tongue lolling out as the lust for speed takes control.

Poetry in motion.

The ringer, too, was completely wrapped up in the thrill of the moment. He yelled with excitement as he cracked the whip again and again, over the big bird's head, oblivious to the foam splashing back from its gaping beak.

They were so caught up in their charge that they forgot about the Daly Street intersection. Again, no traffic lights . . . and a bloody great Shell road train steaming into the intersection. There was no brake on the little sulky and the chook, not being the brightest creature on God's earth, paid no attention to the ringer's panic-driven screams.

The sound of the collision was sickening.

A crowd gathered. A couple of days later, a twelve-year-old policeman fronted up.

'Has there been an accident here?' he inquired perceptively.

Someone gave him a few basic details, gesturing towards the smouldering wreckage of the road train slap bang in the middle of the intersection. The copper wandered over to where the ringer was sitting disconsolately in the gutter, his head in his hands.

'I have reason to believe you are the driver of a vehicle involved in an accident.'

The ringer nodded.

'Did you suffer any injury in the aforementioned accident?' asked the walloper. The ringer shook his head.

'And how about your vehicle?'

The ringer looked across at the little sulky, on its side with its wheel in the air . . . then across to the chook lying flat on its back with its legs in the air, the big yellow feet hooked pathetically.

'I think me big 'en's stuffed.'

5

THE GUNDAROO CONNECTION

The hamlet of Gundaroo, about 35 kilometres from Canberra, is probably no different from any other tiny Australian community struggling to retain its character in the soul-destroying shadow of a big city. The fact that I intend devoting this whole chapter to Gundaroo yarns isn't, however, merely a piece of self-indulgence. True, Gundaroo stories were very kind to me for a number of years. Again, although my Prickle Farm stories in print and on ABC Radio were largely about Gundaroo between 1979 and when we left in 1985, the truth is, they could well have been written about any small Australian rural community at any point in time.

That's not to say Gundaroo hasn't got a character and flavour all its own. All similar small Australian communities have—or, at least, did have. My old cronies in Gundaroo assure me that, these days, the place is a mere shadow of its former self. It's far more a dormitory suburb of Canberra now, with all the middle-class and 'respectable' influences that implies. Therefore, I feel a certain duty in trying to give some idea of the spirit of the place we knew.

The character of Gundaroo has largely been forged in that esteemed drinking parlour, Matt Crowe's Wine Bar. No trendy little bistro, this. The wine bar is one of only about four left in New South Wales. It was demoted from being a full-time pub about the turn of the century, when Matt's mother forgot to renew the licence. Its rough-hewn weatherboard and bush pole structure takes you right back to last century. Matt and his wife, Beat, could almost claim to go back that far themselves. Needless to say, these Gundaroo yarns either originated from Matt himself, or from his gutsy little establishment.

THE VERDICT

Gundaroo, in the middle of the week, is pretty sleepy. These days, most of its residents commute to Canberra to work. However, it was quite a thriving metropolis in its day. Did you know it was one of the places that was seriously considered as a site for our National Capital. Well, back about the turn of the century, a lot of little joints were being considered. A parliamentary select committee was set up to travel the country, enjoying the hospitality of countless bush communities, sussing out all the candidates. Many communities, like Gundaroo, saw fit to build grand buildings (comparatively speaking) in the hope that they might catch the committee members' freeloading eyes.

Gundaroo had its courthouse. These days it's St Mark's Anglican Church, and doesn't provide half the laughs it used to back when the circuit magistrate would front from Queanbeyan every so often to put erring locals through the mincer of justice. They reckon court days were pretty well attended by curious Gundaroonatics interested in what their neighbours had been up to.

So you can imagine the interest back in about 1902, when a local shearer came up on a charge of indecent exposure. He drew a far bigger crowd than if he'd been caught riding a horse with an altered brand, let me tell you. In fact, the court was chock-a-block.

The local copper, a bloke called Walmsley, got up in the witness box, raised the Bible and droned the oath.

'Your Worship, on 22 October 1902, I was proceeding in a northerly direction along Cork Street, Gundaroo, when I espied the defendant walking towards me clad only in his singlet. I arrested him and charged him.'

The magistrate noted Walmsley's evidence, then looked over his glasses at the poor little skinny shearer bloke shivering in the dock.

He warned him that he could either give sworn evidence, make an unsworn statement or keep mum. But the shearer decided to speak from the dock.

'I really don't know if what the constable said is true or not,' he began shakily. 'I could have been wandering round town just in me singlet. But I just don't know. You see, Your Majesty, whenever things are going bad for me, I have these turns. And when I have these turns, I'm likely to do anything. The thing is, afterwards, I don't remember a blessed thing. I could well have had a turn and been walkin' round in me singlet, I just don't know. Because, Your Lordship, that particular day had been a bugger of a day.

'I'd been sacked orf the board at Bowylie station. I walked through the pouring rain all the way back home. When I got home, I found all me kids in bed with the infloo-enza. Me missus wasn't feelin' too well and she announced then and there she was pregnant again. I guess I may well have snapped, Your Grace, but I don't remember a thing.'

The magistrate, obviously moved by the little bloke's tale, adopted a far less formidable mien.

'Well, how many children *have* you got?' he asked.

'Seventeen, Your Worship.'

And the old judge banged down his gavel and announced, 'Case dismissed. This man was in his working clothes.'

Matt Crowe's Wine Bar was always much more than just a watering hole. For decades, it was Gundaroo's equivalent to the Forum, in Athens. We gathered there to discuss art, philosophy, politics, the meaning of life . . . and the weather. The fact that we left there invariably wearing extremely unstable footwear was purely a freak of nature. Everyone became larger than life after a few ports at Matt's. And the genial host was always quick with a yarn. Even solemn occasions such as funerals didn't escape Matt's wit.

THE ART OF DYING

Our port's a good body builder. We never had anyone complain. It cleans the blood and improves the muscles. All the old fellers around Gundaroo live to a great age. Why, an undertaker'd go broke here. We had one feller, a carpenter bloke, come to set himself up in business. He got himself a black horse and carriage with the little round balls up the top, and invested in a big billy hat. But no one died round here for seventeen years. He went broke.

There's one tombstone up in the old graveyard there. It reads, Patrick O'Shaughnessy, born 1847, died at Fairfield Gundaroo, 1902. Then, where most of them say something like 'Rest In Peace' or 'Into the Arms of Jesus', this one just says 'I told you I was crook'.

Funny thing is, when Matt told that yarn on the ABC's *Big Country* program, people actually wrote in asking for more details, saying they were related to Patrick O'Shaughnessy and would like to visit his grave.

I've read every tombstone in and around Gundaroo and there's no Patrick O'Shaughnessy buried there. Not that I'm suggesting that Matt's not telling the truth. Maybe he just got the name wrong. It's an easy thing to do.

Now in his eighties, Matt's seen them all come and go. It's little wonder that he's a font of knowledge about what's happening around Gundaroo. Here's a selection from the wine bar.

TALKING OF HORSES

These days, Gundaroo is really just a dormitory suburb of Canberra. Crikey, it's only about 35 kilometres from the National Capital, so it's lucky it held onto its character for so long. There aren't nearly as many laughs in the place as there were in the old days. The rot tended to set in during the seventies, with the big boom in hobby farmers—most of them $40,000 a year people from Canberra. They bought their blocks in the bush and moved out there for pretty much the same reason they bought their powder blue Volvos—to prove to the world how much they were earning. They weren't nearly as colourful as the old-time bush characters. They didn't even avail upon the intellectual services provided by the wine bar mob.

One public service family, in particular, worried the more socially aware of us down here. They'd lived in Gundaroo for a couple of years, but they hadn't socialised at all. He was a little skinny bald bloke and she was a big battleship of a woman. They'd hardly said boo to anyone since they arrived. What they did do, however, was drive these little horses and jinkers around the village. At any time of the night or day, you'd hear and see them exercising their teams. You'd first hear the clip-clop of little hoofs, and then they'd come into sight, sitting bolt upright in their seats, solemnly driving one or more little grey ponies around the village. They wouldn't look to the right or left. They just stared straight ahead without acknowledging anyone. Bloody hell! Sometimes they even wore nifty little matching deerstalker caps and rugs across their knees—a different bloody outfit for every occasion.

You can only try so hard to get people involved in a community and, eventually, we all gave up and tended to forget this pair. One icy winter's night, a swag of us were down the wine bar practicing our deep breathing exercises at the bottom of several glasses of Matt's cheapest port. Most of the talk, as it had been since the 1830s, was about the weather, which had been pretty dry and cold. Suddenly, we could hear the familiar clip-clop of those little hoofs on bitumen. No one took much notice, until the hoof noises came to a stop right outside the wine bar door. Even Matt, behind the counter, showed some interest.

'Crikey! Don't tell me they're actually coming in,' someone remarked. Such an unusual situation motivated a few of the troops to get up and go to the door to see what was going on. There was the little public service bloke, in his deerstalker cap, taking his natty little driving gloves off and carefully folding the rug he'd had over his knees.

'Jesus! He's actually coming in,' whispered Cec Burgess. Sure enough, the bloke stepped down from his carriage, looped the pony's reins around the front veranda post of the wine bar and moved towards us. Right at the last minute, he stopped behind the pony and, to everyone's amazement, lifted its tail and kissed it fair on the date. You can imagine how *that* put a damper on further conversation. By the time the bloke came into the wine bar, everyone was back on their stools, staring into their empty glasses without saying a word.

Now Matt, being a garrulous sort of bloke, realised the mood of the evening had somehow changed for the worse. He tried breaking the suddenly materialised ice.

'Would'ya like a drink?'

'Ooooh yes,' lisped the bloke. 'I'll just have a small glass of moselle.' Matt poured the drink, still mindful of the stunned silence in his normally noisy little bar and realising that he needed to brighten things up a bit.

'The weather's been a bit chilly,' he observed sagely, feeling sure that the revitalisation of life's main topic of conversation would get tongues wagging again. Only the newcomer responded.

'Yes . . . and you really feel it riding round in these open carriages.' No one else took the bait so Matt charged on.

'Yeah, I noticed your little pony and that. It's a lovely little animal.' As a horse owner himself, he had an eye for a decent nag.

'Mmm, yes. He's beaut. We've been breeding them like that for years now. Before we came here, he was named champion at the Mittagong Show. We paid over $10,000 for his sire.' Still dead silence—and most of us there were horse people. Matt realised he'd have to try harder.

'And that little jinker of yours doesn't look too bad, either.'

'Well, no. And there's an interesting story behind that. We found it in bits and pieces at a clearing sale near Camden. We paid a couple of hundred dollars for the bits and pieces, then took them to this wonderful Swiss man at Bellingen, who did it up for us. It cost close to $15,000 but still, we think it was worth it.'

Now everyone there was a died in the wool clearing sale buff, but still no one else deigned to enter the conversation. Matt bit the bullet and realised he'd have to ask *the* question if the atmosphere in the bar was to be thawed.

'I couldn't help but notice, just before you came in here, you walked behind that little horse there . . . and kissed him on the arsehole.'

The hobby farmer fellow laughed. 'Oh that?' he twittered. 'Yes, well, I find that driving around in this dry cold weather makes my lips all cracked and sore and . . .'

'Be buggered,' roared Geoff White, finally unable to control himself. 'Kissing your horse on the bum doesn't prevent chapped lips, does it?'

'No, silly . . . but it does stop me licking them.'

ROAD SERVICE

One of the wine bar's greatest characters was also one of Gundaroo's worst drivers. He had an old brown Belmont ute which, after a few ports, always seemed to take on a will of its own. One morning, the Child Bride noticed it on its side at the bottom of our lane and, fearing the worst, went down to investigate. She found the driver fast asleep behind the wheel, still strapped firmly in his seat belt. When she shook him awake, it was obvious he hadn't the slightest idea what had happened.

'Wake up. You've had an accident.'

'Why, what happened?'

'You've slid into the creek and the ute's lying on its side.'

'Thank God for that. I spent hours last night trying to work out how come the car lights on the highway were going vertically up the windscreen instead of across it.'

This same bloke used up nearly a whole tank full of juice in that same ute, revving like buggery on Wattie Brown's Lane, quite oblivious to the fact that he was bogged and not going anywhere.

'I thought I was taking a long time getting to Murrumbateman,' he observed, when someone finally came to his rescue. 'And when you walked up just now and tapped on me window to let me know what happened, I thought "Shit. That bloke's runnin' fast."'

As you can imagine, such motoring adventures took quite a toll on the old Belmont ute and it was always resting on chocks at Steve Darmody's repair place in Sutton. Steve worked out he replaced the clutch in the ute nine times in one year—including two in a twenty-four-hour period.

So it wasn't uncommon to have our valiant motorist stumble into the wine bar and announce he was in trouble yet again. And sure enough, one night, there he was again.

'Matt, I'd like you to ring up for me.' On top of his motoring woes, this local had a bit of a problem with reading. No one made any big deal about it, but if he needed anything difficult nutted out, he usually came to Matt, who was quite happy to help out. One of his problem areas was using the phone book and Matt was quite used to not only finding numbers, but dialling them.

'What number would you like me to look up?'

'The RSPCA.'

Everyone showed an interest. 'What's up? One of your dogs crook or something?'

'Dogs be blowed. It's that bloody old ute of mine. She's buggered again. I reckon that Steve Darmody isn't doing it right. I'm gonna get the RSPCA to check it out.'

Everyone had to be tactful. 'But mate, they won't be able to do much . . .'

'Be buggered. I've been paying me membership for twenty-eight years and I've never called them before. It's about time I got me money's worth.'

Perhaps we all could have tried a bit harder to convince him, but I reckon, like Matt, we all wanted to see what would happen. Matt dialled the RSPCA in Canberra and we all sat round like idiots awaiting the outcome.

Now picture the scene in Canberra. There's the animal refuge, late at night, being run by one poor old volunteer worker. Over in one corner of the compound, there's the condemned dogs all yowling their last. In the other, unwanted cats are venting their misery. What this poor old volunteer craves is human contact. And it comes. The phone rings. With shaking hands, he picks it up. The voice he hears is barely human.

'Is that the RSPCA?'

'Yes sir, it is.'

'Could I have road service, please?'

'I beg your pardon?'

'Road service. Give me road service, you bastard.'

'Look, I'm sorry, sir, I don't think we can help you . . .'

'You'd better be able to bloody well help me. Me ute's buggered and I demand service.'

'But sir, we can't give it to you.'

'What do you mean, can't give it to me? I've been a member for twenty-eight years and I've never called you before. You better bloody give it to me.'

'Look, you don't seem to understand. We're the RSPCA, we look after sick, neglected and injured animals.'

Then, without batting an eyelid . . . 'I should bloody well hope so. If I thought you didn't, I'd dob you straight in to the NRMA.'

HIGH FLYING

Of course, being so close to Canberra, Gundaroo was always in danger of being overrun by wankers. And, being a wine bar, Matt's was in the greatest danger of all . . . because there's no greater wanker than a wine snob. Strangely enough, in my day, we always seemed to have less than our fair share of them. I don't know why. Perhaps the strong local character in those days warned them off. But we could never hope to avoid them entirely. Occasionally, a couple would make it through the invisible force field that seemed to operate at the Yass River and would turn up in town. In Matt's, the wankers were always hoping to find a few wine gems, legendary vintages that they imagined we were all too stupid to appreciate—

Grange Hermitages from before the Deluge perhaps, which they could pick up for two and ninepence.

One such pair, complete with sunglasses perched on top of their heads, La Coste shirts and Reebok everything elses, made real dick-heads of themselves in Matt's one Saturday afternoon. They found out pretty quickly that Matt's wine stock was fairly ordinary. Anything really special had been snapped up by the locals when it came. What remained was just decent, honest stuff for the passing trade. On the very top shelf, though, Matt kept a few collectables—festering bottles of Barossa rosé from the fifties; greening Porphyry Pearls from the same era and evil, smouldering containers of sparkling something or other, slowly eating away the labels from the inside. Matt had resigned himself years ago to never selling the stuff and now only kept it there for interest's sake. It was amazing how a few nostalgic reminiscences about an old bottle of Porphyry Pearl could prompt the punters of a Certain Generation to invest in something far more acceptable and profitable. Then the old bottle could go back on the top shelf until the next lot of 1960s romantics dropped by.

But these two Canberra wankers weren't interested in nostalgia. Once they realised they couldn't exercise their wine snobbery at Matt's, they decided to get pissed. By midafternoon, they'd achieved their aim, but didn't know when to stop. They started tossing money about and demanding that Matt serve them from his top shelf.

The money they were offering was pretty good, but Matt at least showed some reluctance as he opened some of his less rare collectables. It must have tasted horrendous, but these blokes were beyond noticing. They had green and purple stains around their mouths and strange discharges from their nostrils, but still they demanded more exotic fare. Eventually, Matt had had enough and refused to serve them.

'But we want more . . . more, more, more . . .' sang the drunks.

'There isn't any more. And I could do my licence if I serve you in that condition.'

'More, more . . . just one more drinky winky.'

'I told you, I haven't got any more. You've drunk nearly all my collection of fine vintage wine.' He started steering them out of the door but one of them suddenly turned and pointed to the furthest, dustiest corner of the top shelf.

'Wozzat then? Wozzat bottle over there? Give us some of that and we'll go without another word.' It seemed a fair enough deal. Matt felt he was a bit long in the dentures to still be wrestling drunks off the premises. He honestly had no idea what the dusty bottle in the corner contained, until he got it down and wiped the cobwebs off the label.

'Crikey! I'm not giving you blokes any of this.'

'What's it, what's it, what's it?'

Matt took the old bottle outside to get a better look at the label. It was a simple bit of white paper with one word written on it in what appeared to be pencil: Concorde.

'I didn't know there was any of this stuff left,' he muttered. 'I thought we'd got rid of it all up the tip.'

'What is it?' someone asked.

'It's a wine called Concorde. A bloke who lived here years ago used to brew it up himself. He was some scientist who worked in Canberra and he fancied himself as a bit of a wine buff. But this stuff was vile and sent people off their heads, so we dumped the lot.'

'Beauty, beauty, beauty,' chirruped one of the drunks, snatching the bottle from Matt. 'Give us a drinky poos and we'll go.'

Matt thought carefully. God knows what time had done to the Concorde wine . . . but these blokes seemed to have survived some pretty awful stuff during the afternoon . . . and, it would get rid of them . . . so why not? He went outside, put on a pair of rubber gloves and several condoms and carefully wrenched the cork out of the top of the bottle. Deciding to go for broke to get rid of the wankers, he poured two schooner glasses of Concorde. That would make sure they kept their promise and went without asking for more. We all sat around in amazement watching them chug-a-lug the noxious-looking brew. Then they were gone.

God knows how they got home. In fact, they didn't quite make it straightaway. Some time in the wee small hours of the next morning, one of them woke up in a strange room. He hadn't any idea where he was, only that he seemed to be in a motel somewhere. He felt like death warmed up, and a strange ringing started in his ears. It took him a couple of minutes to twig that it was the phone beside his bed. Gingerly, he picked it up.

'Is that you Marty?' came a pathetic voice on the blower.

'Yeah, mate.'

'How do you feel?'

'Bloody dreadful. That Concorde wine was powerful bloody stuff.'

'You're not wrong mate. Have you had a look in the mirror this morning? That Concorde was stronger than we thought.'

'What d'you mean? Hang on a sec.' He juggled with the phone cord and moved into the bathroom, where he could see himself in the mirror.

'Do you notice how your nose has sort of gone all long and pointy?'

He looked. 'Now you mention it mate, I do.'

'And look at your eyes—have they gone sort of square and glassy and moved closer together at the front of your head?'

'Jesus! So they have.'

'And your ears, Marty . . . have your ears got longer and sort of flattened out and swept back?'

'Bloody hell, you're right.'

'Well for God's sake mate, don't fart. I'm ringing from Singapore.'

THE LITTLE JOINT UP THE BACK

But my years at Gundaroo shouldn't be seen as witnessing the death knell of an old-fashioned bush community. The place still had its characters. Sure, a lot of them have passed on, but maybe there's a new generation there. I hope so.

In Australia, we tend to take a lot of our bush characters for granted. It's odd that sometimes, people from overseas know more about that sort of thing than we do. Certainly, a lot of them seem to care more about it. That's why we were all intrigued the day a big stretched limo turned up from Canberra with an American couple on board. They were from New York and were interested in tracking down a couple of old-timers who lived out on the Back Creek Road. Tom and Jack were good blokes. They were brothers and lived in an old slab place, half an hour's drive from the village. The Americans reckoned they were related to the two old blokes and were mighty interested in getting in touch. We were only too pleased to draw a mud map for them.

When they turned up at the old place in their big car, they gave Tom and Jack quite a start. They weren't all that used to getting visitors. But they took the two Yanks into their little kitchen, complete with white-washed fireplace and wood stove, offered them a couple of Vegemite glasses of Matt's finest port and started yarning.

It turned out they were indeed related, a long way back on the track. The Americans were ecstatic. They had reams of paperwork of family trees and what-have-you, and they took copious notes and roll after roll of photos.

While scarcely the sort of blokes to become ecstatic themselves, Tom and Jack at least did make some attempts to be gracious hosts — bearing in mind that they didn't usually get a lot of social callers. They got a fair way through most of the port in the house. They took the Americans on a guided tour of the old place, which was quite an eye-opener for their visitors. They'd never before seen the traditional Australian bush home, with the slab walls and the kitchen separate from the rest of the place, so a careless cook wouldn't burn the whole joint down if a fire escaped from the old wood stove. They marvelled at the old-time ways of their hosts. Around there, the real old bush people believed that if someone died in a house, you took out the doors and windows, so their spirits could move freely about. Tom and Jack's parents had both

died there and the draughty old place was exactly as they'd left it. Because it was so cold, the two old blokes actually lived in the kitchen, where there were doors and windows and the old stove kept them warm.

They took their American relatives out the back to the big shed, where their old man had stored a great collection of old horse-drawn vehicles—including one he'd knocked off years earlier when he worked on the Shire.

They even wandered with them up the back paddock to look at the sinkhole where they gathered water. Because the old place still had a bark roof, it wasn't safe collecting their water in a tank. The tannin in the bark made any run-off poisonous. All these things kept the Americans amused for hours.

Towards the end of the afternoon, however, the good lady whispered to her husband, Howard, that she was desirous of straining the old potatoes. Howard coughed discreetly and asked the old-timers, 'Excuse me, but do you happen to have a ladies' powder room?'

Old Jack knew what he was after, immediately. 'Aww! You mean the dunny? That's it up there on the hill.'

And, sure enough, it was, too—your traditional Aussie outhouse, of a design universal throughout the bush, but with one important difference. At this point, it's perhaps prudent to explain that the country along that particular stretch of the Yass River is particularly stony. As a result, the good burghers of that parish have never been able to enjoy the services of the common, or garden, long-drop dunny. Instead of being able to dig a big hole, all they've ever been able to make do with is a 4-gallon kero drum with a motor tyre round the top for comfort—the general idea being that, once a week, the youngest kid in the family would be responsible for taking the drum out, digging a hole somewhere, and burying the contents. Tom and Jack, bachelors from way back, were a bit light on ankle-biters to perform that particular duty, so the hygiene of their particular operation was, to say the least, a bit on the marginal side. They were quite used to it, but the big city New York woman was mortified. She came galloping back down the path from the dunny, screaming hysterically, 'Howard! Howard! It's disgusting in there. It's so unsanitary . . . and there isn't even a lock on the door.'

Howard was a bit embarrassed by his wife's outburst, but felt he had to defend the good lady's honour—so he feigned grave concern. 'Is this true, Tom and Jack, that here in Orstralia, you don't even have a lock on the door of the john?'

Old Jack thought for a while, tilted his hat back and scratched his head.

'Well, to tell you the truth, Howard, we never seen no need

to. In seventy-two years, we've only had three drums pinched—
and two of them weren't full.'

BATTLING THE RED STEERS OF SUMMER

It's a startling fact of life that, despite all the advantages of living
in the bush, we still face one danger which has the potential to
wipe us all out. There's some danger in the Big Smoke (no pun
intended), but city folk don't ever have to face anything as potentially
disastrous as bushfire. And do you know what's even worse? This
monster, this enormous threat, has to be dealt with, largely, by
amateurs. Every year, bushfire brigade members have to go to the
government, cap in hand, to beg for funds to help them protect
their loved ones from death and destruction. Sometimes they get
what they ask for. Sometimes not.

Well, at Gundaroo, we got well and truly pissed off with the
situation. But did we whinge? Did we complain? Well, not much,
anyway. No, we decided to bite the bullet—take control of the
situation ourselves. So we did what political leaders of various
persuasions have been urging Australians to do for years. We
privatised. It wasn't an easy process, and we had hundreds of meetings down at Matt's before getting it organised.

First of all, we needed a new corporate image. To do that, we
had to have a catchy name. So instead of sticking to the boring
old 'Gundaroo Bushfire Brigade', we elected to call ourselves 'The
Flamebusters'. With a flash name like that, we couldn't have the
troops bowling along to meetings, training sessions and fires, just
in Stubbies and thongs. We needed a corporate look.

So a couple of the wives who went into Gunning every Thursday
night for TAFE dressmaking classes, knocked us up these beaut
luminous green overalls. The postmistress, who was a dab hand
with Hobbytex, drew big logos on the back—'The Flamebusters'.

One of the blokes worked on the Gunning Shire, and he managed
to knock off a few of those luminous orange hard hats the Stop/Go
men wear to prevent being run down by speeding motorists. Once
we had all the gear, we posed for the official photographs. By crikey,
we looked swish.

With a new look, we progressed to the next step of our meta-
morphosis. It was no good sounding and looking good but still
wasting our time putting out piddling little fires in someone's
hayshed, or along the railway line whenever trains went past in
summer. We had to specialise. It was unanimous. The big money
could be had fighting oil rig fires, so that's the way we'd go.

Of course, there didn't happen to be many oil rigs in Gunning
Shire. In fact, there weren't any at all. Nevertheless, if we were

going to do this properly, we had to look beyond our own shores. There was no way our old ex-World War Two blitz wagon, with the big tank on, could make it on any call we got overseas, so we had to find a better means of transport.

We put in for an Arts Council Grant and used the money to buy one of those second-hand ex-RAAF Hercules aircraft that Bob Geldoff hadn't wanted to freight famine relief to Ethiopia. We parked it behind the hall, and the ankle-biters in the Tuesday morning playgroup used their artistic skills to decorate it. And *then*, we were ready to go.

As it turned out, there was a decided dearth of oil rig fires around Gundaroo (or anywhere else) that summer. In fact, the only call we got was to the Shell servo in Gunning. Apparently, some vandal had used a washer to try to get a free drink out of the Coke machine. It was stinking hot, and with the machine gummed up, the truckies were getting thirsty. The Flamebusters were called in to cut the lock off the machine with our bolt cutters, and try to get the bloody thing working again.

It mightn't sound like much, but, for our first call out, it proved a copy book exercise. Everyone turned up on time, in full uniform, and the whole thing went off without a hitch. It proved, once and for all, that The Flamebusters were a fire-fighting force to be reckoned with. And so we sat around for a couple of more years, waiting for the Big One to prove our worth.

And, one day, it came.

Over in the Middle East, a big rig caught fire. Millions of barrels of oil a day were going up in smoke. In desperation, the oil company did the only thing they could do. They rang the only other oil rig firefighter in the world—the legendary Red Adair.

'You've got to help us, Red. We're in big trouble.'

'Well, suh, ah'd lahk too, yes ah would, but ah cain't help right this very moment,' explained Red. 'Ah'm just on mah way out the door to fly to Bolivia, where some commie terrorists have blown up a big installation. There's people bin killed, villages destroyed and everythang! I gotta get down there right away.'

'But, Red, what about your son? Surely he can help us?'

'Ah'm afraid not. He's bin workin' off the coast of Scotland now for three weeks. Some big storms in the North Sea have blown over rigs all over the place there . . . so he's flat out.'

'But, Red . . . ain't there no one who can help us?'

'Well, jest you settle down a bit. Ah read in the *Oil Rig Firefighter's Newsletter* that a new lot have started out somewhere down in Orstralia. Jest hang on now and I'll get their number. Here it is. The Flamebusters. Jest ring Orstralia 062-368195 and ask for Neville.'

It just so happened that Neville was Gundaroo's chartered

accountant. Because he was at home most of the time, doing all our tax returns, he was the best man to stay on the phone. So he was The Flamebusters' secretary, treasurer and duty officer. So there he was, lying brilliantly on behalf of all of us to the Deputy Commissioner of Taxation, when it came—the call from God.

It just so happened that poor old Nev had a bit of difficulty getting a quorum. A lot of the troops were in Canberra at work. Some of the others were doing things like hay-carting or shearing, but he did a ring round and eventually managed to muster a crew. In a couple of hours, they were into the gear, aboard the old Hercules . . . and off.

What no one realised was that oil rig fires are always a big media event. While the old Herc was limping out to Sidi Ben Somewhere, the oil company PR people were ringing round the papers and television stations. It was only a matter of time before the air strip near the rig fire was lined with reporters and TV cameras—every lens pointed towards the south, awaiting the arrival of The Flamebusters.

And then, they all heard it, the steady chug-chug-chug of a well-tuned Australian aero engine, or four. Every lens zoomed in on the white-hot desert sky. Soon, through their viewfinders, the cameramen made out the ever-enlarging spec heading towards them. It wasn't long before the Hercules flew low over the desert air strip, towards the huge column of fire and smoke at the end of it. The big plane flew slowly around the burning rig, then straight through the smoke. Finally, with every camera recording its every move, it landed in a cloud of white talc dust. At the end of the runway, the Hercules came about and, like a huge dinosaur laying an egg, it opened its rear end and out came The Flamebusters, clinging to the back of Peter Dyce's Mazda ute.

With its red light flashing, the ute hurtled down the strip at 120 kmh. The cameramen followed it as it zoomed across the desert and, without even slowing, hurtled straight into the pillar of fire and smoke.

The press contingent surged forward in horror to get a better view of the tragedy. As they neared the holocaust, they could just make out a handful of black, pathetic stick figures leaping down from the back and sides of the Mazda ute. Some tried to get closer, but the sheer heat of the fire threatened to melt the lenses of their cameras. All they could do was stare in horror at the drama unfolding in front of them. The black figures raced around in confusion and, over the angry crackle of the flames, people could hear the muffled cries of 'Shit!' 'Jesus Christ!' and a few pathetic attempts to slap out or blow out the flames.

Suddenly, the tide seemed to turn. 'Hey, the goddamn fire's dying down!' And, sure enough, it was. Gradually, the smoke cleared,

then dwindled. The flames died down and, soon, the only evidence of the conflagration was a black smear in the desert sand. Hardened reporters and cameramen, who thought they'd seen everything, actually wept and cheered. Because there, staggering towards them, came the charred, but unbowed crew from The Flamebusters.

The press contingent ran forward, but the chairman of the oil company, sensing a huge PR coup, managed to keep ahead of them. As he ran, he whipped out his chequebook and signed it with a flourish as he went. He reached the Gundaroo team ahead of the first reporters, turned to face the cameras, and, waving the cheque for all to see, spluttered, 'Never in the history of mankind, have I seen such a valiant effort. On behalf of my board of directors, I'm proud to present you with a cheque for 1.4 million dollars!' That sure was a lot of knapsack sprays.

As he handed the cheque to Neville, a spotty little reporter with one of those great big microphones nicked under his elbow and asked, 'Sir, sir! What's the first thing you're going to do with all that money?'

Neville thought for only a second.

'Get the bloody brakes fixed on Peter Dyce's ute.'

That was the Gundaroo we knew. For us, it's the way it'll always be.

THE WIDE
WILD WORLD
OF SPORTS

If there's one area in which I can honestly admit I have no expertise
whatsoever, it's sport. My dear old mum always put it down to
the fact that I had TB as an ankle-biter. That's a pretty good yarn
in itself. But even if I *had* been fighting fit, I probably wouldn't
have bothered. Me and my best mate at high school got by pretty
well by claiming to be chronically unfit. We could watch the girls'
dressing sheds from the third storey art room, where all we poor,
fragile little invalids were doomed to spend sports classes . . . and
that's another yarn again.

But, really, my lack of interest in sport had at least one drawback,
because some of the best yarns in existence are sporting tales.
There's many an Aussie sporting identity who's feathered their nest
on retirement from the Wide World of Jockstraps by having
published copious volumes of sporting yarns. So, it's with great
pleasure that I turn you over to my yarn-spinning contemporaries
for a collection of their sporting greats. Hang on! Before I do . . . I
just can't resist the temptation to pass on to you just this one . . .

THE LUCK OF THE DRAW

Families are funny sorts of institutions. These days, when I hear
do-gooders moaning about the forces working against the traditional
family unit, I get a bit confused. The idea that all families are
traditionally fun little groups where everyone works together for
the common good, has no place in a volume like this, where truth
and harmony is everything.

The intrigues within the average family are complex and disturbing. And nowhere is it more so than in the relationship that
exists between brothers. Really, Rolf Harris's immortal 'Two Little
Boys' greatly oversimplified the situation.

When I was a teenager in inner Melbourne, I went to school

with a lot of Jewish kids. Just down the road in Carlton were a couple of brothers who, even as teenagers, were constantly pissed off at the way their family played them off against each other. All the time at high school, their performances were monitored and used to try to goad them on to greater efforts. When they left school, things didn't improve. Their parents were always comparing the stunning career moves of the older brother against the valiant, but less successful, efforts of the younger one. He wasn't a dill, or anything. Far from it. In fact, both of them did far better in their business dealings than the rest of us. Still, they were played off against each other.

The older brother already owned BHP, had discovered Posiedon and was leasing the entire state of South Australia back to the government. The younger bloke owned a couple of Kentucky Fried Chicken outlets, was introducing something called McDonald's to Australia, and had won a few land deeds and one or two promising mining claims from some old bloke called Hancock in Western Australia—but still was being goaded by his family to do as well as his older sibling.

Eventually, both brothers had had enough. They got on really well together, and, over a quiet beer at the local, the older bloke announced he was giving it all away.

'I know you probably don't believe me,' he told the younger feller, 'But I'm sick and tired of the way the family always holds me up as having been more successful than you. I've done all right. I've got nothing more to prove, so I'm going overseas to give you room to do your own thing. I'm selling all my Australian interests and moving to Israel.'

His younger brother had mixed feelings about the announcement. Sure, he loved his older brother and was deeply moved by his unselfish gesture. On the other hand, he couldn't help but be a bit jealous of the older bloke's successes, and yes, it would be easier for him if his brother moved overseas.

'Hey, whatever you do, keep in touch, okay?'

The older bloke promised he would.

And so he flew off to Israel, hoping for a quiet life farming in some kibbutz, away from the continuous pressures of his family. What a hope. For a start, even in his new country, he couldn't help but be successful. Soon, as though by magic, he was enjoying stunning business success in Israel, where there was great interest shown in the Australian way of doing things. And didn't his family rub it in to his younger brother?

'Look at Hymie,' they'd say. 'Slaving away overseas and *still* doing better than you.'

The younger brother tried to shrug it off, but it still hurt. On the other hand, he stayed in contact with his brother on a regular basis. One day, he received a phone call from Tel Aviv. His brother was ringing with a great idea.

'Look,' he explained. 'The one thing they haven't got over here that you have at home is horseracing. People are fascinated by it. So I've hit on this great idea. I want to raffle a genuine racehorse. It'll have great novelty value and I've already sold millions of tickets. Of course, as there are no racehorses over here, I'll need you to organise the prize. What I want you to do, is go to the yearling sales in Sydney next week and buy me a reasonable-looking horse. It doesn't have to be much chop. Don't buy a real nag—but get something that's reasonably priced and looks like a champion. I'll fix you up for it and pay for it to be shipped here to Israel. By the time it turns up, I'll have sold all the tickets and we can draw the raffle. I should make a fortune.'

The younger brother was only too happy to oblige. At the yearling sales, he snapped up a lovely-looking thoroughbred for only ten thousand bucks. Then, according to his older brother's wishes, he arranged to have the horse shipped off to Israel.

Down at the docks, disaster struck. The wharfies had rigged up a special sling to have the horse winched onto a freighter, leaving that night for the Middle East. However, when the crane had winched the horse up off the dock, the bloody thing started playing up. Tragically, it wriggled out of the sling and plummeted to its death on the wharf.

The wharfies sat around looking at the dead horse. 'What'll we do now?' one of them asked the younger brother.

He was just going to organise them to cart the thing away, when a solitary wicked thought entered his mind. For once in his life, a little malicious twinge overrode his normal, easygoing nature. 'Bugger it,' he thought to himself. 'All these years and Hymie's been getting the better of me. Now let's see how he handles *this* situation. He thinks he's so smart . . . let's see what he can do with a dead horse.'

'Keep going,' he told the wharfies. 'Wrap it up and bung it in the ship's cool room. We'll *still* send the bloody thing to my brother in Israel.'

And so they did. It took the freighter a couple of weeks to complete its journey, and during that time, the younger brother grew more and more impatient. How would his brother react? How would he get himself out of *this* predicament? How would the rest of their family view *this* particular stuff-up? Who'd be the clever brother *then*?

Several more weeks passed, and still, no word from Israel. Finally, unable to contain himself any longer, he dialled his brother's number. For the first few minutes, he endured a painful amount of unnecessary small talk. All his older brother seemed to want to discuss was the weather. Finally, he couldn't bear the suspense and broke the ice himself.

'By the way, Hymie, how did your horse raffle go?'

'Aww. Bloody ace, mate. I cleaned up. You know how many tickets I sold? Three million—at the equivalent of ten dollars Australian each. It's the biggest, single most successful venture I've ever been involved in.'

'Y . . . yeah . . . but the horse . . . the flaming horse I sent you . . .'

'Yeah, what about it?'

'Well, it was *dead*.'

'Yeah, I know, but I still went ahead with the raffle. I had to. It was still the single most successful venture I've run.'

'But it was *dead*. Didn't anybody complain?'

'Only the bloke who won the raffle—and I gave him back his money.'

And that's about as far as I go in relation to sporting activity. But there are other yarn spinners with a swag of great sports stories . . . especially racing yarns. Take old Frank Hardy, for instance.

THEY'RE RACING IN DARWIN

These days, the Darwin racetrack's got computerised results from every state. It's got a members' stand. It's got multicoloured umbrellas everywhere. But when Tex Tyrell and I were telling yarns there twenty-three years ago, the Darwin racetrack was a rough place. I want to tell you about the smart bookmaker from the south, who brought his horse up to Darwin.

He wanted to run it in the Darwin Cup and to lay the book on the races in Melbourne, Adelaide, Sydney and Brisbane.

So the smart bookmaker from the south sets himself up—puts up the prices for the interstate races, and the Darwin punters are punting away like mad. There are more punters in the Northern Territory per head of population than any other place in the world . . . and they're pretty shrewd.

So it comes the time for the Darwin Cup. The smart bookmaker from the south puts his horse, Smartfella, up 3 to 1 on. The Darwin bookmakers have a look and they copy him—Smartfella, 3 to 1 on. Anyway, they're getting away in Melbourne and Sydney and Brisbane and Adelaide, when all of a sudden, the smart bookmaker from the south thinks, 'Hey! There's nothing doing on my horse.' So he says, 'Anyone want a bit of even money?'

But there's no move from the Darwin punters. They've checked the papers. They've seen nothing about him, but they have a feeling it might have won a race at Morphettville or Gawler.

So the bookmaker says, 'What about 2 to 1? You can have 2 to 1.' And with that, a ringer from down the Track, in laughin' sided boots, pink and white shirt with studs on it and big ten-gallon hat comes forward.

'You just named a great price for that horse, mister. Can I have two hundred for a hundred?'

And the bookmaker says, 'Two hundred to a hundred?'

'That's a very good horse,' says the ringer. 'It won a race at Gawler.'

'I don't want you to give me a bloody form guide. Two hundred to a hundred—do you want it again?'

'Yes. I'll have it again.'

The bookie looks at this mug from down the Track and can't stand the look on his face. So he says, 'Do you want it again?' and the ringer says, 'Just give me a few minutes will you mister?' and he delouses his wallet—a five dollar bill, a two dollar bill, a ten dollar bill—till he rakes up another $100. So he's got three tickets worth $900.

Suddenly, the smart bookmaker from the south thinks, 'I've outsmarted meself.' So he says to his clerk, 'Go round to the jockeys' room for Christ's sake and tell them to pull it up. Here I am, running a horse in a race with a five hundred dollar prize, and a mug's got on for six hundred.'

So the race starts and they jump away. Smartfella's jockey's pulling against it. He's easing it back. Nothing comes up to him and they come to the turn into the straight . . . and he's looking round and he's pulling on the horse until its head's between its legs. But nothing's coming behind him. He wins by a length.

The smart bookmaker from the south's not very happy. Then up comes the ringer, with a half-shrewd look on his face and his three tickets. He passes them to the clerk and the clerk gives him the $900. The bookmaker can't stand it. His horse has just won the Darwin Cup, and he's lost $100.

He says, 'Listen here, mate, you think you're smart, don't ya?'

'Awww no,' says the ringer. 'I told you it was a good horse. I told you it had won a race at Gawler.'

'One thing you didn't know. You think you're smart, but you're a mug. I *own* that horse and it was dead.'

And the ringer from down the Track says, 'Yeah. I know you own it. But what *you* didn't know, was I own the other four.'

The sport of kings is also the sport of bull artists. In fact, there are probably more yarns about racing than any other field, outside the bush. That's probably got to do with the fact that once we all travelled on horseback—so, traditionally, horsy yarns were universal. The ABC's yarn competition—surprise, surprise—also unveiled some beauties. This one's from Shirley George, of Gunnedah, New South Wales.

A TOUCH OF THE DOINGS

This yarn was told to me by my dad, who owned a few racehorses in his day.

There was this bloke called Nev, whose one wish was to win a race with a horse he owned, but, for a long time, he didn't do much good at all. One day, in desperation, he got on to some sugar-coated pep pills and took them to the stables just prior to a big race.

He was just popping a pill into the horse's mouth, when a voice behind him said, 'Hey! What are you giving that horse?'

Nev turned to see the stipendiary steward walking towards him. Quick as a flash, he replied, 'Oh, I'm just giving him a boiled lolly. He loves one before a race.'

'Gee!' said the steward. 'I don't mind them myself.' So Nev had no choice but to offer him the bag. To make it look good, he popped one into his own mouth.

Later, as Nev was helping the jockey onto the horse in the saddling paddock, he told the hoop, in soft voice, 'When he jumps at the start, give him his head and let him go. Don't worry if anything flies past you in the straight. It'll either be me, or the bloody stipe.'

Pete Steel, dubbed the Coonawarra Kid, after the Darwin onshore naval base he served on, now lives in Melbourne. He was a real breath of fresh air on the yarn-spinning scene, because, being half a generation younger than the rest of us, his stuff is valid *today*. His sporting stories are the same . . . told through his alter ego, Richard. As Pete says, Richard is no ordinary bloke. Pete swears he remembers the time Richard came second to Rob De Castella in the Boston Marathon, after being run over by a wheelchair in the first 10 kilometres, breaking both his ankles, and running the last 32 on his hands. Richard is cool and Pete has no problem recounting the time he went to the surf . . .

HANGING ELEVEN

'Six o'clock,' declared my clock radio, 'and it's two degrees centigrade outside.' But I leapt off the bed, chucked off the doona and got into the boardies—'cos it's never too cold for surfing. So there I was, board on roof, fag in mouth, in my fuel-injected, high-speed pursuit, turbo police-special Volkswagen. Flipping round the dial, I tuned into the surf report.

'Six foot and building at Bondi.' Not bad.

'Five foot dumpers with a ground swell at Collaroy.' I pulled to the left. 'But nice crests at Bronte.'

Finally, I heard it—the one I'd been waiting for. 'Krakatoa has erupted, tidal wave heading for Sydney.'

So there I was, lying on the boogie board, picking up some practice on the 15 foot swells just outside South Head. Then I saw it— 2½ inches of solid black, lining the horizon. The sky was dark; the sea, grey. Relentlessly, the monster moved in on Sydney, feeding and growing on the very ocean. Silent, alone, defiantly exposed, I waited—the riptide pulling me in, courage driving me on.

I think it might have been about when the third supertanker dashed against the rocks that it first crossed my mind that this tidal wave surfing caper mightn't have been all it was cracked up to be.

I stared it straight in the teeth. Ninety-six snarling feet of wild animal power. I flipped my board and began to paddle, but stopped, turned around and thought, 'No. Mother Nature, do your worst!'

I ducked under to wait for the big one, right behind. I was not disappointed.

North Head had ceased to exist. South Head disappeared in the spray. I think that if I could have changed my underpants right there and then, I may have.

But I was there to surf this mountain of destruction, and surf it I did. Steam hissed from below my board as I roared down the face at speeds approaching 196 kilometres an hour. Red Dog! Hand Stand! Board Walk! I did the lot . . . my dual tail fins smashing the great wave apart.

Then, emerging from the mist—a giant grey coat-hanger. Oh no! . . . the Sydney Harbour Bridge (with Mother Teresa on it), dead ahead, right in my way. Now I really wished I'd changed my underpants.

I still had a chance—the Opera House, coming up on my left. If I could just ride down those curves to safety . . . oh, but there she was . . . alone on the highest pylon of the Harbour Bridge, a damsel in distress—all dressed in white.

A split-second decision . . . a tidal wave special . . . double-edged, cutback . . . 'Hang on, baby, I'm on my way.'

Tears were welling in her eyes, when I plucked her away to safety, the instant before she would have surely crashed to her death. With her head cradled to my chest, tenderly, softly, did I hold her. Gently, I looked at her. I couldn't resist. Yes . . . and you must forgive me . . . above the Harbour Bridge, surfing a tidal wave on a boogie board, a defenceless maiden safely in my arms, I hung ten toes over the end of the board.

Richard, you're a devil.

Do you know what I hate?

I hate it when you're surfing a tidal wave, she starts to tube and you're on the wrong side. There was one move that could save us. I sucked my breath in, tensed my body and prepared to pump some big white wash . . . a finger-touch, double switchback with a backhand, sideswipe, spinround, reo-clamp, split-side, whiplash, punched-out with a banana split, portside to the wall, triple-whammy hotdog!

Man, I was flying.

Now you're supposed to ask me, 'What about the girl?' Well, for that, you're going to have to wait for my next yarn.

You know what? We did—several times. And he still hasn't let on.

Don't let on to anyone, but I personally think this next one is the yarn that ensured Kev Naughton knocked me off as World Yarn Spinning Champion in 1992. At the time, the Brisbane Bears were at the very bottom of the AFL ladder, and casting round keenly to knock off some Territory sporting talent. The hero of this, and others of Kev's excellent footy yarns is Patrick Puruntalimeri, the great Tiwi footballer from Bathurst and Melville islands. As Kevin tells us, Patrick proved a prodigious punt kicker of points through the perpendiculars from the pocket. If you don't already understand what Aussie Rules football's about, don't expect me to explain what *that* means.

PATRICK PURUNTALIMERI — THE PRODIGIOUS PUNT KICKER

In all the years Patrick Puruntalimeri played for Pularumpi, they never ever won a premiership—and they bloody well should have. They had some of the very best players in the game. There was the Tungatalums and the Tipaclippas, the Puruntalimeris and the Pulimjimis. They were brilliant footballers, but never did Pularumpi win a premiership, the reason being that, in the five Grand Finals that they played, they never received a single free kick. And I think that that explains the Curse of Martin Luther King.

Now I'm sure you've heard about Martin Luther King. He was assassinated in 1964 after he told the world that he had a dream. Patrick Puruntalimeri and I were sitting in the front bar of the Humpty Doo Hotel one night, discussing the fact that Pularumpi had never won a premiership and no bloody umpire in the world had ever given Pularumpi a free kick in any Grand Final played on Nguiu. It was a sad thing for Patrick, because after 467 games, he'd retired from football without a premiership win—a sad, sad thing indeed for the greatest footballer ever known in this world.

I sat there with Patrick Puruntalimeri and we had beer, after beer, after beer. All of a sudden, at the far corner of the room, an apparition appeared. Yes, 19 years after his death, Martin Luther King had come to visit Patrick Puruntalimeri in the front bar of the Humpty Doo Hotel. You might ask why? Well, he had nothing better to do that particular night.

Anyway, Martin Luther King walked over to us, and said, 'You seem sad. You don't have a dream, brothers. There is no dream in your life.'

Patrick said, 'That's right.' And I said, 'Bloody oath.'

Martin Luther King looked at me. 'Look at yourself—five foot nothing; you're bald on top; you've got everything going for you. You must have a dream.'

I said, 'I do have a dream. I dream that Collingwood will win every premiership between now and the year 2000, and I dream that in every Grand Final, they'll win against Carlton, with the last kick of the day, and they'll win by a point. That is *my* dream . . . and I dream of furniture factories that make a profit . . . and I dream of international hotels that run without subsidies. (Territory local jokes.) I dream of a land where tall men are slaves and short men their masters. I dream of a land where every woman fantasises about making love to a bald man. That is my dream.'

He said, 'Your dream's very bloody self-centred, isn't it?'

I said, 'I don't think so.'

He said, 'A real dream is a dream that demands something from every man and woman in the world. I have a dream. I dream that all of America will rise up and live in truth and justice. I have a dream. I have a dream that one day my children will go to the mountain top and they will see their dream, and from the mountain top they will sing, "Let freedom ring, let freedom ring". I have a dream this day. I have a dream. I have a dream that when that day comes, they shall all join together as the children sing from the mountain top. I have a dream that when that day comes, we shall all join together, black men and white men, Jews and gentiles, Catholics and Protestants. We shall join our hands together and sing, "Freedom at last, freedom at last. Thank God Almighty, freedom at last." I have a dream this day.'

Patrick Puruntalimeri said, 'Big bloody deal.'

He jumped up on on the bar and said, 'I have a dream. I have a dream that the progeny of Patrick Puruntalimeri, will punt prolifically and prodigiously for Pularumpi and pierce the perpendiculars prolifically with punts from the pocket and one day clinch the elusive premiership for Pularumpi. That is my dream. I have a dream that one day I'll be sitting under the raintree at Nguiu and the scores are tied with seconds to go. I have a dream that my son, Patrick Puruntalimeri, will pirouette above the pack and pluck the ball from the clouds. That is my dream . . . and it's my nightmare. My nightmare says that, as Patrick Puruntalimeri junior pirouettes above the pack, he grabs the ball only to see it tumble from his fingers—the chance of glory gone. Then I have my *real* dream—a man in white runs in and says, "Interference to Patrick Puruntalimeri from Pularumpi."

'Two metres out from the goal . . . and I have a dream that I shall see Patrick Puruntalimeri poignantly punt through the perpendiculars to win for Pularumpi. And I will say to you, "A free at last! A free at last for Pularumpi!" '

Martin Luther King said, 'You bloody idiot. How bloody selfish is that? For *that* and your little mate's selfish attitude . . . the curse of Martin Luther King will sit above you forever.'

Now Patrick Puruntalimeri never believed him. We left the Humpty Doo pub for the airport and we caught the Air North charter to Pularumpi. And just as we walked towards Patrick Puruntalimeri's place, we saw the ghostlike figure of Martin Luther King leaving the house.

Patrick was slightly concerned that this could be the curse of Martin Luther King. He rushed inside and there they all were, his fifteen children . . . all named Patrick one, two, etcetera . . . fifteen Patrick Puruntalimeris, all holding a piece of paper.

Yes, ladies and gentlemen, the curse of Martin Luther King had struck. He'd signed fifteen Puruntalimeris to play for the Brisbane bloody Bears.

Despite my personal doubts as to whether stories in verse are technically yarns or bush poems, I couldn't resist the temptation to sneak in another fine piece of doggerel. Not only does it enter the extremely dubious realm of golf stories, but it's written by a woman.

I've already mentioned that, comparatively speaking, relatively few yarns are spun by women. But the delicate subject matter covered herein makes this particular saga fairly unusual.

It was another entry in the ABC Great Aussie Yarn competition. I don't know whether it warrants Jill Steen, of Florida Gardens, Queensland, congratulations or a 'Shame, Jill, shame!'

BALL BEARINGS

The dawn was breaking. The alarm clock rang.
So out of bed, I happily sprang.
I gobbled some toast, then rang up me mate
'Get out of bed, Fred, or we'll be late.'

I loaded the car with my golf clubs and buggy
Then drove around, to pick up my buddy.
Fred jumped in the car, all happy and bright
A day playing golf would be sheer delight.

We paid our money in the pro shop
Then walked our way down to the very first stop.
I hit a beauty, right up near the green
And Fred's went so high, it could hardly be seen.

I got a six and was one over par
Fred got a four and was acting like a star.
Then we heard an almighty roar!
A big burly woman was screaming out 'Fore'.

Down the fairway her golf ball flew
And down went Fred, he began turning blue.
Fred held his hands tightly down to his crutch,
I tried to help, but couldn't do much.

The big burly woman said, 'I am a nurse, I will give it a rub'.
So she helped him up and they walked into the scrub.
I couldn't see much, but the noise was horrendous,
When I finally saw Fred, he looked tremendous.

He had a big grin and his face was all pink
Then the nurse said, 'Well, what do you think?'
Fred scratched his head and said, 'Did you see the ball land?
My crutch was the warmest place to put my throbbing hand.'

All of a sudden, the conversation did stop,
And the big burly woman, boy, did her mouth drop!
For the rest of the game, Fred seemed distant and calm
But when we got to the clubhouse—did he spin a yarn!

There's a motto to this story
About Fred in all his glory.
Next time you see a ball fly by,
Remember, there is more to it than meets the eye.

Cricket has its fair share of yarn spinners, which may surprise people who don't follow the game. Perhaps it's due to the fact that old cricketers don't die, they just become commentators and, therefore, a gift of the gab is considered as important as a good bowling arm or batting eye.

Tom Hall, of Mt Gambier, wasn't one of our Test greats. Nor is he a cricket commentator, but he entered this little bit of nonsense in the yarn competition.

THE LAST LAUGH

There's little doubt that the most notorious individual performances in the history of Australian cricket have been Dennis Lillee's attempt to kick the backside of Javed Miandad, the Pakistan captain . . . and Trevor Chappell's infamous underarm delivery that denied New Zealand of a possible chance of winning a one day match against Australia off the last ball of the game. Chappell's effort created so much animosity across the Tasman that serious consideration was given to calling off the pending visit to New Zealand by an Australian XI. However, sanity prevailed and the tour was allowed to proceed.

So concerned about the enmity between the two teams was the New Zealand prime minister, that the day before the Australians departed on their tour, he cabled the Australian Cricket Board and sought permission to honour Dennis Lillee for his outstanding contribution to the game by naming one of its towns after him. Anxious to accept the olive branch, the board gave its consent and, much to its surprise, the New Zealand government renamed one of its towns 'Whykickapaki'.

This next offering, a real cricketing gem, is, without doubt, my favourite yarn. I first heard it from Frank Hardy—although he, in turn, admits it originated elsewhere. In true, yarn-spinning style, Frank has fine tuned and polished it, and so (at least I reckon) it's the jewel in the crown of his personal empire.

AND THE SCORE NOW STANDS AT . . .

You've all heard of Don Tallon, the famous wicket-keeper? He was captain of Queensland, and a selector. But he had a brother called Bill Tallon . Bill sometimes got a game for Queensland, but some rather narrow-minded people suggested he only got a game because he was Don's brother. He opened the bowling. He was a fast medium-paced bowler and he had just *one* day of glory at the Gabba. He also had a stutter. This is how he told of his day of glory at the Gabba.

'Th . . . there I was b . . . b . . . bowling at the G . . . G . . . Gabba. And in c . . . c . . . came a b . . . b . . . batsman called N . . . N . . . Ninski. A b . . . b . . . bloody good bat. B . . . b . . . but I swung one away from him and he s . . . s . . . nicked it. F . . . f . . . first slip went for it, s . . . s . . . second slip went for it, b . . . b . . . but, you b . . . b . . . bloody beauty, my b . . . b . . . brother Don leapt over and caught it in one hand.

'One for n . . . n . . . none.

'Who comes in next, b . . . b . . . but a f . . . f . . . feller called B . . . B . . . Babcock. He used to c . . . c . . . come from T . . . T . . . Tassie, but he was playing for New South Wales this d . . . d . . . day. So I b . . . b . . . bowled an outs . . . s . . . swinger outside of his legs and he snicked it. S . . . s . . . square leg ran for it. F . . . f . . . fine leg ran for it, b . . . b . . . but, b . . . b . . . bloody beauty, my brother D . . . D . . . Don, dashed over and c . . . c . . . caught it.

'T . . . t . . . two for none.

'Then who comes in, but D . . . D . . . Don B . . . B . . . Bradman. Bradman himself. But I'm not w . . . w . . . worried about B . . . B . . . Bradman. I'm swinging the ball b . . . b . . . both ways and I'm on at the G . . . G . . . Gabba, amongst me own p . . . p . . . people.

'All of a sudden, B . . . B . . . Bradman went for a big hit. It went so high I couldn't see it. B . . . b . . . ut I d . . . d . . . dashed back. I'm looking for it. I'm running back towards the f . . . f . . . fence. I get to the fence and I'm waiting for it to come d . . . d . . . down. I got s . . . s . . . sunburned lips w . . . w . . . waiting for it.

'And I'll t . . . t . . . tell you another thing. M . . . m . . . mid-off ran back for it. M . . . m . . . mid-on ran back for it but, bloody beauty, me brother D . . . D . . . Don ran right down the ground, got under it . . . and caught it.

'B . . . b . . . bloody beauty.

'Three for four hundred and fifty.'

Such is the public outcry against the irresponsible, indiscriminate and downright psychopathic use of firearms in Australia that it's no longer considered ideologically sound to enjoy a spot of shooting. The opposition of environmental and animal welfare groups has also contributed to the demise of hunting as a universally accepted sport. Of course, in saner times, it was more than mere sport. Many of us who grew up in the bush can remember the times when the family relied on a bit of game to supplement the diet. I must admit to being a bit of a hunter in my youth, but, to be honest, these days I tend to side with the anti-gunners. Although, at times I wish the debate, on both sides, wasn't so extreme.

Here are some hunting yarns, contributed to the ABC contest by others who, in different times, obviously enjoyed a bit of honest, outdoor sport—or at least the yarns about it.

The first is a yarn by Vic Forrest, of Sale, Victoria.

THE FICKLE FINGER OF FATE

A hunter was out duck shooting on the Victorian side of the Murray, when he was approached by a Fisheries and Game Inspector.

'Hey!' called the inspector. 'Don't you know you're shooting ducks out of season?'

'That's all right,' said the shooter. 'These are New South Wales ducks.

'No, they're not!' asserted the inspector. 'They're Victorian ducks. I've been in this game for fifteen years and I ought to know.'

'Oh yeah?' sneered the hunter smugly. 'How can you tell the difference?'

With that, the inspector picked up a dead duck, turned it over and shoved his finger up its backside. He then extracted the digit, sniffed it, put it to his lips and pronounced, 'That's definitely a Victorian duck.' He proceeded with the same method for the other six ducks lying at the hunter's feet, before finally announcing, 'You've got five Victorian ducks there and only two New South Wales ones. I'm officially informing you that you're going to be charged with breaching the Victorian wildlife protection act. Now, what's your name?'

'John Smith,' replied the shooter.

The inspector jotted the name in his official government-issue notebook. 'Right. And where do you live?'

Quick as a flash, the hunter turned around, pulled down his trousers and bent over.

'You're the expert. You tell me!'

Bob Fisher, of Mareeba, in north Queensland, sometimes blames his yarns on the head stockman of Speewa Station, but he takes full credit for this one.

THE BRAVE LITTLE TAILOR

It was during a stay in a road camp in my youth when I was working on a peninsula road job. I was the camp truck driver/cook's offsider/odd-job person. Our camp was about two miles from a lagoon that was always teeming with wildlife, so, as it was a couple of weeks since we'd had fresh provisions, the foreman said to me, 'Take my old gun and go over to that swamp and bag a couple of ducks for Cookie to put in the cook pot.'

That old gun was a muzzle loader, with a very touchy trigger. The foreman told me not to load it until I was ready to shoot, as it was far too dangerous to carry while loaded.

I crawled up to the very edge of a large swamp and spotted

a nice lot of ducks. By the time I'd loaded the old muzzle loader, the ducks had swum over to the other side of the lagoon. To get within range of them, I waded out, waist-deep, into the water, took careful aim and fired.

I must have put too strong a charge into the old gun. It had a boot like a donkey and the recoil lifted me right out of the water and up the bank onto a patch of grass, where I landed on a nice fat pig. Thinking quickly, I wrestled it down to the ground and used my belt to tie it up.

Feeling pretty good about it all, I looked out across the lagoon to see how many ducks I'd shot. Well, there were six floating on the water . . . but something bigger was flapping about on the distant bank. I went around the lagoon to get the ducks and see what was making all that commotion on the bank. When I got there, I found that I'd forgotten to take the ramrod out of the gun after I'd loaded it. It had shot out the barrel and impaled two plains turkeys. Maybe that was why the old gun had kicked so much.

I collected the turkey and ducks and took them back to where I'd left the pig. I suddenly realised I had no boots on. Thinking they must have still been in the water, I waded back out and found them. When I got them back to the bank, I found a nice-sized cod in each boot.

I now had so much, it needed two trips to carry it all back to camp.

To this day, I've never been able to understand, why, after struggling back with that lot, all the other blokes treated me as some sort of hero, but wouldn't believe I'd got it all with one shot. After all, I was just getting a bit of fresh food for the camp. Why would I have needed a second shot?

Why indeed? Ron Hurst, of Mullaway, New South Wales, would have believed Bob's story. It's just as plausible as his reminiscences about duck hunting.

HAND OVER HAND

Years ago, I was with a duck-shooting party in the upper reaches of the Hume Weir and saw something I feel is worth repeating.

In those days, the ducks were very large and plentiful. In fact, when we approached one lagoon, we disturbed a large flock and they took off towards the weir. As they flew into the air, they nearly blotted out the sun—which was fairly normal in those days— but the strange thing this time was that the sky wouldn't hold them all. A lot had to just walk away.

However, I digress. We were camped near a party of fishermen, who were trying their luck on the river itself. We had suspicions they were using crosslines, which, of course, were illegal. In case you don't know, a crossline is one that stretches *across* a stream, with many baited hooks fixed to it at short intervals. This crossline was baited with small green frogs. Suddenly, some of the ducks who'd been forced to walk reached the river where the line was set and immediately began to eagerly eat the frogs. Seeing that, the fishermen ran to the edge of the stream, shouting and waving to frighten the ducks from taking their bait. Now they had room to fly, the ducks took to the air, but each, of course, had a hook in its craw, so they took the line with them, pulling out the small shrubs it was fixed to.

One of the fishermen grabbed a shrub and held on, only to be lifted into the air with the line.

'Shoot the ducks!' he bellowed. But we were too frightened to shoot, in case we hit him, so away they all went, heading towards the lake.

The other fishermen started singing out, 'He can't swim. He'll land in the lake and drown.'

However, the bloke in the air remained cool. He just climbed the line, hand over hand, and, as he came to each duck, wrung its neck, then climbed to the next one and did the same.

With each duck killed, there were less to fly. That factor, plus the added weight of the dead ducks on the crossline, meant that the bloke came down to earth again in a long glide, landing quite safely with a gentle bump on the ground.

Which, of course, brings us to a whole different concept of what truth really is—fishing stories.

Without a doubt, fishing is Australia's number one participation sport. Sadly, a lot of our fisheries have been thrashed close to death and the big catches are nowhere near as common as they used to be. In many areas, that's an environmental disaster, but on the yarn-spinning side of things, that's probably not a bad thing. After all, a scarcity of fish provides the motivation for fishermen, like Joe Compton, of Nundle, New South Wales, to do what they all seem to do best—spin a yarn or two.

IF ONLY

In the early sixties, I was living in a border town in northern New South Wales. It was midmorning and, on the Queensland side, the paddocks had been hot, dry and brown. The awning of the pub in town actually seemed to nod 'G'day' as I neared it. The old FC must have noticed it, too, because I could feel its steering wheel take on a life of its own and pull us over to stop in the shade.

The usual group was at the bar, reciting and giving all the words of wisdom needed to fix the world's problems. I willingly added my two-bob's worth.

We hadn't been at it long, when in bustled Herby with his old army haversack on his hip. Herby ran a pub on the New South Wales side. Like the rest of us, he had the usual run-of-the-mill weaknesses, but his one great passion was fishing. Herby announced that the cod were really on and he was going down the river to get himself three or four.

Somewhat tentatively, I asked Herby could he 'just possibly' get me one?

No worries. 'What about you other blokes?'

I can still recall who else was there, and the answers they gave. The brothers, Tim and Geoff, said they only needed the one cod, but a big one. 'Something you can scale with a hoe.' John, the publican, said the Bullwarrie shearers were in and he'd need one about 20 pounds.

Herby did his sums, pushing back the fingers of his right hand as he counted up. 'You want one. You two will share—that's two. A big 'un for you, Dilla, makes three. One for you, John, three for meself . . . that's oh, let's say, ten cod. Best be off. Gotta be back to get behind the bar at three. See ya!'

Herby downed his glass and headed for the door. I called out after him, 'Hey, Herby! Will you be able to catch ten cod before three o'clock?'

'No worries,' he replied, without even a pause in his stride. I felt I should press the issue, so I followed him out.

'Herby, what are you using for bait to catch so many cod?'

He stopped in mid stride and looked back over his shoulder at me. He was frowning and on his face was a querying expression. 'Bait? Bait? I've got no bait!'

Then his face lit up and he slowly shook his head. 'Oh, Joe. If *only* I had *bait*.'

Joe notes that like a lot of those present, old Herby's gone onto the great big cod hole in the sky. 'He never got to catch me a murray cod, but over the years, he gave me much more—fond memories of the days when it was still possible to drink that Barwon water.'

A bit like Herby, another old-timer, Old Bill, is the hero of the fishing yarn told by Ann Duffy, of Canowindra, New South Wales.

OLD MATES

We first met him at Lake Cargelligo in 1956. We knew he was a fisherman from his daughter, Marge. Bill's wife was dead and he lived with Marge. She told us how she'd found Bill's new nylon socks in her fridge. He reckoned they weren't much good for wearing, so he'd put frogs in them and stored them in the fridge for the next time he went fishing.

Bill had been a farmer all his life. He was eighty-three then, and very active. Small and wiry, slightly stooped and with a deeply wrinkled face, he wasn't much to look at. His skin was dark brown and looked like leather. He had small eyes, bright and full of humour—although he didn't say much. When he did speak, his voice was high pitched and his words were slow and drawling.

Because we were very young, very newly married and from the city, Bill decided we needed to be introduced to the Lachlan.

Even in Bill's little blue Morris ute (with me sandwiched between the two men with the gearstick between my legs), it wasn't far to the river. When we got there, Bill set us up in two of his favourite fishing spots. Before long, the redfin started biting. In our excitement at really catching fish, we actually forgot about Bill for a while—until we heard him.

'Come on! Come on!' he was saying in his high-pitched drawl.

We looked at each other, shrugged and went off to have a look. Bill was inching his way backwards down an old tree that sloped out over the river, clinging on with his feet and one hand. His other arm was stretched out above his head. He was holding a piece of fencing wire. Caught in the loop at the end of the wire, was the head of a very large goanna.

Slowly—very slowly—Bill backed down the tree, encouraging the goanna every step of the way.

'Ran out of bait,' he explained, as he killed the goanna. We went back to our fishing.

It must have been half an hour later that we heard a great commotion upriver. We couldn't see anything from where we were fishing, so we left the lot and rushed to Bill's aid. What we saw transfixed us. There was Bill, halfway into the river, yelling and jigging up and down. Suddenly, his whole body disappeared beneath the water. We were petrified. We scrambled down the steep bank, ready to dive in and rescue Bill, but his head broke the surface and he had a great grin on his silly face. Then he stood up. The water wasn't that deep after all. Bill wasn't on his own. In his arms, he had the biggest fish I've ever seen in my whole life.

'Got you, ya bastard!' he said, looking the big fish in the eye. He struggled over to the bank, then, ignoring us, turned around and without a word let the big feller slide back into the water.

As we all watched the huge cod swim away, I swear I heard Bill say, 'See ya!'

The thing about fishing yarns is that there's always somebody ready to outdo you—with something that was bigger and better. In fact, yarns like the next one from Evan Farley, of North Rockhampton, Queensland, lead you to believe that some of our fishermen tend to exaggerate a wee bit.

TOM CREEDY'S BIG COD

Tom had the best eighteen-yoke bullock team this side of the black stump . . . or the other side, for that matter. He'd been bringing back parts for a boring plant for Sunnydale Station. After three months, they'd crossed the border and were only 100 miles from Sunnydale, when he had wagon problems. Then it started to rain. Tom camped on Tonga Creek to wait till the weather cleared. But it rained and rained until Tonga Creek was like the bloody Murray.

After a second week, having lost two dogs and a spare bullock, Tom reckoned there was something big in the creek. He thought of crocs and 'gators, but he knew they wouldn't hang round the swirling water. Therefore, it *had* to be a fish.

So Tom set some lines. But every line he set snapped like cotton— even the big hitching rope, an inch thick.

'Break my new hitchin' rope, would yer?' growled Tom. 'I'll get you . . . and I ain't leavin' this crik till I do.'

On board the dray, he had a winch drum and 500 feet of steel cable for the boring plant. He dragged them to the bank and anchored them to a big gum. Tom always travelled with two wagons, hauling them in tandem. While one was only bogged, the other was completely buggered—the axle bent and both back wheels smashed. First, Tom made himself a shelter to keep out the pouring rain, then he dragged some big logs up to make a roaring fire. Next, he heated up the bent axle and twisted it further to make a hook big enough to catch a whale.

There was this one young bullock that was pretty lazy and kept wandering off. Tom knocked it on the head, kept enough meat for himself and used the rest to bait the hook.

It took three days before he got a bite.

At first he thought he'd just got snagged, but when he saw the steel cable tearing off upstream against the current, he started winching. He'd just got whatever it was back midstream, when the hook tore out of the bait and he lost the fish. The bait had been too tender. This time, Tom shot an old bull buffalo that wandered past. It was so tough, he gapped his axe and bent his crowbar cutting a hole to get the hook in. In two days, he was ready to go again. Of course, with a belly full of tender young bullock, the fish didn't feel hungry enough to bite again for five days.

This time, Tom let it run until it was well and truly hooked before he started winching. That fish pulled so hard, the big gum started to lean towards the creek. Tom decided to play safe and yoked up twelve of his best bullocks. As soon as there was some slack in the rope, he moved quickly and hooked his heavy snig chains on and started them pulling.

The bullocks pulled and came to a stop. Tom swore and cracked his whip. The team went down on their knees. They were moving slowly forward, but that fish was still in the water. Then Tom saw why. He'd pulled the whole creek five chains out of line. That's why, to this very day, that bit's called Creedy's Elbow.

Next, Tom drove his team round and round a big old ironbark tree and anchored the cable and the fish to it.

'Wait there till the next drought,' he yelled at the fish. 'Then we'll see who's in the water and who's out! This is Queensland, remember, so we won't have to wait all that long.'

In fact, the rain had started easing already. When it stopped. Tom abandoned the broken wagon, unbogged the other, and completed his job, doing two trips with the one wagon.

For various reasons, it was five years before he went back. The drought had well and truly set in.

It was a humdinger. Most of the sheep had died, so there was no wool to cart and Tom made a crust carting water to the homesteads—and that's how he came back to the elbow. It was the only waterhole with any decent water. The others were all nearly dry.

And yes, the fish was still there—or at least its skeleton was. The bones were too big for even Ringo the Dingo to drag away. Tom, being a practical man who wouldn't waste anything, could see a use for them. Every time he went for a load of water, he'd hook up some bones and drag them back to Murray Downs homestead. Sometimes he only managed to get one big one out at a time. At the homestead, he bolted them together and built the finest shearing shed in the country from them. Any shearer who couldn't shear 500 a day in that shed wasn't worth his salt, and gangs would fight each other to see who could shear in the Murray Downs shed.

For seventy-five years it stood, solid as a rock, and nobody knows how many thousands of bales of greasy wool came through it. And it stayed like that until all that rain early this year. Yep! It stayed at Murray Downs right until that big flood came up over the flat— and the whole shed swum away.

7

BEATING
ABOUT
THE BUSH

It doesn't matter how hard any of us try to avoid it, sooner or later, we've got to come back to spinning yarns about the bush. There's no way out of it.

On the other hand, it doesn't *all* have to be corks around the hats, blowflies around the bullockies or dogs doing unspeakable things in tuckerboxes. There *are* bush yarns that tell of country life in the 1990s, pretty much the way they did in the 1890s. It's just that bush people these days seem to feel a bit less like spinning the odd yarn or two. In a way, you can see their point—with the worst rural recession in our history running riot everywhere. However, you'll hear lots of bush people swear that the only thing that got them through hard times in the past was their sense of humour. Perhaps, like putting a steel rim on a cartwheel, hand shearing or lynching the bank manager, yarn spinning is a rural craft that's been swamped by the twentieth century. I hope not. I hope the bush yarn spinners who still pop up from time to time aren't verbal dinosaurs, plodding through the dusty remnants of a world that existed before the nuclear winter of *Full House* and *Paradise Beach*.

My own passion for bush yarns was rewakened in the late 1960s, when I became the primary industries writer for the Melbourne *Age*. After a few years in the city, I felt I'd lost my bush trappings, until a fateful afternoon in a Victorian country town, when I was born again. Hallelujah!

TELLING THE TIME

There was an institution back in Victorian farm writing circles in the 1960s called the Shell Royal Agricultural Society Journalists' Tour. It was supposed to be about promoting Victoria's September extravaganza, the Royal Melbourne Show. Every year, the RAS would select an area of Victoria for special scrutiny by the rural press. They'd hire a big air-conditioned bus, herd a mob of feral journalists aboard, and head off to the nominated lucky district. All the local stud breeders, carrot growers and chook fanciers would be teed up to show their finest to us. Councils throughout the area would be asked to bung on civic receptions, afternoon teas and banquets. They did so with gusto. Usually, by eleven o'clock in the morning, after four or five receptions and twenty or thirty morning teas, the diligent members of the rural press would be too stuffed to jump. Once the grog was broken out at lunchtime—and fifty or sixty times during the afternoon—we'd all be in pretty marginal nick. God knows why it took the RAS so long to work it out, but overindulgence was the main reason those bunfights got very little real coverage. We were *supposed* to take photos and interview leading primary producers as a publicity prelude to the show. Sad to say, we rarely did.

On my first Shell tour (the Shell part was because of the benevolent oil company sponsoring it), I'd arranged to telephone head office every afternoon at three precisely, to see if there were any messages or stories requiring my attention. That appointment was also a ploy by an alert chief of staff to make sure I was doing what I was supposed to be doing. Unfortunately, on this particular junket, my watch had given up the ghost towards the climax of an impromptu arm wrestle with a government agronomist about one o'clock one morning, during an in-depth discussion about molybdenum deficiencies in the lighter grey soils of that region.

We'd all been bussed to a showground in a largish country town, where the local stud breeders had trotted out their best stock for the cameramen's attention.

To be fair, there wasn't a lot in the story for my good self, so I wasn't really showing much interest. As the afternoon wore on, I realised it was about time to check in with the office. I'd spotted a public phone across the other side of the arena but, being watchless, I wasn't sure what the time was. As I hurried towards the phone box, I passed a Hereford cattle breeder, all done up in a spotless white coat, who'd obviously brought his best bull out to show off to the media. He was crouched down polishing the bull's front hoofs with a chamois. Still uncertain of the time, I stopped and interrupted him.

'Excuse me, mate. Can you please tell me what the time is?'

He gave the hoof a last polish, neatly folded his chamois, placed it in the pocket of his white coat, then, to my amazement, leaned across, grabbed the bull's scrotum and moved it slowly to one side. Then he let it fall back into place and announced, 'Five minutes to three.'

I was dumbfounded. Surely I'd chanced apon some age-old

method of telling the time that city folk had long forgotten. Way in the background of my subconscious, I could hear kookaburras laughing and sheep bleating. The bush. I'd almost forgotten the bush and its old time ways. There *had* to be a story in this bloke and his bull. But I had to be sure, so I asked him again.

'Sorry, mate. I didn't hear what you said. What was the time again?'

Once more, he gently moved the bull's scrotum to one side for a second or two, then released it and announced, 'Four minutes to three.'

I hadn't imagined it. I *had* stumbled on a forgotten piece of folklore. I *would* be able to file a story. Ever the professional, I whipped out my notebook and introduced myself.

'Look, mate. I'm Mike Hayes, from the *Age* newspaper. I couldn't help but notice what you did just then. It's amazing. I've always been interested in old, dying bush skills. Now, could you tell me how you tell the time by moving your bull's testicles like that?'

The bloke shrugged. 'Had to,' he said. 'It's the only bloody way I can see the town hall clock.'

I know there's been a rash of stories about working dogs in recent years. They're usually a good source of yarns . . . and there's quite a few in this book. Second to dogs, cattle, in particular, bulls, seem to be a favoured topic for bush yarn spinners. Maybe it's something to do with the male dominance of yarn spinning. After all, as in the above yarn, bulls are undeniably macho.

Although we're supposed to have ridden to the Mess We're Currently in, on the Sheep's Back, there are relatively few yarns about sheep. Perhaps we've subconsciously allowed New Zealand to enjoy the monopoly there. Here's a bull yarn from Tex Tyrell.

TAKEN THREE TIMES A DAY AFTER MEALS

A cocky somewhere down in New South Wales decided to invest some big money in a bull. He'd never bothered before, but he realised that if he was to stay ahead in the cattle game, he had to have good stock. He shopped around a bit and finally found an older bull, with an impeccable pedigree, going for only $300. That probably wasn't much, as far as bull prices go, but this bloke was a bit of a battler, so it was quite a sum for him. He paid the money and arranged to have the new bull trucked to his place. It ambled off the truck, into the paddock of heifers and went and sat down under a big old tree. And for the next three weeks, that's all the bastard did.

The cocky started getting a bit worried. He'd paid $300 for the blessed bull, and so far, he wasn't getting a cracker back. The old bull just wasn't performing. He tried ringing the bloke he'd bought the bull from, but he wasn't much help.

'No. He was all right when he left here. He always worked good and regular at *our* place,' the bloke told him.

So the cocky consulted his mate down the road, who ran a few cattle himself. He hadn't much to offer, but he finally suggested the cocky ring the local vet.

The vet came out and had a look at the bull.

'Well, there's nothing wrong with him at all. Although he's a bit long in the tooth, you should get a few good years out of him. What I reckon's wrong, is that he's disorientated. The trip, all the way here in a truck, has thrown him off a bit. His system's out of balance and until it settles down, he's not likely to work.'

'Crikey, doc,' said the cocky. 'I need him to start on my cows *now*. Otherwise my whole year's program'll be out of whack. Isn't there something you can give him?'

'Sure,' said the vet. 'I've got these pills—they're a mixture of vitamins and hormones. Whack a couple into him, morning and night, and he'll come good in no time.' The vet produced a big bottle from his bag, handed over his account and left.

The cocky yarded the bull immediately and administered the first dose.

What a difference. In no time, the old bull was up and about— at 'em and into 'em. In only a couple of days, he'd done over all the cockie's cattle. The next thing he did was jump the fence and get stuck into the neighbour's herd. By the end of the week, he was four properties away, still going hammer and tongs.

The cocky rang his mate and thanked him for advising him to go with the vet. 'It's a bloody miracle,' he told him. 'That old bull is going at it full bore.'

'What made the difference?' his mate asked.

'Those flaming pills the vet gave me.'

'What sort of pills are they?'

'I don't know, but they're a blue colour and taste of peppermint.'

Of course, bush yarns go back further than bulls, or cockies, or white people. Our greatest storytellers are our Aboriginal people. While many of their traditional stories are of a sacred nature— preserving the records of creation and spirituality—others are passed on pretty much in the same way as our traditional folk stories . . . and yarns.

I once asked a traditional storyteller in outback New South Wales whether there was an Aboriginal tale about the Darling lily—that beautiful plant that appears as if by magic in some of Australia's most hostile country, growing in unseen sandy beds across the desert. My friend thought for a moment and said, 'You know, we *don't* have a story about it. But next time you come back, I'll tell you one.'

During white Australia's Bicentennial celebrations, a quest was mounted for the Two Hundred Greatest Stories Never Told. The idea was to identify 200 unsung heroes and heroines and recount their achievements to the world.

It was launched at a turn in the Argyle Tavern at Sydney's Rocks. A whole swag of noted storytellers were teed up to spin a few yarns as a curtain-raiser to the official launch. Also present was a small contingent of Aboriginal people. They explained to the organisers that, as storytelling was part of their culture, they felt they should be given a chance to participate in the opening. Maybe because most of Aboriginal Australia was, at that time, allegedly opposing the Bicentennial celebrations, they were given a mumbled knock-back, along the lines that 'The official program's full and we can't change it now.' Perhaps the organisers feared some sort of political process . . . who knows?

A small group of us adjourned to the next bar in some semblance of protest. We continued to enjoy the free refreshments being offered, but didn't take part in the rest of the proceedings. It wasn't much of a protest, admittedly, but our hearts were in the right place. It was there that Bob Maza spun a yarn that, with hindsight, may sum up the whole Aboriginal condition.

BUSH BAPTISM

Years ago, in a western New South Wales town, there was a priest who became renowned as a fire-and-brimstone merchant. He tolerated no strays from the straight and narrow. Most of all, he waged war on those Catholics who dared disobey the Pope's ruling that meat shouldn't be eaten on Fridays. It's not hard to work out how, almost single-handedly, he'd managed to bludgeon to death almost all traces of Aboriginal culture in the district.

One Friday afternoon, he was sitting in the shady grounds of the presbytery, working on the vitriolic text of next Sunday's sermon, when he detected a slight movement out of the corner of his eye. He investigated and, sure enough, there was a figure slipping silently through the river gums down towards the sluggish Macquarie River. Instantly, the priest recognised who it was—old Ernie Cockatoo, a grizzled veteran of many a hellfire sermon. And, to the priest's immediate fury, the old bloke was carrying a huge goanna over his shoulders. To the God Botherer, it was obvious what the old backslider was going to do. He was going to disobey the Holy Father's rock solid decree.

Without a sound, the priest let himself out by a side gate and followed the old man through the trees. Creeping from tree to tree, he managed to make up quite a bit of ground between them by the time the old feller had reached the river. There, crouched out of sight, the priest watched.

Old Ernie threw the 7 foot goanna on the ground and set about lighting a fire. He soon had a handful of twigs smouldering at the water's edge. Then, as the priest's anger grew, he picked up the old goanna, bunged it on the fire for a few seconds, turned it over, cooked the other side for a few seconds more, then rinsed it in the Macquarie.

Just as the old man was about to take a huge bite out of the goanna, the priest leapt from his hiding place, frothing at the mouth. Old Ernie nearly had kittens on the spot.

'Jesus, Father. You give me a hell of a fright.'

'That's nothing to what the Good Lord has in store for you, Ernie Cockatoo. How many times have I told you about not eating meat on Friday?'

The old bloke looked a bit crestfallen. 'Too many times, Father.'

'Then why do you always go out of your way to disobey God's holy instructions?'

Ernie didn't hesitate. 'Hey, Father, you remember the time my little bloke Bingara was born?'

'I do, indeed. And what a poor example you're setting him.'

'And you remember when you came and took Bingara from me and carried him to your church and put water on him and renamed him Freddie?'

'I certainly do.'

'Well, I just put water on that bugger and renamed him Fish.'

And while we're slinging off at the clergy . . .

TENDING THE FLOCK

According to ABC yarn-spinning entrant Frank Holland, of Neereman, via Maldon, Victoria, a parson went to a small country church one wet, cold Sunday night and found the lamps burning brightly, but only one person in attendance—an old cocky.

'Do you reckon we should still have a service?' he asked the old farmer.

'Definitely,' the cocky replied. 'If I went to feed my sheep and only one turned up, I'd still feed it.'

'Fair enough,' the parson decided and launched into a full-length service—four hymns, a prayer and a thirty-minute sermon—the whole kit and caboodle.

After the Benediction, he shook hands with the old farmer and asked, 'Well, how was that?'

The old bloke thought for a minute, then drawled slowly, 'Like I said, if I went to feed my sheep and only one turned up, I'd still feed it . . . but I wouldn't give it the whole blinking' bag full.'

Not long ago, I dropped in on the fine folk at the Gill-Waminda Nursing Home in Goulburn, New South Wales. I was introduced to Stella Young, from the nearby St John of God Hospital. She'd come up with a mob from the hospital for an afternoon of culture and yarn spinning. I was warned that Stella had a swag full of yarns.

'I haven't got time to tell many,' she whispered conspiratorially, 'but I will tell you one. It's not dirty or anything like that, but . . .'

A CHAMBER OF MIRACLES

Two nuns were on a mission of mercy way outback. They'd driven for most of the day along rough bush roads and were almost at their destination, when their car ran out of petrol.

'What will we do?' asked the junior sister.

'We'll just have to get some petrol from somewhere,' her companion told her. 'We won't need much. We're only a few kilometres from town.'

The nuns noticed an old bloke in a nearby paddock, cutting burrs. They found a saggy bit of the fence, wriggled through and walked over to him. He showed some surprise at finding two nuns suddenly alongside him.

'Crikey. You give me a bit of a scare, sisters. You never strike many people out here.'

The sisters apologised and explained their plight. 'We were on our way into town and ran out of fuel. Is there a farmhouse or anything around here where we can borrow a litre or so of petrol?'

'You'll be right as rain,' the burr cutter told them. 'There's a homestead just out of sight over the next hill. If you pop in there, you shouldn't have any worries.'

The nuns thanked him and headed off in the direction he'd indicated. Sure enough, there was the silver roof shining among the pine trees, just over the crest of the hill. In no time at all, they were knocking on the back door. A cocky came to the fly-wire screen, chewing on a camp pie sandwich. When he saw who his visitors were, he quickly shoved the bulk of it into his face and signalled them in.

'We won't stay,' said the senior sister. 'We're already late for an appointment in town. We were just wondering if you could spare us a drop of petrol? Our car seems to have run out.'

The bloke swallowed his sandwich and nodded vigorously. 'No worries, sisters. I've got a two thousand litre tank out behind the shed. Just let me get me boots on, and I'll have you fixed up in a tick.'

The nuns followed him out to the tank. Excusing himself, the farmer went back into the shed and started fossicking about. After a few minutes, he returned.

'Sorry to keep you waiting, but you wouldn't by any chance have some sort of receptacle to carry the petrol in, would you?'

'We don't, I'm sorry,' said the nun.

'Well, I don't seem to have a spare drum or anything like that. The missus made me clean out the shed only a week or so ago.' Then he seemed to remember something. 'Hang on. You won't need much, will you? I'll be back in a sec.'

The farmer hurried back to the house and came back in a minute or two with an old enamel chamber pot.

'I'm sorry, sisters. It's the best I can do. But, like I said, you won't need much, will you?'

The nuns agreed that the chamber pot would do nicely. The farmer filled it to the brim for them, then remembered that his wife had the car in town and he couldn't even give them a lift back to their vehicle.

'Don't worry,' he was assured. 'It's a lovely afternoon and the car's only back over the hill. If we're careful with how we carry the petrol, we'll be fine.' And off they went.

Gingerly, the nuns carried the pot of petrol down to their car. They took the cap off their petrol tank and carefully poured the fuel in. The senior sister got back in, pumped the accelerator a few times and turned the ignition key. Instantly, the motor roared into life. The second nun ran around to the passenger seat and jumped in. They were just about to roar off, when the burr cutter appeared suddenly right in front of the car, his hat in his hands and a look of wonderment on his dial.

The senior nun wound down her window and asked, 'Is something wrong?'

'No, sisters. Everything's fine. In fact, you've brought new faith into my life. In recent years, I'd never had much time for religion, but when I saw from over there, how you two got that car started . . . I believe in miracles again.'

Stella's yarn brings me back to the claim that I made in the introduction to this fine publication that yarn spinning tends to be a male province. Her yarn, and some of the beauties in the ABC competition, might seem to make a liar of me (heaven forbid!). But I stick to my guns. The *telling* of yarns is the male go. Even in these liberated times, women do not tend to spend much time around a few cold ones swapping yarns like blows in a duel. But they *do* tell some rippers—usually being more prepared to take the time and write them down, rather than indulge in the oral traditions of yarn spinning.

Take Leona Ward's true yarn, sent in from Nyngan, New South Wales.

HAZEL

During the 1985 drought . . . or was it the 1987 drought? Hang on, now I think about it, I'm almost sure it was the '89 drought . . . Anyway, during the drought, we were given two pups, reported to be by that most prolific sire, The Australian Champion.

We called them Bob and Hazel (after our Honourable Leader of the time and his good lady). As the pups grew, Bob began to display symptoms of some type of mental disorder. He spent his days going round and round in circles, chasing his tail and yapping madly. He had to be put down. Hazel developed into a great lovable dog—no brains, but she had a great smile and a sweet personality.

We were taking wether weaners into the sale and had to get them across the Bogan River Bridge into Nyngan. As the bridge was on the Mitchell Highway, traffic was held up on both sides while *himself* on the motorbike, with Hazel and This Little Woman, on foot, worked frantically to get the sheep across without holding up traffic for too long.

Only those who have ever tried to get weaners anywhere, let alone across a bridge, will understand the degree of difficulty we faced. *Himself* roared about on the bike, screaming abuse in the direction of Hazel and TLW.

Up and down flew Hazel and I, under the bridge, over the levee banks, back up the road—our ears constantly being blasted with,

'*Stop the breakaways!* Back over the levee!'

'*Hazel, you bitch!* Don't let them down that side!'

'*Hazel! What the bloody hell are you doing?*'

'Get the bloody hell out o' there! *Hazel . . . You stupid bloody bitch!*'

'Ring 'um! Ring 'um! *For God's bloody sake, Hazel!*'

As the dog and TLW worked frantically to this string of explicit directions, we passed backwards and forwards by a car with caravan behind, waiting to cross the bridge. The driver and his lady passenger watched, with great interest, our rich tapestry of bush life—the terrified sheep, the red-faced man, his faithful dog . . . and TLW.

Finally, one weaner stepped onto the bridge . . . then two, three . . . and then they were all over, running madly off the other side . . . in the *wrong* direction, of course. *Himself*, with smiling dog behind him on the bike, roared over the bridge to fend off the next disaster.

As I walked, puffed and perspiring, back past the lady in the car, she lent out of the window and said, 'I think you did a really good job, Hazel.'

Poor Leona. Her yarn, though, does reflect the fact that country women *are* capable of far more than just baking scones, breeding neanderthal sons and boiling up tonnes of ram chops in pure cholesterol to keep their men happy. However, that doesn't mean everything's sweetness and light on the feminist front.

HUMAN RELATIONSHIPS

A lawyer round our way told me this story in strictest confidence. You know how careful they are about confidentiality, so don't pass a word of this on to anybody, eh?

He got a phone call the other day from a cockie's wife, down the road. I won't tell you any names. But they're *well known* round here. Anyway, this woman gave him a bell and told him, right up front, 'I want you to arrange a divorce for me.'

'I'd be more than happy to,' said the lawyer, 'but I'm playing golf for the next three weeks, so I'm a bit tied up for the moment. But don't worry, I won't neglect your case. I'll take a few notes now and while I'm on the putting green, I'll give it some thought.'

'Oh thank you,' gasped the grateful client.

'Right. Now, you want a divorce? What grounds do you have?'

'Well, we've got three and a half thousand acres here and a half acre building block down the South Coast.'

'No, no,' laughed the lawyer, 'you don't get my drift. Do you have a grudge or anything like that?'

'A grudge? No, just a big double car port and the old machinery shed out the back.'

'Hang on. Hang on. We seem to be on the wrong wavelength. Does he beat you up, or anything?'

'No. I'm always awake first.'

The lawyer finally did his block. 'Good God, woman! Why do you want a divorce?'

The good woman gave a sad sign of resignation. 'We just don't seem to be able to carry on a sensible conversation any more.'

These days, your traditional gnarled old bushman, with a face like old leather, hat brim pulled down over eyes grown wrinkled at the side from too many October long weekends watching the car races at Bathurst on the telly, size ten boots and a size three hat, doesn't always have the final say over TLW, slaving over a red-hot slow combustion stove in a bark hut on the furthermost fringe of the F3 freeway, as B. G. Hazeldine, of Wodonga, Victoria, told us.

WHEN THINGS AREN'T LOOKING UP

Things hadn't been good on the farm for the past few years, and among a host of other problems, Wally was desperate for a new pair of boots. His old Blundstones had just about carked it, and badly needed replacement. They were just about on their last legs, as it were, and Wally's last legs had never been real good. He'd always dreamed of owning a pair of renowned R. M. Williams boots, but had never had the readies to afford them. But one week, Wally's luck changed with a small Lotto win, information about which Wally somehow neglected to pass on to his devoted wife, Roma.

The next time he hit town, Wally headed for the boot shop and got fitted with a brand spanking new pair of R. M. Williams boots. He told the sales assistant he'd wear the new boots home and asked him to box the old ones.

Wally was really excited about his new boots and when he got home, he marched into the kitchen, where Roma was preparing the evening meal, threw his arms up and said, 'Roma, d'you notice anything different?'

Roma looked up from her chores, eyed Wally up and down and replied, 'Wally, what's different? The same bushy moustache, the belly out over the belt. Have you been drinking?'

With that, Wally headed off into the bedroom, took off all his clothes, except for his socks . . . and his brand spanking new R. M. Williams boots. Then he strode back into the kitchen.

'Hey, Roma, *now* do you notice anything different about me?'

Roma looked up again, eyed Wally up and down again, and said, 'The same bushy moustache, the same belly over the belt and that little thing pointing down.'

Wally fairly exploded. 'For God's sake, Roma . . . that little thing, as you call it, is pointing down at my brand new R. M. Williams boots!'

'For God's sake, Wally,' retorted Roma, 'then why didn't you buy an Akubra?'

Hang on, folks. We better not write off the old bushie stereotype altogether, eh? Where else would we be able to record the patient wisdom of blokes like Des O'Sullivan's mate Harry, of Blackheath, New South Wales.

HARRY ON THE ROAD TO MUNGINDI

Harry was a funny bloke. He made no attempt to be humorous—things just happened around him. He had a dry old voice and he didn't talk much—only when he had something to say. He had a simple theory: 'If you're talking, you're not listening.'

One day, we were driving from Cunnamulla to Mungindi. The road was unsealed and had few signposts. The day wore on and then, out of nowhere, a lone fencer came into view. After exchanging notes on the weather and the state of the road, we asked him, 'How far to Mungindi?'

'Well,' said the fencer, 'I reckon you're dead set on a hundred mile out. Yeah. See that tank over there? I always reckon that's a hundred mile out.'

An hour or so later, we came upon the mailman. After disposing of the weather and the season generally, we asked, 'How far to Mungindi?'

'Now then,' said the mailman, 'd'you see that mailbox just over there? Well, that's Steve King's, and he's just on a hundred mile out.'

Not real long before dark, we came up with a drover setting up for the night. We told him about the track behind us and he told us about the track ahead of us. Then, 'How far d'you reckon we are from Mungindi?'

Said the drover, 'You're just on a hundred mile out. You can't go wrong from here, mate.'

We drove on in silence. Then Harry uttered his first words for a couple of hours.

'Well, there's one thing for sure. Mungindi ain't gettin' any further away.'

There are lots of bush yarns about snakes. There are lots about goannas. And there are some about dingoes. Goannas and snakes could take up quite a few volumes on their own, so here's a dingo yarn to go on with.

HOODWINKED

Trevor Duncan, of Cairns, reports that in his grandfather's time, around Nebo, west of Mackay, in Queensland, the dingoes were still in large numbers. One year in particular, the dogs were really causing havoc, and to try to minimise the damage, the manager of a property where old Ted was working, between Nebo and Collinsville, offered a bounty of a shilling for each pair of dingo ears. Ted and a couple of his mates thought it'd be a pretty easy way of picking up a bit of extra drinking money, so they sat down after tea one night to decide how best to go about it.

They quickly worked out that they wouldn't make much if they only shot the dogs they saw as they moved about during the day. And if they went chasing them at night, a light bright enough to spot the dogs could scare them off. Anyway, without sleep, they wouldn't be much good for work the next day. So they had to find a way to bring the dogs to them, so that one could keep watch, while the rest slept until the dingoes arrived.

They worked out that if they took an old boiler from the chook house and strung it up in a tree, the squawking and flapping would be sure to attract the dogs. Then they could string a carbide lamp over the hen, to give just enough light to reflect the dogs' eyes, so they had something to aim at.

On the first night, the plan worked to perfection. In the morning, the lads had ten bob's worth to put in the kitty. In those days, that was the better part of a bloke's weekly wage.

The second and third nights were more of the same. Ted and his mates could see a big binge coming up in town, come rodeo week. Then, on the fourth night—nothing—not a solitary hair. The dogs were coming down in the same big numbers, but the hunters' shots weren't having any effect. It was a night of clean misses and wasted ammunition.

Something had to be drastically wrong. Maybe one shooter might have an off night, but not all of them at once.

So then next night, after tea, out came the old jam tins and down to the creek they trooped to check their sights. They all checked out perfectly. That night was the same as the one before— plenty of dingoes' eyes in the light, plenty of shots fired, but absolutely nothing to show for it.

On the following night, instead of shooting when the dogs came in, Ted climbed up the tree, and as soon as he heard the dogs, he turned the lamp up, so they could see what was happening.

Those blokes always knew the old dingo was a pretty smart animal, but the sight that met their eyes astounded even them.

There were the dogs, in pairs, walking side by side, about 6 inches apart. The dog on the right had his right eye closed and the one on the left had his left eye closed. The bullets were passing straight between them.

G. J. McGoady, of Dubbo, New South Wales, came up with a bush yarn that, to me, at least, is *the* great horse story.

FAIR EXCHANGE

It wouldn't be proper to mention names, as, from time to time, I see references to them in the results of camp drafts and kindred sporting events in the newspapers and horsy magazines. This yarn was told to me by a stockman who lived and worked in the Outback during the 1920s and 30s.

The head of this family was on holidays, visiting capital city racecourses seeking a mount fit to represent his station at nearby meetings. He finally selected a good-looking brown thoroughbred, complete with papers and an assurance that it 'wasn't good enough for the city, but would win anywhere in the bush'.

By the time the horse finally arrived at the station, spare time to work him was a bit scarce, so he was turned out for a spell. When the work slackened, he was brought in and the lightest stockman was given the task of bringing the horse to racing condition. All went well for a fortnight, until one morning, the horse objected to all the new found attention and threw the trainer. The boss's response was 'Put the big saddle (the stock saddle) on him, and show him who's boss.'

That move wasn't a success. The only difference being that the rider went a trifle higher when he vacated the big saddle.

Eventually, an invitation went out that anyone who fancied himself as a rider could try his luck. Quite a few ringers made the effort, but all of them were unloaded in short time. So once more, the big brown horse was 'hit over the rump with the bridle' and turned out.

Time passed and one afternoon, when the boss was sitting on the front veranda, a horseman approached. He rode a bay gelding. But what took the boss's eye was a beautiful-looking grey mare being used as a packhorse.

After the usual small talk, the boss asked if there was any chance of buying the mare. The traveller explained that if he sold the mare, he would need something else to carry the pack. The boss big-heartedly acknowledged his logic, but persisted by suggesting a swap. 'We've got the ideal animal for a job like that.'

The response was 'Why don't we sleep on it?'

Both men were at the horse yards early next morning . . . as was everyone else on the station. The big hope was that the visitor would try out the 'swap horse'.

When the station horses were yarded, the boss pointed out his half of the bargain. 'That bloody good-looking brown horse. Yes, that's him there!'

The mare's owner asked quietly, 'Does he buck at all?'

'Well, he hasn't had a strap on him for a couple of months, so he *might* hump up a bit.'

With that doubtful assurance, the visitor caught the big brown feller and saddled him without any trouble. In fact, there wasn't the slightest hint of bother until he swung into the saddle . . .

For months afterwards, the only topic of conversation was that bloke's amazing display of horsemanship. No one had ever seen anything quite like it.

Finally, the dust settled with the rider still comfortably aboard. After a few laps around the yard, the word came, 'Open it up!'

Out across the plain, past the mill and tank, between the woodheap and the fowl house and then . . . he brought the big brown horse back to the yard.

Pulling up in front of where the boss still sat on the top rail of the yard, the rider said, 'Boss, this is a good horse—a real good horse and I'll take him as a swap for that grey mare. Y'see, I can ride this bloke orright. But I can't ride that mare.'

It's probably significant that so many bush yarns refer us back to yesteryear. While yarn spinning appears alive and well in the 1990s, it's obvious that time has taken a little toll on this great Aussie tradition. Of course, it's not the only one to have undergone change in the last few decades—as David Ridgewell, of Mannilla, New South Wales, reports.

PROGRESS

April 1965—a Red Letter Month for New England and northwestern New South Wales. Television had, at last, arrived. Who would ever forget the first ad for Streets' ice-cream or that initial movie on Saturday night, *The African Queen*, starring Katharine Hepburn and Humphrey Bogart? It was all too much to imagine, and to think—there it was, in our lounge room.

For many households, the HMV battery radio was still their eyes and ears to the world. The convenience of electricity had not yet lit up their lives.

The Manilla district was no exception. For many families to the north and west of this river junction town, there would be disappointment at not being able to join in the celebrations of the long-awaited new form of entertainment.

However, Dolly and Mont, from their abode on the flat at West Manilla, were more than anxious to participate. That bush-born pair, whose whole lives revolved around their boys, horses, saddles, rabbit traps and pigs, only asked for the simple, but happy things of life. Pictures in the front room were something they had to have, at any cost. So the first Monday morning following the commencement of television, the bay pony was harnessed to a light spring cart and they headed for town, crossing the Namoi via the low-level bridge.

Any journey from the homestead, Old Fairhaven, was only embarked upon on important occasions—the show, elections or funerals. This latest venture was considered notable enough to fall within those important categories.

Tethering the pony beneath a kurrajong with a feedbag on her nose, Dolly and Mont headed for the Popular Corner Store and their appointment with the proprietor, C. F. 'Dougie' Hayward. There was nothing quite like that sort of country emporium, where all the purchases were wrapped in brown paper and tied with thick white string; with all the customers treated as family—whether they be gentry from the vast holdings, or the families of fettlers who camped in tents by the rail line. Credit was extended annually, and the selection of goods offered varied from a Sunshine Header to half-a-dozen saveloys.

Dolly, the spokesperson, explained to Mr Hayward the urgency of their calling—highlighting not only a keenness to purchase a television set, but the possibility of also investing in a pop-up toaster.

Regretfully, it was explained that neither a TV or a toaster was currently in stock at the moment, but, luckily, both items could be trucked to Manilla by Friday, at the latest.

Smoko, an Australian tradition, was prepared for all customers— Dolly and Mont being no exception. C. F. Hayward sought details as to the brands required. Kreisler was promoted as an excellent make of TV . . . as was AWA or Pye. And definitely, the 21 inch screen was the most popular. As far as a toaster was concerned, the Sunbeam or Hotpoint displayed, proved reliable and had room for two or four slices of bread.

Strangely, details of cost and brand names stimulated little response from either Dolly or Mont, so the manager assumed the pumpkin and date scones, generously supplied by the Laird girls, had distracted them from their mission. Then, of course, the bush pair, used to sitting by a camp fire on old spindle backs, were probably being lulled by the sheer comfort of the tilting, revolving office chairs—excuse enough for their seemingly indifferent response.

Clutching a steaming cup of the famous Billy tea, Dolly politely, finally broke the ice.

'Any sort of television or pop-up toaster will be okay with Montie and me, Mr Hayward, so long as they can both run on Plume kerosene, rather than Atlantic, because it's a penny ha'penny a gallon cheaper.'

GETTING
WHAT WE
DESERVE

If the traditional 'Corks-around-the-hat' yarn has had its day, what's replaced it? Well, thankfully, there *are* yarns around the traps that capture the spirit of the 90s. Sometimes it takes a little time, but usually, the Issues of Today are eventually expressed in yarns. As Kevin Naughton observed at the 1992 World Yarn Spinning Contest, 'I'm glad to see a crew from *A Current Affair* here, as it *is* a Jana Wendt.' Take politics, for example. We're told that nearly 30 per cent of our nightly television news has a Canberra slant. Well, if that's the case, we certainly can't let the mediocrats of the media have sole rights to discussing politics. We yarn spinners have just as great a right to be crashing bores as they do.

The Little Bush Princess, aged eleven, came bopping in the other day.

'Can men have babies?' she inquired to no one in particular.

'No!' chorused the rest of the household, with complete confidence in their statement.

'Then, how come Paul Keating's in Labour?' she shrilled, cackled hysterically, then zotted out into the afternoon to wreck yet another pair of new school shoes on her bike.

The political yarn as an entity isn't new. Nor are most of the yarns themselves.

The tradition of slinging off at our pollies goes back to the First Fleet. Somewhere in a secluded park on Sydney Cove, is a colonial public toilet on which the following has been inscribed in Georgian felt pen.

THE FIRST GREAT AUSSIE POLITICAL YARN

Captain Arthur Phillip was in a pensive mood as he sat on an exposed granite outcrop, looking over the placid waters of Sydney Cove. One of his senior officers, Lieutenant Nigel Groyne, walked slowly up to where our first governor was sitting and stood quietly beside him, sharing his reverie. Finally, the governor spoke.

'Y'know, Groyne, fate plays strange tricks with we mere mortals.'

'If you say so, sir.'

'I do, Groyne. I do.'

They shared another moment's silence.

'D'you realise, Groyne, that I never sought this position as Governor of the colony of New South Wales?'

'No, I didn't, sir.'

'Well, it's true . . . or sort of,' replied Phillip with a sigh. 'At least, I never wanted to be governor of a penal colony.'

'You don't say so, sir.'

'I do, Groyne. I do. Y'see, Lieutenant, I'm a simple man. The navy's been my life, but, really, I wanted more than it could offer me.'

'And what was it you wanted, sir?'

'You might think it strange, Groyne, after all those years at sea, but, deep down, all I ever wanted to do was to grow things. I love the soil. I love plants. I love putting things in the ground and watching them germinate and grow.'

'Do you, sir?'

'I do, Groyne. I do. And when His Majesty asked me to come all the way over here and start a colony, I jumped at the chance. You see, originally, he wanted me to establish an agricultural commune.'

'Did he, sir?'

'Oh, yes Groyne. He told me no expense was too great. Anything I needed to establish my little farming colony, I could have. So I put in an official requisition for the supplies I needed.'

'And what did you need, sir?'

'Agricultural implements, Groyne. The tools for planting and collecting our harvest. I asked for two hundred hoes and eight hundred wicker baskets. But you know what the public service is like. They buggered it up.'

'How's that, sir?'

'They sent me two hundred whores and eight hundred wicked bastards.'

Although modern political yarns can be quite vitriolic at times, there's nothing really political in their intent. Like all yarns, they're there to amuse or express one's feeling at the time. In reality, if today's political yarns tend to be scathing about the government in power, they're just as likely to be as scathing to the other side of the political fence once power changes hands in the next election. There's nothing *personal* meant in political yarns—although they name names and hold public figures up to ridicule. The truth is, that it's usually the government of the day that's the butt of these jokes. So now, in 1993, it's Labor that gets a blasting from your traditional Aussie yarn spinner. A few elections back, and probably in the not-too-distant future, it's the Libs who'll get the pasting. Where a political yarn names Paul Keating, it could just as well be Bob Hawke, John Hewson, Malcolm Fraser or Joh Bjelke-Petersen. There's no real personal or political malice intended. The yarn itself is always more important than the party or the individuals it's about.

Take the next offering. I first heard it in the Northern Territory, but variants have cropped up elsewhere. It's about the late Russ Hinze, but it could be about any politician of bulk.

TURTLE POWER

It had been a wild old long weekend a few years back at the Barry Caves Roadhouse on the Barkly Highway, which links central Australia with western Queensland. A big mob had come in for the races, rodeo and needlepoint competition. They'd drunk and eaten everything in the place. At first light on Tuesday morning, the boss staggered out the front to survey the mess. For as far as the eye could see, there was litter and garbage. It'd be a hell of a job cleaning it up.

Suddenly, he detected the distant roar of a motor. Minutes later, a sleek white limousine, with black-smoked windows, pulled up in a cloud of dust beside him. The publican noted the limo had Queensland Government numberplates.

A chauffeur in full uniform, complete with a peaked cap, got out, adjusted his leather gloves and cleared his throat.

'Any chance of a feed here?'

'You've got to be joking,' spluttered the publican. 'We've just had the biggest long weekend booze-up we've ever had. Bastards came in from all over. They've drunk everything in the joint and eaten every skerrick of food we had.'

The chauffeur gave a knowing wink, grabbed the publican gently by the arm and led him inside.

'Look, mate,' he whispered. 'I've got big Russ Hinze outside in the car. Porky Everingham's asked him to come up here and sort out a few local political problems.'

'So?'

'Well, we left the Isa at sparrow fart this morning and Big Russ hasn't had his breakfast. He's famished and when Big Russ's hungry, he gets impossible to handle.'

'Well, that's stiff, mate, because, with the best of intentions, I haven't anything to offer you until tomorrow, when the truck comes in to replenish our supplies.'

The chauffeur shook his head in disbelief. 'Surely there's something in your fridge? Or maybe a bag of chips . . . anything to get Big Russ of my back.'

'Nope. Not a thing. We've been cleaned out.'

The chauffeur lowered his voice a bit. 'Look, mate. You still don't understand. Russ goes ape-shit if he doesn't keep his blood sugar levels up. Surely there's a dog, or a cat . . . maybe a budgie or a goldfish you could knock on the head and bung in the microwave?'

'Look. I've told you. There's sweet bugger-all. In fact, even me missus and kids shot through for the weekend. They're not coming back till tonight. There's only me and me old pet tortoise.'

The chauffeur's eyes lit up. 'Tortoise? Look, money's no problem. Couldn't you just knock it on the head and boil it up? Russ is so hungry he won't notice what it is.' He started peeling bills from a big roll.

The publican gave in. 'Hang on. I'll go and get the tortoise.'

The chauffeur kept peeling bills off the roll.

The publican came back with a fairly big tortoise—about half a metre across the shell—and put it on the bar. As soon as it saw the chauffeur, the tortoise stuck its head under the shell.

'Jesus! Now, how am I going to kill the bloody thing?' groaned the publican. 'I can't whip his head off when he's got it tucked in like that.'

Together the chauffeur and the publican tried to get the tortoise to stick its head out again, so they could deliver a coup de grâce, but the old feller wouldn't budge. Finally, the chauffeur took over.

'Look, grab a cleaver or something from the kitchen and stand up the front of the tortoise. When I give you the nod, it'll stick its head out and you can do it in.' The publican did what he was told and came back with a little tomahawk. To his amazement, the chauffeur went to the rear end of the tortoise and stuck his index finger fair up its bum. With a look of complete surprise, the tortoise stuck its head out. 'Whack!' The publican brought the axe down . . . and Russ's dinner was almost ready to be served.

Half an hour or so later, after the poor old tortoise had been cooked and apparently enjoyed by the big politician lurking in the dark recesses of the limo, the chauffeur made ready to head off to Darwin.

'Just one thing,' mentioned the publican, relishing the thick wad of notes that had been transferred to his pocket. 'Where on earth did you come up with that idea to get the tortoise to extend his neck like that?'

The chauffeur didn't bat an eyelid. 'How do you think we get Big Russ's tie on every morning?'

During the Hawke years, there were any number of yarns about the Honourable R. J. and his offsider, the World's Greatest Treasurer. Usually, they started off, 'Bob Hawke and Paul Keating died in a plane crash . . .' It seemed a great example of national wishful thinking.

Bill Hay, of Chinchilla, Queensland, goes by the nom de pun of the Yahoo from the Barcoo. He's a great yarn spinner of the old school. At the 1992 titles, he delivered his rendition of an old Aussie political yarn. Sure, it's about Hawkie. But it could just about be any politician.

YOU'RE STANDING IN IT

Old Bob goes right up to the Edward River Mission in Queensland on this big election campaign, see. The whole population's Aboriginal. There's one old bloke standing over there on one leg with a spear . . . another one over there. So old Bob gets going, the full bit. You'd swear he was in some big football stadium in Melbourne. But he's not doing any good. There's a stony silence. He can't break through. So he turns around to the administrator of the mission and asks, 'What am I going to do? How'll I get through?'

This administrator is a white bloke and he tells Bob, 'Just let 'em know what you're going to do for 'em.'

'Well, okay,' says Bob and off he goes. 'We're gonna make beer the same price as sausages, a dollar a skin full.'

Not a word. So he keeps going. At last, when he's explaining what he's going to do for Australia, what he's going to do for the Aborigines, what he's going to do for land rights, one of these fellers says, 'Koondarra!'

Then his mate over there says, 'Koondarra!' Then another, then another.

Bob thinks, 'At last, I'm getting through to them . . . at last.' And off he goes again. Then more blokes start saying, 'Koondarra! Koondarra!'

Bob thinks, 'That'll do. I've got 'em. I've got 'em.' And the Koondarras are rolling along and Bob thinks, 'That's great.'

When he finishes, he asks the administrator, 'How d'you reckon I went? D'you reckon I got 'em?'

'Oh great, you went great. They're all going to vote.'

So Bob asks, 'What happens now?'

'Well, Bob, when any VIPs come up here—National Party, Labor Party, Liberal Party—it doesn't matter what mob they're from, the people here always kill the fatted calf and put on a big feed.'

'Yeah, but what's that got to do with me?'

'Well, you go down to the cow yard there, go in and put

your hand on the vealer you want killed—and they'll kill that one.'

They go down to the cow yard and Bob's just about to open the gate and go in, when the administrator says, 'Hang on a minute Bob—one thing.'

'What's up? What do you want?'

'Be careful. Don't put your foot in the koondarra.'

So the government of the day really cops it from yarn spinners. A perfect example is a story I first heard from my American mate Billy Ed Wheeler. He told it to me using Ronald Reagan as the butt of the joke. At the time, all anyone needed to do was change the names to fit the Australian political climate, and it immediately became fully naturalised. For a while after the 1992 Federal election, this yarn didn't have quite the same impact. But times change. Euphoria fades and so . . .

THE BEST RABBIT BLOCK IN NSW

Until the drought caught up with us and we had to sell it, we had a block of land out on the Lachlan River, which those in the know regarded as the best rabbit block in the whole state. The local Pastures Protection Board didn't appreciate the accolade, but at any time of the year you could go over there and bowl over plenty of bunnies.

The trouble was, its reputation was known far and wide and we often had trouble with shooters. Sometimes, when we were working out there with the sheep, there'd be bullets whizzing around everywhere—fired by people whose identity we wouldn't have known in a thousand years. We eventually had to clamp down on people using the block without our permission. We weren't too hard, because we needed help keeping those rabbit numbers down. Our attitude was, if anyone bothered to ask us if they could go out there and shoot, we'd let them. However, if we sprung anyone shooting there without our permission, we'd come down on them like a ton of bricks. Eventually, the word got round and people stopped cutting the chains on the gates, wrecking fences and shooting the sheep.

Like I said, we eventually decided to sell the block. Just before we were due to hand it over to its new owner, one of our regular shooters rang up to see if he could go out for one last hunt. We didn't mind at all. He'd always been more than co-operative. He came from Sydney's western suburbs—around Blacktown. He always asked permission to shoot on our block. He was always careful and considerate, never careless with fire and always took his rubbish with him. Once we'd given him permission to go out to Blacksnake, we didn't really give him another thought.

The city bloke went out there all on his own. It's a pretty isolated spot—one of those places you like to get away to by yourself. He had a pretty good time and managed to bag quite a few rabbits. Late in the afternoon, it started to rain. The Blacktown feller was still quite a long way from his car, so he looked for some shelter. The rain was fairly heavy, so he needed something fairly good to protect him. Then he found it. Halfway down a bit of a rise over the Lachlan River, was a huge hollow log. The bloke wriggled inside it and there, nice and dry, prepared to wait out the storm.

In fact, it was so nice and dry in the hollow log that he dropped off to sleep. When he woke up the rain had finished, but, to his horror, the Blacktown feller found that the rain had caused the wood of the old hollow log to swell . . . and he was jammed tight inside.

Try as he might, he couldn't extricate himself from the log. He managed to free his arms, but that wasn't much help. Panic set in. He used up his last remaining ammunition trying to blast his way out of the log. But although it was old, grey and desiccated, it was also solid redgum, and he could barely make a dent in that tough old wood.

He reached down and wriggled his sheath knife out of his belt, hoping to carve his way out. But that was just as hopeless. And, of course, he tried calling for help. But, like I said, that paddock's in an isolated spot. There wasn't anybody for miles.

Finally, the dreadful truth sank in. There was no one coming to his rescue. He was on his own. He was going to die in that old hollow log.

God knows how long he lay there, cursing his fate. Eventually, hopelessness and the lack of food and water started to affect him and his mind began to wander. He'd always imagined it was just a myth, but, like they said in the classics, his life began to replay in his head.

He thought about his parents and early childhood in the western Sydney suburbs. He thought about his school days; his first girlfriend; the committed years of his youth in the turbulent sixties. He remembered great sporting events such as Australia winning the Ashes and our America's Cup win. He recalled the major historical events in his lifetime—Cyclone Tracy in Darwin in 1974; how Whitlam was sacked in '75; the Bicentennial year in '88.

He even remembered seemingly little details, like the colour of his old dog Blue, the purple flares his girlfriend gave him for his eighteenth birthday and how he'd voted for Paul Keating in the last Federal election.

Suddenly, he felt so small, he was able to get up and walk right out of that old hollow log and make it back to his car in time to drive home before dark.

Sorry Paul, sir. Nothing personal—you just happened to be the Man for the Time. As you can see, all you need to do is change that one name at the end, and that yarn is good for all time and for all politicians in any country. How's that for value?

Of course, one of the most controversial political topics discussed in Australia these days is our relationship with the British monarchy. Will we cast them off, or not? If we do, what will the women's magazines have to write about? It's a worry.

In order to demonstrate a royal yarn that never made it to their pages, I've had to draw on a story from years back—the first World War, in fact. I thank ardent royal watcher, Mr Charlie Pearmain, of Two Dogs, Gundaroo, New South Wales, for this stirring tale.

ONE HAD TO ASK, DIDN'T ONE?

Good old King George V was doing the rounds of the trenches. At the request of the army bigwigs, he also visited wounded soldiers in field hospitals. At one hospital, he received a special request from the staff to call in on troops who hadn't been wounded— they were just down with relatively run-of-the-mill ailments.

'But they're a bit downcast, Your Majesty,' one of his military advisers told him. 'They feel as though they've let the side down a bit by just being ill. A visit from your Gracious Majesty will help lift their spirits and, hopefully, get them back to the Front just that little bit sooner.'

How could the monarch refuse?

Accompanied by a huge crew of doctors, nurses and senior officers, the King went from bed to bed, talking to the patients.

'Good morning, my man, and what are you in here for?' he'd ask.

'Piles, sir!'

'Hmm, piles, eh? And what sort of treatment are you getting?'

'Wire brush and a Dettol rinse, sir!'

'Good show. And what's your ambition once you're out of here, soldier?'

'To go out again and fight the Hun, sir!'

'Good show!' And His Majesty moved on to the next bed.

'And what are you in for, corporal?'

'Gonorrhoea, sir!'

'Hmmm! And how do they treat that, corporal?'

'Wire brush and a Dettol rinse, sir!'

'Good show, and what do you want to do once you're out of here?'

'Get back to the Front and fight the Hun, sir!'

'Good show.'

And so His Majesty went to the next bed, a miserable-looking little Aussie digger.

'And what's up with you, my faithful colonial?'

'Laryngitis!' replied the mournful Australian.

'And how are they treating *that*?'

'Wire brush and Dettol rinse, like the others, mate.'

'Hmmmm. And what's your main ambition in life, my good man?'

'First go with the wire brush!'

It's been obvious for the last 200 years that, despite the avowals of our monarchists, there's always been a fragment of the Australian character out of touch with our once overwhelming British heritage. I first heard a version of this yarn from Rolf Harris, about twenty-five years ago, when we were all far more accepting of Their Gracious Majesties—but it still reflects that glimmer of cheeky disrespect evident in the Australian character.

SETTING IT STRAIGHT

It occurred during one of Queen Elizabeth's earliest grand tours of her antipodean holdings. She and Prince Philip were in Tasmania, where huge crowds turned out to greet their royal visitors. Now, Tassie is renowned for its axemen and the tour organisers planned a whole contingent of the state's finest wood choppers to form a guard of honour for their royal guests.

Resplendent in white singlets and white daks, Tassie's finest paraded past the royal couple and then formed a tidy guard of honour in front of them. At the invitation of the local dignitaries, the Queen and her consort moved down the ranks of axemen for the obligatory 'informal chat'.

The Queen went out of her way to make the extremely nervous bushmen at ease, and patiently listened to their stumbling replies to her questions. Finally, she pulled up in front of a bloke about as tall as a King Billy Pine, and about eight axe handles across the shoulders.

'And where do you come from?' she asked.

'Err, Liena, near Mole Creek,' the big feller mumbled.

'You look very strong. How much wood can you cut in one day?'

'Err. Umm. About twenty fuckin' ton, Your Majesty.'

At this unprecedented outburst of totally unacceptable foul language, Prince Philip stepped forward, frowning with total disapproval.

160

'I say, that's going a bit far,' he admonished.

The big bloke looked down at his boots, shuffled his feet and replied, 'Yeah, you're right. I suppose it'd really be more like fifteen fuckin' ton.'

Of course, our monarch's day-to-day representative in Australia is the governor-general, whose role has increasingly been to Australianise the working relationship between the great unwashed and the Palace. My favourite GG has always been the late Paul Hasluck. Again, he operated in more formal times, but, as this next incident shows, was capable of demonstrating the Aussie character along with the best (and worst) of us.

LUIGI

Back in the early 1970s, the biggest postwar event in the Northern Territory was obviously the development of the huge bauxite mining operation on the Gove Peninsular, off eastern Arnhem Land. Working, as I did, for the ABC news service, we were always eager to get good, informative stories about how work on the development of the bauxite mine, the associated alumina processing plant and the proposed town of Nhulunbuy were proceeding. As is the way of big companies, the developers, Nabalco, weren't always as cooperative as we would have liked.

For instance, we'd never received clearance for a film crew to visit Gove to shoot some television footage of the place. Then it was arranged for the governor-general, Sir Paul Hasluck, to inspect the project. Surprise, surprise, a media contingent was actually invited to record the event.

A small group of us crowded into a light plane and flew there to film the viceregal visit.

At Nhulunbuy, the Nabalco lackeys weren't at all sure how far they should allow us to go, so they played it safe and organised an itinerary that ensured we were always about ten minutes behind the official party. Which meant that we always turned up just as the GG was finishing his inspection of whatever it was, and could only jump back in our borrowed vehicle and eat his dust to the next destination. It was obvious that Sir Paul, a one-time journo himself, and thoroughly used to dealing with the media, didn't mind us doing our jobs, but the company bods seemed bent on frustrating us—something that he seemed to realise. Towards the end of the tour, we managed to catch up with the official party as Sir Paul was shown some massive concrete formwork, obviously part of the alumina plant.

Imagine the brown-nosing company officials' horror when His

Excellency rounded a piece of formwork to be confronted by a huge concrete wall on which someone had written in white paint, 'Luigi roots dogs'.

They instantly went into panic mode, trying to steer the GG away from the wall.

'And over here, Your Excellency, we can show you the site where the main smelter is to be constructed.'

'Oh dear,' grinned Hasluck. 'I was rather hoping you'd point out Luigi.'

One of the most heartbreaking aspects of the times in which we Australians find ourselves is the decline in the fortunes of our bush people. The so-called rural recession in recent years seems far more final in its destructiveness than previous hard times on the land. We country people often espouse that, when things are tough, it's only our sense of humour that gets us through. An indication of the depth of the current rural recession may arise from the fact that there's been relatively few yarns to come out of it . . . but here goes.

SO IT'S COME TO THIS

Imagine how it feels for a cocky to come to the end of the trail. It's happening to more and more of them these days. Imagine how it feels to load up the old ute with your last six bales of hay and take them to the last of your sheep, starving out in the drought-ravaged paddocks. It feels miserable.

This poor old wool grower drove the bales out to the dam, where the last of his stud ewes were sheltering, weak and thin, in the black slash of shade thrown in the dust by the high earthen wall. He kicked the light, mouldy bales off the tailgate and watched them explode into pathetic, desiccated fragments on the ground. The old ewes, their sides sucked in and their backs arched, limped half-heartedly towards him, ready to suck the last bits of stick-like straw out of the dust. In a few seconds, nothing remained of the hay and some of the ewes, those with a bit more strength left than the others, gazed at him inquiringly through unfocused, glazed eyes.

The wool grower had nothing more for them. He climbed back off the tray, slammed the tailgate shut and slid behind the steering wheel. The sheep watched, uncomprehendingly, as he drove away, the dust from the vehicle's wheels hanging in a grey line in the still air. The cocky didn't bother shutting any gates. The sheep were too weak to move far and if they did, what would they eat? The paddocks were absolutely bare, as far as the eye could see.

The cocky pulled up with a jerk outside the homestead. As he moved towards the back door, two large crows flapped lazily from where they'd been watching proceedings from the top of the big, empty, house water tank—a grim omen of what might lie ahead.

As his boot heels echoed through the house, the farmer walked into the kitchen . . . and knew immediately that something was wrong.

The washing-up from breakfast was still cluttering up the sink. A quick check showed that the fire in the big Aga stove had gone out—for the first time in ten years. Something clawed inside him as he hurried down the main passageway. What could be wrong?

He was vaguely aware of the open bedrooms on each side of the dusty hall. They'd been the kids' rooms. But they'd been unused for years. The younger members of the family had been quick to realise the hopelessness of life on the land. They'd bailed out ages ago. Their rooms were as they'd left them, with their childhood teddy bears still lying back on the pillows, sightless eyes gazing at the gloomy ceilings.

The cocky found his wife in the main bedroom. She had on her only good frock and was packing clothes into the big leather suitcase.

'What's going on?' he asked her.

She didn't look up at him as she spoke.

'I've had enough,' she said, wearily. 'I'm finally giving up. For twenty-eight years, I've stood beside you, shoulder to shoulder, slaving away, sacrificing everything to try to wrench a living from the godforsaken place. I've never complained. I've worked my guts out trying to hold things together for you and the kids. It's been a total waste of time. And you know what? I'd still keep doing it, if only I thought I was being appreciated. In all that time, there's never been a glimmer of recognition of the role I've played. There's never been a word of thanks. Well, I've had it. I can't go on like this. I'm going somewhere where I'll be appreciated.'

The poor old cocky struggled to find words. 'W . . . what d'y' mean? Where are y' goin'?'

'I'm going to the Big Smoke—to Sydney. Do you know, I read somewhere that they pay $100 a time for sex in places like Sydney. That's what I call appreciation.'

The cocky didn't say anything more. He reached into the old wardrobe, pulled out another suitcase and started putting undies and socks into it.

'What d'you think you're doin'?' his wife asked.

'I'm comin' with youse.'

'What on earth for?'

'I just want to see, how, in an expensive joint like Sydney, you're gonna be able to live on $200 a year.'

The truth is, these days farm families have to face far more than your traditional droughts, floods and low prices. From every quarter comes new concerns to plague them. Not the least of these has been the environmental movement.

It probably wouldn't have been so difficult for cockies to cope with if it hadn't been politicised to the extent it has. There are strong elements in the so-called green movement that stereotype farmers as The Enemy, with no regard to the fact that, to be successful, cockies *have* to work in harmony with their environment. Instead of bringing people together to reach a common goal, concern for our environment seems to have driven a wedge between groups that have to combine forces if we're going to be able to survive as a species.

I don't know if these next two yarns will help—but here's hoping . . .

THE FERAL ANIMAL CONTROL MEETING AT THE JINDABYNE SPORTS CLUB

Ever since the government turfed the mountain sheep and cattle-men off the alpine grazing leases in New South Wales, there's been bad blood between them. It's probably more the result of how the government went about things, than any disrespect for the mountain environment by the mountain people. It's taken a few decades but, today, there's a grudging acceptance that perhaps it was necessary to end the practice of taking stock up onto the highly vulnerable high plains to graze every summer.

It didn't help the situation at all when government expenditure pruning and cock-eyed policies often interfered with the management practices required to keep the Kosciusko National Park environmentally healthy.

One of the big complaints from graziers whose properties ad-joined the KNP, was the lack of suitable control of feral animals— ranging from wild pigs to wild dogs. These days there are probably few true dingoes roaming the NSW High Country. But there's any number of crossbred wild dogs. Some resulted from truant sheep and cattle dogs mating with dingoes—others from pets deliberately dumped by irresponsible owners. Some of the worst stock-killers were results of the latter crosses. Dingo and samoyed crosses, often being talked about in hushed whispers by the mountain people. Ex-dog trapper Ernie Bale even talks about finally nabbing a purebred Alsatian, accompanied by a purebred corgi, that'd caused havoc on stock in the Snowy Mountains area.

What the land-holders objected to most of all was that, no matter how hard they worked at controlling wild dogs on their holdings, nothing was being done by the park management. Dogs allowed to roam the park could just jump the fence and kill stock on private land, and nothing was being done to stop them. Things finally came to a head and land-holders in the Jindabyne area organised a protest meeting at the local sports club to discuss a campaign to force the government to do something about the wild dogs in the national park.

Fairly close to the date, groups of animal libbers and conservationists in nearby Canberra heard of the meeting and decided to stick their bib in. Some wanted to ensure any control measures were carried out humanely, others objected to what they regarded as a threat to native wildlife and others just hated cockies and fancied a bit of a barney.

The actual meeting was a ripper—the clash of the titans. Tempers flared, allegations were made, motions were moved, amended, lost and passed.

One of the highlights was when one land-holder from the Brindabella Valley walked the full length of the auditorium and flung a grisly collection of dried scalps across the disco floor to show how many wild dogs he'd recently shot on his place—all of them having snuck in from the adjoining national park.

In the general hubbub, the animal libbers and the conservationists had their two bob's worth. Late in the evening, someone up the back moved a motion asking the premier to ensure that money was provided for extra dingo trappers to be immediately appointed to the park staff to reduce the risk of dogs invading the neighbouring properties. One of the most vocal animal libbers leapt up to the microphone and immediately spoke against the motion. Amid loud heckling from the body of the hall, she was adamant that trapping and killing of wild dogs was too drastic.

'I would amend the motion, Mr Chairman, to provide for any wild dogs caught by the trappers to be taken to the park headquarters and humanely sterilised. These are magnificent wild creatures, which should be allowed to live out their days, roaming the wilderness areas of these mountains as they have since time began. They have a right to live. A simple operation is all that's needed to prevent them from breeding and becoming a nuisance.'

A hand went up at the back of the hall.

'Point of order, Mr Chairman,' drawled a voice familiar to the mountain people. 'I'd like to point out that the wild dogs have been killing our sheep—not screwing them.'

Finally, a yarn that combines so many of the elements covered in this modest volume of contemporary Australian folklore. It's current, it's theatrical (in that it involves a courtroom drama), its roots are in the bush, and it takes no prisoners.

NOT GUILTY, YOUR WORSHIP

One of the worries about today's widely publicised concern for the environment is that one day it will cease to be flavour of the month and drop from the public arena. I think it's too important an issue to ever be replaced at the head of Australia's consciousness. Only the other day, there was a mere three paragraphs in a Victorian paper about this particular case, with little indication on what an important issue it really was. I hope to rectify that.

What those meagre three pars reported was that a local farmer was due to appear in court in eastern Gippsland, charged with violating the Victorian Wildlife Protection Act by killing and eating a protected animal, to wit, one platypus.

Well, once the big-time media mob got onto it, you can imagine how they reacted. A farmer . . . eating a platypus. The full media circus went into full gear. Jana Wendt was immediately hired back by the Nine Network to do a special program. Derryn Hinch announced that he was boycotting the whole thing. On the big day, the court was packed with people—most of them from the Big City media.

The sole crown witness was a highly experienced twelve-year-old National Parks and Wildlife Service Ranger, who'd been on the job for almost three weeks and was keen to see justice done. He got up in the dock, swore on a copy of *Dot and the Kangaroo*, and gave his evidence in a loud, clear voice.

'Your Worship, last Friday I was on patrol in the Port Albert area, when I became temporarily disoriented on the rough, unmarked, back country roads. After spending most of the day trying to get my bearings, I was somewhat inconvenienced by the eventual arrival of nightfall. Then, to my relief, I noticed a light up on the hillside. In a few hours, I'd managed to find my way through approximately two hundred yards of thick grassland to the source of the light, which I ascertained to be a farmhouse.

'After a while, I located what I assumed to be the back door of the farmhouse and knocked loudly. A voice from within invited me to enter, which I subsequently did.

'There in what appeared to be the kitchen of the aforementioned farmhouse, I espied a group of people, who I later ascertained to be the accused and his family, sitting around an item of furniture, which I later established to be a kitchen table. On the middle of the table was a blue and white willow pattern serving dish, on which I observed a charred, blackened mess that looked suspiciously like a cooked platypus.

'The defendant reached out with a large fork, stuck it in the leg of the aforementioned carcass, and using his other hand, containing a carving knife, cut off the aforementioned leg. He then raised the fork to his mouth, took a bite, chewed for several seconds and said, "Can I help you, mate?"

'Showing him my official identification, I informed him I believed he was in breach of the Victorian Wildlife Protection Act and formally charged him.'

An ugly silence reigned in court. The entire media contingent was in shock. Jana was white-faced. So would Derryn have been, if he wasn't boycotting the whole thing. Imagine anyone stooping so low as to kill and eat a platypus.

Finally, the magistrate broke the silence. He stared grimly at the defendant, standing self-consciously in the dock, wearing his best blue suit with the brown trousers.

'Accused, I am appalled by what I have just heard,' he told the farmer. 'I am so appalled at this total disregard for the sanctity of Australian wildlife that I'm going to take a very unusual step. My legal colleagues could well criticise me for this, but I feel duty bound to warn you as to the depth of my repugnance at what I've just heard. I personally regard all Australian wildlife as sacred. And for someone to violate something as precious as a platypus, one of only two species of montremes currently in existence on this planet, is totally beyond me.

'So I hereby give notice that unless you have a very good explanation about your behaviour—and it will have to be *extremely* good—I intend coming down on you with the fullest weight of the law.'

The cocky appeared only slightly nonplussed.

'Well, crikey, thanks a lot, Your Worship. I appreciate that, so I'll do me best to explain what went on.' And with that, he swore on the Bible and started his story.

'As you know, Your Worship, things have been crook in the bush recently. Well, round our way, things have been crooker than anywhere else.

'We've had no rain since 1947. Now, I know Gippsland's supposed to be a rainy place, but every time it's rained everywhere else, it hasn't quite made it to our place. This lack of rain has had a distinct bad effect on our income. For a start, our wool hasn't been too crash hot. Now, I know, Your Worship, that the Port Albert area's not really regarded as a wool-growing area. But me old grand-dad went into it years ago and I've been stuck with it. Sheep don't do too well round here at any time and, since we've had no rain since 1947 on top of that, well, it's tended to make our wool crooker than it would have been otherwise.

'So, we haven't had much of an income for the last generation or so. At first, that wasn't much of a worry. We could eat our sheep, right? And that's what we done. One by one, we slaughtered the useless bludgers and ate them. They weren't much of a feed, bearing in mind that we hadn't had no rain since 1947 and the grass was pretty thin on the ground.

'It took a few years, but eventually, the sheep were gone. So we moved on to the house cows—Bossie and Strawb. They weren't much chop either, but beggars couldn't be choosers. After that, we moved onto the chooks. Then the cats. Then the sheepdogs, Your Worship. Have you any idea what it's like to look down into the brown, trusting eyes of your best work mate, then blast him with twenty-three shots from the under and over . . . and then eat him? It's pretty crook, Your Worship, and that amount of shot tends to stick in your teeth. But we had no choice. Things were *that* crook.

'Last Christmas, we ate the budgie.

'After that, we resigned ourselves to grazing what used to be the front lawn—only it weren't much of a feed, 'cos as you know, we ain't had no rain round our neck of the woods since 1947.

'It was about this time, Your Worship, that it struck me how I'd failed, not only as a farmer, but as a father and provider. Things were so bad, it seemed the only honourable thing for me to do was to do meself in. I'd used up all the shotgun shells on the dogs, so the only avenue left open for me was to throw meself orf the bridge over the little dry creek down the end of the road.

'I plucked up the courage to do it, and was almost halfway down there, when I noticed a red smear on the white line in the middle of the main road. Bugger me dead, if a timber truck hadn't run over a poor old platypus.

'I didn't eat him then and there, Your Worship. In fact, I sat by the side of that road for hours, wrestling with me conscience.

'Your Worship, me family's been on the land around here for five generations. Like his dad before him, my father used to take my little hand, from the time I could first walk, and lead me out into the bush. He'd stop at every little flower, kneel down and show it to me. Over the years, I learned all their names. He did the same thing with all the trees . . . and the birds and animals. And I've done the same thing with my kids. We've all grown to love the bush, Your Worship, and we all appreciate how precious each and every living thing is on this great island continent of ours.

'That's why I couldn't bring meself to eat that old platypus, Your Worship. I regarded it as one of the jewels in our country's crown. I had to ask meself, did me loyalties lie with the precious wildlife of this great land, or did they lie with Mavis and the kids?

'Then the wind musta changed, Your Worship, because I suddenly heard the little ones back in the house, whimpering with hunger. That did it. I knew where me loyalties lay.

'I went back to the house, grabbed a shovel, and scraped that poor old platypus orf the road. Mavis bunged it in the microwave, cooked it up and we were just sitting down to our first reasonable sort of meal since we ate the budgie last Christmas, when the ranger come up and busted me.'

There wasn't a dry eye in the court. Jana had her teeth out on the bench in front of her and was sobbing into her folded arms. The magistrate was white-faced, with large tears coursing down his cheeks. He spoke in a strangled whisper.

'What an experience this has been for all of us,' he gurgled. 'What a huge lesson we can learn from this. How easy it is for those of us who live in the cities, to forget the true plight of the families on the land. How easy it is for us to forget the strong ties our bush folk have always had with their harsh environment. How easy it is for law-makers and legislators to draw up rules and regulations without due consideration of how they'll really affect the real people living out here in the real world. This case will affect my work on the bench from here on in. Your evidence has been the most moving account of human endeavour I have ever experienced. Naturally, I dismiss the charges.'

A weak cheer came from the equally distraught, cynical members of the media.

The magistrate banged his gavel for order. 'I am so shaken by this experience that I intend calling a ten-minute adjournment before hearing any other cases.'

He addressed himself to the cocky. 'Look, this must have been fairly shattering for you, too. I'd like you to come back to my chambers with me. I'm sure you could handle a quick snort to settle your nerves. I know I could.'

'Don't mind if I do,' replied the cocky and followed him into his rooms behind the bench.

The magistrate poured each one of them a stiff sparkling tawny port and took a hefty slug before speaking.

'Your story really is remarkable,' he said again. 'But, you know, while you were telling it, there was one question nagging at the back of my mind.'

'What was that?'

'Well, and don't think I'm awful . . . but I couldn't help but wonder, what does a platypus taste like?'

The cocky thought carefully for a moment.

'Well, Your Worship, about halfway between a koala and a dolphin.'

Tell Us Anotheree!

More yarns from all round Australia

"YOU AIN'T GUNNA BELIEVE THIS, WALLY!"

Chapter 1

LIES, DAMN LIES, STATISTICS AND YARNS

It might come as a shock to you, but there are some terrible liars out there. I know this book was never meant to be an incisive piece of investigative journalism, but I feel I owe it to my fellow Australians to expose the sort of people we have living amongst us. Many of these liars look just like normal folk. You'd never suspect their deep dark secrets. Why so many of them felt a need to contribute to the Search for the Great Australian Yarn is totally beyond me. Now is the time for them to be revealed. I intend including names and addresses so everyone will know who they are. The sort of lying I'm talking about isn't the clean, healthy sort we've come to expect from politicians, journalists, car salesmen or real estate agents. This is dark, sinister stuff. It obviously starts at an early age, as one of my dogged reporting team found out. Here's the full story from Lockie Beauzeville of Lake Cargelligo, New South Wales ...

Late for School

In this particular small country school, one pupil, Jack, was generally late attending class. The teacher decided it was time to put a stop to his nonsense ... and the lame excuses he offered for being late.

One Monday morning, Jack arrived, as usual, thirty minutes late. The teacher demanded to know why.

'Well, sir,' said Jack, 'it's because my old man wears a short pyjama coat.'

'Go on,' said the teacher, dreading what was coming next.

'Mum had washed the old man's pyjamas, but a shower of rain came and the pants got wet on the line. That meant he had to sleep in his short pyjama coat.

'During the night, a fox got amongst the chooks. Dad jumped out of bed in his short pyjama coat, got the double-barrelled gun out of the laundry and went sneaking across the backyard with both barrels cocked and the gun thrust out in front of him. He didn't know that our old staghound, who's half blind and totally deaf, was following him across the yard.

'Dad stopped suddenly and bent over to peer at the chook yards, hoping he could see the fox. The old dog, not realising Dad had stopped, kept on going. His cold nose went in under Dad's short coat and touched him on the behind.

'Both barrels of the gun went off, and sir, I've been plucking chooks ever since six o'clock. That's why I'm late for school.'

In case you don't believe Lockie's report, I feel it necessary to bring to your attention the case of young Lizzie Webster, of Five Mile Tree School on the Southern Tablelands of New South Wales. Where's Five Mile Tree? Between Binda and Bigga, of course. Don't you know anything?

It's one of New South Wales' smallest schools—with about thirteen kids there last time I visited. I went there at the invitation of chalkie Jeanette Parker, to talk to her students about yarn-spinning. It seems that within this state's enlightened education system, someone came up with the idea of having kids spin yarns as part of their language courses. Great idea! Jeanette was a bit worried that some of her ankle-biters didn't quite know about the finer points of yarn-spinning. Lizzie Webster, in Year 6, proved she wasn't one of them. It may have something to do with the fact that her dad is Robert Webster, State minister and Upper House member in the NSW Parliament. Here's Lizzie's yarn, delivered with all the wide-eyed innocence a politician's daughter could be expected to muster . . .

The Time Mum Sent Me to Buy Some Mangoes

Well, we were down the coast last weekend and Mum asked me if I'd go to the shop and buy two mangoes. I went to the shop and asked the lady for some mangoes. While she was getting them, an elderly woman came in and said to me, 'Hello Belinda.' I said to her, 'My name's not Belinda, it's Lizzie.'

'I know it's not Belinda,' she said, 'but you look exactly like my little girl, whose name *was* Belinda. She's dead now. You look so like her, do you mind if I call you Belinda while I do my shopping?'

She looked so sad that I said I didn't mind.

'And would you mind calling me Mum?' she asked.

I said I didn't and while she did her shopping, she kept calling me Belinda and I kept calling her Mum. Although I'd only gone there for two mangoes, I kept talking to her and let her go out ahead of me.

'Bye, bye Belinda, see you at home,' she called.

'See you later, Mum,' I replied.

When I went to pay for my mangoes, the shop lady said, 'That'll be fifty dollars, thanks.'

'But I only wanted two mangoes. That's a lot to pay for two mangoes,' I said.

'But your mother, who just went out, said you'd pay for her groceries, too,' the shop lady said.

I ran out to the car park and saw the old lady putting things in her car boot. She saw me coming and started getting into the car. I got there just as she was closing the door.

Do you know what I did?

I pulled her leg . . . just like I'm pulling yours.

At least Lizzie had the common decency to admit that her story was a bit smoky. I don't know what it is about yarn-spinning, but many of the entrants in the ABC competition had no qualms about claiming their scurrilous tales were true. That's why I felt duty-bound to include so many of them in this opening chapter. Of course, the true stories all appear later in the book.

Cop this particularly tall tale from J Wills of Ouyen, Victoria . . .

Ducks

I purchased a second-hand double-barrelled shotgun at a farm clearing sale in 1953, for thirty bob. Next day, I cleaned it on the kitchen table and placed a cartridge in each barrel. Later, looking out the window, I saw about forty ducks heading straight for the house.

I didn't have time to go outside to have a shot at them, so I put the barrels up the chimney and pulled both triggers.

To my surprise, sixteen ducks fell dead in the garden.

You might wonder how a serious academic like my good self manages to sift the out-and-out porkies from the fair dinkum yarns with so many competition entries. Well, a dead give-away is the fact that occasionally, the same story pops up a couple of times—with only minor variations. For instance, Lizzie Webster's yarn was very similar to one submitted by J Davies of Wauchope, New South Wales.

A couple of versions of this next yarn turned up in the competition. In fact, it was the only one that was repeated more than once. This full-blown version from Horrie Gartner, also of Wauchope (is there a message there somewhere?), was about the most downright, bloody outrageous.

Wingham Storms

Horrie had just arrived at the Wauchope Country Club. He picked up his schooner and headed up to Deena at the end of the bar.

'One hell of a storm coming, Deena,' said Horrie as he knocked off the top quarter of the schooner. 'Don't think I've ever seen clouds that black in my life,' he continued, staring out the south-facing windows.

'Reminds me of the storms they get up the back of Wingham,' observed Deena. 'Bloody terrible storms they get up there. My poor old Uncle Bert got caught up in the worst one they ever had that way, back in the thirties.'

'Yair? Tell us about it Deena,' said Horrie as he ordered his next schooner.

'Well, you see, Uncle Bert owned this mare. Miss Australia was her name. When she was a filly, Uncle Bert won a lot of races with her. Mainly at Wingham and Taree and Wauchope. Went like the wind, she did. Won most of her races by ten lengths or more. Everyone reckoned she'd kill them in Sydney, too.

'Well, what with a couple of bad years on the farm, the cost of feed and training and problems with transport, Uncle Bert gave up on the racing and ended up breaking Miss Australia into the shafts for the old spring cart he used on the farm. She was OK, but bloody flighty, and he was always bewares of her and always kept a tight rein on her.

'Well, this day, Uncle Bert's fencing up in the top paddock. He's taken all his gear up in the spring cart and he's got Miss Australia tied up in the shade nearby. It's about four in the afternoon and he's stood up about thirty posts. Bloody good worker, was Uncle Bert, I don't mind telling you.

'Anyway, he's still got his head down reckoning on doing a few more posts, when he hears Miss Australia whinny. He turns around to see what the trouble is and... Holy Hell! The wildest-looking storm he's ever seen is coming up on him. The clouds were that black they were purple, and it was coming terrible fast.

'Uncle Bert drops the crowbar, bolts over and unhitches Miss Australia. He leaps into the cart and, for the first time, lets her have her head.

'Well, did she go? A lot don't believe it now, but her front hoofs were throwing up dust, her hind hoofs were throwing up clods of mud and the dog behind was swimming.

'And what's more, when he got home, the spring cart was three parts full of water, even though it had two floorboards missing.

'Terrible storms up the back of Wingham,' reflected Deena, as the sun broke out over the Wauchope Country Club.

I've mentioned before that one of the most intriguing things about the Search for the Great Australian Yarn was the number of entries sent in by women. Nearly all of them put a great deal of thought into writing their stories. A lot were more along the line of short stories, like this one from Denise Sheridan of the scarcely-outback community of Strathfield, New South Wales. It was that city address that gave me the first inkling that Denise may have been bending the truth a bit.

The Alice Anecdote

I wouldn't have picked him for a Jimmy Woodser, but you can never be sure in an outback pub. He was leaning alone against the bar—a real old-timer with his trousers suspended on a piece of twine and his pale, rheumy eyes gazing moodily into a half empty glass. The only other company in the bar when I walked in were three prospecting types, who looked as though they might have been drinking there all day. They'd managed to propel each other on to a bench near the door and were watching it intently, aiming to go through it as soon as it stayed in the same place long enough.

When you've been driving a few hundred kilometres, what you want is a quiet beer and maybe a bit of convivial conversation. I decided to invite the publican to have a drink with me and I indicated the old-timer with the back of my thumb. The publican was quite reassuring.

'He's orright. He's old Smithy. Been rabbiting round here all his life. Him and his mate, Fred—both rabbiters. But Fred had a bit of trouble a while ago and it's affected old Smithy real bad.'

'Poor old fellow,' I said. 'All on his tod, at his age.'

'How's it going, Smithy?' called out the publican.

'Well, me mate's went to sleep, so I'll maybe have another beer,' Smithy replied without any noticeable enthusiasm.

I took my glass and moved up a few paces so I could talk to him.

'So you've been a rabbit trapper round here all your life?'

'Yairs, me and me mate, Fred ... what was. A great rabbiter was old Fred. His father taught him all about rabbiting.'

'You don't say?'

'Yairs. A great rabbiter was old Fred's father.' He thought quietly for a while and finally surmised, 'And *his* father before him, probably.'

I've never been particularly interestd in genealogies and this one seemed to have an almost infinite potential. I tried a diversion.

'And, so that's what you do every day—go round setting rabbit traps?'

'Nah! Not any more I don't. Not any more.'

'How's that?'

'Well, I spend all me time now out looking fer mushrooms.'

In the bush, the line between eccentricity and plain lunacy is a pretty dubious one, and I began to have serious doubts about the publican's ability to recognise it at all.

'I wouldn't have thought you'd find many mushrooms out here,' I suggested.

'You're right there,' he replied gloomily. 'There ain't many mushrooms out here. That's a fact—not many at all.'

He sighed deeply and we spent a few silent minutes in sorrowing reflection on the paucity of mushrooms in the outback. I was thinking the topic was exhausted when he confided, 'Trouble is, it's a very pertickler sort of mushroom that I'm lookin' fer. It needs to have a little ticket on it saying, "Eat Me".'

'You don't tell me?' I said. 'Sounds straight out of *Alice in Wonderland.*'

He turned and studied me closely. 'Well, now. I'd never have took you for a literary bloke. But, yairs, that's about the size of it. *Alice in Wonderland.* It's a terrible book. It were the end of poor Fred. Undone him completely it did.'

The connection escaped me, but he seemed anxious enough to tell me the rest of the story, so I ordered us each another beer and waited.

'One day, Fred comes into camp arter checking the traps,' he said, after taking a large swallow. 'And he reckons he seen this big white rabbit come up outa burrer with a gold watch hangin' round its neck. Couldn't talk him outa it. Claimed he hadn't had a drink all day. Jus' insisted he'd seen what he'd seen and that was it. He went round telling everyone he met about that rabbit— even total strangers. Got to be a bit embarrassing really, Fred always was known as a steady sort of bloke before.

'Well, eventually, he meets this cove out on the road who tells him it's all explained in *Alice in Wonderland* ... and, so help me, he's got a bloody copy with him in his bedroll and gives it to Fred. And that were the end of him ... Fred, I mean. Once he read it, there was no holding him. Spent all his time from then on wanderin' around the bush, lookin' fer a mushroom that had a notice on it saying "Eat Me". But you see, Fred weren't thorough enough. What Fred didn't realise was that he oughta had been lookin' fer was *two* mushrooms. One of them is the "anecdote" fer the other, see. I read the book meself arterwards and I seen it straight away. You need two ... One grows you smaller and then you eat the other and it grows you bigger again. Nah! Fred weren't thorough enough with his reading ... and, yairs ...' he agreed, anticipating my offer, 'I jest might have another beer.'

'Well, it were the end of Fred, like I said. He went and bought this old chess set and every night, he'd sit there puttin' the pieces here and there and talkin' to them and he grew this giant moustache because he thought he might have really been a walrus. And every day, rain or shine, he'd be out in the bush and, if he weren't lookin' up in the trees fer Cheshire cats, he'd be lookin' all over for mushrooms. In a real bad way, he was, poor old Fred.'

It had been a long time since I'd read *Alice in Wonderland*, but I seemed to remember there were a lot of characters and I thought it likely that the list of poor old Fred's aberrations might be fairly lengthy.

It was one of those pubs where the bar didn't close until the publican decided to go to bed. I had to make an early start next morning, so I broke in rather briskly, 'And so he never found his mushroom?'

Smithy eyed me with disgust. 'Ain't you been follerin' at all?' he asked. 'I've been tellin' you, it were the ruination of him. 'Course he found it. He come back into camp one night carryin' it ... a mushroom with a little bit of paper stuck to it that says "Eat Me". And he did, right there in front of me. And it shrinked him. Right there. Shrinked him right down—right there in front of me eyes. It were a terrible sight ... poor ol' Fred shrinkin' down in front of me eyes. And like I told you, he never had the anecdote mushroom. Ruint, he was.'

His eyes filled with tears at the terrible memory, so he must have felt, rather than seen, my look of disbelief. Then he sighed in a resigned sort of way and plunged his hand into his shirt pocket.

He pulled out a little man, blinking angrily at the light. He would have been about the size of your hand. He was wearing a tiny pair of moleskins and he had a black handlebar moustache that hung down as far as his microscopic collar ... a sort of miniature Jimmy Edwards.

Smithy propped him gently against the glass. 'Yairs,' he said morosely. 'Poor old Fred.' Then he wiped his eyes and addressed the little man with passionate fervour. 'But don't you worry none, Fred. I'll find that mushroom fer you. S' help me, I'll find it, if it takes the rest of me bloody life.'

I think the little man said something back, but I didn't hear it. I didn't want to hear it, anyway. I had a long way to drive next day, so I gulped down the rest of my beer and went to bed. And I've never been back that way, but I wonder sometimes whether Smithy ever managed to find that 'anecdote' mushroom.

Of course, I could be way off the track. I may have misjudged Denise entirely. She may well have *not* been stretching the truth. On the other hand, I must express grave reservations about Lewis Carroll, the bloke who wrote *Alice in Wonderland*.

Tom Winters, of Cairns in Queensland, is pretty proud of the fact that he's over eighty. I'm not sure he has any right to be proud about the yarn he promotes as his all-time favourite.

Baaa!

I was with a mob of Australian tourists on a bush safari in the outback of Queensland. The weather was quite balmy and we were sitting round the campfire, swapping yarns and experiences. The subject came up of the wonderful work the doctors were doing transplanting human organs. One of the company suddenly spoke up.

'I think I witnessed the very first human transplant ever performed,' he announced. 'I was working as a medical orderly at an army hospital, outside a little town in England during the last war. A soldier was brought in with most of his stomach blown away. The doctor was working frantically to keep him alive. Suddenly, he looked out the hospital window and saw some sheep grazing out there in a field. The doctor turned to me and said, "Quick, get some help and slaughter one of those sheep. Bring its stomach back to me as quickly as possible."

'We did what he asked and he transplanted that sheep's stomach into the wounded digger. After he'd sewn the bloke up, the doctor declared proudly, "Well, he'll live."'

Everyone around the campfire was all ears.

'Well, *did* he live?' someone finally asked.

The storyteller paused awhile, stirring the fire with a stick. 'Yeah, I'll say he did. And what's more ... three weeks later, he lambed!'

Some of the most successful stories published by the ABC have concerned working dogs. Of course, all of them have been true. But this one from John O'Brien, of Marrickville, New South Wales, sounds a bit suss. John writes about the Crookwell district, where I've lived for the past few years, and I certainly haven't heard this particular yarn before ...

The True Story of Rex

Mate, this is only half a yarn, 'cos it's true. But since it's as wide as a yarn and nearly as long, I thought I'd pass it on to you, anyway.

I don't know if you know what an eye dog is. The dog in Footrot Flats is an eye dog, and they're mighty around the yards and in the paddocks. An eye dog has the knack of mesmerising sheep. They stand stock-still, stare straight at the woolly bugger and fix it with an eye. The sheep freezes like it's hypnotised. Then it can be worked back into the mob ... or wherever.

We had one great eye dog named Rex—not to be confused with Tex, a dog Dad sadly ran over one Christmas Eve. Tex was probably my favourite sheepdog of all time. He was border collie cross with thick, soft fur, but he must have had something else in him, because his legs were terribly short. That meant Tex wasn't as fast as the sheep. But he was smart.

Crookwell's a fairly hilly place, apart from the Mulligans' new patio, and even that lists a bit after a couple of beers. Tex used those hills to his advantage. Dad'd say, 'Go way back, Tex!'—which, for you smog hoppers, means 'Go to the back of the mob'—and Tex would disappear over the side of the hill and reappear a few seconds later behind the sheep.

When Tex got old, he became the house dog—not that he was allowed into the house. Sheepdogs smell something awful, and there are odours some sheepdog's collect that a thousand baths can't wash out. But Tex *was* allowed to sleep on the back doormat and keep us company in the backyard . . . until that sad Christmas Eve when Dad felt that telltale 'Ba-dump-bump' that spells the end of a dog.

Rex on the other hand, was the only dog we ever had that *didn't* smell. So he was allowed inside when he retired. We rigged a flap so he could get in and out and he lived like a proper house dog. One weekend, we all went down to my Nanna and Grandpa's in Wollongong. Rex was left captain of the house. While we were away something unthinkable for a small country town in New South Wales happened. A burglar broke in.

Rex was onto him in a flash—tail wagging, tongue hanging out, angling for a pat. Great guard dog, that Rex!

So the burglar gave him a pat and started doing the rounds, picking up the silverware, Mum's jewellery and the odd bit of cash, while Rex followed him round the house, keeping him company.

When he was ready to go, the burglar reached down and gave Rex one last little pat. That's when the dog fixed him with his eye. The burglar couldn't move . . . not a bloody inch.

If you've ever been hypnotised, you'll know how it was. You feel like you're normal, but you're doing these blasted ridiculous things that you're going to be reminded about for the rest of your life. That's how it was for this bloke. He just couldn't budge an inch.

Then, slowly, slowly, Rex backed the burglar out of the living room, up the hallway, into my parents' bedroom, shut the door, locked it and rang the police.

In honour of the achievement, Dad always drove much more carefully whenever he was near the house.

That yarn is so typical of the Australian bush—a man, his dog and his imagination. Robert Corkhill of Boorowa, New South Wales, was quite right to question this tale (or should it be tail?).

Tiger's Tail

G'day mate. The name's Jack—Jack O'Shea.

I've just retired. Worked all me life on an outback station. It belonged to this old bloke named Bulla McKenzie—so named because he had a face just like a bulldog... and a bite to match. On his eightieth birthday, I'm putting up this new fence for him, see, when along he comes and says, 'Make a good job of it, Jack. We don't want to be replacing it in twenty years' time.' He reckoned he was going to live forever, the poor old bloke. And mean ... he'd skin a flea and nurse it back to health just so he could skin it again.

Have I got some stories about that station and old Bulla? This one's about the time he sent me out into the scrub to muster about 800 wethers for shearing. It was a day's work just to get out of the scrub, let alone back to the shed, so I start out about five in the morning on the old grey mare with me trusty dog, Tiger.

We're travelling at a fairly steady rate to the far side of the scrub, when these big black storm-clouds roll in on us. I can see we're in for one hell of a drenching, so I turn and start heading for safety. The old mare is fairly tearing. She wants to get home, too, before the storm breaks, and its starting to get so dark, even an owl'd have no chance seeing where he's heading.

Just when it seems disaster's about to strike, a flash of lightning reveals this enormous tree just in front of us. There's no time for the old girl to go round it. That tree's about forty foot in diameter. Just as I'm getting ready to meet the Boss upstairs, this great flash of lightning splits that tree fair down the centre and the horse and me pass through. The dog's right on our tail, but, sadly, the tree closes up again, catching poor old Tiger right in the middle.

There's nothing I can do to save him. That tree's taken him as its own. So the old mare and me head off home.

You know, to this day, every time I go past that tree, I swear I can hear a muffled barking noise and scratching inside it.

Some time later, this young bloke that worked on the station came into town and called up to see me. He said, 'Jack, you're not going to believe this, but t'other day, as I was going through the scrub, I passed the tree where you told me your dog Tiger got entombed that time. You're still not going to believe me, but all the new spring leaves on that tree have sprouted and they're all shaped exactly like your dog—with a long tail.'

'You're right,' I replied. 'I don't believe you. You're the one with the long tale. My Tiger had a short one, his mother bit it off when she was cleaning him up after he was born.'

The things these young fellers try to tell a man.

It is amazing, isn't it?

Variations of this next yarn were submitted by a couple of contestants. I chose the version from Beverley Hamilton, of Bordertown in South Australia, because her particular fib seemed the most plausible. In fact, if GL Minett of Tamworth hadn't also tried to bamboozle me with a similar yarn, I mightn't have twigged that it was a tall story at all.

Goanna Oil

I've always had a bit of a soft spot for goannas, from way back before there were any cooked-up Greenies. Goannas are swift of foot and can climb a tree in half a blink—helped by their lengthy tails. But woe betide any spectator who gets in the way. That's the easiest way of becoming a substitute if there's no tree close by—especially when the goanna's being chased by a couple of rambunctious dogs. One of the best things about goannas is the magnificent oil that can be produced from them. To be truthful, that's always upset me a bit. I always liked to think of them running free.

Now, this story took place way back in the petrol rationing days, during, or just after, the Second World War. My old man told me about some of the sneaky ways some people used to get a bit extra allowance of petrol. Any old engine they had, even if it had not been used for yonks, was doused with oil to make it look as if it was still in use. That way they could increase their ration. If tricks like that failed, people sometimes were forced to use substitutes for petrol to keep themselves mobile.

It was from my old man that I heard this story about the mail man out bush. He might have heard the story third-hand, but I can personally vouch for its truth, because my old man always told it like it was.

This mail man one day made an appearance with a significant dent in the front of his bus. Of course everyone asked the question, 'Whatever happened to you?'

He'd sadly explain. 'I was running a bit low on juice and I still hadn't finished me run. It was also getting a bit too late to go into town for petrol, and anyway, I'd used up all me ration. So I put in a pint of goanna oil. The old bus went pretty well. In fact, everything woulda been all right if Harry's greyhounds hadn't come rushing across the paddock at me. The old truck took fright and headed for the nearest gum tree.

'Stone the crows if she didn't miss her footing on the first branch and down we came.'

One thing about these sorts of lies is that they seem to be infectious. Instead of admonishing the perpetrator, you instantly get sucked in and are suddenly overcome by an irresistible desire to outdo them. It's a terrible affliction ... and probably a good reason the ABC never elected to bung on a barbecue or a garden party for its yarn spinners. If you got a lot of them in one spot, they'd probably start going hammer and tongs trying to outdo each other. The resulting explosion would probably re-create the universe.

For instance, if you asked Dave McBain, from Merbein in the Victorian Sunraysia, something relatively innocuous, like if the insects were bothering him, he'd come out with something like this ...

Mossies

Mosquitoes are a bit of a problem up our way, especially since the red gum sawmill started up at Merbein. Pulling out the red gum logs along the river tracks causes problems when the river's high. Tractors can't get along the tracks close to the river's edge. In fact, quite a few areas further back are inaccessible, too, when the water's really high.

However, sometimes the problem can be overcome by using the old bullock team. It was a time of high water when the old bullocky *really* got into strife ... and it wasn't that long ago.

Archie Wilson was the bloke working along the river with his team. As usual, at dusk he unharnessed his team, tied the bells around the bullocks' necks so he could hear them as they fed along the bank, and let them go for the night.

Everything seemed fine. He made camp, set up a beaut campfire so the smoke'd keep the mosquitoes away and slept peacefully. However, when he got up in the morning and went looking for the bullocks, he couldn't find them. He listened for the tinkling of their bells. Not a sound. He looked for hoof marks and when he found them, started following them along the river. Every now and then, he came across a bell, lying on the ground ... but never a sign of a beast. Finally, coming round a bend, he saw a great big red gum log lying on the side of the track. Sitting on the log was a row of fairly big mosquitoes, cleaning their teeth with bullocks' horns.

You've sure got to be careful along the river up our way.

Speaking of rivers ... I think I managed to demonstrate in *Yarns!* that there are one or two members of the angling fraternity who are prone to stretching the truth. But none of the examples I gave there came within a cooee of the following one from Ted

Barraclough, of Peregian Beach, Queensland. As you'll quickly see, Ted feels so dubious about his own yarn that he's had a pang of conscience. He starts it off by trying to blame someone else for it . . .

Splash!

A bloke told me this yarn in a pub once, but I don't believe a word of it.

Once upon a time, a fisherman stood on a beach casting his line into the sea . . . but without any luck. He decided to go for one last try.

Suddenly, he felt a great weight on the end of the line. When he reeled it in, he found he'd caught the strangest sea creature he'd ever seen. It had a long shiny tail, blonde hair . . . and various other interesting bits.

'Struth! I've never caught one of these before,' he said to himself. 'It's pretty big . . . *must* be over the legal limit. I wonder if they're good to eat.'

'Please throw me back into the foaming brine, where my father rules,' begged the fish.

'I don't know about that,' replied the fisherman. 'You're a fair size. I might get me photo took with you down at Davo's Bait Bar, although normally he only worries about flathead and cod . . . or mangrove jack, when they're running.

'Nah! On second thoughts, I can't do that. I'd look pretty silly holding *you* up by the tail.'

'Please, *please* throw me back into the foaming brine, where my father rules,' begged the fish with the blonde hair and interesting bits, yet again.

'Can't take you home,' mused the angler. 'The missus'd go crook if I walked in with *you* under me arm.'

'*Please* throw me back into the foaming brine where my father rules,' repeated the fish, 'and I will grant you a wish.'

'Now you're talking,' said the fisherman enthusiastically. 'A wish, eh? Lemme see . . . What about the Sydney Swans winning two

in a row? Nah! That'd be a bit too much to expect. Yair! I know! Gold Lotto! Yair, I want to know which numbers'll win first prize in Gold Lotto next Saturday.'

'Your wish is my command,' intoned the fish, promptly dictating a list of numbers to the fisherman. 'Now, please throw me ...'

'Yair, yair,' said the fisherman, and he took the strange fish with the blonde hair and the interesting bits and threw it back into the foaming brine, where ... etc. etc. etc.

He made his first stop, the local Lotto agency, and sure enough, come Saturday night, he did *indeed* win Gold Lotto. Great was his joy. He watched the TV news, waiting eagerly for the newsreader to declare the dividend. Eventually, there it was.

'Last night's Gold Lotto win was the lowest on record. First Division paid only $5.80. According to a Lotto spokesman, the same six numbers seemed to have been extremely popular.

'Now, before the weather, here's Macca with his weekly fishing report.' With that, the newsreader turned around to the television fishing commentator.

'Thanks mate. Well, fishing has been good on most beaches, with anglers reporting especially good catches of mermaids. They seem to be running at the moment. The best time to catch them is between low and high tide, around sunset. Mullet gut and worms seem to be the go. Back to you, Brian.'

On the other hand, the Barwon River, out west a bit from the coast and the Big Smoke, is too far away from the major television networks to warrant attention from the news journos. Perhaps, in a strange way, we should be grateful to Max Overton, of Dubbo, for his conservative and unembellished fishing report.

Hatchem, Latchem and Catchem

These three pretty keen fishermen operated back when there were *real* fish in these here western rivers like the Barwon.

Hatchem was a real crafty geezer. Seeing he only used water for fishing in, or mixing sparingly with thick black Bundy rum, he

was also pretty easy to find—even after dark—on the river bank . . .
and sorta attracted fish with his special scent.

Latchem was a different kettle o' fish altogether. He had
enormous, smelly 'plates o' meat'—better known as 'feet' in more
cultured society—although *he* wasn't cultured *or* what you'd call
a member of society. But he had this uncanny ability to attract
bait by dangling his big plates o' meat in the stream.

Then there was Catchem—an important bloke, seeing as how he
was the business head of the trio.

What I want to talk about is their best and biggest catch and
how they profited from it (apart from winning the Australian
cod-fishing championship).

Hatchem was camped on the river bank after a particularly hot,
sweaty day. Having drunk lots of Bundy rum, he imagined he
could see the telltale signs indicating the size of fish that could
certainly win the championship. Those signs were small tidal
waves lapping the bank at regular intervals.

Now Latchem was around the bend, busily attracting bait by
dangling his great big plates o' meat over a huge gum log. He'd
sewn three woolpacks together and draped them over the log,
too. Sure enough, the biggest crawfish you ever imagined was
lured past his big smelly big toe, into the woolpack trap.

Catchem, on the other hand, had borrowed the heaviest fishing
gear he could find—a two inch mooring rope and an anchor
salvaged from a paddle steamer burned at its moorings at Brewarrina
a few years before.

All as set.

While Hatchem marked the spot where most of the tidal waves
were crashing into the bank, Latchem was having a bit of a tussle
with his three hundredweight, six foot craw fish. Eventually, he
shoved a couple of them hoop iron bands from round a beer
barrel over its nippers and subdued it. Catchem, who, as I said,
was equipped with the two inch rope, sharpened the flukes of
the old anchor and, setting the whole cray on it for bait, slung
the line over the thickest limb of the biggest river gum around . . .
and ran it back to where their three horses was tethered. Tying
the tails to the line, Latchem, a fair sort of horse tailer, yelled

'Giddap!' and the nags pulled the bait into midstream.

Well, holy hell! Hatchem hadn't the time to pour another rum; or Latchem to untie the horses' tails; or catchem to get his springer set when *Wham!* ... the big 'un hit the bait.

First of all, a big tidal wave almost knocked them down. Water splashed onto Hatchem and the shock made him pass out. Latchem's huge, stinkin' plates o' meat was washed clean from under him, while Catchem just watched helplessly as the horses was drug up over the limb of the big gum tree.

They was all chestnut horses, and I understand their celebrated flight created the symbol of the Flying Red Horse what Mobil used on their kero tins. Perhaps you've seen them about?

But back to the drama.

Just down the stream from the big fishing hole, where Hatchem first located the fish, near where Latchem caught the bait and Catchem borrowed the old anchor, the Maritime Services Board or the DMR ... or *somebody* ... had built one of them big steel lift-up bridges for vehicles to go over or boats to go under—depending on whichever you happened to be passing in. That bridge came in pretty handy once Hatchem, Latchem and Catchem got over the shock.

Hatchem had a quick snort of rum. Latchem gathered his big stinkin' plates o' meat under him and Catchem dodged the falling twenty foot springer he'd been hanging onto ... and off they run just downstream of the bridge. They winched down the lift-up part ... and blocked the fish. Then rejigged the winch a bit and got it going again to pull their catch, and the horses, up onto the roadway.

Of course, the fish had to be weighed in, so they rigged up a sky hook (there being no crane around big enough).

It topped the record, winning them the Australian cod title and prize money of two and six.

But now, what to do with it?

Well, although it was Friday, all the pubs and cafes had enough fish for their guests. So they had quite a problem on their hands—not to mention the added one of the stink that'd build up if the fish was left blocking the bridge in the middle of summer.

By then, buggies, carts and teams was banking up way back to the Cato creek, and Cobb and Co's four in hand was tearing up the bridge with the Goodooga mail on board, the driver anxious to be on time, as they always was in them days.

It looked like things might get real ugly, what with the cranky riverboat captains wanting to pass underneath; the rod travellers itching to get over the top, so as not to miss the dawn line-up at the Middle Pub; and the local cop stewing about being drug out so early because of the noise. But just then a toffy bloke stepped out of the Cobb and Co coach.

He cleared his throat a bit, held his nose and approached Hatchem, Latchem and Catchem, exuding a fair bit of pomp and authority. It turned out the Toff was a pastoral company inspector from London, doing a tour around the stations.

You couldn't hear what was said, but everyone saw the size of the wallet the Toff flashed in front of the fishermen.

It had the desired effect. In no time, while Hatchem had a quick swig of neat rum, Latchem had their horses untied, grazing safely in a nearby paddock and Catchem grabbed the earholes of a couple of mates who had their bullock and horse teams handy.

Encouraged by the smell of Hatchem's rum, twenty blokes with pinch bars and crosscut saws offered to help. It turned out they was sleeper cutters from Pilliga who'd come across for a bit of a do at Bre'.

With their pinch bars, they prised off the cod's huge scales. They was resold by the Toff later as windowpanes for that Crystal Palace joint in London—or so they say.

The jawbones, after being displayed at the Sydney Royal Show for a few years, was donated to the builders of the Harbour Bridge to form the main span.

Once them sleeper cutter fellers sawed the cod in half, the two teams of bullocks and horses was able to drag it off the roadway. It took them two days to cut it into fillets, salt it, cart it to the railway and load it into fifteen rail trucks.

That's when it became just like this yarn—the biggest load of codswallop ever seen or heard in the west.

Max's dubious fish story seems to be a big brother of Tom
Creedy's Big cod, the tale that won Evan Farley, of North
Rockhampton, the Queensland state prize in the Search for the
Great Australian Yarn. I won't repeat it here. You can catch up
with it in *Yarns!*

Before we leave the smoky world of fish stories, here's one in
verse. Throughout this whole exercise, I've tended to avoid poetry,
because bush poems have their own distinct niche in Australian
heritage. Rules are always meant to be broken, however—especially
ones you make yourself—so I couldn't resist including a couple.

Here's one from Jack Gillis, of Harrington, New South Wales.

Barramundi Bob

I've listened to the stories of the fishes lost and caught,
And I have had some highs and lows, indulging in this sport.
This yarn, I'd like to share with you, of a top man at his job.
He's known around the mangrove creeks as Barramundi
    Bob.

He knows every nook and cranny and where the big ones
    hide.
He's aware of all their habits and which lure will tempt a
    strike.
Bob works the 'Gator River, South, East and in between,
And he's caught the biggest barras the north has ever seen.

They held a competition. T'was a handicap event.
Bob read the rules, gave a grin, then packed his gear and
    went.
The judges, checking out the gear, they only took one look,
And made him fish for two long hours, without the aid of
    hooks.

Now Bob felt harshly treated but sighed, 'Ah, what the hell?
'I've travelled miles to get here. I'll fish and win, as well.'
He chose a good-sized yabbie, put a half-hitch round its tail,

195

Uncapped a Darwin stubby and began to lay his trail.

Boats were whipping here and there, the contest had begun.
Bob drifted round the mangroves and dozed off in the sun.
He dreamed of club conditions and said, 'I will appeal.'
But was jerked back to reality by the screaming of the reel.

He grabbed the rod, took the weight and tightened up the
  drag,
And thought, 'That bloody yabbie has wrapped me round a
  snag.'
Bob said, 'I must be dreaming. You're still asleep, you fool.'
But then found out that it was real, as the smoke flew off
  the spool.

The line whipped through the water. He thought his
  chances slim,
But slowly, oh so slowly, he began to bring it in.
It took an hour to tire that fish and get him to the boat,
And Bob's 'good-sized' yabbie had that monster by the
  throat.

They didn't weigh Bob's fish that day—the scales were far too
  small.
But that was naught to my old mate, he didn't mind at all.
He rolled his swag, gave a grin, headed back home to the
  'Gator,
And as he cranked his old jeep up, he said, 'I'll see you
  later.'

You may not believe this story of Barramundi Bob,
Or how he improvises when he's out there on the job.
I haven't seen him for a while, but I'll strike him on my
  rounds,
But he sent a photo of the fish *and the print weighed seven
  pounds.*

Get the idea with all this downright lying? Everything's got to be
bigger and better. It reminds of the sad tale I heard about the
yarn spinner who died in a small country town. He was a big

bigbloke—so big they didn't have a coffin that'd fit him. However, someone had the bright idea of giving him an enema—and they buried him in a shoe box.

Could Barry Simes meet a similar fate? He had the temerity to submit a gardening story, from that greenest of places—Broken Hill.

Ye Olde Vegie Garden

After months of planning, reading all the latest tips on gardening, digging out all the family secrets handed down through the ages, it was time to put everything into practice.

Six o'clock—the sun just starting to rise. What could be a more perfect start to the day that was going to be one to look back on for the rest of my life?

After much deliberation on whether the chook poop should be raked through the plot first ... or should I add the prized treasure I had collected from the winners' stables after the annual bush races? I decided a mixture of both would be the best solution. After much digging, spreading, raking, mixing, levelling and the odd cuppa here and there, it was time to water it all in and wait.

The seeds, the best stock available, were sown into their seed mixture, so only time and TLC were needed to bring the results of my labour to fruition.

The previous year had seen my first attempt at satisfying our family's lust for fresh, home-grown vegetables. That time, I bunged in a packet of ordinary old carrot seeds. At least they might have been labelled ordinary, but the consequences were nothing short of horrific—one hernia and plenty of back strain from just trying to pull them out of the ground. This year, it was Back To The Old Drawing Board.

After many sleepless nights, a whole swag of computer programs and stacks of calculations ... at last, a solution! It seemed to make sense to dig down eighteen inches and bury a piece of

quarter inch steel plate, so the carrots couldn't grow any deeper this time around.

Every morning we followed the same procedure. I'd go out to the seed boxes, check the pumpkins (Queensland Blues, of course), water the carrots, turn the beetroots towards the sunshine, keep the cat away from the cherry tomatoes and last—but by no means least—carefully tend the sweet corn.

Well, after a few weeks, the waiting was over and little seedlings were popping up everywhere, as though eager to be part of this memorable undertaking which, I could see, was going to occupy all my spare time for the next few months.

So far, everything had progressed to plan and now, the time had come to transplant. So out they went—the pumpkins alongside the chook house; tomatoes against the shed; carrots in their space-age bed; beetroot and corn along the back fence.

At last, the fruits of my labour were rewarded. Fresh, home-grown cherry tomatoes were the first to appear and they just seemed to keep on getting better.

I don't mean to brag, but I'd reached the stage that whenever anyone asked me for a couple of kilos, I had to reply, 'You either take a full one, or none at all. I'm not going to cut 'em.'

The next to respond to my TLC were the carrots. Had all those sleepless nights paid off?

The next morning, up early to try to pull some up for a lunchtime coleslaw, it all came to no avail. You just wouldn't believe it. They'd grown down, hit the quarter inch plate, turned around and come back up again. Not only did they have soil all around them, but in the middle, too. That's how I discovered a backhoe cost fifty dollars an hour to hire.

Was the project really going to be worthwhile? I wondered. But, seeing the family loved fresh beetroot, I persevered.

This time, the wife pulled the beetroot, but, being in somewhat of a hurry, forgot to fill in the craters. You can guess the outcome. The kids got down in the craters playing ... and no way did they want to come out for their meals.

I really didn't think things could get any worse, until I returned home from work a couple of days later and found the same kids had turned my pride and joy—a nice little Queensland Blue—into a two-roomed cubbyhouse, complete with doors and windows. Ahh well, kids'll be kids . . . and we did end up with two years' supply of pumpkin scones made from the bits they'd dug out.

With all the dramas of those few weeks still fresh in mind, I actually formed a strategy for picking the sweet corn. The first step was to borrow the neighbours' extension ladder, stand it against the corn and secure it to a trunk. I don't know what I'd ever done to Murphy, but his law sure seemed to be alive and well in our vegie garden. No corn got picked that first day, but I scored a ride in the district's newest ambulance and survived my first broken leg—all courtesy of a fifteen foot fall.

Well, lying here in hospital, I've had plenty of time to do some serious thinking. Was it really the result of mixing the chook poop with the dobbin dung? Or was it that touch of moo poo I added to that liquid concoction? I'll never know.

From now on, you can bet your bottom dollar I'll stick to bunging those plastic bags of vegies into the shopping trolley. It's got to be cheaper and safer.

And on and on it goes. There's very little anyone can say about this yarn from Garth Madsen of Horsham, Victoria.

The Finger

A few years ago, Lazy Ted got lucky in this little bar in Mayfield. She was a good-looking girl, too. He drove her around to this park, the local lovers' lane, for a little privacy and they were getting along just fine, when some local louts happened by.

Luckily, all the doors of the car were locked and the larrikins had to content themselves with rocking it backwards and forwards. Lazy Ted wasn't going to hang around for any nonsense. He stuck the car into reverse and revved out of the car park. Bodies scattered in his wake. He ended up taking the girl to the safety of a nearby hotel.

Lazy Ted might have forgotten all about the incident but, the very next day, as he was watching his wife, Betty, washing the car, you'll never guess what he saw—a finger, just sitting there in the grille in front of the motor.

Well, he shook his head and was about to tell Betty to put it in the rubbish, when she stopped him short.

'That finger must belong to someone. We'd better take it down the road to the Lost and Found. You'd be surprised what they can do with microsurgery these days.'

Lazy Ted followed his missus down to the local cop shop, where they were extra helpful. While Betty was out of earshot, he told them the full story—exactly what had happened, how, when, where and why.

Afterwards, Lazy Ted went home and forgot all about the whole business until one day, this cop came to the door and presented him with this little frozen container ... and in it—the finger.

'According to Section 4 of Article 8 of the Mislaid Articles Act of 1893,' the cop spouted off, 'found goods, if unclaimed by the owner and the loser of the aforementioned lost goods, after a period of three months, should be returned to the finder, who will be thereafter considered the owner and therefore the loser, in the event of the goods ever being re-lost.'

Lazy Ted didn't really know what to do, but he took the finger and thanked the cop for his trouble. He told Betty to put it in the freezer.

Soon afterwards, the phone calls started. A man, his voice deep, husky and mean, would ring and say, 'You got my finger. You better give it back ... or you'll get rubbed.'

Night after night, the same man rang with the same message. Then, during the day, the Health Department started ringing and a man with a high, piping voice, would tell Ted, 'Keeping a finger in your freezer contravenes Section 1, Article 12, of the Body Parts in the Kitchen Act of 1923, and if you persist in infringing this regulation, we will be forced to carry out immediate legal action.'

The final straw was when the surgeon started calling up daily, too.

'Listen, we get kids in here every day, with their fingers missing—

car accidents, gun accidents . . . you name it. Some will never be able to use their hands again. With that finger, you could at least help one . . . just one of them.'

Finally, it got too much for Betty. 'Listen Ted, do something. Give that finger back to the gangster. Give it to the Health Department. Even give it to the hospital. Just get rid of it. It's no use to us.'

But it was all to no avail. Lazy Ted wouldn't hear of it. You know what he's like. He'd never lift a finger to help himself or anyone else.

Sometimes you have to wonder what inspires some of these yarns. And then you have to wonder why anyone would go to the huge amount of trouble Eric Williamson, of Lawson, New South Wales, did just to destroy his own credibility . . . in verse (of sorts).

The Disappearing Toads

When I was heading north one year, I saw the Theebine
        pub,
And stopped awhile to quench my thirst and grab a bit of
        grub.
A friendly local said 'G'day' and 'Where y'headed to?'
I said, 'I plan to go up north and look at Kakadu.'
The local had to laugh and said, 'That might be risky, mate.
'You'd better talk to Scraper here and let him put you
        straight.

'His name is really Skyscraper—his stories are so tall.
'Old Scraper's standing over there, against the other wall.'
'Well, thanks,' I said and walked across to where old Scraper
        stood,
And asked him if he'd drink with me. Of course, he said he
        would.
I said, 'I'm heading north to have a look at Kakadu.

'They tell me you're the sort of bloke I should be talking to.'

'You're lucky you saw me,' he said, 'and not some tourist
  chap.
'You'll never get the truth from all that coloured brochure
  crap.
'You look a decent sort of bloke, so my advice to you,
'Is turn around and head back south, away from Kakadu.
'That may seem strange advice to give a stranger passing by,
'But if you've got the time to spare, well, I can tell you why.

'I lived up north for years,' he said, 'when jobs was very few.
'And only kept from starving with me special cane toad stew.
'When I was out of tucker and fast foods was quite
  unknown,
'I'd boil a Queensland cane toad in a billy with a stone.
'And when the stone got soft from being boiled a week or
  two,
'I'd thrown away the toad and eat the stone up with the
  stew.

'With all those years of catching toads and making cane toad
  stew,
'I thought I'd use me expertise to earn a quid or two.
'I got a council contract catching giant Queensland toads.
'And using them for patching up the holes in all their roads.
'And here's where me intelligence and native cunning
  showed,
'By working out a clever way to catch and kill a toad.

'I used to use a football boot to finish off a toad,
'Until I broke me ankle on a rock beside the road.
'A wallop with a golf club is another way I've tried,
'It makes a lovely sound but tends to mutilate the hide.
'So when it comes to choices, I prefer the cricket bat.
'It doesn't mark the skin and gives a better sounding "splat!"

'So every night just after dark, when toads are mostly found,
'I'd set me special gear up on the local cricket ground.
'I'd stick a lighted lantern on an old twelve gallon drum.

'The light attracted all the moths ... and then the toads'd
  come.
'I'd grab me trusty cricket bat and stand there at the crease,
'And toads would come in hundreds, hopping straight to
  their decrease.

'I'd hit them all for four or six and drive and cut and hook,
'And belt them round the field with every shot that's in the
  book.
'I could've played Test cricket with me batting prowess, mate.
'But all that tropic sunshine made me body dehydrate.
'That medical condition caused me cricket hopes to shrink,
'Because doctors told me not to go too long without a drink.

'Well, anyway, these toads I killed, I stacked them in a heap,
'And put them through a process I invented on the cheap.
'I got an ancient washer with a wringer at the top,
'And squeezed out all their innards and collected all the
  slop.
'I boiled this up for seven days and made a sticky brew,
'And put it in a watering can to make a patching glue.

'I mixed the glue with toad skins in the hole I had to fix,
'Then packed it down real tight and firm, with special
  ramming sticks.
'The finished job was concrete hard and wore extremely well,
'Much better than the road itself, as far as you could tell.
'I thought I'd make a fortune, 'cause there's always roads to
  patch,
'When suddenly I found the toads was getting hard to catch.

'The toad supply was falling far behind the toad demands.
'I thought I was exterminating toads throughout the land.
'And then I found I'd see some toads, but when I got up
  near,
'The ugly little devils would completely disappear.
'One night I saw a single toad and crept up, bit by bit,
'Until I got up close enough to nearly have a hit.

'But then I made a little noise and gave the toad a fright,

'The toad looked sort of furtive, then he looked to left and
   right.
'He flexed that giant mouth of his and opened up real wide,
'Then did a sort of backward flip and disappeared inside.
'Jumped right through his mouth, he did, completely out of
   sight.
'I tell you, mate, there's nothing ever give me such a fright.

'Well, after that I'd sneak right up behind them toads at
   night,
'And when I got up close, I'd see them disappear from sight.
'I'd grab me faithful cricket bat and rush where they was at,
'And make a brilliant cover drive and listen to the splat.
'But nothing ever happened, mate, me swipes all went astray.
'They knew I couldn't see them and then calmly hopped
   away.

'So, catching toads for patching roads got harder every day.
'It wasn't long before I had to give the game away.
'The council used old-fashioned ways for patching up a hole,
'And I was out of business, so I finished on the dole.
'But I don't give up easy, I decided there and then,
'To find a way to catch them toads and get some work again.

'For years I studied up them toads and one thing soon came
   clear.
'They couldn't make their calling cards and footprints
   disappear.
'Although I couldn't see him, I could track the warty pest,
'And soon I found the toads were all migrating further west.
'I tracked them past Mt Isa and, as far as I could see,
'They'd spread across the border to the Northern Territory.

'About this time, a pair of experts came to count the toads,
'And talk about some bulldust mate, well, those two blokes
   had loads.
'The first one was a loudmouth and he sounded insincere.
'He'd open up his mouth before his brain got into gear.
'The other one spoke Latin and was smarter than most men.

'He didn't take his boots off when he counted over ten.

'But when it come to animals, they didn't have a clue.
'And pulled out this big photo of a toad—full frontal view.
'They seemed to think that I was only two bob in the quid.
' "That's Bufo," said the loudmouthed bloke, as if I was a
      kid.
' "Bufo, my anus," said his mate and spoke as if he knowed.
' "The both of you is wrong," I said, "That thing's a bloody
      toad."

'Well, once I'd put them straight on that, I asked how long
      they'd stay.
'They said, with modern methods, they would only need a
      day.
'I asked them how they'd count the toads. They seemed
      stupid drips.
' "It's easy," said the loudmouthed one. "We count them up
      in strips.
' "We drive across the paddocks for a kilometre, then,
' "We count up all the toads we see, and multiply by ten."

'Then off they drove, to look for toads and when they got
      too near,
'The toads would do their backward flip and simply
      disappear.
'And after all that fancy work, it turned out like I thought,
'They finished with a figure that was simply ten times
      naught.
'So back down south they headed, with their big consultant
      fees,
'And said the toads had all been killed by some unknown
      disease.

'Of course, I knew meself that all the toads were far from
      dead.
'But no one took no notice after what the experts said.
'So I kept on tracking them, by following their poo.
'I trailed them right around the Gulf and up to Kakadu.

'And all the time I worried, 'cause I noticed on the way,
'The calling cards I tracked were getting bigger every day.

'I learned a thing about the toads those experts wouldn't
    know,
'They haven't got a finished size and while they eat, they
    grow.
'They keep on growing bigger while there's food to get them
    by,
'And buffaloes and tourists are in plentiful supply.
'The heat and wet round Kakadu just suits them all the
    more,
'They're up there, growing bigger than a flaming dinosaur.

'One day I watched some cattle graze, this ain't bulldust,
    now,
'When, suddenly, this toad appeared and swallowed up a
    cow.
'That sort of shook me up a bit. It made me contemplate.
'It made me stop and wonder if I had a future, mate.
'I tells meself, "It's not safe here. It's time a bloke shot
    through.
' "Next time a giant toad appears, it might be after you."

'Now you might think that's not a pretty picture that I've
    sketched,
'And all these things I'm telling you might seem a bit far-
    fetched.
'But think about the things that's going on up north just
    now,
'And I'm not talking just about that disappearing cow.
'There's truckies feeling thumps, but kangaroos aren't near
    the road,
'Each bump they feel is probably a disappearing toad.

'And what about the tourists disappearing all the time?
'Officials tack them on the list, another unsolved crime.
'I'll bet those poor dumb tourists know they'd ended their
    careers,

'When suddenly an evil, grinning monster toad appears,
'From out of bloody nowhere, right beside them on the
    ground,
'And all the cops can tell you is, "They're missing, can't be
    found."

'And all those missing animals you hear of every week,
'That keep on getting taken up some muddy mangrove
    creek.
'A pig, a dog, a straying horse, a careless kangaroo,
'And buffaloes and emus—and a fisherman or two.
'It's not what people's blaming, mate, it's not the crocodiles.
'It's giant Queensland toads, mate, with their disappearing
    smiles.

'And then, last week, I heard the news, the thing I've always
    feared.
'A semitrailer full of grog completely disappeared.
'It's time good men like you and me got into fighting mode,
'And started taking steps to stop the disappearing toad.
'I'm starting up a club to fund research to tell us how,
'For only twenty dollars, mate, I'll let you join up now.'

Peter Dargin, of Dubbo, New South Wales, is a man with quite
a reputation for his factual and historical writing. But it seems
even he gets carried away at times. He attributes this gem of a
yarn to one Lizard McGuiness, who takes up the story . . .

Coffin Charlie and
the Innamincka Bike Race

Bikes! They spread like rabbits and they went about as fast. Nearly
all the shearers and shed hands had 'em. Cheaper than a 'orse—
no need to feed or water 'em on a dry stretch and a sight easier
to catch in the mornin', too. Yet know, a bike carried more and
went further. Still needed shoein', but you could always make do
when a tyre blew. The bike carried the bush in them days.

One of the great bike rides was to Cordillo Downs, the big stone shed on the edge of Sturt's Stony Desert. Blokes came from Bourke and Tasmania to shear there. It was a bloke called Bass Strait—a real big blow 'e was—who started the Innamincka Bike Race. 'E'd come by boat to Melbourne, trained it to Adelaide, then up to Lyndhurst, where 'e and 'is mates pedalled the Cobbler and the Strzelecki Track to Innamincka. They added a few bottles to the Innamincka bottle dump, then pushed on to Cordillo Downs. Them Tasmanians thought themselves pretty good with the bike, an' Bass Strait was always blowin' about anythink. 'E reckoned 'e could beat anyone over a distance.

'I challenge the shed!' he screamed like a crosscut saw.

The shed squirmed, but didn't say anything.

'From 'ere, straight to the Innaminka Pub?' drawled Coffin Charlie. Everyone looked up.

'Yeah. At cut out. Are yers on?' Bass Strait stuck his head forward.

Coffin Charlie's beady black eyes read the shed. 'Well, I'll take yer on fer ten quid, if yer game.'

Someone choked on his pipe. They all looked at Bass Strait to see if he'd blow out.

'Game? Charlie, you'll be in your coffin before you get there.'

The shed was game, too. It put up the ten pound, which was a lot of money, with the promise of a skinful at the Innamincka Pub.

Bass Strait took the challenge seriously. He ate big steaks, drank vinegar water and rubbed his legs with goanna oil. He pulled his bike down half a dozen times, then did a few laps around the smithy to show how good he was. Instead of blowing all night and boring everyone to death, Bass Strait slept long, sound sleeps and went real regular. The shearing went like clockwork.

A couple of rousies, concerned for their stake, gave Coffin Charlie's bike a good going over. Charlie had been the last to reach the shed. His front tyre was stuffed with strips of towel and bound with bits of singlet and one of his socks after the long puff from Bourke. They swapped their tyres for his—then threw in a new tube. The bike was like new.

Charlie was a short, wrinkled, ageless bloke, who tended to smell a bit off. He took all the carry-on without any hassle. The only thing he called training was to wobble off like a drunken sailor on a few afternoons with a couple of sugarbags and a broomstick. Mostly, he sat around smoking and yarning with the station cook. On the last night, he got a bit talkative, reciting 'Mulga Bill's Bicycle' (it being all the rage at the time) and telling yarns. Bass Strait went to bed.

At cut out, all except the racers set off. They had their own race to the Innamincka Pub—whoever came last had to shout. Although Bass Strait retired early, Charlie had a good night—winning at cards and enjoying a few grogs with the cook and the blacksmith.

First light saw Bass Strait ready to go. He was chewing a chop and swallowing hot tea when Coffin Charlie rolled out. Charlie slowly strapped his swag and broomsticks to the rear carrier, then wobbled off.

'Come on, Charlie. Shake a leg. It's time!' bawled Bass Strait.

Charlie returned with two sugarbags, tied with strips of greenhide. He dropped them over the front fork.

'Yer ready?' The cook hit the triangle.

Bass Strait skidded around the blacksmith's shop and through the sliprails before Charlie reached the cookhouse.

'Coffin Charlie's goin' to need a bloody miracle,' shrugged the blacksmith.

Bass Strait pedalled flat out over the sandhills and gibbers, through willy-willies and punctures. An hour before sunset, he splashed through the Crossing to make a spirited dash to the hotel. The waiting men cheered, slapped him on the back and pushed him, panting, into the bar.

'What kept yers, Bass Strait?' drawled a very dusty, bleary-eyed Coffin Charlie. 'I thought youse was comin' straight here.'

Bass Strait was punctured. All the blow went out of him.

'How?' he croaked. 'How could an old bugger like you beat me?'

'I know this country like the back of me 'and, Bass Strait. I took the wet weather track.'

'But that's long.' Bass Strait crumpled at the knees.

'Yeah, but it runs onto the Willy Track. I just spread me swag across me back and 'ad a willy push me all the way to the Crossin'.'

Lizard McGuiness, accepting our disbelief and another beer, lowered his voice.

'Well, Charlie took the wet weather track all right, but yer remember I said 'e had two sugarbags? Well, *that* was 'ow 'e done it. 'E 'ad it in the bag. Yer know ... springtime it brings on the shearin' ... an' about everythink else ... an' in them two sugarbags, 'e 'ad a pair of 'oop snakes. Yer know—they whips into an 'oop an' roll along faster than a 'orse?

'Well, 'e turned 'is bike over, pulled the wheels an' tyres orf an' strapped them two 'oop snakes onto the rims with green 'ide. Put the female on the front and the male on the back. An' didn't 'e go? Soon as 'e turned the bike over, the male was tryin' to catch the female ... all the way to the Crossin' ... where 'e let them go. Got in hours ahead of Bass Strait, 'e did. Dinkum!

I feel obliged to finish this chapter by inflicting upon you another piece of alleged verse. Not just *any* piece of doggerel, mind you, but the Victorian state prize winner in the ABC competition. Strangely enough, a straightforward version of the same yarn was also sent in from Victoria, by Margot Jones of Bendigo. However, the honours went to Beatty Blennerhasset of Bengworden, who proved one of the real truths of yarn-spinning—you really *can* go too far. Sorry folks!

Tourists

They came to the Northern Territory
From their homes across the sea.
They wanted to see Australia
And how their lives could be.

From Czechoslovakia and Yugoslavia
They crossed throughout the land,
Visiting the sites of the Dreamtime
And the pleasures of Arnhem Land.

They camped among the gorges
They marvelled at The Rock.
Then they decided to do some fishing
After they'd looked at the stock.

'Don't camp there in that area,'
A local man told them.
'The crocs are as big as elephants
'And so fast you won't see 'em.'

'We'll be all right,' the tourists said,
'From crocs we'll keep away.
'We only want to stop awhile
'And look, and fish and play.'

They tried their hand at fishing
The fish they caught were big.
They tried to live like the natives
And for food they had to dig.

The locals smiled and watched them
And kept an eye on the pair.
Then one day the locals noticed,
The tourists were not there.

A search was mounted quickly,
There was no time to waste,
For those crocs could strike swiftly
And gobble them up in haste.

The locals went out looking
With their guns all ready at hand.
They checked out every billabong
And all around the land.

In pretty quick time they noticed
The tracks along the edge.

Two huge crocs had been there
And were sunning themselves on the ledge.

They saw the tracks of the humans,
They saw the smiles on the crocs.
And realised just what they'd been eating
Why, they weren't just sucking on rocks.

Their guns went to their shoulders,
The bullets found the heads,
And there upon the river bank
Two crocodiles lay dead.

With knives they opened up those crocs,
They slit them from the tail.
They found the Slav in the girl croc
And the *Czech was in the male.*

HAD MUCH EXPERIENCE IN EMU SEXING?

PERSONNEL

VISA

Chapter 2

NEW CHUMS

As far as bush yarns are concerned, the fairest of fair game has always been the newcomer–the new chum. There's a stereotyped picture in everyone's mind of just what a new chum is. The first thing that we picture is, invariably, the gangling, chinless, dithering Englishman. But when you come to think about it, the new chum comes in many forms. The following yarns reveal him or her as the city slicker, the new bride, the teacher just out of college ... the list goes on and on.

We all appreciate a joke on the new chum—mainly because we've all been in the same boat, whether as a butt of similar jokes, or as the perpetrator of them. The new chum is indeed, everyman ... oh, all right, then ... *and* everywoman.

Perhaps the best known new chum yarn is this next one. It was often quoted to me during our early hobby farm existence on the Prickle Farm. I include this version from Rowena Walker of Missabotti, New South Wales, simply because she, too, has had the temerity to reduce it to verse.

The New Chum

When I came out from London town, a man of thirty years,
I wasn't 'Quick' or 'In the Know', just 'Wet Behind the
    Ears'.
I hankered for a country life and soon was on the go,
To buy a half an acre block and build a bungalow.

The air was fresh, the weather warm, the next-door neigh-
    bour nice.
He leaned upon the paling fence and gave me good advice.
Like, 'You don't need to mow that lawn. I've got a better
    way.
'A mate of mine has got a sheep he wants to give away.'

The woolly wether soon arrived and stripped the garden
    bare,
But left the grass untidy with sheep pellets everywhere.
As well, the reason for the 'gift' soon became quite clear,
At every chance, the sheep would charge and butt me in the
    rear.

And soon my next-door neighbour, one early summer's
    morn,
Said, 'Cripes! That sheep is shaggy, mate. You'd better get
    'im shorn.'
I looked at advertisements and unbeknownst to me,
Found the largest shearing contract company from Dubbo
    to the sea.

I felt so very nervous about ringing up the place,
And I stuttered, ummed and faltered, heart hammering on
    apace.

'G'day,' they answered. 'How'd ya be? How many hundred sheep?

'The blokes aren't through with Walgett way till the middle of next week.

'OK now, what's the tally? Let's have 'em by the ton.

'How many sheep?' he shouted. I whispered, 'Only one.'

Silence ... then, 'By cripes!' he said. 'You poms are all the same.

'Well, OK mate, this sheep of yours ... let's 'ave 'is bloody name.'

I'm always heartened when kids take up the art of yarn-spinning. Their yarns can't be expected to be full of the sort of insight that we get from older people—but they can certainly find some amusement in our old mate the new chum, as thirteen-year-old Annette Donnell showed.

The Bouncing City Kid

Shearing was in the school holidays, so we had to help Mum while she helped with the shed handing and assorted other jobs. The shearer arrived with his nephew, a city kid, so we introduced him to some of our activities. His name was Shane and he was about ten. There was also my brother Dean, seven, sister Samantha, eleven, and me.

Most of the morning involved helping feed the pigs. Then we ran in the sheep and helped get the lunch and smoko. After that, we had to check a couple of cows due to calve in the back paddocks.

We checked the first paddock, and everything was OK. We were riding on the back of the Land Cruiser, hanging on to the rail and 'bouncing' over the bumps—having a great time. Shane was on the right side of the ute, me next, then Dean and Sam. As we finished checking the second paddock, Mum swung around a sharp left hand to get straight at the gate. Well, me, Sam and

Dean all did the usual—which was to hang on with a death grip, with our feet planted—and swung our behinds with the corner. We forgot that Shane was one of the uninitiated and when we went right, we found he wasn't hanging on tightly enough.

Shane sailed off over the side, landing on his arms and shoulder. Mum rammed on the brakes and came out with steam coming out of her ears—yelling at us and asking Shane if he was all right. He was a game kid, so he got up grinning, with only a sore wrist to show for his impromptu flight. Mum tore strips off us and we were all very subdued—for all of five minutes.

From then on, Shane decided to stand in the middle.

Poor old Shane. But did you notice the sympathy in Annette's simple little yarn? We might laugh at the poor old new chum ... but there's usually a hope expressed that they'll eventually come good. A lot of them do, of course, because some of the best new chum yarns come from people having a joke at their own expense.

Typical of these is a yarn from Anne Welling of Dubbo, New South Wales, reminiscing about her days as that newest of new chums—the schoolie, not just out of college, but fresh off the boat as well.

Birds of the Bush

It was a hot Monday morning in a small country town in the central west of New South Wales, right at the beginning of the new school year. I was just nineteen, a recent migrant from England, in charge of my very first class. They were six year olds. We were about to have 'News'.

Jimmy stood up in front of the class, gave a wicked grin and stated, very loudly, 'Paul showed me his dicky bird on the way to school.'

Mistaking the sharp intakes of breath from the class for gasps of approval, and ignoring Paul's hissed, 'Did not!', I turned encouragingly to Jimmy and said, 'Wasn't that so very kind of him? Is this bird very special?', to which Jimmy nodded a doubtful assent.

'Do you know what kind of bird it is?' I queried.

Jimmy became intensely interested in the floorboards and shook his head.

'Well, what colour is it ... blue, green or maybe yellow?'

After describing semicircles with his feet on the floor, Jimmy eventually dragged out, 'Pink, I s'pose.'

'Oh!' I said brightly. 'A galah?'

'No,' said Jimmy. 'Not a galah.'

By now, very curious about this bird, I asked Paul to come out the front and stand beside Jimmy.

'Paul,' I said, 'can you tell me what sort of bird it is you have?'

'No,' stated Paul. He didn't know either.

'Do you keep it in a cage?' I asked, becoming more and more puzzled.

'No. It didn't have a cage.'

'Oh. It must be very tame and friendly not to have it locked up. Will it sit on your finger?' Paul cast a venomous look at Jimmy and muttered, 'If you want it to.'

Reluctantly admitting defeat in working out the exact breed and nature of this mysterious bird, I told them both to sit down and we went on to hear other people's 'News'.

During morning recess, I asked the staff if any of them knew anything about a special bird kept by Paul and related all the blanks I had drawn in my questioning. Light dawned. One male staff member asked, 'Anne, exactly what did Jimmy say to begin with?'

Some time later, when the staff had quite finished choking, this pommy school teacher learned, to her acute embarrassment, that the fondly remembered 'dicky birds' of her English girlhood were not quite the same species as those owned by little boys in the central west of New South Wales.

Anne postscripted her yarn with a wistful, 'I wonder if the two young lads concerned, who would now be in their early thirties, ever recall the day when a very innocent teacher accidentally called their bluff.'

Like most new chums, Anne 'came good'.

Another prerequisite for a new chum is to walk, wide-eyed and innocent, into a situation where his or her ignorance and/or innocence can be exploited to the fullest advantage. Typical is the situation that one JE Averkoff, of Mt Carbine in far north Queensland, observed as he watched the main players in one of outback Australia's rich little comedies.

Take the Map

During the end of the forties and early fifties, in the early part of each year, when the wet season rains made it impossible to do much work on the coast, I would spend my time in the outback of central west and south-west Queensland. I looked for work crutching sheep, when it was available. When nothing was doing in that area of work, I used to team up with an old bushman called Billabong. We'd indulge in odd jobs of fencing, yard-building or windmill-experting—whichever came up. We'd do any kind of work to earn a quid.

Billabong was quite a character, with a sense of humour a mile wide.

One day, we were constructing a fence alongside a road—such as roads *were* in those days on the black soil plains. Suddenly, out of the distance, came a great black cloud of dust which eventually materialised into a large, flash car. It pulled up adjacent to us, and a gent in an expensive silk shirt and tie leaned out of the window and inquired as to how he could find the way to a neighbouring station. It didn't take Billabong long to stroll up to the car. I shuddered as I saw the lopsided grin on his sunburned dial.

'Yeah, mate,' he drawled, as he squatted down beside the car and began drawing a map in the black soil dust. 'You go about five miles down from here. There's a grid. As soon as you cross the grid, you take the road along the right-hand side. After you follow the fence for about three miles, you find a turn-off to the left. Follow this road for about six miles and you come to a bore drain. You have to go *through* the gate here, then you're in the home paddock. You follow the road alongside the bore drain for about a mile and a half ... and you're there.'

The bloke in the car, who had been watching intently, thanked him very much. Billabong asked him, 'Are you sure you won't forget? Just in case—you'd better take the map with you.'

So saying, he scooped up a couple of big handfuls of the black soil dust where he'd scratched the map and turned towards the car. Too slow. By the time he'd straightened up, the vehicle was hidden behind a great cloud of black dust and doing every last bit on a ton.

I felt certain Billabong was going to split a rib before he stopped laughing.

For some obscure reason, a significant number of the new chum yarns submitted to the Search for the Great Australian Yarn seem to dwell, somewhat nauseously, on food and eating. It's strange, bearing in mind that today, rural Australia is renowned for its conservative palate. Perhaps the rough-and-ready gastronomic feats of bygone days have in fact spurred this lack of adventure at the trough as a defence mechanism. On the other hand, maybe yarn spinners like Ken Williams, of Macksville, New South Wales, just like making people feel queasy.

Not Bloody Rabbit Again?

A farmer in Western Australia took on a new hand. For breakfast, lunch and tea—day in, day out, week after week—he was fed a ration of rabbits—baked, fried, grilled, braised and roasted.

Eventually, the new hand became quite violently ill. The boss scratched his head and, when that did no good, gave the patient a strong dose of Epsom salts. The new hand showed no signs of recovery, so the farmer decided it would be cheaper to bring out the local doctor than to bury the poor bloke.

'Hmmm!' said the doctor. 'Looks like food poisoning. What have you been eating?'

'Rabbits, Doc,' moaned the new hand. 'I've ate rabbits for breakfast, lunch and tea, for past three weeks.'

'What treatment have you had?'

'Epsom salts, Doc.'

'My good man,' exclaimed the doctor, 'you don't need Epsom salts. You need ferrets.'

Of course, even the most adventurous palate in the world can't be expected to cope with that ultimate atrocity—a dodgy egg. Martin Bell, of Parkes, New South Wales, came across a mixture of new chum and cackleberries that could make the strongest stomach churn.

Scrambled Eggs

Back in the steam days on the western line, crews would work trains from their depot in Parkes to Ivanhoe over a four or five day period. They'd leave on Monday, work to Euabalong, where they'd camp, then sign on again and work to Ivanhoe, where they'd once again camp before repeating the process on the return journey. They were required to carry all their provisions, and quite often, supplemented their rations with bush tucker.

On this particular trip, the driver and fireman were required to work a ballast train, which was to drop its load between Euabalong and Ivanhoe. The old driver was a pommy migrant with a dubious past, shrouded in mystery and rumour. But one thing was sure—he was a rough diamond, used to living by himself and not having to worry about others. The fireman, on the other hand, was a new chum, just out of training and new to life 'on the road'.

After leaving Euabalong, the train proceeded to the spot where the ballast was to be unloaded. That involved the driver moving his train at a slow walk while a gang of labourers toiled inside each wagon, shovelling the ballast, which consisted mainly of ash, onto the track. The process took a considerable amount of time.

While the train was moving slowly, it was not uncommon for one member of the crew to take the opportunity to walk along beside the track. That's how come the driver decided to take a break and, after handing the controls to the fireman, wandered along the firebreak.

While he was walking, he stumbled across a large plover's nest full of eggs, and being an Englishman, thought that nothing would be better for breakfast the next morning. Returning to the engine, he showed the fireman the eggs and proudly announced that tomorrow's breakfast would be on him.

On reaching Ivanhoe, it was almost tradition that the crew would venture down to the local watering hole to wash the day's dust down. But on this occasion, the dust was very, very stubborn and they didn't return to the barracks until late.

The next morning, the driver was up early frying up the delightful plover's eggs, when the slightly hungover fireman came into the room.

'Breakfast's nearly ready,' he called, as the fireman came over to take a look.

Peering into the frying pan, the young fireman was greeted with the sight of the fried eggs, complete with eyes, half-formed legs and wings, bubbling away in a pool of fat.

With a look of horror, he gasped, 'Urrrrgh! I don't like fried eggs very much . . . ' and raced for the door.

'That's all right,' the driver said, reaching for a fork. 'We can have 'em scrambled.'

Look, it's probably politically incorrect to point it out, but an awful lot of these new chum yarns are about . . . well, let's be daring and face it . . . pommies. We'll get into some more politically incorrect material later, but while we're pommy-bashing, here's a scurrilous tale from Jim Foster of Mount Gambier, South Australia.

The Pommy and the Emus

A long time ago, when I was just a young fellow, I worked on a cattle station in south-west Queensland. It was there I met a young pommy bloke. His name was Jim Corbett. I've a suspicion it wasn't his real name—rather, one he chose for himself—but we didn't ask questions. The real Jim Corbett was a famous boxer, world champion heavyweight of years gone by, if I remember right. This Jim didn't measure up to his namesake—not by a long chalk, if the fight outside the pub at Hungerford was any indication. Jim and I ended up in the brand-new gaolhouse, the one that was so new it didn't have any locks on the doors. We didn't notice at the time ... but that's another story.

I was the station windmill expert. It was my job to fix any of the windmills when they broke down ... and they often did. One day, the mill in the back paddock, seventy-five kilometres out from the homestead, stopped pumping. It was the deepest bore on the property and I needed help to pull the pump—so I was given Jim and a jackeroo (whose name escapes me) to help out.

We made our camp a few hundred metres away from the tank and windmill inside a small stand of mulga trees. We never bothered with a tent or anything—just an old wire stretcher to unroll our swags on, was good enough. Sleeping in a swag is a great way to sleep in the bush. A good swag is waterproof and warm. They keep out the cold and the wind. You can camp out snug in a white frost in a good swag. I always liked a swag, but Jim Corbett didn't. It wasn't that they were uncomfortable. He just hated his head to be uncovered when he was sleeping. To overcome that, he placed the head of his stretcher next to a mulga tree and draped a sheet of snowy white new canvas above his head, down over his bed. It kept the dew off his face and was less trouble than a proper tent. We unloaded the gear and left it piled about the camp. It was pretty much of a mess, but it was easy to find things.

I woke the next morning, just when there was enough light to see, but still a long time before sun-up. The camp was full of emus. Well, I just lay there and watched them. They're very inquisitive, but usually can't do any harm or damage unless they receive a sudden scare.

One of the emus, a huge bird, began strutting around Jim's bed, drumming low in his chest like they do. The white canvas had him fascinated. A couple more emus began to follow the lead of the big bloke and soon there were half a dozen of them circling the poor pommy's bed—like a mob of Indians circling a wagon train.

Suddenly, the big bull emu stopped, stretched his neck out and peered down under the canvas. Moving from side to side and from one foot to the other with an urgent curiosity that made his tail feathers look as if they belonged to an excited puppy, he strained forward another quivering step.

I lay on my bed, cramming my mouth with dusty canvas as I fought to suppress the mirth that threatened to interrupt the almost unbelievable comedy unfolding in front of me.

As the bull emu stepped closer, so did the others, with their straggly necks stretched to the fullest. The poor pommy was totally surrounded but oblivious of his peculiar audience. He slumbered peacefully on.

Finally, the big emu could restrain himself no longer. Stepping up to the unsuspecting pommy's bed, he thrust his head down under the white canvas while the rest of the mob looked on. At the same time, he gave out with a loud drumming that reverberated among the dawn-lit mulga trees like a Harley Davidson accelerating up a steep hill at full throttle.

For the length of time it takes to draw one deep breath, nothing happened. But then there was the most incredible hair-raising shriek from the pommy. Half a dozen emus fell over backwards. In their haste to remove themselves from the vicinity of the white-draped apparition that flew straight up in the air in front of them, they forgot they weren't equipped with legs capable of moving backwards. The result was a dozen long scaly legs thrashing in the air as feathers flew in clouds that almost obscured my view of poor Jim smashing his canvas-draped head into the mulga tree and rendering himself unconscious.

Finding their feet, the whole mob of emus dashed panic-stricken and wild-eyed back and forth through the camp, kicking everything in it to pieces. They blundered into the jackeroo's bed and tipped him out of it, scaring the poor blighter half to death as they stampeded off through the trees.

I lay back in my swag, totally helpless. I was so overcome with mirth that the jackeroo began to think that I was in dreadful pain.

It took most of the morning to put the camp back in order. When Jim woke up, he quit. He said no one had told him how dangerous the job was. I had to take him back to the homestead, so I lost a whole day's work. But it was worth it. Seeing the pommy's bed surrounded by those emus with their long legs in the air, was the funniest thing I'd ever seen.

Max Overton, another resident of Dubbo, New South Wales, is a yarn spinner of the 'bigger and better' school. In other words, he's a liar. The only reason I didn't include him in the previous chapter was that his particular lies concern a new chum—a breed of rarely considered bigger or better than anyone or anything.

The Horse Tailer

I'd like to tell you this story about a young city bloke named Jim, who wanted a job in the bush. He read about this job at Lake Splash Station, way up in the cattle country of Queensland: 'Wanted—horse tailer; some cattle experience an advantage.'

Well, he'd had a ride or two on a baker's cart, so he knew about horses' tails. And he'd spent a couple of hours in the yard of a local dairy, so he applied ... and got the job.

He got a letter telling him to catch the train to Longreach, then the mail coach to Lake Splash.

A ticket to Lake Splash via Longreach? It had the ticket bloke at Flinders Street Station tossed. They eventually sorted it out. It took three days to reach Longreach, but the mail coach bloke said, 'No go, mate. She's rained a bit out there and the creeks are up. It'll be a couple of months before we can drive through. Better put up at the pub.'

The poor young feller was down to the last quid his old man had given him. Cried all night, he did.

Early next morning, the coppers came to see if the water pipes had busted, because the gully back of the pub was a banker. Gawd! he cried. When the cops found out what was up, they sent a smoke signal to the manager of Lake Splash about the kid, and the boss just hopped into his plane and picked him up, then dropped him off at the mustering camp with his swag had a chunder over Jundah, the poor kid.

'Here's your new horse tailer, Fred,' the boss told his head stockman. 'He's done a bit of horse tailing and cattle work down in Victoria.'

'He'll be right,' said Fred.

So, he showed the kid the night horse and told him to slip around the spare horses and water them and then help the cook get tea—it being the horse tailer's job to help the cook.

Horses? Hell, he'd never seen 700 in one mob, or imagined there was that many anywhere . . . and all of them crippled in the front legs (or that's what he thought, with the hobbles on them). Once he'd fixed the horses, the cook said he wanted to do over a couple of killers.

'Killers? Hell, this must be pretty wild country. Where'd they escape from?'

'Silly bugger—the ringers eat them.'

'Ringers? What's ringers?'

'The ringers what ring up the cattle, lad.'

'Come off it, Fred. There ain't no phones. Even the cops had to send smoke signals to the boss. You're having me on.'

The killers, of course, were a couple of lumpy bullocks to feed the 250 ringers.

That camp was beside one of them flowing artesian bores. The killers were just shot, pulled up on a sky hook and dropped into the hot water in the bore tank with a couple of bags of Kiwi cure.

'Why don't you skin 'em?' asked Jim.

'Nah,' said the cook. 'They're best boiled in their jackets, like spuds.'

While the meat was cooking, the cook announced he'd better knock up a damper—that's some damper for 250 ringers. First they dragged a few carcasses out of the overflow hole near the tanks, snigged over a couple of dozen bags of flour and tipped them in. How'd they mix it? No trouble. The kid was sent to get about twenty of his horses and drove them round and round (without their hobbles, of course).

He mixed it up really good. Of course, he had a bag of baking powder and a bit of salt on the pommel and spread it as he rode round behind the horses. A bit of hot water from the bore—and she was soon a lovely, fluffy dough. You won't believe it when I tell you how they cooked it.

Well, in Queensland, they always take out plenty of turps (rum, for the uninitiated) so the ringers can wash out their gobs after a hard day's branding. Then they all sit around yarning. This time, as the ringers rode into camp, they let their horses go for the horse tailer to water and hobble out. Then they grabbed their quart pots, filled them with rum and sat around the nice, fluffy damper. In no time, the hot air from the lies they told, the fumes off the rum, and methane gas from the bull shit, had cooked the damper to perfection.

As soon as the beef was cooked and pulled outa the tank, the cook chucked in a couple of chests of tea—that's how they made beef tea, see—and the ringers just dipped it out as they wanted it. A chainsaw was handy to cut off a slab of meat and a chunk of damper.

On the first long weekend, the head stockman said Jim could leave the horses on grass and have the weekend off. So he borrowed a big roan night horse and slipped home to tell his old man how he was getting on. He got away about sunrise on Saturday and pulled up at home in Carlton, Victoria, about sundown. Gee his dad was pleased to see him. They went into

Young and Jacksons for a few beers and a look at Chloe, the nude sheila. Jim told his old man about his job and all the cattle, horses and ringers and that the place was bigger than Victoria. He told him about how one morning he was told to steady the lead of a mob they were counting out at a big bronco yard. They started about sun up. At eleven o'clock, he cantered back eight miles and they were just counting out the tailers. It was a big mob, all right.

After Sunday at home with his mum, Jim left Carlton on Monday afternoon and, by taking the short cut back to camp, had the horses up for the ringers and helped the cook get breakfast on Tuesday morning. That roan was a good horse, eh?

I suppose you're wondering where this kid Jim got to. Well, after a couple of years horse tailing, he went back to Melbourne and joined the police RUI squad—that's Riding Under the Influence—checking on horsemen and women jockeys. But he reckons after all the bull he's been through and the lies he's heard, he's set to become a successful politician.

Again, our new chum eventually made it.

But sometimes, making it can be a bit dangerous. Often, when a new chum came good, he started to make the local knuckle draggers feel threatened.

Max Ward of Miles, Queensland, was able to combine a lot of new chum elements in his little yarn. I'm therefore prepared to forgive him for putting it into verse. It's got poms, bush cuisine . . . the lot.

Spider and the Pom

We were sitting around the campfire, telling jokes and
　　spinning yarns.
A few of the young fellows were trying to break each other's
　　arms.
But they soon found out the strongest and the toughest of
　　them all,

Was a skinny-looking Englishman, about six seven tall.

Now the Aussie boys don't like it when they're beaten at
  their game,
And they swore they would get this pommy with the lanky-
  looking frame.
Now a young fellow known as Spider, horse tailer with some
  pride,
Came up with a bright idea to burn this pommy's hide.

Well, he went down to the kitchen. He knew just what to
  do,
To teach this pommy so-and-so, a few things he never knew.
Well, there upon the pantry shelf, he thought, 'Why here
  they are!'
Just what he was looking for—red hot chillies in a jar.

Now chillies are a tasty treat, used sparingly in a stew,
But when eaten from the bottle can have strange effects on
  you.
He looked through all the bottles, there was one in the lot
That had 'Mild' written on it. The rest were marked 'Hot!'

So he took two of the bottles and he smiled an evil grin,
One was for the pommy bloke—the other was for him.
Then he went back to the campfire where the boys were
  telling lies,
And he noticed that the pommy's head had grown some-
  what in size.

He was still there bragging about his special powers.
If Spider hadn't stopped him then he would have bragged
  for hours.
Now Spider saw an opening. He said, 'I've seen enough.
'I bet your sickly gizzard wouldn't be so tough.'

Well, the pommy came in quickly, as fire showed in his eye,
'I could live out in the desert, where the rest of you
  would die.
'And I've eaten snakes and lizards, saddle flaps and uncooked
  'roo,

'And I've even had a go at cats, with a salt bush stew.

'If you think your stomach's better and can take much more
   than mine,
'Have you ever followed crows along for the scraps they've
   left behind?'
It was there that Spider stopped him. He said, 'I know
   you're pretty good.
'I was going to make you a challenge, but I don't know if I
   should.

'You see, I've got two bottles of chillies—not too hot.
'But I don't think that you should eat them, if your sto-
   mach's apt to rot.'
The pom said, 'You'll never beat me but I'll tell you what I'll
   do,
'I'll bet you fifty dollars, I eat twice as much as you.'

Well, Spider produced the chillies and two forks that he had
   found,
While the pommy's face was smiling as his foot tapped on
   the ground.
He said, 'Mother fed me chillies when I was just a child,
'And the curries that my father made would make this stuff
   taste mild.'

Well, the jars were quickly opened and the contest had
   begun,
As the ringers gathered round them to enjoy a bit of fun.
Now Spider ate in silence but the pom, he liked to brag.
He said, 'They're bloody lovely, I must carry some in my
   swag.'

Well, his jar was nearly empty, taking two to Spider's one,
But he looked a little worried about the swelling of his
   tongue.
He ate the last red chilli and mumbled they were good,
Though his eyes were rolling sideways and not looking
   where they should.

'Well, I've eaten all your chillies, now you'll have to pay your bet.'
But Spider said, 'I don't think so, it's a little early yet.
'I'll pay you in the morning, when I see you fit and well,
'But if you're not out on the job, you'll have no hope in hell.'

'I think you're trying to do me and take me for a ride,
'But if you don't pay up tomorrow, then I'll have your bloody hide.'
His colour started changing, you could almost smell the fire,
As he headed for the quarters and said, 'I think I might retire.'

Well, all night long, the pommy moaned and called out for his mum,
As Spider smiled and listened, he thought, 'The best is still to come.
'I'll get him in the morning when it sneaks up from behind,
'For chillies have a habit that they burn a second time.'

Well at breakfast in the morning, the poor bloke, he didn't show,
And the boss was asking where he was, but no one seemed to know.
Then Spider said he saw him heading down towards the loo,
He reckoned he was acting queer and looked about to spew.

Then they heard a mighty shout. It came from in the loo.
The language was unacceptable. The air was turning blue.
Well, he came out of the dunny door, his trousers at half mast,
For all the world it looked as though he was trying to outrun his past.

He headed for the station dam. He passed a startled 'roo.
They reckon you can still see his tracks from back in sixty-two.
He climbed out of the muddy dam, badly shaken, but never beat.

He said, 'I don't know what you fed me, but it surely had
    some heat.'

'Now if you blokes will excuse me, it must be getting late,
'And I'm absolutely starving. It's been a long time since I ate.'
Well, Spider shook him by the hand and humbly paid his
    bet.
He said, 'You've got the toughest gut that I've run into yet.'

It wasn't long before these two became the best of mates.
They both agreed the past was gone and that friendship
    highly rates.
But Spider knew one day he'd tell, he'd probably write a
    letter,
And apologise for the night he laced the chillies with
    cayenne pepper.

Wasn't that sweet?

Of course, not all poms of 'young men from the city' attempted anything as tough as becoming stockmen. There's a school of short story writing and yarn-spinning I rather self-indulgently call the Prickle Farm School—based on my very own writings in the 1980s about urban people trying to scratch a living out of the land. I'd like to think it's a result of my influence that so many people adopt that scenario to write and spin their own yarns. However, it's obviously been around for a lot longer than I have.

Of course, at the Prickle Farm School, the villains of the piece don't have to be horse teams, disgruntled bigoted ringers, continuous drought or the vast outback. You can come to grief with long drop dunnies, garden hoses and chooks.

Beatty Blennerhesset of Bengworden, Victoria, has already appeared in this slim and enlightening volume. Yes, folks, it's more verse. Sorry.

Trying the Country Life

A young man from the city,
Thought he'd like to try Country Life,
So he headed on up to a bush block,
The man, and his dog and his wife.
'Chook farming's the type I'd like to try.'
So he sent off in the mail.
'Please send me three hundred chickens,
'And send them COD, without fail.'
Soon those chickens all arrived
But in a few days, all were dead,
So off he sent for three hundred more,
'And COD,' he said.
In time arrived *those* chickens,
But in time, they, too, had died.
He didn't know what had gone wrong,
But at least he knew he'd tried.
Again he sent for some *more* chickens,
Again, to be sent COD,
But this time the wily chook farmer said,
'I'd better go up there and see.'
He took a box of chickens,
And drove on up to the farm.
'I've brought you up those chickens,
'And to see why they've come to harm.
'What happened to those chickens?
'Why did those chickens die?'
'Please come and look,' said the new chum,
'You'll see I really did try.'
He took him to a ploughed paddock,
Ploughed up as well as could be,
And pointed to little stick things
(They looked like legs to me).
'What did I do wrong?' the new chum asked.
The cry came from his heart.
'Did I plant those chickens in too deep?
'Or did I plant them too far apart?'

Oh, Beatty.

New chums always seemed to have more problems back in the days when we relied on horses for transport, and on-farm muscle. That's when this yarn, from Ernie Bowers, of Edmonton, Queensland, dates from.

Vice Squad

During the Great Depression, this unemployed fitter and turner couldn't find work at his particular trade in his local surroundings, so he decided, like many others, to hump his swag.

After travelling many miles, and receiving plenty of knock-backs, one day he came across a very well-to-do station owner.

This station owner had a number of well-bred blood horses. He interviewed the fitter and turner and asked him if he had any experience with horses. The city bloke decided to change his story and said that horses were what he was best at. The owner agreed to give him a go. He gave the fitter a set of horse shoes and told him to go into the big shed at the back and shoe his blood mare.

After some time, the boss thought he'd better take a look to see how the new bloke was going. When he got to the shed, he found the valuable mare lying on her back, with her legs up in the air.

'What the hell happened?' asked the boss.

The city bloke replied, 'I don't know. She was all right till I took her legs out of the vice.'

Isn't it strange how bosses seem to get preferential treatment in new chum yarns? Long suffering they may well be, but it's not often anyone gets the better of them. To set the record straight, I thought I'd best include this yarn from Ted Evans, of Coonamble, New South Wales.

A Trick of the Light

When I was a young fellow, many years ago, I was working on a property out past Moree. It was a good two days' sulky drive to town, and that was with a bloody good horse, too.

On this particular trip to town, in the sulky with the boss, we came to this large lake. Would you believe it? Two ducks were sitting up in the middle.

As it was almost lunchtime, the boss stopped the horse and grabbed the single-barrelled shotgun from under the seat. He then stalked the two ducks through the 'lignum, until he lined them up and fired, shooting both of them with one shot.

He then rolled his trousers, removed his boots and waded out to get them.

When he got there, he found he had shot two plovers sitting out on a mirage.

These days, the ultimate new chum in the bush is, undoubtedly, the poor old tourist. Tourist operators could probably knock together half a million volumes simply of quotable lines from their charges.

Here's just one, from Bob McLean, of Wodonga, Victoria.

The Aboriginal Carving

The holiday bus tour set off to Darwin with a full complement of passengers. They were all anxious to see and experience the numerous scenes and attractions along the route. They saw parks, sacred sites and a host of outstanding attractions. In short, the passengers were delighted.

On leaving Katherine, the guide made an announcement, 'We will soon be approaching an Aboriginal carving which I know you'd love to have a look at.'

When they reached their destination, the guide said, 'Everyone out to see the Aboriginal carving.' They trooped off—all except one lady, who refused to move from the bus.

'Don't you want to see the Aboriginal carving, lady?' the guide asked.

'Not on your life. I once saw a cow calving—and it nearly made me sick.'

Chapter 3

WHO HAVEN'T WE OFFENDED?

Isn't it interesting that in these times, when we're supposed to be working flat out to be Politically Correct in everything we say, that no one has exactly stood up and admitted responsibility for it? No one's said, 'Yes, it's all my idea and you have to do what I say.' God knows whose idea it originally was, but there seems to be an awful lot of people (in every sense of the word), prepared to enforce the dreary doctrine.

And when you look at what's going on in the world today, you can't help but wonder why more effort isn't made to ensure that Political Correctness applies to what people actually *do* rather than what they merely *say*.

Sadly, humour looks like being the first victim of Political Correctness ... which isn't fair. I'm fairly certain no one's ever been incited to hatred, violence or bitterness by a good yarn. Look, there are stories I wouldn't give any recognition to because they are out-and-out sexist, racist or bigoted. In fact, perhaps the best yarn I ever heard is terribly racist. It's funny, clever and everything else. Unfortunately, its true colours don't reveal themselves until the very last sentence. That's why it's not included in any of my books.

On the other hand, I found very few of the entries in the Search for the Great Australian Yarn objectionable. From the hundreds of entries, there was *none* from men poking fun at women—in any shape or form. There were a lot from women poking fun at themselves and scores from them poking gentle fun at mere males. Homosexuals weren't vilified (or even mentioned, for that matter). And the rest? Well, there are a lot of yarns concerning the differences between various races and cultures—but they all exuded good humour.

It's odd, isn't it, that the accusations of racist humour tend to be levelled at yarns about some of the most naturally laughter-prone people of earth—Aborigines, the Irish, the aged and the disabled? As one disgruntled Kiwi once complained after several hours of being bombarded with non-stop New Zealand one-liners: 'It's not fair. I come to Australia and hear all these great jokes—but once I get home I won't be able to use them.'

So here, then, is a chapter of yarns that some poor souls may consider Politically Incorrect. If they offend you, I'm saddened rather than sorry, but I personally take full responsibility.

And just who am I, to be so magnanimous?

I'm just a half-Irish, long-haired, rapidly ageing migrant from pommy land, with more than a touch of the Sri Lankan tarbrush. I have kids with learning disabilities and epilepsy; a swag of Aboriginal in-laws; a few of my best mates flap their wrists most suspiciously when they talk; and I grew up with an Italian family living on one side, and Hungarians on the other. I'm a pretty average Australian.

I'd like to think the truth about Australian attitudes is somewhere along the lines suggested by a snippet sent in to the ABC's competition by Ken Hodgson, of Port Macquarie, New South Wales.

The Lucky Country

'Wonderful country, this Australia', said migrant Hans. 'Everyone's very hospitable, too.'

'Why are you being so complimentary, mate?' asked his Aussie companion.

'Well, over here, you meet someone, he invites you home for dinner, gives you the best wine and whisky, asks you to stay the night, gives you breakfast and puts fifty dollars under the pillow.'

'Come off it,' scoffed his mate. 'How often has that happened to you?'

'Never,' came the reply. 'But five times, it's happened to my sister.'

But we can't deny there is racism in our community. Back in my childhood, I can remember the same sort of irrational bigotry being levelled at our Italian and Hungarian neighbours that is now directed at Aborigines, Asians and people from the Middle East (often by people whose own roots might well be Italian or Hungarian). Sadly, in many areas, the times aren't really changing all that much—only the names are.

Reg Della Bosca, of Orange, New South Wales, knows what I'm talking about. Here's his yarn.

Awkward Pause

Despite our belief in our tolerance and image of equality, there have been some glaring examples of racism, sexism and, on occasions, fascist-like bullying of minority groups in Australia. The Mabo decision brought utterances from the business and mining interests, National Party and significant community leaders, which would have made Mussolini blush.

Racism has always been around. People who are different or do things differently are always a source of suspicion to the uninformed, or those who just don't have minds broad enough to see past their noses.

At the turn of the century, there was racism against Italian migrants. The white Anglo-Saxon Protestants in the Australian Workers Union caused such a ruckus about their jobs being in danger that the union was continually attacking the 'illiterate and dirty dagoes', who according to the union, were stealing their jobs. A government report, commissioned under pressure, found there was less crime among the Italians and, even more interestingly from a union point of view, less scab labour. Anyway, my story is set in Lithgow, much later.

Mary Renshaw was a popular dancing widow, who conscientiously looked after her ageing father. In country towns in those days, good dancers were in great demand and Mary could dance like a fairy.

Accordingly, she was in demand by a couple of old friends— men who sought her out for her dancing skills as much as for her great sense of humour. Her blue eyes and aquiline good looks indicated a quick intelligence and she was always shown the deep respect which, in working class areas, indicates a family held in high regard.

Mary was in the company of two long-term dancing friends on this particular evening, at the Wednesday night Scottish Old Time dance in the Lithgow Town Hall, when a conversation started up. The talk was about a new man in town—a recently arrived Italian, who had bought a local popular cafe.

'Been to the Silver Bird Cafe lately?' asked Number One friend.

'Yes, mate,' replied Number Two. 'Bloody New Australian dago's bought it. Geez it's dirty.'

Mary looked up intently at the use of the word 'dago'.

'Dirty lot, these wogs,' observed friend Number One.

There was an *awkward pause* as Mary put her stole on slowly and checked her handbag.

'Where are you going, Mary?' both men asked.

'Well, I'm off home. I'm going to get my father out of bed, get a big scrubbing brush, put him in the bloody bath and scrub him clean.'

With that, she walked out of the dance imperiously.

Both friends suddenly recalled the name of Mary's father—Giuseppe Antonia Della Bosca.

It's interesting what Reg said about prejudices against people just because they *did* things differently. It's like the criticism that's always been made of Aborigines simply because they don't seem to share the same work ethic as Europeans. That's conveniently counterbalanced by that other prejudice, levelled against most migrants since the Chinese in the goldrush days, and extended to our postwar Mediterranean Australians and today's Asian Australians—because they allegedly work *too* bloody hard!

Around Crookwell, where we lived for some years, a yarn's still told about an old Chinese market gardener called Sunday Tommy.

Me Next!

Like a lot of so-called foreigners, Sunday Tommy endured an odd mixture of respect for his diligence and hard work, and harassment because he was 'different'. He used to grow vegies in a series of plots on what's now the property Norfolk Rise, and take them a couple of kilometres into town in an old horse and cart.

One morning, a local cockie, riding into town, found Sunday Tommy's horse and cart slap-bang in the middle of the road. The old Chinaman was around the front end, trying unsuccessfully to get the ancient nag to move.

'What seems to be the trouble?' asked the cockie.

'This bloody horse, he no go,' complained Tommy. 'He just stop and no start again.'

The cockie climbed down from his mount and inspected Tommy's horse.

'Get him out of the traces, Tommy. Maybe you've got too heavy a load for him to pull.' Together they undid the harness and pushed the horse out of the shafts. It still didn't seem too keen to move.

'No good. He properly buggered,' observed the old market gardener.

'No worries, Tommy. He's just lost heart. He needs something to spur him on. Do you have any methylated spirits?'

'Sure, sure,' muttered the old bloke, rummaging under the seat of his cart. Sure enough, he pulled out an old brown bottle stoppered up with a piece of rag. The cockie took the bottle, removed the bung and used it to smear some metho around the horse's arsehole.

In seconds, the old nag let out a whinny of pain and fright and started galloping full bore into Crookwell.

'There you are, Tommy,' said the cockie, full of self-satisfaction. 'That got him going.'

Without saying a word, the old Chinese man dropped his strides and turned his back on the cockie.

'Geez! What the hell are you trying to do Tommy?'

'All right. Now you do the same thing to me. I've got to catch the bastard.'

Similarly, the hardworking migrant in the yarn sent in by Bill McKay, of Lakes Entrance, Victoria, could be about any of the hundreds of thousands of people, from all over the world, who played a vital role in developing rural Australia.

Self-defence

Well, it was like this, you see.

Old Tony had lost his wife and was living alone. He lived on a fair-sized block, about an acre or more, and he really did grow beautiful fruit.

And that's where the trouble began. Tony's block was close to a fair-sized town, and in that town were a lot of lads with taking ways—and they gave poor old Tony a hard time. They took his peaches, nectarines, plums and apples.

He was a good-hearted old bloke and would have *given* the lads a feed if they'd asked for it, but no, they had to come and pinch his fruit. Worse still, they had a habit of breaking the limbs off the trees. Tony used to call out to them, telling them to come to him if they wanted fruit but that wasn't their game at all. And they called old Tony names that could only be described as very, very rude!

Finally, Tony had had enough. He got out the old shotgun and a cartridge. He emptied out the shot, filled the cartridge with wheat, tamped it down neatly and poured candle grease over the top to keep it firm.

The next time the lads came back, Tony shoved the cartridge back into the shotgun and let fly. The local villains let out a bellow of pain and they all shot through.

But Tony had hit the lad much harder than he had anticipated and it was a good job for the doctor. Then the police were notified and Tony was charged with unlawful wounding.

When the time came for Tony to tell the magistrate of his woes, he went into the witness box and explained, 'Alla time, they come to my place and steala da fruit. They calla me the wog bastard. I notta the wog bastard. I bloody good wog. I giva plenny fruit for nothing. They smasha down my trees. They breaka the limbs. So I tella them, "You keep away my place or I shoot!" I getta the gun and the shot—notta the *real* shot—only the wheat.'

By the time the magistrate had got the hang of things, he was feeling a bit sorry for Tony and he said, 'Well, then, you fired the gun and shot the man in defence?'

'No,' insisted Tony, 'I not shoot him in defence.'

The magistrate was intrigued. 'Well, what did you do?'

'I shoot him in the arse and he *jumpa* da fence.'

And so, on to the Irish.

Perhaps the Irish joke thing *has* gone a bit too far. There was something on the news recently about an Irishman in Britain being sacked because he'd decided he'd had enough of his mates constantly joking about his nationality—and had stopped laughing at the jokes. On the other hand, the best collection of Irish jokes I ever saw was in fact put out by the Irish Tourist Board. Cynics might suggest that's an Irish joke in itself. But really, despite that troubled island's centuries of woe, the Irish can justifiably claim to have put the twinkle in most of the Western world's eye. And they've been doing it for some time, too. So, just for the record, here's a couple of yarns that shouldn't upset anyone from Ireland.

The first comes from G McLeod, of Swan Hill, Victoria.

Pleased to Meet You

This yarn has to be told with an Irish accent, where required.

This old Irishman was standing on a bridge over the Yarra River in Melbourne. He was leaning on the rail, with his lunch bag in his hand, looking intently down into the water. He'd been there for some time looking down when two young policemen, patrolling the bridge, noticed him. One of them approached the old bloke and asked, 'Is there anything wrong?'

The old feller answered, 'Me mate fell in the water. Me mate fell in the water.'

The young constable called to his colleague, 'Hey! The old bloke's mate has fallen into the river.'

Both of them ran to the end of the bridge, then down the embankment to the river. They stripped off and started duck diving. After fifteen minutes or so, they were both exhausted but hadn't found anybody.

'We'd better go and break the news to the old bloke, I suppose,' said one of the constables. He walked slowly to where the old Irishman had been watching the proceedings with some interest. The young policeman put this hand on Paddy's shoulder and said softly, 'I'm sorry, but we couldn't find your lost friend. The water's too deep and murky.'

'What d'y' mean?' the bloke cackled. 'I don't know nothing about no lost friend. I meant the mate out of me sandwiches.'

Then there's a touch of Blarney from John Scott, of Condobolin, New South Wales.

Tom

Tom was as Irish as Paddy's pigs. He came to Australia as a teenager in 1910, worked hard as a farm hand in the central west of New South Wales and bought his first farm in 1935.

Tom had a comment for every situation, always delivered without cracking a smile.

A neighbour called on Tom one day while he was ploughing. One of the plough wheels was squeaking like a demented politician.

'How often do you oil your plough, Tom?' asked the visitor.

'Once a week, whether it needs it or not,' was the reply.

During their few minutes of conversation, Tom said he aimed to finish the paddock next day. Two days later, they met again at a sheep sale.

'Did you finish your paddock, Tom?'

'No, I had to knock off yesterday. That wind was so strong, it kept blowing the plough out of the furrow.'

Tom was sensitive to changes in the usage of words but always came out on top of any situation. At the same time, he was always polite to the opposite sex.

One day, he went into a department store and a young lady came to serve him.

'A roll of sanitary paper, please Miss.'

'You mean toilet paper, sir?'

'We call it sanitary paper at our place, Miss.'

'Well, sir, it's called toilet paper now.'

'OK! A roll of toilet paper please, Miss.'

'Anything else, sir?'

'Yes, a cake of soap please, Miss.'

'Toilet soap, sir?'

'No thank you, Miss. I only want to wash my face with it.'

Another rarely recognised group of 'different' people who helped develop the outback were the so-called Afghan traders. In truth, they came from many Eastern countries, but were mostly catalogued under the generic nationality of Afghan. They did the rounds of the small, embryonic bush towns and lonely stations, selling general merchandise, hardware and food. It's interesting that, usually, they seem to have been regarded far more charitably than other 'foreigners'. Perhaps it was because their wares were otherwise so hard to come by.

John Scott has another reminiscence about hawkers.

Death Becomes Nerang

The brothers Kissan and Nerang were Indians and farmed a fairly rough block from 1925 to 1950. They spoke their own arrangement of the English language. If they borrowed something without first asking, they explained it: 'No like stealem; just takem.'

In those days, cracked and broken wheat was called 'chick wheat'. But to Kissan and Nerang, it was 'rooster feed'.

They were usually placid, but sometimes quite the opposite. When they encountered a problem which they could not handle, one or both of the brothers walked or ran across the paddocks to their very good neighbour, Walter.

One day Kissan arrived in a state of great agitation.

'Oh Walter, Walter, you come quick. Old Nerang—he dead.'

Nerang was prone to passing out, and fortunately, a sister from the hospital had told Walter that if Nerang was in a coma, he would need a tablet placed under his tongue. So Walter hurried to the brothers' humble dwelling, found the tablets beside the bed, put one in place and stayed until Nerang revived. At the same time, he tried to explain to Kissan the importance of the life-saving procedure.

However, about a week later, Kissan repeated the performance.

'Oh Walter, Walter, you come quick. Old Nerang—he dead again!'

I mentioned in *Yarns!* how Aboriginal Australians are probably the world's greatest natural yarn spinners. And their sense of humour, put to far greater test than even that of the Irish, is second to none. Sadly, most yarns about Aborigines serve only to denigrate them. However, I couldn't resist this one from Leo Davis of the Eventide Home in Canowindra, New South Wales.

On the Right Track

I was out on a property called Bahloo, between Nyngan and Bourke. Sixteen thousand acres—if you can take it away in one shovel full, you can have it!

The property belongs to my daughter and husband. They run 2000 sheep, plus kangaroos, goats and wild pigs. One time, we lost 1000 sheep, a week off shearing. The fence wasn't too good in places, but I didn't think they got out that way.

Rhonda was just lying there in the shade. Feeling fit, I decided to mount her. Hang on! Don't get the wrong idea. Rhonda's just my four-wheel drive Honda.

Anyway, I set sail looking for those lost sheep. But I couldn't find any.

So I went to Bourke trying to find a black tracker. Again, no luck, so I went out along a little track, about a mile out of town, and there I came across an old Aboriginal man moving around on his hands and knees, staring intently at the ground.

'What's up, mate?' I asked.

'I'm doing a bit of tracking.'

My ears pricked up. 'What are you tracking?'

'A car.'

'What sort of car?'

'A Holden ute.'

Uncanny. 'What else do you know about it?'

He paused for a while, still looking at the tracks in the sand. 'There's two black ladies sitting in front, with a white man driving.'

Amazing.

'In the back there's an old army blanket, a Rinso box full of groceries and four slabs of VB.'

'Crikey!' I said. 'You're really good. I'm looking for a tracker like you. How do you know all that stuff?'

'Easy, I only fell out of the bloody ute twenty minutes ago.'

Some of the greatest culture shock endured by bush Australians has been a result of the massive increase in Japanese tourism. The only thing to compare with it is the culture shock endured by our Japanese visitors. The advent of farm holidays for these tourists has resulted in a lot of a good-natured misunderstanding. I'm sure the laughter eventually generated by those 'clashes' has done more to strengthen relationships between ourselves and the real Japanese people than all the seminars, trade delegations and cultural missions put together.

A typical collision between two alien worlds was recorded by Elizabeth Walker of Mt Gambier, South Australia.

Making Do

My daughter Anne is a university exchange student in Tokyo, Japan. After several visits, she's quite familiar with the traditional Japanese way of life. However, to some of her Japanese friends, Australia is shrouded in mystery. So it was with great joy that two male colleagues of her's told her they were at last off on their great adventure—a trip to the great south land of Australia. They knew that tourist attractions would be readily available to them, but they desired to see the way that Australians lived and sought her help in achieving that.

Her two friends wanted very much to see inside a real Australian home. Anne contacted me and I agreed to show them mine. As most Japanese holidays are only a week long, the time for the visit was set for an afternoon they'd be travelling through Mt Gambier. I set to work to make my home look as attractive as possible. I thoroughly spring-cleaned all the rooms and placed fresh flowers in the lounge and hall. Satisfied with my efforts, I sat back to await the visitors.

As the time drew near, I decided to take a last look through the house to make sure that everything was all right. I was feeling quite happy, until I cast my eyes around the toilet. I gasped in horror when I realised we had run out of toilet paper. What was I to do?

There was no time to race to the shop and I certainly couldn't have the Japanese thinking Australians were like the Balinese, who dispense with paper and use their hands. My daughter was never going to forgive me for neglecting this detail. At this stage, there seemed to be nothing that could be done. My mind had gone blank.

Suddenly, my eye fell upon the sewing machine and I saw a way out. I ran to the drawer and got out a heap of paper patterns which I used often to cut out garments. The paper was the right texture, surely?

Holding my breath and praying that there would be no knock, I put together a tidy pile. Then, seizing the scissors, I quickly cut several thicknesses into squares and placed them neatly above the cistern. Hardly had I finished, when I heard the discreet knock, and trying to appear cool yet welcoming, I opened the door to the two young Japanese.

After bowing and pleasantries had been exchanged in halting English, we began a tour of my house. The visitors smiled and exclaimed over different items, but as they spoke only in their own language, I was unable to gauge their true impressions. They left me with many bows and I could only hope that they would take a good report back to Anne.

I waited in great apprehension to hear the result. It came via the telephone, with Anne immediately asking, 'What did you do? How did you do it?'

My heart sank. 'Your friends . . .' I began timidly. 'They weren't impressed with our way of life? The house wasn't grand enough?'

'But they *were*. They *were* impressed,' cried Anne. 'They were amazed. They noted dishwasher, the computer, the microwave oven, the video recorder . . . They just couldn't get over the toilet. How did you do it?'

'What was wrong with the toilet?' I dreaded what I might hear.

'My friends,' replied Anne, 'decided that, with all the mod cons,

Australia's technology did indeed compare with Japan's. But they couldn't stop talking about the toilet being different from theirs, which is usually just a recess in the floor. And they were full of admiration for—of all things—the toilet paper.'

'Oh no!' I gasped. 'I didn't think they'd notice.'

'They did,' said Anne. 'They gave full marks to Australia. They said that even though Japan leads the world in many things, their manufacturers never came up with the idea of marking their toilet paper "Centre Front" and "Centre Back".'

How's that for Australian made?

I'm sorry, but I just can't resist the temptation to sneak in another yarn about our dear old mates, the poms. Having been born in England my good self, I can honestly say I never took offence at being called a pom until some pedant somewhere decreed that it was a nasty, offensive racist term. To my memory, it was always used by true-blue dinki-di Aussies as a term of affection. As this yarn from AE Spiller of Mildura, Victoria, shows, that affection sometimes went too far.

A Travel Yarn

During the Second World War, as a crowded inter-city train was leaving London for Exeter, a rather reserved English country gentleman, who was just a little hard of hearing, accompanied by his public schoolboy son, boarded the train.

They found themselves seats in a compartment with two noisy Australian army lads—a couple of rough diamonds.

In an effort to appear friendly, the elderly deaf bloke said to the soldiers, 'How far are you lads going?'

'All the way to bloody Exeter, mate.'

'Eh? What'd they say?' blustered the old bloke to his son.

'They're travelling to Exeter, Daddy,' replied the son in his father's ear.

'Do you know Exeter very well?' asked the gent.

'My bloody oath we do,' was the retort.

'Eh? What'd they say?' he asked his son again.

'They're very familiar with our city, Daddy.'

The gent's next question was, 'Do you lads happen to know the Duchess of Devonshire?'

'Know her? We've both slept with her.'

'Eh? What'd they say?'

'They know Mummy very well.'

In our odyssey through the minefield of multicultural Australian yarns, this next masterpiece probably doesn't really have a place— except that it's too good to let slide. So, although we don't have many native American Australians, let's hear from K Boothman of Morwell, Victoria.

Preventative Medicine

A tribe of Indians asked their chief how bad the coming winter would be and how much firewood they'd need. The whole tribe had nearly frozen to death halfway through the previous winter, when their firewood ran out. So the chief summoned his medicine man and asked him how bad the coming winter would be. The medicine man, remembering the previous winter's disastrous prediction, decided to cover himself. So he did a medicine dance, threw some spirit dust around and proclaimed, 'Winter will be bad. You must gather much firewood.'

The Indians raced out and gathered heaps of firewood. Still unsure of the amount needed, they quizzed the chief again. He immediately fronted up to the medicine man and asked *exactly* how bad the winter would be.

'Oh gosh!' thought the medicine man. So he did his little dance again, threw some more spirit dust and again stated, 'It will be very, very bad. You must gather more firewood.'

The Indians freaked right out and flew into the surrounding forest, dragging back and piling up huge amounts of wood. Once again, they queried the chief, who got serious and demanded from the medicine man the *full* story for the coming winter.

The poor medicine man, now scared stiff, proclaimed, 'This winter will be the worst ever—very, very cold. We need *more* firewood.'

The tribe attacked the forest with a frenzy, ripping into the trees like ants when their nest's disturbed—denuding the land around the village.

Fearing ecological damage, the medicine man decided he needed some expert white man's advice, so he travelled many days to civilisation to speak to the men from the weather bureau.

They confirmed his predictions of an extremely bad winter.

'Thank God for that!' the medicine man said. 'But how do you know a bad winter's coming?'

'Well,' the weather man explained, 'it must be. The Indians out west are gathering heaps of firewood.'

With the racial stuff neatly out of the way, let's dwell a while on Those Less Fortunate Than Ourselves. In short, we're not supposed to laugh at the disabled. Fair enough. But what do you do when someone like John Black, of French's Forest, New South Wales, comes up with a yarn like this? John's disabled himself . . . being deaf.

It's a Miracle!

For some reason or other, three handicapped people were trekking across a sandy desert. One was deaf, one was blind and the third was a paraplegic in a wheelchair. The deaf bloke was leading the way and helping the blind one push the wheelchair. They were out of water and almost dying from thirst, when they came to an oasis. There they found a pool of water under the palm trees.

The deaf man ran on ahead, jumped into the pool and splashed about, drinking the water. When he came out, he suddenly yelled, 'I can hear! I can hear!' Sure enough, his deafness seemed to have been cured.

The blind man was amazed, so he stumbled in after him. He too splashed around in the water and sure enough, when he came out, he yelled, 'I can see! I can see!' His sight was restored.

The paraplegic bloke wheeled his chair into the water and he also splashed around and drank deeply.

When he came out, he had two new tyres on his chair.

And, of course, we all recognise how Politically Incorrect it is to poke fun at those of us who suffer some form of mental aberration, don't we? Shame on you, F Robbins of Woolgoolga, New South Wales.

Horticulture

A psychiatrist decided to test a new patient.

He pointed to three trees outside his window and asked the patient, 'How many trees can you see?'

'Nine,' replied the patient.

'How do you work *that* out?' asked the psychiatrist.

'Well, it's easy,' replied the patient. 'Tree and tree and tree make nine!'

The psychiatrist decided to try again.

'How many trees do you see?'

'Twenty-seven,' the patient answered most definitely.

'How come?'

'Obvious, tree, by tree, by tree, equals twenty-seven.'

The poor old psychiatrist decided to have one more try.

'Again . . . how many trees do you see?'

The patient sighed. 'Ninety.'

'Eh?'

'It's easy . . . fir tree, plus fir tree, plus fir tree equals ninety. Can I go home now?'

Raymond Martin, of Orbost, Victoria, was no better when discussing the mental capabilities of two blokes I can only surmise to be locals.

Smarter Pills

These two young fellers arranged to meet down the river to do a spot of fishing. One of them was running late, so his mate decided to start without him. He was lying back on the river bank, fishing, with the line in the water and the other end around his big toe. Beside him he had all these little black pills and was idly throwing them in the air. Eventually, along came his mate.

'G'day, where have you been?' the first bloke asked.

'Had to do some chores for Mum. Hey, what are those little black pills you're throwing in the air?'

'These are Smarter Pills,' the fisherman explained. 'You oughta try some.'

'What do they do?'

'They just make you smarter.'

So the second bloke took a couple. 'Hey, they're not making me any smarter,' he duly reported.

'Well, take a whole handful.'

So the second bloke did. He chewed them up until he had black juice running all down his chin.

Suddenly he stopped. 'Hey, this is just sheep poop,' he bellowed.

The fisherman laughed. 'I told you they'd eventually make you smarter.'

And AJ Monaghan, of St Thomas, New South Wales, was prepared to take the dicey subject of lunacy even further.

Neighbourly Love

A bloke by the name of Brown had just shifted to a new town. One afternoon, he was digging in his garden when his neighbour from across the road came over.

'G'day, mate! My name is Jonesy. Do you know anything about motor cars?'

'Yes, I do. I'm a mechanic by trade.'

'You beaut!' Jonesy replied. 'Would you come over to my place and help me start my car?'

'Yes, of course I will,' Brown answered and went over to Jonesy's home.

Jonesy opened the roller door on the garage but there wasn't a car in there—only an ordinary chair sitting in the middle of the garage floor. Jonesy immediately sat in the chair and said to Brown, 'Righto, mate, give it a crank with the crank handle.'

'Where *is* the crank handle?' Brown asked.

'Over there on the bench.' Although there was no crank handle to be seen, Brown went over and picked up an imaginary one ... and gave an imaginary car a few imaginary cranks.

Suddenly Jonesy made a sound like a motor running. 'Brmmmmm! Brmmmm!' Then he got up, ran down the street and disappeared.

'Crikey! That Jonesy's a nut,' Brown thought to himself. 'He's definitely got a few marbles missing.'

Anyway, he went back home and soon started digging in his garden again. A short time later, another bloke from a few doors away wandered over and introduced himself as Smith. 'I'm pleased to meet you.'

After exchanging pleasantries, Smith said, 'I saw you going over to Jonesy's place. Did you start his car for him?'

'But he doesn't *have* a car,' Brown pointed out.

'Hey, you won't ever tell him that, will you?' asked Smith with some concern.

'Why not?'

'Because he pays me ten dollars a week to wash the bloody thing for him.'

Right, loonies out of the way ... who'd like to hear a yarn about speech impediments? While we are in Politically Incorrect mode, let's tune in to Robert Dansie, of Toowoomba, Queensland.

The Diesel Fitter

A few months ago, an ill-assorted pair of fellows turned up at the CES office in a big provincial town in Queensland. One of the men was a tall skinny bloke called Jim. The other, called Joe, was a somewhat rotund, shorter bloke with a large, completely bald head. Neither looked 'the full quid', as the saying goes. Indeed, the CES officer who interviewed them was heard to say later that both were several sausages short of a barbecue.

When they breasted the counter, the CES officer asked them what they were able to do. The short bloke didn't answer, but Jim, who spoke very hesitantly, with a considerable stammer, said, 'I-I-I'm, a 'l-'l-'l-'lastic thr-thr-threader for a l-l-l-ladies' p-p-p-pantie f-f-f-factory.'

'Oh!' exclaimed the CES bloke. 'That's great. There's a ladies' lingerie factory just starting up here, and I'm sure they'll give you a job. Now, what about your mate?'

'Oh!' said Jim. 'H-h-h-he c-c-c-can't t-t-t-talk too well, b-b-b-but he's a d-d-diesel f-f-f-fitter.'

'Well,' said the CES man, 'aren't you in luck? The tractor dealer just down the road wants a diesel fitter, so I'll ring him and the factory up. I'll take your mate down to the dealer and you can go over to the lingerie plant.'

'B-b-but,' protested Jim, 'J-J-J-Joe and I are a t-t-team. We always w-w-w-work together.'

'Well, you can't this time,' said the CES bloke, who was getting a bit annoyed. 'The manager at the lingerie factory hasn't got any diesels. Now get over there if you want the job and I'll take Joe down to the tractor works.'

Still protesting, the lanky one went off. The CES officer took Joe down to the tractor dealer and came back to the office, congratulating himself. He'd hardly got back, when a very upset tractor dealer burst in with Joe in tow.

'What the hell do yer think you're doing?' he said. 'This bloke knows bugger-all about machines. He wouldn't know a diesel engine from a country dunny. I'll leave him with yer. He's no good to me.'

The CES bloke looked at Joe. 'Come on,' he said, 'let's go and find Jim and see what this is all about.' So off they went to the lingerie factory, where they found Jim already at work, deftly threading elastic into newly sewn pairs of panties.

'G-g-gee, I'm g-g-glad to see Joe,' he said. 'I n-n-need him here. The w-w-w-work's piling up.'

The CES bloke was completely nonplussed. 'Show me what he does,' he said.

Joe sat down opposite Jim and Jim handed him a completed pair of panties. With a beatific smile, Joe pulled the waist of the panties down over his head as far as his ears.

'Dese'll fit 'er!' he said, and placed the pants in a pile marked 'Inspected and passed'.

Now that we're totally committed to poor taste yarns, let's go the whole hog and have a chuckle at the expense of that growing number of Australians—the aged. The first offering is from Pam Reissen of North Beach, Western Australia. Hers is a beaut example of the short story style of yarn that a lot of women sent in to the competition.

Getting Rid of Gran

'You still got that Gran, Mavis?' the woman in front of me in the bus queue said to her companion.

'Yes, that's her down there,' Mavis indicated with her head, to where a frail, little old lady, leaning on a stick, stood at the head of the queue.

'Shouldn't she be up here with you?'

'Are you joking? She never queues up. You just wait till the bus comes, then you'll see what she uses that stick for.'

The day was hot. The queue was long and straggly. The bus was late and I couldn't be bothered reading. This seemed just the sort of diversion I needed. I discreetly tried to lean my head towards them, so I could catch any further gems. Fortunately, my hearing was very good, so I could really be quite discreet. I was looking forward to the bus coming . . . and not just for me getting on it.

'Funny thing, that, the way you got her,' continued Mavis's companion.

'Funny? We weren't bloomin' laughing, I can tell you that,' Mavis replied.

'I didn't mean funny *that* way. You know what I mean—funny . . . like . . . '

I just stopped myself from saying, 'Peculiar!'

'Yes, I know what you mean,' Mavis grudgingly admitted.

'You were at the beach, weren't you?'

'Yes. Supposed to be our day out. We'd all been looking forward to it. Then *this* happened.'

They both fell silent and looked rather gloomily to the head of the queue. Surely they weren't going to leave me up in the air like that—not knowing what happened? Perhaps I could ask them . . . I was saved from such impudence by Mavis taking up the story again.

'We were having our sandwiches . . . you know, the ones Bill likes.'

'Yes, you mean those salmon and onion ones. They're nice.'

'I've got a special way of doing them. I'll give you the recipe. Got a bit of paper?'

Oh no! My thoughts raced . . . just tell us what happened. I don't want to know about your stupid sandwiches. Thankfully, her companion didn't want to know either. 'I'll get that another time, Mavis. Go on about this Gran of yours. I can't make head nor tail out of it.'

'Well, as I said, we were having our sandwiches on that nice grassy bit. You know the place where the trees are? It's very popular—everyone likes going there.' I could see I was going to be a nervous wreck before we got anywhere near the end of the story.

'Yes, I know. Was that where it happened?'

Surely Mavis would take the hint and get on with it now?

'Yes, it was.' Mavis took a deep breath and laid her hand on her companion's arm. 'As I said, we were just sitting there, when this young girl pushing an old lady in a wheelchair comes up to us ... such a pretty little thing she was, too. Who'd ever have thought ...?'

'Who'd ever have thought what?'

'That she'd do a thing like that.'

What thing? I hoped I hadn't said it out loud. But this story could go on forever. For heaven's sake, Mavis ... hurry up!

'Yes, she just comes up and asks us if we would mind keeping an eye on her Gran while she went and powdered her nose. And being good Christians, we said we didn't mind.'

'And she didn't come back? That right?'

'Never saw her again ... and we waited hours.'

Now we were getting somewhere and I was intrigued. What a way to get a rid of unwanted relatives.

'But didn't you take her to the police?' Mavis's companion went on.

'Oh yes. Soon as we knew the girl wasn't coming back, but the old hag told them we were just trying to get rid of her and we were only after her money. If she's got any, we've never seen any sign of it ... and she eats like a flamin' horse.'

'Well I never ... here, what about the wheelchair? Doesn't she need it any more?'

'She didn't need it in the first place. That was just for show ... same as that stick she's got.'

At last, after that build-up, I finally knew about the Gran. I leaned back and sighed with relief. A bit tough on poor old Mavis and her family—but that's life. As I stood there idly thinking who I could tell the story to, I just caught Mavis's companion's voice saying in an almost whispered tone, 'Here, why don't you get rid of her the same way you got her?'

'You mean, ask someone to ...?'

'Yes.'

There was silence for a few seconds. Then Mavis touched my arm.

'Errr, love ... I was wondering if you would mind ...'

I didn't wait to hear any more.

'I've got to catch that bus down there,' I blurted and ran. I just made the bus and collapsed into a seat, perspiration dripping from my face. I didn't know where the bus was going, and I didn't care ... as long as it took me away from the clutches of that Gran.

As the bus pulled out, I looked back. There was Mavis, her companion and Gran, waving her stick in the air—all of them clutching each other, doubled up with laughter ... and pointing at my bus.

Poor old Grans. At least some people appreciate them, as Pearl Smith pointed out in her yarn ...

Drought

Each day the drought became more desperate, till, by January 1981, we realised that something had to be done. We were at the end of our tether. I thought we should cut our losses and go, but Peter quietly said, 'Mardi, things are so bad, they can only get better. You'd be sad to uproot the family, then find that the rains arrived the next week. The grass *will* grow again and the cattle *will* get fat ... rolling fat. The children would hate to live in the city. Things can't get any worse.'

'You're right ... as usual. We'd all hate living in the city. Things *must* get better.'

Alas! They didn't.

Another three years dragged on. Promising rain clouds gathered each evening, but blew away before morning. Daily, Peter rode the fences, putting the cattle out of their misery. One swift bullet was enough.

Five hundred cattle were being hand-fed in the home paddock, but the chips were down and they, too, would have to be shot if they could no longer stand on their feet. Our youngest daughter was badly affected by the sad plight of the animals. She would wail hysterically each time a shot rang out. Then she'd register a cross on her little blackboard.

Grandma was coming to help her cope with the situation. Today was the day and we were gathered on the verandah, awaiting the arrival of the mailman and Grandma. Our daughter was hopping up and down singing, 'Hooray! Hooray! Grandma's coming today!'

'Yes, and you'd better behave yourself. She won't want to listen to you wailing like a banshee,' scoffed her seven-year-old brother.

'So will *you*, smarty! You'll have to clean your teeth.'

'Bang!' The rifle shot seemed close. Again. 'Bang!'

'That's two,' wailed our little one as she rushed to her room to add another two crosses to the blackboard.

'Mother, she's getting morbid,' observed our eldest girl. 'I hope Grandma can do something with her.'

'Look, there's the mailman. Run and open the gate.'

'OK, Mum.'

It took some time to unfold Grandma from the back of the utility, but eventually we were all seated around a huge pot of tea and sponge cake, discussing the trip.

'Perhaps you would like a rest before dinner, Mother?' I suggested.

'Yes, that *would* be nice, dear.' She held out her hand, but couldn't get to her feet. She just sat there. 'Leave me for a moment, Mardi. I'm *so* stiff, I can hardly feel my feet. I'll just sit a little while longer.'

Bang! The rifle shot sounded clear and close again. Our baby ran to her room, wailing. She drew two more crosses and rushed back. She threw her arms around Grandma and cried, 'Don't you worry, Grandma. I won't let Daddy shoot you.'

The thing about most of the yarns about the aged is that they're invariably told by people not that far away from being the butt of the very same stories. This emphasises the point that the best yarns are when people are in fact laughing at themselves. I first heard this next one from Russell Wong, of Laggan, New South Wales, but it was entered in the yarn-spinning contest by a namesake—Russ Gribble, of Broadbeach, Queensland.

Knock! Knock!

These three old blokes had been good mates for most of their lives. Their wives had predeceased them, and because of frequent memory lapses and other difficulties associated with living alone, they decided to move in together and help each other cope with individual problems.

They were seated around the table talking one evening, when Bert stood up and announced that he'd go upstairs and have a bath.

It was about ten minutes later that he called out from the bathroom, 'Fred, I've got a problem. Could you come up and help me please?'

'What's the problem, Bert?' asked Fred, rising from his seat at the table.

'Well, I've got one foot in the bath and one foot on the floor . . . but I can't remember whether I'm about to get in or get out.'

'Hang on,' called Fred. 'I'm coming up.'

But when he was halfway up the stairs, Fred slipped, twisted his ankle and couldn't stand up. 'Charlie, I've got a problem,' he called out.

'What's the problem?' asked Charlie, who was still seated at the table.

'Well, Bert was having difficulty remembering whether he was getting *into* the bath or getting *out*. I've fallen and twisted my ankle and can't remember whether I was on my way upstairs to help Bert, or whether I've already sorted out his problem and was on my way downstairs again.'

'All right. I'm coming,' said Charlie.

As he rose from the table, he smiled to himself, rapped his knuckles on the top and said quietly, 'Touch wood I'm not as bad as those two silly old buggers.'

He'd only moved a couple of paces when he stopped in his tracks, a puzzled expression on his face.

'Hmmmmm . . . Was that the front door, or the back?'

Finally, an offering from Leith Ryan, of The Rock, New South

Wales. It could well be about those same old blokes, sharing the confusion of their twilight years ... well, at least a couple of them.

Come Along and Have a Peter's Ice-cream

'You know what I really miss sometimes?' asked Bert pensively.

Charlie rustled the pages of his paper to show his annoyance at being interrupted in his reading and replied gruffly, 'No. What?'

'I miss those ice-creams we used to get in the cones. Do you remember them? Most of the ones they have these days come on sticks and in plastic buckets and things. They aren't the same.'

Charlie put down his paper and showed some uncharacteristic interest. 'Do I remember them? Crikey, I can almost *taste* them. Great big creamy ice-creams they were ... in cones that got all soft and soggy if you left them too long ...'

'Yeah, and you could bite the end off them and suck the melted stuff down through them ...'

'You're right,' Charlie agreed. 'They don't make them like that any more.'

'Well, that's where you're wrong,' Bert whispered almost conspiratorially. 'There's a little joint up the main street that's just been taken over by an Eye-talian family. And they sell ice-creams just like the ones we used to like.'

'You're kidding!' gasped Charlie. 'Oh what I'd give to have just one of them.'

'Well, no worries. I'll nick up the street and get us a couple,' volunteered Bert enthusiastically.

'Nick up the street? You, you silly old bugger? With your arthuritis and crook memory, by the time you got up there you'd have forgotten what it was you'd gone to get.'

'Rubbish!' shouted Bert. 'My memory's as good as it ever was. I'll have no trouble remembering two great big vanilla ice-creams.'

'I want chocolate ...'

'Yeah, well, one vanilla and one chocolate. See, I remember it as clear as a bell.'

'Well, all right. And do you think you can remember to have hundreds and thousands sprinkled on mine?'

'Hundreds and thousands? Not a worry in the world. Let's see ... that's one big vanilla ice-cream and one chocolate one with hundreds and thousands sprinkled on it. Piece of cake. And you know what? Now you've mentioned hundreds and thousands, I think I'll have mine with a big red cherry sitting on it. Me mum always used to get me one like that as a special treat.'

'OK,' said Charlie challengingly. 'Go over it again ... just in case you have one of your turns.'

'No worries. Two big ice-creams ... a vanilla one for me and a chockie one for you. Yours'll have hundreds and thousands sprinkled on top and mine'll have a big red cherry.'

'Well see you don't forget, you stupid old fart,' muttered Charlie.

Bert fossicked round till he found his wallet, then shuffled off up the main street. He appeared about an hour and a half later clutching a brown paper bag.

'Did you remember what you were meant to get?' asked Charlie accusingly.

'Of course I did. Here, have a look for yourself.' He handed Charlie the brown paper bag.

'You silly old bugger ...' Charlie began.

'What do you mean?' asked poor old Bert, a mite confused.

'Look at this,' hissed Charlie in disgust, producing two meat pies from the brown paper bag. 'I knew your memory wasn't up to the job.'

'What d'y' mean?' asked Bert.

'You've forgotten the bloody sauce.'

MURPHY'S DUNNY
(circa 1949)

REFUSED BY THE
NATIONAL TRUST 1961

← KIOSK

Chapter 4

DREADFUL DUNNIES

There have been times with my own humble yarn-spinning when
I've mentally whizzed through my stunning repertoire and thought,
'Crikey! There's a lot of them about ... ahem! ... bodily
functions.' Over the millennia, I've come to rationalise this seeming
fascination with the potentially embarrassing aforementioned
topic by the realisation that bush life—especially farming—is top-
weighted with them.

I call the subject 'knackers, knickers and knockers'—and that
only describes part of the fascinating thing we have to contend
with in the all-consuming world of animal husbandry. A cockie's
life is filled with considerations about mating, giving birth and
feeding small quadrupeds. If an animal's sick, your first hint of
trouble is usually gleaned through inspecting their poo. It's also
usually how best to tell when the animal's well again.

And things are not all that different in the average human family. No matter how the more sensitive of us recoil from it, bringing up ankle-biters involves more than a reasonable share of piddle, poop, chuck and yuk. That's why I sometimes wonder why people are so coy about discussing bodily functions. On the other hand, none of our yarn-spinning contestants seems to have any qualms.

Now, don't worry, I'm not going to sully the following pages with festoons of yarns about bodily functions. Because we probably managed to get a goodly swag of people offside with the preceding chapter, I've decided to limit the ensuing pages to learned scientific discussion of perhaps the most popular of bodily function yarns— the old bush dunny. There were too many entries to ignore.

Out in polite society, it seems even dunnies can offend. That great Australian, Rolf Harris, once admitted to me that even now, he still can't bring himself to say the word 'dunny'. 'I don't know why,' he said. 'It must just have something to do with my upbringing.'

During my earliest broadcasting days, waxing poetic about the Prickle Farm on ABC Radio, I had some trouble—bearing in mind that our old dunny, a disgusting Hygaeia Dissolvinator, was one of my earliest heroes. Although the stories were being broadcast all over Australia, the ABC in Canberra (where else?) wouldn't play them, because I mentioned that dreaded word on the odd occasion. Apparently, there were good, urban, middle-class folk in our national capital who felt that any discussion of a topic so down market was definitely offensive.

But, like I said, our yarn spinners are made of sterner stuff. This first one actually came from my bank manager.

On the Road to Gundagai

One of the most amazing stories in our part of the world concerned a young bloke who grew up in the Snowy Mountains, near Tumut. His family scratched a living way back in the scrub, and he didn't get much schooling. In fact, as soon as he could handle money, he went out rouseabouting, fencing and fruit picking. In the early sixties that didn't cause many problems. However, by the time he was thirty, it became obvious that the world had changed and the era of the non-skilled farm worker was over. This bloke took stock of his life and decided that he needed to broaden his horizons—something that wasn't going to be too easy for someone who couldn't read or write. He gradually became more and more depressed. He got on the booze. He was fast becoming a derro. Then, one hungover morning, he decided he needed to pull hmself up by his boot straps and smarten up his act. Quite by coincidence, that was the day one of his mates down the pub mentioned there was a job going on the neighbouring Gundagai Shire Council. 'It's been advertised for weeks, so apparently no one's put in for it,' his mate observed.

'What's the job?'

'Well, the ad in the paper is for a nightsoil removal engineer.' Despite its highfalutin title, our hero knew what the job meant— doing the rounds of the outlying villages in the shire and collecting their toilet pans. There were still a few of those in Gundagai in those days.

Our hero gave the matter some thought and decided that, despite the obvious drawbacks of the job, it *would* be a foot in the door for anyone seeking a career in the highly lucrative and potentially advancing arena of local government. So he gave the Gundagai Shire Clerk a bell.

The Shire Clerk was almost grateful to have someone apply for the job.

'Look, as far as I'm concerned, you can have it. You're the only person to show the slightest interest. All you have to do is come in, fill in a few forms and the job's yours.'

'Beauty!' chortled the young bloke, seeing, at last, the light at the end of his long personal tunnel. 'But I may need a hand with those forms. You see, I can't read or write.'

There was an embarrassed silence at the other end of the phone.

'Look, I'm terribly sorry,' apologised the Shire Clerk, 'but according to the Local Government Act of 1972, all shire employees have to be able to read and write. It's not *my* decision, but I just can't give you the job.'

Well, that did it for the Tumut bloke. This time he *really* got on the grog and made a nice old mess of himself. When he finally came to, weeks later, he'd managed to con himself a job with a travelling showman and had left the district half-drunk on the back of a truck hauling one of those laughing clowns games.

They say travel broadens the mind, and it certainly did for our hero. Despite the knockabout life of a showman, he prospered. Within three months, he actually owned his own laughing clowns game. In a year he had six of them, two dodgem car tents and a huge machine that whizzed people around at a million miles an hour and made them chuck up the entire contents of their liquorice show bags. He had found his niche.

And that's how my bank manager got to know this bloke. He managed one of several large accounts the Tumut feller had salted away in banks all over the bush. On this particular occasion, he'd come into town to deposit thousands of dollars taken from show-goers throughout our region.

'You know,' the bank manager said as he finalised the formalities for depositing the Tumut bloke's tidy sum, 'apart from a few well-established wool cockies around here, you're probably my biggest single depositor.'

The Tumut blike grinned. 'Yeah, well, I've done pretty well.'

'Pretty well! You've cleaned up. It's quite an achievement for a bloke who never really went to school.'

'Yeah, I suppose so.'

'It's amazing. Have you ever wondered what you might have achieved if you *had* been able to read and write?'

The Tumut feller thought for a while. 'Yeah, I'd be the Shire of Gundagai dunny carter.'

And while we're on the subject of local government, here's a contribution on its important role in dealing with our bodily functions, from Ken Dodd, of Fernmount, New South Wales.

Terminology

The shire council meeting was nearing the lunchbreak. After a morning thick with accounts, debates and comments, Bill and Jack moved a resolution that a new urinal be erected in the town park. To their astonishment, the resolution was hotly contested by Paddy, who maintained that he was sick and tired of the wastage of public money. In her wisdom, the president decided that the matter could best be resolved by personal discussion, so she declared the meeting adjourned for lunch.

On their way to the local rubbidy for an amber sandwich, Bill and Jack proceeded to tell Paddy what they thought of his lack of support for a public amenity. Things became very heated until Paddy confessed, 'I don't really know what this 'ere urinal is.'

An explanation was given. Paddy apologised for his error and some time later, they returned to the meeting. After the president reopened proceedings, Paddy indicated that he now supported the resolution on the urinal, but wanted to have a few words to say to the Health Inspector.

'When you build this 'ere urinal, I think it would be a good idea to include a couple of arsenals as well.'

There is a certain innocence about toilet humour. After all, it's probably the first sort of humour we embrace as kids—once we feel we've grown out of knock! knock! jokes and riddles. That innocence is reflected in the number of dunny yarns which involve mistaken views about bodily functions and the hardware and methodology surrounding them. Like our local government representative just dealt with, the heroine of the next yarn, from Marj Wood, of Benalla, Victoria, doesn't quite get hold of the right end of the stick.

Finished?

Mrs McGregor was having afternoon tea with her good friend, Mrs Dunn, in her little cottage in the Scottish highlands. Mrs

Dunn was looking very sad and burst into tears when Mrs McGregor asked the reason for her gloom.

'Oh, Mrs McGregor,' she sobbed. 'I'm so worried about my son. I haven't heard from him for ages. The last letter I had from him was five years ago.'

Mrs McGregor was shocked at this thoughtlessness of Mrs Dunn's son. 'Where is he living now?' she asked.

'In a little white house in Kalgoorlie in Australia,' said Mrs Dunn, blowing her nose on a lace-edged handkerchief.

Mrs McGregor hugged her friend. 'The problem is solved,' she said. 'I'm going to Australia in a few weeks. I'll go and see him and find out why he hasn't written to you.'

Several weeks later, a very determined Mrs McGregor was on her way to Kalgoorlie. A plane ride, several taxi rides, bus rides and a long train journey later saw her standing on the platform of the Kalgoorlie railway station. She approached the stationmaster and asked directions to the little white house. He pointed towards the end of the platform, where there was a small white building. Thanking him, Mrs McGregor gathered up her bags and headed off towards the small house. She noticed a man going in the door and quickened her pace. She reached the house and knocked briskly on the wall. The man emerged.

'Are you Dunn?' she demanded.

'Yes, lady, I'm done,' he replied.

'Well,' snapped Mrs McGregor, 'then why haven't you written to your mother?'

This next yarn is, without a doubt, probably the best known dunny story. I'd be very surprised if you haven't heard it before. This version comes from Bob McLean, of Wodonga, Victoria. It is included here purely for scientific reasons.

Mistaken Identity

A bloke had just returned from a party and was telling his wife about the grandeur he'd experienced while there.

'You know,' he said, 'it was the most beautiful, opulent house I have ever seen. Everything was expensive. There were beautiful tapestries, paintings, marble everywhere ... and gold-plated taps. But what impressed me more than anything else ... now wait for it ... was a gold-plated toilet. I reckon *that* is wealth and opulence.

'I have to go back there in the morning, because I left my hat behind.'

When he returned to the scene of the previous night's festivities, he rang the doorbell and the lady of the house opened it.

'I've come to collect my hat,' he told her. 'I left it here last night. Let me just say what a wonderful time I had at your party ... and I've never seen a grander house.'

'Hey, I remember you,' said the woman. 'I saw you swinging from a chandelier about three this morning. You certainly enjoyed yourself.'

'Too right I did. And I told my wife what a wonderful setting your place was for a party. I must say, what impressed me more than anything was your gold-plated toilet.'

'Gold-plated toilet?' mused the woman. 'Harry!' she suddenly sang out. 'Here's the bloke who piddled in your saxophone.'

Believe it or not, there's a great tradition of yarn-spinning among the clergy. They seem to like their yarns as rough as anyone else. Those still with a few qualms left, however, stay away from the nudge-nudge, wink-wink stuff and concentrate on dunny yarns, like this one from Moyses Marjan, of Cleve, South Australia. The confusion about terminology here used to be a common one in my troubled youth—especially on trains, where the official sign 'WC' often had my good self bamboozled. I came to the conclusion that it stood for 'Wee Cupboard'.

It's WC ... See!

A young couple, about to be married, were looking for a house to rent in the country. They found one, and after satisfying themselves that it was suitable, they returned to the city. During the journey, the young woman was thoughtful. When asked why, she replied, 'Did you notice any WC, Edward?'

Edward, not having noticed any, decided to rectify the problem by writing immediately to the landlord inquiring as to its locality. The landlord didn't know what the letters 'WC' stood for. After thinking it over for some time, he came to the conclusion that it meant Wesley Chapel.

So he replied to the young man . . .

Dear Sir,

I regret very much the delay in the matter of the WC, but have much pleasure in informing you that it is situated nine miles away from the house and is capable of seating 250 people.

This is an unfortunate situation if you are in the habit of going regularly, but no doubt, you will be glad to know that a number of people take their lunch with them and make a day of it, while others who cannot spare the time, go by car and although they arrive in time, they're generally in too great a hurry to wait long.

It may interest you to know that our daughter was married in our WC. In fact, it was there that she met her husband. I remember the wedding so well, on account of the rush for seats. There were ten people on the one I usually occupy—in various positions, standing, kneeling and sitting. My father was there, too. He has been going regularly since the day he was christened in its waters.

A wealthy resident of the district donated a bell for our WC, to be rung every time a member entered. The people living near there have had no sleep since.

My wife and I are old now and it is six years since we went and we had to stand all the time.

It pains me not to be able to go more often.

Yours truly,
The Landlord.

But it's the old bush dunny, with its unique personality, air of mystery (especially to the new chum), and disgusting little quirks that inspires most yarn spinners. Maisie White, of Crookwell, New South Wales, is a dear friend. Her dunny story is 100 per cent true. I know. She told me it was, personally.

Toad Down the Hole

Erections have always been the blight of man. Well they were for Harry, anyway. And when he couldn't even erect a shed, things were more serious than you might at first think.

It all started when Rose won a trip for two to the UK. She decided to use the tickets to her best advantage ... but Harry had to *earn* his.

'Harry, you'll get your ticket if you put in a new earth closet (the technical name for a long drop dunny). It won't be difficult. In fact, it'll be a piece of cake,' Rose told him.

'You seem to forget that I'm a truck driver—not a handyman,' Harry replied indignantly.

'Take it or leave it, Harry. Your big trouble is that you can drive a truck, but not a screw. That old toilet's been there since the turn of the century. Just ask the tarantulas that live in it. No Harry, enough's enough. I'm ordering one of those do-it-yourself sheds, and at the weekend, it'll be all hands on deck.'

The following Saturday morning, Rose was up with the larks. Her new pre-fab earth closet was going to put Thomas Crapper's finest brainchild to shame. She'd acquired a new spade, a big square of board for the floor, a new pan ... and the shed, all ready to erect.

After breakfast, she summoned Eddie, their son, outside and put the spade in his hands.

'Right, Ed. Dig a hole and keep digging down till we can't see you,' Rose ordered.

'Well, what else do you want done?' Harry asked tentatively. He'd been slowly coming round to Rose's way of thinking.

'OK, Harry. We need a hole cut in the board. You can put the pan on the timber, mark around the base, and cut the hole out while I go into town.'

Rose arrived back at home to be greeted by Harry.

'You'll have to pull Ed out of the hole,' he mumbled. 'I've thrown a rope down to him. He just needs hauling up. And then I'll need someone to help me put up that shed. I can't do it on my own.' Harry seemed pretty agitated.

Rose sang out, 'Sandy, will you help your father erect his shed round his hole while I get the tea?'

She almost had it ready to serve, when Sandy came running into the house, screaming, 'Mum, Dad's going to kill me!'

Harry was hot on her heels. He came running to the house, and then stood in the doorway, all limp-wristed and his fingers dripping with blood. 'How did you ever give birth to a daughter like that? She's pop-riveted me fingers,' he roared.

Rose didn't dare look. She was laughing fit to bust. After taking a few deep breaths, she gasped, 'Harry, put your eyes back in their sockets and wipe the steam off your glasses. Be calm. I'll bandage your fingers. I'm sure Sandy didn't mean it.'

After Rose officially postponed the taking of tea, everyone rallied to finish the wondrous galvanised structure. Finally, there it stood, pan over hole, ready to go.

What a great effort. Rose was elated.

After tea, Harry announced he was going to christen the new loo. An hour went by and still he didn't come back.

'Eddie!' Rose called. 'Just go up the back and see where your father is.'

Within minutes, Eddie was back. 'Come quick! Dad's fallen down the toilet.'

Rose and Sandy headed off in the direction of Harry's screams. It was as plain as day what had happened. Harry had jack-knifed down the pan and the pan, in turn, had gone down the hole in the board—which *someone* had made too big. All that was showing was the toilet seat on the floor, with feet, bandaged fingers and Harry's head protruding.

Again, Rose was finding it hard to contain herself.

'Hold on, Harry. I'm going to phone the patents office. What a novel idea—dropping the toilet seat flush with the floor.'

They eventually got Harry out with little more than a sprained back.

'Well, Harry,' Rose said, 'I hope you're feeling better by tomorrow, because that's when we're up, up and away to the old UK.'

As it turned out, Harry hobbled aboard the plane like a man of ninety-three. Rose called the flight attendant and asked if they could fix Harry a stiff whisky. The flight attendant looked strangely at him and his bandages.

'Don't worry—he's just accident prone,' Rose explained.

The flight attendant rolled her eyes. 'That's *all* we need on this flight,' she said. 'Just remember, the safest place on board a plane is the toilets.'

Harry didn't even let her finish. 'No, not the toilets! Not the toilets!' he whimpered.

Yes folks, even building the dunny can provide material for yarns, so you can imagine what happens when people actually start to use the thing. Ask Brian Scammel, of Glenrowan, Victoria.

It Indoors

Me and Dad was standing out in the garden the other day, when I looked over at the old dunny and said, 'Hey Daird! Don't ya reckon it was time we put a new dunny inside the house like the Joneses have?'

Well, did he get upperty? Straight away he yelled at me, 'Listen Dave, that dunny was good enough fer yer grandfather and it's good enough fer me ... so it'll be good enough fer you. Fair dinkum!'

Well, that gave me a bit of a shock, but I wasn't going to be put off that easily, so I thought I'd fix him and get a dunny in the house like the Joneses.

So I snuck over to the shed, grabbed a stick of 'jelly' and snuck back to the dunny—making sure Dad wasn't around to see me. Then I lit the wick, lifted the night door and in she went. Quick as a flash, I made a beeline to the old gum tree.

'Boom!' Up she went—wood splinters, wee, poo and tin ... everywhere.

'Bewdy!' I thought. Then ... Hell's bells. Out of the steam comes Dad, with the dunny seat around his neck, his trousers tripping him ... and covered in it. It gave me a heck of a fright.

'Cripes Daird!' I said. 'Are yer orright? Are yer orright?'

'Yeah, Dave,' he said. 'But by cripes, it's lucky I didn't let that one go in the kitchen.'

Of course, dunnies and other forms of life don't always combine well. Phil Tod, of Port Broughton, South Australia, has just such a story. And guess what? He heard it from a man of the cloth.

The Pup and the Long Drop

Another funny dunny story I heard was told to me by a Lutheran minister. It happened in the New South Wales wheat belt during the fifties, when he was on his pastoral duties. The kids of the cockie he was visiting had a cattle dog puppy. While playing around the long drop, they'd dropped the puppy down the hole. The little dog was OK (it was, after all, a soft landing), but he was barking from deep down the long drop. The kids pleaded with their father to save the puppy, so Dad went and got his torch and a long piece of eight gauge fencing wire. With a hook on the end and straightening the wire as he went, Dad guided it down to the puppy ... in ideal working conditions, what with the hot day, the smell and the droning bluebottles. The minister heard him mumbling and thought, 'If it was me I'd be swearing.'

Finally, success! The father managed to hook the collar and started to haul the puppy up. Carefully, he lifted the 'blob' up and over the seat and set him down on the ground. What a sight! The puppy was caked with poop, paper and lime. The odd blowy was hanging around. The puppy looked up at the encircled people and did what all dogs do when they're wet.

He shook.

Margaret Harrison, of Mirboo, Victoria, also had trouble mixing animals and dunnies.

A Different Sort of Fox Hole

For many years we had the old pan type of toilet, and my husband Reg would dig up to fifteen holes at a time with the posthole digger in the orchard near our chook yards to accommodate the dunny's contents. The empty holes would often fill up with water when it rained. Nearby was a galvanised iron tank into which we pumped water, via a two inch poly pipe, from a dam some distance down the paddock, and that filled our cattle troughs. Our country is very steep.

One night we awoke to hear a great commotion—our bedroom is close to the chook yard. Sure enough, a fox was at the chooks. Reg flew out of bed, grabbed the gun and light and raced out at the double. He shot at the fox, which ran up a post and out of the yard into the orchard. Reg aimed again, and this time he got the fox. As he walked across the orchard to check that the fox was indeed dead—yes, you guessed it—he fell into one of the toilet holes and got very wet. As you can also guess, he wasn't very impressed. So, after a bath to warm up, dry clothes and a cup of tea, we eventually got some asleep.

However, in the morning, we discovered that the second shot had gone through the two inch poly pipe ... which meant another job to do before we could pump again.

Nowadays we have an electric fence around the base of the chook yard and that deters our dogs and the foxes.

Then there're the creepy-crawlies lurking in ambush in every country dunny. Peter Beven, of Broken Hill, had a new slant on an old adversary.

The Red Back on the ...

A couple of blokes I know— we'll call them Bob and Steve, because that's their real names and they might recognise themselves—were pulling down the old shearers' dunny. It was one of the old pit drops and stood about fifty yards from the woolshed—like all of them, the door faced away and looked east to catch the early morning sun.

A chunky female redback didn't go much on being shaken out of her dark corner, and gave Bob a good nip. It was bloody painful . . . and a bit of a health hazard, too. So the flying doctor was called for advice. He decided to pick Bob up and take him to town. Bob was out of hospital in a few days and soon back on the job, keeping a sharp lookout for things red and black.

A bit later, a workers' compensation form had to be filled out. Not a problem. Bob wondered if 'accident' was the right word to use, as the spider seemed to have done the job with a definite sense of intent.

One bit of the form had questions to be answered by a reliable witness to the accident. Again, not a worry. Steve had been there and knew all the details.

But when Steve got to the question, 'What action was taken immediately after the accident?' he pondered on it for a while. Finally, he wrote, 'Bob dropped his hammer and said, "Oh shit! Oh shit! I've been bit."'

And it's not only forms of wildlife that threaten the dedicated dunny visitor, as FJ Nation of Howlong, New South Wales, found out.

Closed for Cleaning

We were waiting in a far north Queensland caravan park for the Mt Isa road to be declared passable. When the news came at ten o'clock, my husband, anxious to move, started to hustle us. It was hot and humid and I needed a shower. I noticed the elderly male

attendant hanging a notice on the shower block door, 'Closed For Cleaning'.

As he ambled towards the other block, I decided that the time was right to risk a quick shower. Stripped and soaped, I suddenly heard water being hosed on the floor. A male voice said loudly, 'If anyone's in there, you've got two seconds to come out.'

'I'm here,' I yelled, frantically trying to wash off the soap. Then I remembered that the cleaner was deaf.

Without warning, a jet of cold water shot under the door, saturating my clothes and nearly knocking me over. I cringed in the corner, praying that the door lock would hold. Water hissed around the floor like an irritated snake seeking a victim and I pranced around trying to dodge it, accompanied by the cleaner's off-key version of the 'Blue Danube'.

Dirty water streaked my legs. A squirt of disinfectant added to my discomfort. The door rattled.

'Dratted doors, they're always sticking,' mumbled the cleaner. He withdrew the hose and popped it over the top of the door for a final attack on the upper walls. Buckets clattered, footsteps receded ... but some time elapsed before I had the courage to dress and emerge, dripping wet, from the shower block.

The cleaner passed the van as I opened the door. He eyed my towel and washer bag.

'The Ladies' is done, missus,' he announced loudly. I couldn't have agreed more.

Right, so a caravan shower block isn't really a dunny. If you're disappointed about that, I bet Mrs Nation isn't.

AG O'Rourke, of Newtown, Tasmania, is someone else who's only too aware of what a rogue dunny can do to an unsuspecting member of the general public.

The Destruction of Equanimity

In my time, I have kicked around all over Australia and New Zealand, and as a result, I have worked with many different groups of men. Invariably, it has been my experience that no matter where I've worked, no matter how good, or how easy the conditions have been, there has always been somebody, be it individual or group of individuals, who has taken those conditions and manipulated them to gain personal advantage.

Furthermore, I have noted—and this second observation is quite separate from the first—that when I have worked amongst a group of men, I have often come across an individual of surprising initiative. Please keep both these observations in mind as I relate the following incident.

I went to work at Mount Hercules Mine in the early fifties, in those far off and almost-impossible-to-remember days when anyone who wanted work could get it, so long as you were prepared to get a little dirt on your hands.

I don't suppose many of you have worked as a labourer for a mining company, so I'd better give you a little background detail. When a newcomer arrived at such a place looking for a job, they didn't take him and shove him down into the bowels of the earth ... not on the first day, anyway.

No, it was much more likely that they would take him and put him into a day gang ... that's a surface gang. There he would work for a time while they sized him up and decided where they could best use him to advantage ... *their* advantage, I might add.

The day gang at Mount Hercules was a motley crew. Not all of them were waiting to go underground to work. In fact, that was the last thing that many of them wanted to do. They were quite prepared to potter around on the surface, doing any menial task, as long as it wasn't too hard or too dangerous.

I thought the pick of the bunch was a bloke called Gaddy. He was an unusual type for a labourer. He read a lot—at crib time, smoko, or whenever the opportunity presented itself—and he always had a little dictionary in his back pocket. Whenever he came across a word he didn't know, he would immediately look it up.

The make-up of our day gang was much the same as that of similar gangs anywhere. There was a foreman, a leading hand and us—the diggers, the fetchers and the carriers. It might surprise you, but there was a problem in that small gang. It came around this way . . . you see, the foreman worked underground, and most of the time, we surface workers were bossed by the leading hand. He had a couple of mates who could do no wrong.

Every morning, as soon as the foreman had given his orders and gone off down the mine, the leading hand and his two pink eyes would head straight for the toilets, each with his copy of the daily paper sticking out of his back pocket. And there they would sit until those newspapers had been well and truly read.

I don't suppose you can see our problem yet . . . but there were only three stalls to the thunderboxes at Mount Hercules. I've seen as many as four genuine cases of bowel distension queued up, waiting for a vacancy.

Matters came to a head a couple of weeks after I arrived. My new friend Gaddy had received the call of nature. But he found his way to relief barred by the usual encumbrances. Implore as he might, no one would come forth to make a place for him.

'If they do this to me tomorrow,' he raged as he brushed past me on the way to search for an alternative location down the scrub, 'I'll destroy his equanimity.'

'What's that?' I inquired with bucolic indifference.

'Look it up in your dictionary,' he snarled. 'You should never be without one.' And off he went at a sharp trot, accompanied by the muffled explosions of spontaneously venting gas.

In those days I didn't read anything you'd need to look up in a dictionary, so I did what most young blokes my age would do— I promptly forgot all about it.

At least I did until the next morning, when the now familiar pantomine was again played out before my eyes.

As soon as the foreman had given his orders and had gone off down the mine, the leading hand and his two special cronies made their daily dash for the triple loo. Gaddy watched them go with a fierce look of delight in his eyes.

'Follow me,' he ordered as the last door latch clicked shut.

At this point, I should tell you something about the lavatories at Mount Hercules. They were, in fact, a masterpiece of labour-saving design. Not for them the cluttering paraphernalia of pipes and chains and cisterns. No, they were of far more simple design. You see, they were just a narrow three-box affair which sat directly astride the water race—a torrent rushing below purged the premises instantaneously.

Gaddy led me, stumbling to keep up with him, to this water race and up along the pathway which ran beside it. Around the first bend, he halted. Then he darted into the scrub and reappeared with a long pole and an old four gallon drum, which contained, as far as I could see, a couple of bricks, about a gallon of sump oil and a pile of cotton waste which smelled suspiciously of petrol.

'Stand back,' Gaddy ordered as he lit a match and flicked it into the drum. The result rivalled the biblical pillar of fire.

Next, he took the pole and placed it carefully through the handle of the drum. Then he lifted his portable flamethrower gently onto the surface of the water race. With bated breath I watched it sail away.

I never did get around to looking up the word 'equanimity' in a dictionary, so I guess I can't really tell you exactly what it means. But I can tell you what one looks like ... a destroyed one, that is.

I saw three of them that day, and I can swear on a stack of Bibles that a destroyed equanimity looks almost exactly like a badly barbecued backside.

Far less cerebral is this next yarn from Charlie Chadorowski, of Pemberton, Western Australia.

A Dose of Salts

A few years ago, I was visiting a recently married friend, whom I hadn't seen for years. We'd been yarning away about the old times and having a few sherbets to slake the dryness in the throat, as one is wont to do in good company.

Anyhow, after some time, I needed to use the little boys' room. So, after asking for directions—I had never been to his new house before—I headed off and found the toilet at the end of a long passage.

On opening the door, I discovered the place to be in a frightful mess. Toilet paper was stewn all over the floor, along with excreta and some other dubious-looking stains. Everything—the floor, toilet seat, walls and even the ceiling—was covered with this horrible mess.

When I returned to the lounge where my old mate was waiting, I quizzed him about the condition of the room.

'Oh, that's the missus. She uses salts,' he explained.

I replied, 'Well, my wife and I both use salts, too, but we don't dirty even the ceiling. What sort of salts does your missus use? Epsom salts, Glauber's salts?'

'No—somersaults.'

That yarn was included just in case you thought I'd reformed and was deliberately dodging any mention of bodily functions.

This next one is almost as bad. Another version of it was submitted to the Search for the Great Australian Yarn and included in *Yarns!* This fuller version, with its knowing references to the clergy, is more apt, I think, in this particular context. Quite understandably, the contributor asked to remain anonymous.

Could it be from a ... no, it's unthinkable ... person of the cloth?

Holy... Errr... Shinplasters!

The yarn is told of two Roman Catholic priests who served the Good Lord in neighbouring country parishes. The first was an old priest, nearing retirement, with more than forty years of clerical experience behind him. The second was young, fresh from the seminary, naive to the ways of the Church and of the world. At his ordination, the old priest felt sorry for the young one. 'Poor bugger,' he thought. 'I remember when I was just like that. I'll have to help the lad in every way I can. After all, it *is* my Christian duty.'

So he suggested to the young priest that they meet weekly in a nearby town, have a day off, sink a pint or two, have a yarn or three and discuss the problems of their parishes. The young priest readily agreed and the arrangements for their first meeting were made.

Both of their parishes were very poor and the only means of transportation they could afford was bicycles.

Anyway, at the appointed time, date and place, each rode their bicycle to the local in a nearby town where they could sit down and have their pints and yarns. First and foremost on their agenda was parish finances. How could they raise more money? Each had suggestions—the blend of old and young wisdom—but none seemed practical. There had to be a way.

One day, the young priest arrived first at their meeting place. While he was carefully parking his bicycle, a Rolls Royce drew up to the kerb and a chauffeur hopped out. He held the door open . . . and out stepped the old priest. The young one couldn't believe his eyes and asked the obvious question, 'Hey! Did you win the lottery or something? What gives?'

The old priest smiled. 'Better than that, my son. Come, let's have a drink and I'll tell you about it.'

So off they went to the pub. Over an ale, the old priest said, 'Well, you see it's like this. I bought a new pectoral cross to hang around my neck, and during the sermon last Sunday, I started to sway it from side to side. After a while, I suddenly realised what I had done. I'd hypnotised my congregation. They seemed mesmerised, so I decided to put it to the test. I asked them to stand, and they all stood up. I asked them to sit down, and they all sat down. I asked them to put up their right hands and they all put up their right hands. I asked them to put their hands down and they put them down. Then a brainwave hit me. I asked them to take their wallets out of their pockets and open their purses, which they gladly did. Then I asked them to put all the money from their wallets and purses into the collection plates. Believe me, my son, I have never seen my people so happy in giving to the Lord. And, as you can see, the congregation turned out to not be as poor as it made out to be.'

The young priest was obviously moved by the older priest's good fortune and said, 'Well, I'll be darned. You never know what will happen. Do you think it'd work for me?'

'Well, there's only one way to find out. Try it.'

So at the end of their session, they agreed to meet the following week.

The week went by, and this time, the old priest in his Rolls arrived first at the venue. The young priest arrived late and there was no bicycle. In fact, he was on foot, puffing and panting.

'What's wrong with you?' asked the old priest.

'I've had it. You and your smart ideas for money-raising.'

'Why?'

'Well, you see it's like this. I did as you suggested. I bought a new pectoral cross to hang around my neck and during the sermon last Sunday, I swayed it from side to side, just as you suggested. After a while, I'd hypnotised my congregation, just like you did. I asked them to stand and they all stood up. I asked them to sit and they all sat down. I asked them to put up their right hands, so they all did. I asked them to put their hands down, and they put them down. Then, just as I was about to ask them to take their wallets out of their pockets and open their purses, the string of my new cross snapped.

'All I could say was "Shit!" '

Of course, at the end of it all, the paperwork has to be done, so I'll hand you over to D Mitchell, of Innisfail, Queensland.

Paperwork

This yarn is about what happened at an air show in England many years ago. A firm built an aeroplane which they thought was a world beater. But when they sent it up, one wing used to tear off. On this particular day, a man with a bag over his shoulder turned up and said, 'I can fix that.'

The company officials looked him up and down. 'How can a

fellow like you fix it, when our engineers and designers can't do it?'

'You get me a drill and a very small bit and I'll show you.'

This they did, and the man took the drill and put a line of very small holes all the way around the base of the wing, where it normally tore off. He then told the test pilot to take the aircraft up. The pilot put the plane through a rigorous set of tests. He did everything he could possibly think of with it. The wing stayed on and the plane landed safely.

The company officials were ecstatic. They applauded their saviour.

'But how did you work out that business with the line of small holes?'

'Have you ever known toilet paper to tear along the dotted line?' the man asked.

Finally, there's no way I can allow you to bail out from this enlightening and culturally uplifting chapter without subjecting you to the terror of yet another yarn in verse. It's the work of Jeanette Wormald, of Loxton, South Australia. She swears it's true.

The Enlightened Loo

There's nothing like a long drop loo,
When you're on a camping trip,
With corrugated iron walls and roof,
Guaranteed when it rains, to drip.

As a child I would be terrified
That the wooden floor would give way,
And I'd fall into the depths below
Never to be seen again.

Remember how, with torch at night
Through the eerie bush you'd tramp?
It had taken an hour to get up the courage

To go out in the cold and damp.

You were sure the dreaded boogieman
Was waiting in the dark.
You'd hear the branches snap and leaves rustle
Or maybe a dingo bark.

Finally, with busting bladder
You'd run to the waiting loo.
Only to see a thousand spiders
Beaming down at you.

You'd shudder but decide to go anyway
It was better than wetting your pants,
Or going under a tree somewhere
And sitting on a nest of ants.

But the best loo story that I can recall
Occurred on a weekend trek.
This bloke was with us who'd had 'just a few'
And he was a bit of a wreck.

Finally his bladder could take no more,
It was time for a long drop visit.
So with heavy-duty torch in hand,
He took off and wobbled towards it.

I hope you're aware of male anatomy
So that I don't need to explain.
His plan was to stand with torch under arm
To ensure that he had a good aim.

But suddenly, back at the campfire, we heard
An almighty yell and a 'Splat!'
This bloke had dropped the powerful torch
Straight down the long drop hatch.

There it had landed, right side up,
It lit up the loo like a beacon.
And the heavy-duty batteries inside ensured
It would last all that night ... and then some.

Well, the bloke returned with a sheepish grin,
Wondering what to tell everyone.
'Well, you can no longer see what you're doing,' said he,
'But you can certainly see what you've done.'

Chapter 5

HARD YAKKA

There's a great tradition in Australia of yarns at and about work. We all mightn't like doing it ... but we all seem to enjoy talking about it.

The types of yarns about work are as diverse as the types of work Australians do. Shearers yarn about shed life; drovers and stockmen yarn about buckjumpers and snakes; miners invariably yarn about near disasters and mishaps with explosives; and quantity surveyors yarn about ... ummmmm ... shearers.

The Australian shearer is one of our great bush stereotypes. We imagine him as a brawny, boozing bloke with muscles like whipcords and incredible stamina. That might have been the case fifty or so years ago. In reality, these days, they're usually weedy, whingeing little blokes, with crook backs, arthritic hands, emphysema and a set against the rest of the world. Shearers at smoko and lunch gossip like old women (and here I sincerely apologise to all old women who don't fit *that* stereotype . . . but you know what I mean).

Luckily, our yarn spinners tended to dwell more on the shearers of myth and imagination than the shearers of reality.

Let's kick off with some reminiscences from Bob Redfern of Forbes, New South Wales.

What's the Gentlest Tissue?

I heard this yarn about thirty years ago, when I was in my early twenties, and the storyteller was the wool classer at the shed where I was shearing. I was born in 1937 and he had been born about fifty years before that. The time of the story would almost certainly have been before the turn of the century and may well have been one that had been handed down from a generation previous to that of the narrator. It perhaps reflected the conditions existing in the pastoral industry at that time, or else reflected some cynicism on the part of the workers who were struggling for improvements in their working conditions. It was a common belief among shearers that squatters were exceedingly mean when it had to do with pay and conditions.

I would like to mention also, that it was well and truly during the era when shearing was conducted with a run before breakfast. This practice was changed about 1920. You will appreciate that during the winter months, little was achieved in the first run. Finding the shed on a dark, foggy morning was often a feat.

Before the turn of the century, shearing was, in the most part, conducted in large sheds with a considerable number in the workforce. In this case, the men's quarters ablutions and mess were situated about a quarter of a mile from the shed, and in today's standards, would be rated from inadequate to non-existent.

The squatter was fairly happy about the shearing and wool prospects because the season had been plentiful and even the holding paddocks were nicely grassed up—a rare occurrence. He was looking forward to a good wool clip. As shearing progressed, the pressure of sheep soon caused the holding paddocks to be stripped of their cover, and it was here that quite a few white tufts of wool appeared. Over the next few days, the white tufts increased substantially, to the squatter's alarm. He could see a lot of his best wool going back to the paddock ... or worse.

You see, when the call of nature came, the men were often too far away to make it to the facilities at the huts ... and time was of a premium. Around a woolshed, there's only one substitute for toilet paper.

In order to stop the leakage of his anticipated profit, the squatter addressed the men, and in no uncertain terms, told them to refrain from the practice.

His solution to the problem was, 'Next time, take a lamb. It, at least, will come back.'

A common topic of shearing yarns is the size of sheds they shore in. The bigger the shed, the bigger the kudos. Typical is this gentle yarn from Terry O'Brien, of Dunedoo, New South Wales.

How Big?

One wet day in the local pub, a group of shearers was having a few quiet drinks, when one bloke asked, 'What's the biggest shed you've ever shore in, mate?'

Of course, the usual line of bulldust came from a few of the boys, when one old-timer, sitting quietly in the corner, was asked the same question.

'Well,' he said, 'I don't know how many sheep there were or how many shearers were in the team, but I do know I shore there for seven weeks and while there, I had a letter from Mum, and she told me Dad was shearing in the same shed. Yet I never met him.'

To be fair to the shearers I've worked with, there were occasional bright moments when we managed a decent laugh—but never enough. Others obviously had a better time of it in the sheds than I did—like John Scott, of Condobolin, New South Wales.

Memories of Bill

Bill worked mainly as a shearer and did other jobs to fill in any gaps in his employment, taking his fantastic sense of humour wherever he went. He always had a yarn, either real or homespun, at smoko and his comments on daily events kept the humour bubbling all day.

On one occasion, just as Bill finished shearing a young ewe, it collapsed stone dead. At that moment, my father entered the shed, and not knowing the inert animal was dead, remarked, 'Must be suffering from shock.'

Bill looked at him in wide-eyed innocence. 'Oh, but I never said anything to shock her.'

Mondays were always packed with laughter, because of material gained over the weekend. Artie, the subject of one Monday's merriment, was extremely bow-legged. At the ball the previous Friday night, he had been dressed up like royalty.

'You should have seen Artie at the ball,' chortled Bill. 'He had more regalia on him than one of them knee-knocking trotters.' When we stopped laughing, he added in his 'afterthought voice', 'Of course, Artie might be a knee-knocker.'

Bill had a few beers and a few bets on the horses—but not to excess—so he always had enough to live on and a little left over.

His wife mostly attended to mowing the lawn, but their old mower was just about cactus and sometimes she had to get a neighbour to start it for her. One day, no one could get the damn thing to go, so she bought a new one.

Bill arrived home about sundown to find his wife operating the new machine.

'What's this all about?'

'The old one's had it, Bill, so I thought we might as well spend a bit of money. You can't take it with you.'

'I can't take the bloody mower, either.'

Shearing's hard work—that's why anyone who's been at it for any length of time has every right to get a bit stroppy. The occasional fun and games, however, probably gives the poor buggers some respite . . . for minutes at a time. Jan Beare, of Bordertown, South Australia, collected this little gem from her husband, Malcolm.

Leaping Lizards!

My husband recalls an amusing incident that happened many years ago in his uncle's shearing shed at Nantawarra, north of Adelaide. Uncle Don's son, Rodney, noticed that one shearer seemed to lose concentration halfway through the morning and go into automatic pilot. Rodney went outside and found a sleepy lizard (a shingleback in other states) hiding beneath a sheet of iron. Being a cold day, it didn't move or object to being picked up. Rodney returned to the shed while the shearer was in the pen picking out his next sheep, and replaced the shearing hand piece with the lizard.

True to form, the shearer dragged out his sheep and grabbed for his hand piece—picking up the lizard instead—and tried to adjust its knobs.

Yes indeed, that aforementioned loss of concentration isn't entirely unknown in a shearing shed.

I spent an interesting week shearing with a bloke who was trying to get back into the swing of things after giving up the grog for a whole six months. I've never seen anyone do it so tough. But, by the end of the week, he was back to 100 sheep a day.

Ah yes, the drink's a terrible thing for a working man, as Bob McLean, of Wodonga, Victoria, explains.

The Guessing Game

Two shearers were drinking in a car outback. After many hours of solid imbibing, one turned to the other and said, 'Dave, I've had enough for the moment. I think I'll have a break for ten minutes or so.'

Whereupon Dave responded by saying, 'Well, I think I'll join you. But while we're having our break, let's exercise our minds by having a word game.'

'Word game? You bloody fool,' said Bert, 'I ain't educated or nothing. I'm just no good at that sort of thing.'

'This,' said Dave, 'is not the usual word game, but more or less a guessing game. It's called Actors and Actresses. You must have known a few of them.'

'Yeah? Well give us an example.'

'OK. I am an actor. My Christian name is Marlon and I was a star in a picture called *A Streetcar Called Waterfront*. Do you know who I am?'

'Too right,' exclaimed Bert. 'You're Marlon Brando.'

'Correct,' said Dave. 'See, you're good at this. Now it's your turn.'

Bert immediately called for a beer and started. 'I'm an actress. My Christian name is Marlon, too. God I'm beautiful—lovely body, a figure like a model, beautiful eyes and ears, a turned-up nose, and a throat like a swan. I've got a rose in my cleavage and a dash of Chanel No 5 behind each ear. Who am I?'

'I couldn't give a bugger who you are, you beautiful creature. Quick, kiss me!'

Ah yes, shearers and their famous word games ... come off it, Bob! After a few, your average shearer is more likely to meet the fate of the old-timer mentioned by Mal Darroch, of Atherton, Queensland.

Wake Me at the Next Stop

The shearer had spent his annual cheque in Townsville. On boarding the Inlander to return for another spell of work, he asked the conductor to be sure to wake him up at Julia Creek, as he had arranged to go out to his new shed with the mailman.

He warned the conductor that he was a heavy sleeper and would be annoyed when woken up ... but to make sure he got off at his destination come hell or high water.

Next morning, he awoke to find the train well past Julia Creek. The shearer immediately chased up the conductor and let him know, in no uncertain manner, what he thought about being allowed to sleep past his stop. After several minutes, while the shearer was taking a fresh breath, the conductor got a word in. He expressed his apology for what had happened and congratulated the shearer on his command of the English language.

But he also assured him that it was nothing to the abuse he got from the passenger he put off at Julia Creek.

Bruce Ward, of Wallendbeen, New South Wales, sent in a whole swag of simple bush yarns which captured beautifully the nature of the old-time bush worker. The first couple are typical of the verbal sparring that used to be such an important part of Australian conversation. His last one, especially, is typical of the cerebral discussions you get in a shearing shed, or under a tree out in the paddock during smoko or some other break.

Wallendbeen Reminiscences

I was wool classing in a local shed and one of the shearers, nicknamed Snowy, was intent on finding out as much about everyone as possible. In answer to his questions, I established that, yes, I could shear—I was taught at a shearing school run by the Graziers Association in 1956, during a shearers' strike. No, I wasn't much good, that's why I was wool classing, or wool pressing, instead.

He went on to say he'd worked with another wool classer once, who'd done the experting for the shearers. Snowy reckoned he couldn't get a cut with the tools and asked him, in his polite fashion, 'Who the bloody hell taught you to grind?'

The young wool classer said he'd been taught by the same shearing school at which I'd learned to shear. Snowy replied,

'Well, you might have been taught—but you never bloody learned.'

Here's a yarn I read years ago and haven't heard since. I doubt if it has a copyright. A traveller just returned from overseas was recounting his experiences at the local bush pub with great enthusiasm—probably to the point of being a bit boring. You know how travellers get at times.

An old bushie turned to him and said, 'Eh, mate! Have you ever been to Bourke?'

'No,' replied the traveller.

'Well,' said the bushie, 'have you ever shore a sheep?'

'No,' said the bewildered traveller.

'Well mate,' the bushie observed, 'you ain't been nowhere and you ain't done nothing.'

Scratch a bushman, cockie or shearer and you'll get a philosophical reason as to why it will or it won't rain—based on a variety of obscure and sometimes obvious signs.

My father had quite a few, such as, 'The ants are building up their nests.' I personally found the ants sometimes built them up or cleaned them out after rain or during a drought, and sometimes on any number of occasions that seemed to take their fancy—and never a drop of rain.

His other favourite sign that rain was on its way, without a doubt, was when the wattle bloomed. These trees flowered over a three to four week period in October around Cootamundra. You stood a pretty good chance of rain in October anyway—even if it only came on Show weekend.

The currawongs were another sign heralding the approach of wet weather. Those chortling birds would arrive late April–early May every year, wet or dry. They'd stay till September–October. In a winter–spring rainfall area, they were likely to get it right in most years.

Of all the weather prophets, the moon watchers have the most diverse combinations and observations when it comes to forecasting rain. Old Bill Maher, the first employee I ever had—he came with the farm—based his forecasts on the lunar quarters.

According to Bill, the best rains came in the new moon, half moon and full moon quarters. Any rain in the last quarter was always light and the next two to six weeks would be dry. In the drought of 1982, he was spot on.

A neighbour of mine, CE 'Ted' Brown, took the cake as far as moon-based weather forecasting was concerned. Ted had a voice that oscillated between boy soprano and baritone when he spoke. His forecast for the month was based on the position of the crescent new moon. When the crescent came in looking like a fruit bowl, Ted'd say, 'You won't get any rain till she's full, boy. What we need is to have her sitting up on an angle, so she'll pour the water out.'

Of course, I *had* to ask it. 'Ted, this month the moon came in sitting straight up and down. What's that indicate?'

'Oh well,' he replied, 'it could be wet *or* dry.'

One of the biggest changes in Aussie shearing sheds has been the increase in the number of women taking to the board. There are a small number of female shearers, but any number of rousies. Gone are the days when discreet shearers would call 'Ducks on the pond' to their work mates as a warning that women were approaching the shed—and everyone would modify their language and behaviour accordingly.

Marg Plank, of Woomera, South Australia, was clearly never a duck on a pond.

Doing the Rounds of the Ballroom

Back in the mid-sixties I was on a working holiday in New Zealand and I'd heard of the decent wages women could get on shearing gangs. I wrote to a contractor, enthusiastically giving fictitious experience to secure a job, and I was signed on as a rouseabout.

On the first day in the shed, I joined six shearers, another rousie, the presser, graders and so on—about fourteen people in all. I

grabbed my broom and aped my fellow rouseabout. So far, so good. Then the gun shearer called me over.

'Hey, Marg,' he said, 'this ram shouldn't be with the wethers. Grab the raddle.'

I didn't know what a raddle was and looked blank.

'Grab that chalk by the pen,' he explained, so I bounded back with the blue chalk, eager to show that I'd only suffered a temporary lapse.

'Mark it!' he said. I clutched the chalk and stared at the bollocky ram.

'Come on!' the gun snapped. 'Ring the chalk around his balls so we can sort him out later.'

I squatted down, grabbed the ram's testicles and drew a neat circle around the area.

Two days later, over a beer in the pub, the gun said to me, 'This is your first job in the shed, eh?'

'How did you know?' I asked.

'You shoulda marked that ram's nose,' he laughed. 'How'd they ever see his balls in a mob of thousands.'

Getting away from shearers for the moment, here's a couple of workplace yarns from Fred Chapman, of West Kempsey, New South Wales, starting with a sad tale concerning that nemesis of all bush workers—the bulldog ant.

Ants in His Pants

When employed by the Forestry Commission in the sixties on Tanbar State Forest in the Kempsey district, my job was branding the trees before they were felled for saw logs. I'd also hammer the measurements of logs on their butt ends and record them before they were taken to the sawmills.

On this particular day, I started to hammer numbers on a log. The steel numbers were carried in a leather belt like they were cartridges. Part of my leather belt was flapping about the ground. I suddenly noticed a big red stinging bulldog ant stinging the belt. All my life I'd hated those ants and there, only about forty feet away, was a monstrous nest of them—with hundreds of them heading towards me.

I decided to vacate the area. However, as I still had a job to do, I got up on top of the log I was supposed to be marking and bent down to keep hammering the numbers into its butt.

To my surprise, as soon as I bent down I received a sharp pain in my crutch. I immediately though a bull ant must have crawled up there inside my trouser leg. I applied some pressure to kill the ant, but it stung harder. I applied more pressure, but still the stinging pain continued. I finally applied maximum pressure ... still with no result. I remember thinking what a tough ant it must have been.

The time had come for a more thorough inspection. I lowered my tweeds and found what had happened. My wife, a skilled sewer, often made underpants for me. I was actually wearing a pair on this particular day—and she'd left a pin in the fly of them. There I'd been trying to kill a pin instead of an ant—and only managing to produce a lot of blood spots.

The Date Loaf

Back in the Depression years of the thirties, there were jobs about on dairy farms and grazing properties if you were prepared to work for almost nothing. There wasn't much money about and the farmers and graziers were just surviving.

This particular job I'm about to discuss concerned land clearing. It involved removing hardwood suckers from a paddock of ringbarked trees. We also had to take out the lantana bushes with a mattock. There were three of us in the gang—me, my brother Bert and my nephew Erol Cavanagh.

We moved into the area with horses and a sulky to carry the camping gear. We had to move in daylight as the track was rough and the country thickly timbered. We camped under canvas near a small stream. After about three weeks everything had been going to plan and we thought that if we got an early start the next day, we could finish the job, pack up and vacate the place in daylight. Our estimate proved to be wrong. We just failed to finish the job and that meant another night in camp and some more work for part of the next day. It also meant we had to cook another damper for the night's supper and next day's tucker.

We arrived back at camp at dusk. I stoked up a good campfire, Bert prepared the dry mix for the damper and Erol went to the creek for the necessary water. The water at this time was getting scarce and we only had candlelight in camp. Nevertheless, by the feeble light, our cook added the water to the damper mix and we relaxed and waited for it to cook. Naturally, it was a late supper.

Eventually it was cooked and cooled, and I suggested it was time to attack it. I stuck a knife into the damper and opened it up.

I turned to the others. 'Fancy a date loaf for our last camp supper?'

Bert, the cook said, 'No. There aren't any dates in the damper.'

'Well, a sultana loaf, then?'

'No. There's no sultanas in it, either.'

'Well,' I said, 'we'd better hold a post-mortem on the damper.'

It turned out that although the water level was low in the creek, it also contained dozens of bullfrogs. In the bad light, Bert hadn't noticed them being mixed into the damper dough. We didn't throw the damper out. We prised the frogs out with knives and ate it clean.

If anyone tries to tell you that bullfrogs are poisonous, argue against it, because if they *do* kill you, it's a slow death. This all occurred sixty years ago and I'm still alive at eighty-three. Erol's eighty, and Bert passed away at sixty-nine.

Speaking of the Depression—you have to wonder if those of us who've weathered the current rural recession will reminisce about it like Fred and so many old-timers do about their hard times. It's still pretty hard to get good work in the bush.

It's Dark As a Dungeon Way Down in the Mine

Out where we used to live in a tiny bush community called Fullerton, it's about as isolated as you can get on the Southern Tablelands of New South Wales. There aren't a lot of well-paying jobs out that way. However, about eighty kilometres away, not far past Goulburn, there's a big mining complex at a place called Woodlawn Mine. It's a big base-metals operation and has provided good jobs for people throughout the region from time to time. Work at Woodlawn is usually highly sought after.

Anyway, one Saturday, the company advertised in the *Goulburn Post* for a supervising mining engineer. It wasn't the sort of job they'd expect to fill locally—it was too specialised—but they always paid the local community some respect by advertising such positions, just in case.

Two unemployed spud pickers from Fullerton spotted the ad and studied it closely.

'Have a look at this. It pays one thousand bucks a week,' Jim pointed out. 'We could both live like kings on that amount.'

'Well, why don't we put in for the job?' suggested Charlie.

'Don't be silly, we don't know nothing about mining.'

'Yeah, but they don't know that. And it can't be *that* different from spud pickin'. I bet if we write real snazzy job applications and make it to the interview, *one* of us can con his way into the job. If one of us gets it, we can share the money.'

Jim had to agree it seemed like a good idea, so they nicked into the Crookwell Neighbourhood Centre and dictated the Mature Workers' Program Coordinator a couple of impressive, but totally fictitious, CVs.

Needless to say, the mining company was more than happy to interview two such stunning applications from the local area.

Jim and Charlie reported to the personnel manager's office about a week later—both done up to the nines as if they were attending court again.

Jim was called in first. The personnel manager flipped through his application and CV and remarked that he seemed most qualified for the position. 'However, there are a couple of clarifying questions I'd like to ask.'

'Fire away.'

'In our advertisement, we mentioned we required someone with extensive mining experience. How could you have such experience if you've lived all your life in Fullerton?'

'No worries,' gushed Jim confidently. 'It's not generally known that Fullerton used to be a top mining area—gold, silver, platinum, uranium, everything. My family's been in mining since the middle of last century.'

'Right. Now, we also require someone with a knowledge of heavy mining machinery.'

Jim lowered his voice and answered in almost a whisper, 'Look, mate, I don't generally let this be known, but I've been earning a few extra bob as a maintenance consultant to Caterpillar Australia. They call me in whenever they want advice about the development of their heavy machinery.'

'Most impressive. Now, although Woodlawn's mainly an open-cut mine, we do have plans to develop some underground works. Have you ever worked in deep mines?'

'All the time.'

'How deep have you worked?'

Jim thought for a minute, then replied, 'About five feet.'

That did it. The personnel manager called in the security blokes and Jim was escorted back out into the waiting room, with his arm up his back.

'How'd you go?' asked Charlie, helping him up off the carpet.

'Pretty well. The questions were fairly well along the lines we expected. The only thing is, I blew the last one. They asked me about working deep underground and I told them I'd worked down as far as five feet. I reckon I was being a bit conservative. I should have made it a bit deeper.'

'No worries. I'll remember that,' whispered Charlie. 'If that's all they're worried about, we should be home and hosed.'

A couple of minutes later, Charlie was called in to the personnel manager. He went through pretty much the same process.

He didn't blink an eye at the questions. Why, his family hadn't only mined extensively around Fullerton, they'd branched out to places like Mt Isa, Rum Jungle, Mount Morgan and Jabiru.

Heavy machinery? Charlie had personally designed and built some of the most up-to-date, hi-tech mining gear in use all around the world.

'Finally,' said the manager, 'I want to ask you about deep mining. Have you ever worked a long way under ground?'

'I was born deep underground.'

'Well, what's the deepest you've ever worked?'

Charlie made a great show of estimating the figure. 'Oh, about three hundred and fifty thousand feet.'

The personnel manager gave a low whistle. 'Hey, that's extremely deep. Just one technical question—how did you get light down that far?'

'We never had to,' blurted Charlie. 'We only ever worked day shift.'

In the tough world of mining, it seems you can get into ten times the amount of strife that other workers get into, simply because of the size and weight of the machinery they use. Don't just take my word for it, listen to Toonpan Tom of Townsville, Queensland.

Skiddin' the Dozer Down

Lindsay dumped three spoons of sugar in his battered old cup, added a measure of milk and then made an exaggerated stirring effort. I knew then he had one of his reflections on life to share with us. We were hunting for tuskers on Esmeralda Station on the banks of the Yappar River. Camp was made, the swags were rolled out and we had finished our evening meal. The night was clear and not hot. The billy was warm and we all wanted a couple of cups of tea before calling it a night.

The old bushie just kept slowly stirring and stirring his cup of tea. We all realised what was coming and got as comfortable as we could. Lindsay had the stage. He knew it and didn't rush the chance. Finally, he started.

'I've seen and heard a lot of things in me innings, but the damnedest thing I ever saw and heard was up at Calcium three year ago, where I was operatin' an excavator. A dozer operator shot through 'n' just then, good operators were hard to come by. A grazier on the next property, who was also on the local council, said he had a son who was a good dozer operator. The old man had a D-6, and the son had cleared some regrowth with it 'n' done some other clearin' jobs on their station. The Super couldn't say "no" without giving him a go, so he said we'd trial the son the next day. We decided to start him out on the D-10.

'You blokes that ain't ever run dozers wouldn't know it, but the Caterpillar D-6 'n' D-10 models are nowheres near the same. The D-6 would be like youse crashin' them kiddies' dodgems at the Show. The D-10 would be like drivin' a boltin' 'n' loaded twenty-two wheeler with no brakes in the heart of Sydney when they've dropped the sliprails 'n' all those city loafers are headin' home for a feed.

'The son arrives the next day—six foot six tall, four foot four wide 'n' with almost one full oar in the water. The Super 'n' him completes all that hoo-hah fer a new employee. When that's done, we takes him up to the top where we are to clear an upper ledge for the drillin' drongos 'n' powder monkeys.

'Calcium is this huge limestone deposit. The ore is mined by the gelignite guys blowin' shelves or steps off the face 'n' the ore crashes fearfully to the bottom where it's then loaded into railway carriages 'n' sent to Townsville to the cement factory. The drillers 'n' blowers work from the top down 'n' peel a layer of limestone off just like you would a layer off an onion. When they gets to the bottom, they goes back to the top 'n' start explodin' off another layer. This day, they were ready to dynamite the last step off 'n' we had to clear the top and get it ready fer them to start another cut. It was a good time to study this new cove. So, three thousan' feet up we go; the greenhide, the Super 'n' me.

'It's mornin' smoko time when we gets there, so I starts the fire goin' 'n' the billy boilin'. The Super lights his pipe 'n' watches me. The new feller climbs up into the D-10 that's parked next to the edge 'n' sits there lookin' at the controls. His face is nothin' but befuddlement.

'I pours out three cups of tea 'n' gives one to the Super. He adds his ration of sugar 'n' milk 'n' he hollers fer the kid to come down 'n' have his cup. The bugger says to bring it to him 'n' he'll drink it on the go. I mutters to the Super, "I ain't no tea lady," and the Super tells me to take it to him. I puts the tea makin's on the top truck 'n' climbs up to the cab 'n' gives him the cup, dumps two teaspoons of sugar in, adds some milk 'n' gets down.

'I takes one step back towards the Super 'n' the new bloke starts up the D-10. No bloody joke, that dozer turns smartly right towards the face, knocks me half a chain on me front side 'n' goes over the lip almost before I can swivel me now-bruised head. I'm up in a flash 'n' gets to the face before the Super. It's well over half a mile to the bottom, 'n' while it ain't straight down, it's no more than 10 degrees off plumb.

'In the first hundred feet, that D-10 was goin' quicker than a greyhound with turps on its backside. Time slowed down fer us watching the spectacle, but the D-10, she keeps speedin' up. Soon, she's going faster than that flamin' rocket ship that Flash Gordon used to drive.

'The tracks 'n' rippers were skiddin' down the face 'n' the smoke, sparks and noise 'n' heat they gave off were un-bloody-believable. The smoke was so dense 'n' of such a quantity that it was later seen in Mt Isa 'n' most parts of the Territory. The sparks were so intense that the whole mine area was lit up for three nights afterwards. The noise was so loud that all the birds, bears and possums thereabouts were deafened for life. 'N' the heat ... Hell hasn't put out more heat since Adam's and Cain's time there.

'Well, when the dozer got to the last five hundred, it weren't much more than a smoky and sparkin' blur. It hits the last step which was about a hundred 'n' fifty feet from the dead bottom. The D-10 strikes the outer lip of that step with the leadin' edge of the front blade, 'n' that caused it to spin at a terrible speed. Rocket scientists from the uni told us later that it was both a "centrifugal" force 'n' a "hell-of-a-copter" effect that nearly exactly countered gravity's laws, 'n' it slowed the downward speed of the D-10 to that of a baby's first crawl. That dozer spun just above ground level for a full two minutes, then it landed upright on its tracks with an almighty thud.

'That new operator bloke wasn't conscious when we put him on the stretcher. He had bones stickin' out of him in at least two places, but I've seen more blood the last time I shaved meself. It was clear to all of us that if the doctors didn't make a real mess of the job, he'd pull through. When we loads him in the ambulance, he comes to 'n' with his good hand, he motions me over. I bends close over his face 'n' in quite a loud voice, he says, "Next time, stir me bloody cup of tea!" '

The bush worker who shares with shearers the most notoriety is, of course, the drover. We didn't get a lot of droving yarns entered in the competition, but here's one to go on with, from Phillip Palmer, of Nevertire, New South Wales.

Visions Come to Me of Clancy

Some years ago, we had a drover in the Nevertire district called Bill. Now, Bill looked after sheep for a big dealer down Wellington way, and on occasions, they may not have seen each other for weeks. The stock owner knew Bill lived in pretty harsh and rough conditions, and although his dogs drank water, Bill did not indulge in the stuff himself—for any purpose. He had a habit of getting on the booze if camped within motoring distance of a bush pub, when he disregarded his stock for several days.

To overcome this problem, the dealer didn't pay Bill too often, knowing if he had no money, he couldn't drink too regularly. So every week or so, he would organise his agent in the area to drop

Bill out a box of groceries and a few shillings in case of an emergency.

One Friday, the agent, Tony, had the task of putting together a grocery parcel and dropping it off. Among the basic food itemsTony put in a couple of cakes of soap ... and so it was delivered.

Of course Bill wanted to know why there were no bottles of beer or a cheque from his boss. Tony said the boss was busy, but would get out to see and pay Bill in a fortnight.

True to his word, like all sheep dealers, the owner turned up four weeks later to see Bill and give him some tucker.

Dirty in more ways than one, a quite irate Bill was glad to see him and asked where his money was. The dealer explained he had forgotten his cheque book, but had brought him out another box of tucker.

'Incidentally,' he said, 'how was the tucker I sent out last time with the agent?'

After he'd settled down, Bill replied, 'It wasn't too bad—except that bloody cheese left a bit to be desired.'

One of my most intriguing childhood memories is about being visited on several occasions by the great Australian merchant prince, Sir William Angliss. As kids we all knew how important he was, but two things always struck me about him. If he was so big deal, how come he was so short? And why was his sole topic of conversation always rabbits? 'How are the rabbits?' Sir William would always ask, the moment he shook hands with you. Now I realise that in those pre-myxomatosis days it was as perennial a conversational ice-breaker as the weather is these days.

Lockie Beauzeville, of Lake Cargelligo, New South Wales, looks back on those times.

Rabbit Plague

There has been talk lately of rabbits building up in number in the Western Lands Area. It brings back memories of the immediate postwar era, when millions of rabbits invaded the rich wheat-growing areas around Trundle, Tullamore and Bogan Gate—as well as many others.

In the late forties, I think it was 1948, I was returning to my home in Trundle from a building job between Peak Hill and Trundle, when I noticed three men standing near a car in a gully just off the gravel road. They appeared to be acting suspiciously, since they attempted to hide behind the car as I came along. As the property belonged to a friend of mine, I decided to enquire what they were doing there. I thought, at the time, they may have been stealing sheep.

It turned out that they were scientists from the CSIRO and they were, in fact, releasing several rabbits which had been inoculated with the myxomatosis virus. They had chosen that gully because it was filled with lush green grass, with some run-off water from recent rains. They explained that mosquitoes were helpful in spreading the virus. It was also spread by rabbit fleas. As the gully contained both green grass and water, it seemed an ideal place to release infected rabbits.

In answer to my queries, they explained that they had to be careful who spotted them, as there were scores of families entirely dependent on rabbits for a living. They would not be too pleased to learn that these scientists were releasing rabbits which, they confidently expected, would wipe out the entire rabbit population—thus removing the livelihood of most of those families.

In the area bordered by Tottenham, Nymagee, Euabalong, Fifield and Trundle there were indeed scores of families relying on rabbits for their very existence. It was not unusual, when travelling the roads in those areas, to come across hundreds of pairs of rabbits hanging on poles between trees and covered with sheets of hessian to ward off the flies. The trucks from the various chillers in the district would do the rounds each morning, picking up thousands of pairs of rabbits to take back to the chillers. The trappers lived in very rough bush camps, generally consisting of a camp bed made from saplings and hessian, with a few sheets of iron to keep off the rain, a camp oven and a meat safe hanging in the tree.

Jim and Jean Bissenden of Euabalong operated big chillers at Tottenham during the late forties and early fifties. Those chillers were capable of handling upwards of 5000 pairs of rabbits daily. The rabbits at that time brought about four shilling (forty cents) a pair. The Brissendens had three trucks picking up from the various camps in the area daily. The rabbits were frozen at the Tottenham works for transport to Melbourne, where they went to a large factory which used a chain system for skinning and packing the rabbits for export.

Each of the trappers' camps had a mailbox, where the mailman or truck driver could leave bread and other food items. The men in those rough bush camps usually had an arrangement with a store in town, which would extend them credit until such time as they came to town and picked up their cheque from the managers of the chillers. They would then pay their bills, have a day or two on the scoot, then head back for their camps on pushbikes, in old utes or on shanks's pony. Those who had families in the bigger towns would wire money home to keep the home fires burning until they, too, could get back.

They were hard times. The chiller operators looked after their trappers pretty well so the other chiller operators couldn't steal them.

In 1956, Tom Atkinson of Condobolin was transporting a load of rabbits from the Tottenham area, when his truck became bogged on the road to Tullamore. It was a very wet year and he was unable to get the truck out of the bog in time to save the rabbit carcasses. They were finally unloaded on the side of the road, where they eventually rotted away. The smell of the rotting rabbits carried for miles.

Any person who hasn't seen a rabbit plague would find it hard to believe some of the incidents of those days. An army mate of mine, with an offsider, decided to cash in on the rabbit bonanza. He had an old army blitz wagon and a bit of camping gear. After purchasing rolls of wire netting, they drove to a property about fifteen miles from town and about twelve miles from the nearest chiller. Cutting posts from the scrub, they fenced in an old dam, putting in two entrance chutes. They completed the work about sundown and retired to their camp about half a mile away. They were a bit worried the kangaroos would get in and knock their fences down like they had on previous occasions.

Just on daylight next morning, they drove up quietly to the dam. They couldn't believe their eyes. The fenced-off area was crammed so full of rabbits that some were even in the water. There were thousands and thousands of them. Hundreds had crammed into the corners and suffocated. The two men, still partly in shock, set to work—one inside the fence killing the rabbits, the other on the outside, gutting and pairing them. When they had a truck load, they filled up the blitz. One of them delived the load to the chiller while his mate went on preparing the next load.

They worked until dark that night—delivering four truck loads to the chiller. It went on for three days until, eventually, they were so exhausted and sick of it, they kicked the fence down and let the remaining rabbits free. They returned to town with a very large cheque and a determination never to tackle the rabbits again.

In 1948, I was building a station homestead about twenty miles from town. We were running short of meat because the property was a cattle stud and didn't run any sheep. It looked like I'd have to drive to town to replenish the larder. Late in the afternoon, I noticed a cloud of dust in a lane about half a mile from the homestead. I thought it looked like a mob of sheep coming down the lane. I decided to drive down in the hope of buying a killer from the drover.

I reached the lane and turned into it, expecting to see sheep. I stopped the car and sat there looking, not at a mob of sheep, but rabbits—the full width of the lane and as far back as I could see in the dust. It was a very dry time and the dust was being picked up on the breeze as the rabbits stirred it up. When I returned to the job, the men wouldn't believe me. I had to drive them back to the lane to convince them.

Myxomatosis finally overcame the rabbit, and chillers gradually disappeared from the scene. Many families packed up and drifted to the bigger towns and cities looking for work, and the industry just faded away. It was said at the time that myxomatosis took away the working man's independence. There's one thing for certain—if the rabbits were here now, there would be very few people on the dole in country areas.

And so, to poetry. You didn't think you could escape it this time, did you? When it's all boiled down, perhaps the hardest yakka to be found in the bush comes from trying to work the land itself. It could be argued that shearers, drovers, trappers, miners and quantity surveyors probably never have it so hard for so long as the battling cockie.

 So here's how Gay Donnell, of Bordertown, South Australia, sees it.

I'm Not Complaining, but ...

We started in the red this year
And things have gotten worse.
The kids have learnt an awful lot,
But mostly how to curse.

Summer—and the pumps won't work.
Autumn—still no rain.
Stock are looking skinny, too
Handfeed again, again, again.

Everything got started late,
Then the wheel fell off the plough.
The lifting bar just wouldn't work.
He's sorted that out, now.

We picked the stumps, the yakka lumps.
The rocks were heavy ones—
All piled up in the corner—
The kids are glad *that's* done.

Then it rained, got very wet;

Couldn't level with the bar.
Had to harrow several times
To get it up to par.

The seeder wasn't used last year,
The stars need cleaning well.
Hope this will work without a hitch.
It won't? Oh, what the hell!

It got later all the time,
The seed went in at last.
Rolled it flat—flat *out*, more like,
Hoped all the rain's not past.

The rain came down, the crop came up,
The cockies and mites came in.
What next? we thought. Oh ... rabbits!
Now the top end's getting thin.

The rain cut out, it's awful short,
Won't come to much, this way.
The wind blew hard, sand cut it up,
We'll never get the hay.

It's looking dry, a thirsty green,
Then someone laid hay down.
It's raining now, a good old soak,
Crop's drinking and it's grown.

We'll cut it and we'll bail it,
And store it in the shed.
The stock will have some fodder now ...
But *we're* still in the red.

Chapter 6

Joe Blakes

If there's any topic that challenges dunnies as a favourite for yarn spinners, it must be snakes. Australian men are supposed to be unemotional, secretive blokes, never prepared to let their feelings show. That might be true when dealing with unimportant subjects like personal relationships or how they really feel about things, but mention snakes, and nine out of ten of them will start dribbling, shaking and pouring out all the details about their incredible fears of creatures herpetological.

I'm almost ashamed to admit that snakes don't bother me a bit and I can't understand why people are so scared of them. As an ankle-biter, I used to go out every afternoon after school for years, digging rabbits out of burrows to sell to the local chiller. In that time, I never once came across a snake. When I did finally confront one—and I have been attacked on a number of occasions—

I was an adult, and it certainly didn't engender much panic.

What is it about snakes? Why are people so frightened of them and obsessed with them? Does it date back to biblical times ... you know, Adam and Eve in the Garden of Eden with a big red-bellied black number? I hardly think so. Is it the smell? The only thing that perturbs me about snakes is their smell when you get close to them. Perhaps it's a scent created by nature to cause snakes' victims to panic and lose their sense of priorities. Who knows? Anyway, the Search for the Great Australian Yarn produced a whole swag of snake stories. This one, from Terry McCulloch, of Glenorchy, Tasmania, probably sets the scene as well as any.

Snakes Alive!

'Snakes!' said Harry, whisking his cloth along the bar top. 'Snakes! I hate the slithering bloody things.'

It was Friday afternoon and we were gathered as usual at the end of the long bar in the Wagon and Horses. Oppo had just told us that his wife's best friend's sister's de facto had been bitten by a tiger snake last Tuesday.

'Did he die?' asked Knocker, full of delicious anticipation.

'Nah! But he damn nearly did,' replied Oppo apologetically.

'I hate the bloody things,' said Harry again.

'You'd hate them even more,' old Siddie Evans chipped in, 'if you'd seen snakes like Bern Harris and me seen on Flinners Island.'

Harry filled the empties and my brother-in-law, Wally, said, 'Big fellas were they, Sid?'

'Big!' said Siddie. 'Big and fierce and lively as hell. We'd been roo shooting, way out back of Blue Rocks. We were walking along a wide sandy track in sand so hot it was burning the soles of our feet through our boots, when Bern grabbed me by the arm and pointed ahead. I looked where he was pointing, and bloody near died.'

'Geez!' gasped Oppo. 'A big 'un, was he?'

'*Two* big 'uns,' said Siddie. 'Both as big as your leg and glitterin'' black. Never thought I was scared of snakes till then. Course, we had a couple of good solid snake sticks. You never walk round in that country in summer without one. Anyway, Bern whispered hoarsely, "You go for the front one and I'll git t'other."

"Right!" I said and we laid into 'em . . . Whack! Whack! Whack! Well, when we were sure they was both dead, we decided to see whose snake was the biggest, see? Talk about laugh!'

The Tarraleah Tiger's eyes were sticking out like a Cam River lobster's. 'Laugh? What was there to laugh about?'

Old Siddie wiped his eyes, overcome by the memory. 'When we pulled those snakes out to find their full length, we found we'd killed the same snake. He musta crossed the road once and then doubled back. Probably looking for water. Anyway, Bern had killed his front half and I'd fair murdered the back half. Pass me a beer, Oppo. Snakes always make me dry in the throat.'

'That was some reptile, Siddie,' said Harry, grinning, as he poured the next round. 'Bet you can't top that, Wal.'

My brother-in-law grinned back good-naturedly. 'No, Harry, I can't. But old Skinny Bob Morton could, if he was here.'

'Go on!' we all chorused.

Wally took a long drag on his beer, wiped his mouth and said, 'Skinny Bob was one of the truthfullest blokes I ever knew,' he started. 'So I've got to believe what he told me, especially as he was maudlin' drunk at the time. Anyway, Skinny Bob was with a couple of other blokes chasing wild cattle down round Temma over the Arthur River in the wild, wild west of Tassie.'

'It's wild, all right,' said the Tarraleah Tiger. 'A bunch of us went down to the Arthur fishing a few years back. That was far enough down that way for me.'

'Yair,' said Wally. 'Well, about midafternoon one day, they stopped for a spell. They tied up their horses to some scrubby mimosa trees and sat down on a log for a smoke.

'Skinny Bob had a stinkin' old pipe and he took out his plug and his knife, hacked off a fill of tobacco and shoved it in his pipe. Then stuck his knife into the log beside him and reached for his matches. Suddenly, all hell broke loose.

'As soon as the point of that blade drove into that log, the log jerked into convulsive life and threw the three of them face forwards onto the ground.'

'The bloody log came to life!' gasped Knocker.

'Did it what,' said Wal. 'When they scrambled up, they saw that log they'd been sitting on was the biggest black snake they'd ever seen. It musta been fast asleep until Bob drove his knife into it.

'Anyhow, it disappeared into the scrub,' Wal laughed softly. 'I guess they didn't feel like follering it.'

'Don't reckon they would,' said Oppo.

Wally took a long drag of his beer and shoved the empty glass over the bar. 'Old Skinny Bob had tears running down his face when he told me,' he said. 'He reckoned that knife was the best one he'd ever had. It'd been given to him by his old Dad and he never saw it again. So if you kill a dirty big black snake with a knife sticking into it, remember it belongs to Skinny Bob Morton. Gawd! I'm thirsty. What'd'y' think a man is, Harry, a flamin' camel?'

The question of how big the snakes get that turn up in yarns is a vexing one. Lionel Kennedy, of Nyngan, New South Wales, turned up with a claimant that might give Skinny Bob Morton a run for his money.

How Big?

My neighbour Old Jack was an outrageous yarn spinner and we all took great delight in trying to catch him out.

One day, he had been out cutting Bathurst burrs with a hoe and was on his way home past our house. He called in and was giving his usual resumé of his day's work—how many burrs he'd cut and what he'd seen during the day.

One of the things he *had* seen, was a thirteen foot snake. We asked if he'd got the snake with his hoe.

'No, the snake got away,' replied Jack.

We thought we'd really caught him out this time, so we asked him how he knew the snake was really thirteen feet long if he hadn't killed it.

Quick as a flash, Old Jack replied, 'It was wriggling along the boundary fence line. His head was a foot past one post at the same time his tail was a foot behind the other post—and the posts were definitely eleven feet apart.' With great finality, he added, 'And I ought to know—I put the fence up.'

There's no limit to where, or when, snake yarns come from. They're not something that dwindled, for instance, as Australia became more urbanised. You're just as likely to cop a snake tale from suburbia as you are from way out back.

Tom Winters, of Cairns, Queensland, has treasured his snake yarn for more than half a century.

An Unbelievable Story—but True

In 1931, I was living in my home town of Augathella, Queensland. There wasn't much work around in those days, despite one's capabilities, so my cousin and myself took off for the Carnarvon Ranges, replete with gold prospecting gear. We had a friend up there with his wife, a son aged about ten and a little girl just toddling. He was getting some colour, but he couldn't determine whether it was reef gold or alluvial, so he suggested that my mate and I make our camp about a mile from him, more in towards the foot of the mountains. As he was the expert, we did as he asked. We used to stagger back to our camp, loaded down with specimen rock, which we laboriously crushed with a sledge hammer. After that we washed the crushed dust and found ... nothing!

One glorious moonlit night, we decided to pay the prospector and his family a visit. I don't know whether you've ever walked in mountainous country by the light of the full moon, or seen a more wondrous and glorious sight. We paid the visit, had a bit of a yarn and made our way back to camp, closely followed by a dingo. On the way back we were playing tricks on one another and really enjoying everything. The night lent itself to exhilaration. When we got back to camp, we decided to have some damper and golden syrup. We went into the galley pushing one another about, really skylarking. We didn't light the hurricane lantern, as the moon supplied all the light we needed.

Jim was cutting the damper. I was alongside him, waiting for my slice. He suddenly said, 'Stop, Tom!'

'Stop what, Jim?'

'Stop hitting me on the leg.'

'I'm not, mate,' I said, but something made me look down.

'For God's sake, Jim, don't move your right foot. This is serious. Keep on grinding it down as hard as you can.'

He could tell by my voice that something was wrong. He was standing on the head of a death adder. The tapping on Jim's leg had been the tail of the adder.

We never even knew that there were adders there. Next day we visited our prospector friend to warn him, but he already knew. His beautiful big black and tan dog had been bitten and died.

We packed up next day and went back to Augathella, where we joined the sustenance queue for the next week's handout of food.

Another yarn dating back to the thirties came from A Sadler, of very urban Brunswick in Melbourne. In these days of reversed baseball caps and lurex bicycle pants, many Australians mightn't know what a bowyang is. It was a piece of string or ribbon tied around a bushman's daks, just below the knee. What were they for? Damned if I know. Whether they were meant to keep something out, or something in, I've never been able to work out.

One Less Bowyang

It was the summer of 1936 in the grazing country of north Victoria. Mary stood surveying sun-drenched paddocks from the verandah. Her solemn grey eyes struggled in the glare to detect a sign of the workers due for lunch. They were uncharacteristically late. She wondered at the delay, but could do no more. Turning her back on static fields, she retreated indoors, checking the thermometer as she went. The shade measured 96 degrees Fahrenheit.

Some distance away, in a landscape dominated by the yellows of hay harvest, three men toiled. Sid, the tallest and most talkative, stacked sheaves alongside Arch, whose face lay buried in the shade of a broad-brimmed hat. Jack walked ahead, leaning two sheaves together. This marked the site which, once a further six or so bundles of hay were added, created the stook. Accompanying their circuit was a horse and cart, ready transport for their return to the homestead.

Three men, each of a particular character, were united in one way. Common to all was a handkerchief tied at the neck, wet with perspiration. Each, too, wore a long-sleeved shirt, heavy trousers caught with braces and bowyangs above boots with soles as thick as slabs of beef. They moved slowly—dark figures swimming in the pale hues of a countryside bleached by midday heat. Few trees marked the land. Only the stooks promised any shade.

Arch looked at his watch. 'Time for lunch.'

'Righto!' called Jack, climbing to the seat of the cart. 'Make this the last stook.'

The horse slowed while Arch and Sid stacked sheaves. There was a rhythm in their work; each sheaf being stacked became a beat; each stook became an eight beat bar. As Sid lifted the last sheaf, however, the rhythm of their movement was suddenly abandoned. Arch turned to see a man frozen in his stance with the colour rapidly draining from his face.

'What's up?' he asked.

Sid was mute. As thoroughly as the colour had left his face, so too had the voice departed. Recognition descended on Jack and Arch and they likewise became paralysed. Even the horse sensed trouble and stopped.

To witness the moment was to see time stilled by a sensation as bold as thunder, as sharp as a sickle blade. Sid stood with the sheaf to his chest. His muscles were as good as concrete—arrested by the command of fear. But though muscles freeze, not so the nerves; he felt every detail of a scaled underbelly cool on his flesh. A snake had been in the sheaf and was making its way down Sid's chest and, unhindered by a belt, into his pants.

Arch made no further enquiry, for now there was visible a thickening of his mate's right knee. It was swelling rapidly, pulling the trouser leg tight.

'It's alive,' shouted Jack. 'Keep it clear of the horse.'

'Blimey! You've caught a Joe Blake.' Archie's eyes opened wide.

Sid said something and though there wasn't even a zephyr to speak of, it was as if a wind had caught his words and blown them back in his face. His lips moved again. This time Arch heard the whisper.

'Quick ... undo my bloody bowyang!'

Arch approached tentatively.

'Don't move. Whatever you do, don't move.'

From the sage distance of the cart Jack contributed: 'No worries there, Archie. He couldn't move if you paid him.'

In slow motion, Arch knelt by Sid's leg and tried to release the bowyang. Despite steady hands, his effort was unsuccessful. The weight of the reptile had tightened the knot.

'You've caught a big one, mate,' Arch thought to himself, but said, 'Brace yourself, Sid. I'll have to cut it off.'

In a world clouded so by fear, Sid thought he meant his leg. However, he accepted the diagnosis. Arch took a knife from his pocket. The snake lifted its head and, retracing its passage, began an ascent, curling round its host's thigh. When the blade clicked open, the reptile became agitated. Its head moved quickly from side to side, its tongue lightly pricking Sid's soft inner thigh. He wondered which pain he was going to feel first. Had it been possible to tighten his grip on the sheaf, he would have done so.

With a deft cut, the bowyang sprang open. Arch dropped it at his side as he watched the weight of the reptile sink. The head immediately responded, turning quickly to descend. Arch saw a forked tongue taste the air at Sid's ankle, heralding a thick brown head. Four feet of copper body followed. No move was made to chase it. All three men remained steady until Sid broke the silence with the profound utterance: 'Gawd struth!'

He then got the shakes and Arch had to lift him, still gripping the sheaf, onto the cart.

And so, they did finally arrive for lunch, and in the cool of the kitchen, recounted the story again and again, hoping perhaps that in the repeated telling, the unbelievable would earn credibility.

Jack and Arch said they'd never seen the usually striking tanned visage so pale and void of colour. 'Just like an alabaster statue, he was,' Arch grinned.

Mary said they didn't eat much, but drank many cups of tea. By the time they'd had their last, the atmosphere was almost calm.

'OK, lads. Back to work,' Jack said. 'Seems you've found your nerves, Sid.'

'Yeah, found my nerves but lost a bowyang out there, somewhere.'

So there it lies, somewhere in the paddock—a small price to pay for a life ... and such a story.

Let's go back even further in time for another snake yarn. Colonel George McLean of Tenterden Station, Guyra, New South Wales, sent in a small collection of yarns to the competition. In the accompanying letter, he explained how he'd been jackerooing at Merrywinebone Station, between Rowena and Collarenebri, at the start of the Second World War. Behind what had been the old Avondale Hotel, next to the Merrywinebone Post Office, lived a retired drover, Bill Whitton. He'd known Colonel McLean's father, George, and *his* father (also George), when the most senior McLean owned Collymongle Station, now part of the Collie farms cotton area, in the early 1900s. Bill told the Colonel several yarns about those early days. Here's a reptilian one.

Attacked from Behind

One day at Collymongle, my father and a group of young bloods from the district were out on horseback after wild pigs. The day was hot and all were thirsty, so they stopped at a waterhole for a drink. As normal, they adopted various attitudes to get at the

water—some prone like a goanna, stretched out for direct suction; some squatting on heels and cupping the water up with their hands; others, in between, who knelt carefully on their knees to reach the water.

One of these last, Roly, from a well-known district family, was straightening up with a satisfied smile, when he shot to his feet yelling, 'My God! I've been bitten! A snake!'

Sure enough, just behind him, a snake was slithering into the grass. My father, a recently qualified young doctor and full of authority, ran over and stripped Roly's jodhpurs. There, on the right buttock, were the characteristic twin punctures of a snake bite. He borrowed a stock knife, and applying the accepted first aid of the time, scarified the wound and sucked it to remove the poison. This was all a long way from home, so the wound was covered as well as possible and everyone remounted for the trip back to the homestead.

On the way, to my father's deep concern, Roly started to exhibit the classic symptoms of snakebite poisoning. His pupils dilated. His pulse became faint and erratic. He broke into a cold sweat and became very thirsty.

At the next waterhole, he had to be helped down from his horse, but he was able to kneel again to get a drink. With a relieved sigh, he was straightening up again, when he shouted, 'Caesar's ghost! I've been bitten *again* ... on the other cheek!'

With no snake to be seen, my father examined the patient again and once more found twin punctures. But the absence of the snake led to a more careful investigation. When it was found the puncture marks exactly matched the rowel of Roly's spurs, the patient made a rapid recovery.

With so many people scared witless at the mere thought of snakes, it's amazing that yarns about the poor buggers who get bitten (or *think* they've been bitten) raise such universal laughter. Bill Crane, of Wauchope, New South Wales, you should be ashamed of yourself, having a go at a poor innocent Irishman.

St Patrick, Save Us!

My story is about an Irish family who migrated to Australia and settled on a parcel of land at Bellangry, in the Hastings area. Ireland, being snake free, certainly didn't have any reptiles to worry about like those in the Australian bush. So snakes were first and foremost in these poor people's minds—especially seeing a few tall tales had been told them by old Aussies. They'd become cautious and nervy ... and they *had* seen a black one down near the waterhole, hadn't they?

Electricity hadn't reached the Irish abode then, so hurricane lanterns were in use. There were five in the family—Mum, Dad, a teenager named Mike, a girl of twelve and another lad of eight. One very dark night the family was sitting around the fire planning the following day's chores, when a commotion erupted in the chook house. Mum's pride and joy were her chooks, so she grabbed the lantern and made haste up the back, followed by the rest of the family ... plus their blue heeler dog.

There, wrapped around a young pullet, was a carpet snake, intent on having a Steggles for supper. Pandemonium reigned supreme—the dog barking and growling and Mum shouting, 'Let go, you beast!' Dad arrived with a clothes prop and prodded at the snake, who decided to call it a day and began moving away. Dad made a swing at it and managed to knock the lantern over. Once that went out, it was *very* dark indeed.

The snake had been moving towards the family the last time anyone saw it. They were sure it was poisonous and panic set in.

'Where is it?'

'No one move and it may go away!'

Dad struck a match—creating shadows, everyone of which everybody was sure was a writhing snake. Even Bluey the dog became confused. He rushed in and bit Mike on the leg, thinking it was the snake. In turn, Mike was equally convinced it was the snake which had bitten him. 'Get me to a doctor before I die!'

Dad and the girl ran about a mile down the road to a neighbour who owned an old ute. In the meantime, Mike had almost convinced himself that he was done in.

Eventually, the bloke with the ute arrived, and guessing the culprit was in reality a non-poisonous carpet snake, tried to calm everyone down ... to no avail.

Off to the doctor at Wauchope they all went, with Mike moaning and groaning. Dr Sampson inspected the wound and asked, 'Are you sure it was a snake?'

'Yes!' they all chorused.

'Well,' said the doctor, 'judging by the fang marks, it would have had to be at least thirty feet long.'

'It was!' they all chorused again.

When Mike's leg healed, he returned to Ireland. A friend of mine did a tour of the place a few years later, and at a pub one evening there was a young bloke, name of Mike, showing all who cared to look, the scars of the fang marks where a fifty foot snake had bitten him back when he lived in Australia.

About all that can be said in favour of these confrontations with dreaded Joe Blakes is that a lot of them seem to be family affairs. When there's a scaly monster on the loose, a wonderful sense of togetherness seems to come over your average bush family as they run screaming and yelling in several directions at once. It's quite heart-warming, as Anne Currall, of Molong, New South Wales, proves.

Dad's Annual Event

Every summer, without fail, my father would gather my brother, myself and a various assortment of local children to lecture us on the dangers of snakes. Of course, he had good reason to do so, because of where we lived on the south coast of New South Wales, with our house backing onto bushland. We had numerous snakes pass through or visit, depending on how the mood took them.

On this particular occasion, the lecture started off the same way it always did. The kids were gathered at the front of the house, sitting in a neat row along the verandah, bored and restless. Peter, the old blue cattle dog, was snoozing and twitching, dreaming dreams old dogs dream, under the shade of the lemon tree. My mother was hanging clothes on the drooping, propped clothes line at the back of the house.

Everything started out as per usual, except that this year, Dad was sitting on an old wooden box. He usually leaned up against the rusty green front gate and delivered his lecture. A sense of something different moved through the ragtag audience. Perhaps this year would not be so dull.

Flies buzzed and tormented us as Dad launched into his usual lecture, felt hat tipped back on his head so we could see how serious his face had to be when telling us of the demon snake. The heat from the sun had begun to put half of the kids into a sleep-like state as Dad droned on and on.

At this point, being the showman that he was, Dad stood up, slowly lifted the lid off the box, reached in and pulled out the biggest snake any of us kids had ever seen in our short lives. A collective gasp of horror came from the lips of the children. Many faces, previously red from the heat of the day, became ashen, making the freckles stand out like raisins in a fruit pudding.

My father was delighted. He had made the little tackers sit up and take notice this year—no question about that.

Dad assured us all later that he had not intended to do what he did next. It just happened. None of us believed him.

Raising his voice, he roared, 'This here snake, you young tackers had better believe, is the most poisonous, most vicious and most dangerous snake ever to slither and slide around the earth. In fact, it's a killer snake—mark my words!'

With that, he began to wriggle the snake (which he'd killed the day before), holding it by the tail, swirling it around in the most horrifying, demonic dance us kids had ever witnessed.

Some of the little ones started to clutch onto their older brothers and sisters, sobbing in terror, as the horror continued. Shrieks of fear came from the tightly clenched teeth of the older children as they began to shake and tremble.

Peter the dog, who had been snoozing in the leafy shade, awoke to the cries of terror. He opened his eyes to see his beloved master being attacked by a gigantic serpent. Before he was even fully awake, Peter let out one demented howl of rage and raced to the rescue. With one bound, he jumped into the air, grabbed the snake from his master's hand, sank his teeth into it and worried it back and forth as no dog had ever done before.

The trouble was, the snake was too big and heavy for Peter and before long, he lost control of it. As he swung the snake in a wide arc, it left his mouth, sailed through the air and landed fair in the middle of the little tackers, who, by then, were gathered in a terrified huddle in the middle of the verandah.

Neighbours later related that they thought mass murder had been done. The terrified shrieks of the children could be heard streets away. Kids screamed and ran in all directions, crying and sobbing, trying to escape—except for one. My cousin Ted lay flat on his back in a dead faint, with the huge snake on top of him, nearly covering his small frame.

All that had been accompanied by screams from my father. When Peter the dog had flung the snake into the huddled mass of children, Dad had booted the poor old dog up the rump for his trouble. Peter didn't take lightly to that and he immediately turned on Dad and chomped into the astounded man's leg. Not only did he chomp, but he held on for dear life, clamping his teeth and locking his jaws.

My mother froze when the screaming began. Then she started off at a run to see what was happening ... but the clothes line grabbed her as she tried to duck under it. Engulfed in sheets and undies, she was pulled down to the ground. Finally, she untangled herself and raced to the front yard, just as the shrieking throng of little people galloped past her, white-faced and shaking.

Pandemonium greeted her in the front yard. Dad was lying on the ground, bellowing, with Peter gnawing at his leg. Ted was on the front verandah, apparently dead—killed by the huge snake covering his frail little body.

My mother may have been a small woman, but I had to give her her due. She was a quick thinker. She raced to the front fence, reefed off a grey wooden paling, lifted the snake off poor, seemingly dead Ted with it and pounded the living daylights out of the seemingly live snake. Puffing and panting with exertion, she turned her attention to Dad and Peter.

The dog, by then, had stopped chewing Dad's leg and was eyeing the small, angry woman coming towards him. As he released the bloody leg altogether, Mum swung the paling, hitting the dog fair behind the ear hole. Poor old Peter had no option but to stagger to the shade of the lemon tree to recover, whimpering and snuffling all the way.

But it wasn't over yet. Mum left moaning Dad and gathered up the apparently dead Ted into her arms, sobbing at the sad demise of her nephew. It must have been all the tears falling onto his face that brought Ted back to consciousness. He joined in all the screaming and crying, as he remembered the snake flying towards him, wrapping its cold, scaly body around his, its mouth opened wide ready to devour him. With soothing words, Mum returned Ted to as near to normal as he was ever likely to be after all he'd gone through, and turned her attention to Dad.

He too contributed to the general moaning and groaning as Mum wrapped his leg with her washday apron. By then, all us kids had returned to gather around, still shocked, to view the damage inflicted by Peter's teeth. Suddenly, an indignant high-pitched squeal grabbed our attention. Kids once again raced in all directions as frail little Ted raced towards Dad, raised the grey paling over his head and let him have it. We all cheered!

Never again did Dad give us a lecture on snakes at the beginning of summer. He didn't need to. To this very day, I know of at least a dozen people in various parts of Australia—grey-haired and heading towards old age—who still have a horrible and real fear of snakes and everything associated with them.

When you come to think of it, those last two yarns seem to indicate that it's not so much the snakes we should be worrying about—it's blue cattle dogs.

On the other hand, David Whittaker, of Tarrawingee, Victoria, has added something else to the list of dangerous creatures we all love to hate.

Pet Hates

Do you have a pet hate—cats, rats, politicians, your mother-in-law, or perhaps those mongrels in the supermarket who take full trolleys through express checkouts in front of you when your car's double-parked outside ...?

I have *two* very special hates and they're both connected—overzealous public servants and snakes.

I hate snakes with a passion that would make George Bush and Saddam Hussein look like bosom buddies. You may wonder what would cause such a degree of paranoia in an otherwise normal Australian male. Well, it wasn't the big tiger snake I nearly stood on when I was ten and it wasn't the five foot brown snake that swished by, inches from my face, when I was working underneath the car—even though that resulted in a banged head, concussion and a case of the shakes that required four glasses of medicinal Scotch to cure.

The story goes back many years and was all caused by that other pet hate of mine—one certain overzealous public servant.

It was October 1974. I was a couple of years out of school, a couple of weeks out of work, and having voted for Gough, I was looking forward to a relaxing summer holiday, all expenses paid, under Labor's expanded social security system.

Unfortunately, a just-out-of-school, just-into-the-public-service, overzealous, officious little junior employment officer had other ideas. That little worm of room temperature IQ and I had locked horns about a month before, when he complained I was late putting in my fortnightly form. The reason I was late was that I'd had to ride my motorcycle through a flood to get to town—a point I demonstrated by wringing out my socks on the counter in front of him. It was immensely satisfying at the time, but ultimately proved an action I came to regret.

Two weeks later, he got his revenge.

'Oh boy, have we got a job for you?' he gloated as he gave me the details.

It turned out that a local farmer required someone to help

his son with weed control. It was a beautiful spring day as the farmer's son and I drove the old Land Rover down to the dam, towing a trailer with a pump and a spray tank. At the dam we filled the tank with water and then mixed in the poison.

The farmer's son, Dave, was about my age, and like most farm kids, pretty easy to get on with. Likewise, his approach to his work was rather casual.

'This stuff's pretty dangerous,' he said, waving a five litre container. 'If yer get any of this concentrated stuff on yer, for chrissake wash it off with some of the diluted stuff before it kills yer.'

'Oh, great!' I said. 'Is there anything else I should know?'

'Yeah, watch out fer snakes. I stomped on the tail of a big brown one yesterday to see how frisky it was, and it turned round and bit me boot.'

I had time for a momentary vision of my hands wrapped around the throat of a certain public servant ... and then it was off to work.

It was pretty easy, really. Dave drove slowly around the patches of thistle and Patterson's Curse, while I squirted them with poison from the trailer. When we stopped to boil the billy for lunch, I was feeling pretty smug. The job was a breeze. Over sandwiches and a cuppa, I asked Dave where we were going to spray next.

'Up there.' He pointed to a bloody great hill strewn with fallen trees and boulders and so steep that the sheep had longer legs on one side than on the other.

'We'll never get the Land Rover up there,' I said in horror.

'Not gonna try, mate,' he said. 'We'll do it on foot.'

He then proceeded to drag out of the Land Rover an apparatus that appeared to be left over from an old low-budget science fiction movie.

Ten minutes later, we were ready to go. Just try and visualise the situation I found myself in. I had five litres of highly toxic poison strapped to my chest, a pump powered by a petrol engine that looked and felt like a bloody Victa strapped to my back–

chugging and spluttering away fit to wake the dead—and a trigger-operated spray nozzle attached to a two inch flexi-tube clutched tightly in my right hand. I was so top heavy, I reckon if I'd overbalanced at the top of the hill, I'd have rolled all the way to the bottom—unless, of course, I hit one of the rocks or trees on the way down.

With a momentary vision of myself performing ritual disembowelment on a certain public servant, it was off to work once more.

Up and down that bloody great mountain we went—over rocks and trees, through acres of thistles that were chest high and patches of brilliant purple Patterson's Curse bigger than a footy field. I was drenched in sweat, eaten by flies, pricked by thistles and nearly deaf from the engine. The spare fuel and poison were at the top of the hill and every time I ran out, I was at the bottom. It was truly a living hell ... and couldn't get any worse. Or could it?

It was 4.30 on Friday and the worst day so far, but surprisingly, I wasn't feeling too bad. Thirty minutes to go and I was home free ... for a couple of days, anyway.

I was working a section of hillside so steep it was nearly a cliff. I was keeping myself going by inventing new ways to garrotte a certain public servant.

I was about to step over a fallen tree to get to a patch of thistles, when, coming the other way, was the biggest brown snake I had ever seen.

Brown snakes in that area grow to seven feet in length and that one was no exception.

It was big.

I mean *really* big.

I mean it was so long, it took nearly five minutes to cross over a log ... after which it promptly disappeared into the long grass at my feet.

I quickly backed away up the hill to let it pass.

Suddenly, the grass was moving right *between* my feet.

I backed away, stumbling as I went.

The movement in the grass followed me.

Bloody hell!

I'd heard of snakes being aggressive in springtime, but this was unbelievable. I continued stumbling backwards in frantic haste, the grass moving at my feet wherever I went.

The most terrifying thing about it was the grass was so long, I couldn't see exactly where it was.

I must have gone thirty yards up that hill backwards, positive I was only seconds away from a painful death. I banged into a large boulder, the grass shaking furiously at my feet, and with a backwards leap that any self-respecting ninja would have been proud of, I landed atop that rock.

With trembling hands, I lit a cigarette.

Whew! That was close!

By the time I finished the cigarette, there was no sign of any snake. I climbed down and looked around.

All clear!

I started the pump.

The grass shook violently at my feet.

Oh Christ, here we go again!

I turned and ran blindly up the hill, my mind devoid of rational thought.

Suddenly, I tripped over the spray hose that was dangling from my waist and crashed to the ground.

I got back up on my feet, dripping poison and petrol. I turned off the pump, threw it on the ground and walked to the large gum tree against which I pounded my head for about five minutes. It had finally dawned on me what was going on.

When I first saw the snake, I had let go of the spray handle, allowing it to swing free. The pump was still running ... and blowing a blast of air between my feet ... causing the grass to move.

There was no bloody snake chasing me at all.

It was probably miles away by now.

That all happened twenty years ago, but I still haven't got over my fear of snakes ... or my loathing for a certain public servant.

Anyway, I'm off to see my therapist now. If you ever hear of some deranged bloke spraying an obnoxious little public servant with herbicide and then garrotting him with a dead snake, spare him a thought, because you'll know who he is ... and why he did it.

Eventually, though, we all have to face our fears. Have you ever wondered how you'd react if your greatest nightmare became reality? It happened to Enid Cryer, of Pacific Palms, New South Wales ... and she lived to tell the tale.

Next Time, I'll Do it Myself

I could have done it myself, but it seemed to be a job for experts, so I rang the local National Parks and Wildlife number and got no answer.

Then I tried the local council.

'Yes,' the Community Services man informed me, 'we do have a bloke who's good at handling snakes, but he's on two weeks' holiday. Try the RSPCA.'

I did that, and was given the name and number of the lady who dealt with their wildlife problems. She wanted to be helpful ... until I mentioned 'snake'.

'Look,' she said, 'I'm fine with any other animal, but snakes terrify me. Perhaps you should contact the police.'

At that stage, I'd worked out how I could do it myself ... but decided to be sensible and *did* phone the police.

'A snake in your bath?' He sounded doubtful, so I quickly explained that it was a sunken bath and that the snake could easily have slithered in ... but it couldn't get out. I also explained that I'd rung several other organisations before bothering the police.

'Yeah, well,' I was encouraged, 'we *could* send someone, but it might be a while.'

I gave him the address of our few bush acres out of town and added, 'I don't want the snake hurt. I just need someone to put it back into the bush where it belongs.'

'Lady,' the voice was all authority now, 'we don't get paid enough money to play around with snakes. I'll get someone out there as soon as I can.'

He hung up.

I now had two problems. A ninety centimetre red-bellied black snake in my spa bath *and* the local constabulary eager to shoot, bludgeon or pitchfork it to death in situ.

I went to check my house guest.

It was a young one, about as thick as a good thumb and very restless. How long it had been there I could only guess. It was lunchtime when I'd discovered it. Mentally, I went through my own routine again for shifting it, but the complications of being bitten when I was at home alone outweighed the snake's discomfort.

Then I had another idea.

I phoned the local community radio station ... and wondered why I hadn't thought of it earlier.

No problem at all. They'd be glad to send out an SOS for someone who could handle a snake. Almost immediately, they called me back to say they had a fellow who would be glad to help, but not until about 9.30 that night. I said I could wait (and hoped the snake could, too), gave them directions and cancelled the police.

I was back to having only one problem again. Nicking a few pieces of the cat's meat, I ambled back to the bathroom and dropped them in the bath, thinking the poor creature must be hungry. Then I remembered that red bellies love water, so I dribbled a bit into the bath, too.

As there was nothing more I could do, I busied myself with other things and just checked on him occasionally. The meat remained uneaten and the puddle of water ignored.

My husband was away up north for a few days and I thought about phoning him. However, I decided his well-intentioned advice and instructions would only confuse the issue.

About 10 pm, the young man arrived and we discovered we knew each other from some previous gathering. He put a friendly hand on my shoulder and said, 'Don't worry, Enid. I'll fix him.

Even though I've handled only a couple of snakes, I'm not frightened.'

It seemed pointless to tell him that I wasn't frightened, either. We went through to the bathroom, where I had a bucket and a towel ready. Then I went looking for a flat stick for my Sir Galahad. I also found a pair of heavy gardening gloves ... but he rejected them as being too inhibiting.

Pinning the small snake's head was easy. Trying to get a man-sized finger and thumb behind the head and in front of the stick proved impossible. He just couldn't get a hold. To move the stick further back would have given the red belly, who was by now *very* aggressive, the chance to move his head and maybe make a strike. I was feeling nearly as frustrated as the captive.

Maybe, I thought, my original plan would have been best after all. It was simplicity itself. I would have blocked out a pathway from the bathroom, through the bedroom and down the long hall to the entrance foyer and opened the front door. It meant using lots of boxes, suitcases and upturned tables and, finally, a board slanted into the bath for my house mate to slither out on, but I was convinced it would have worked.

But what could I do now, with a young man's ego to deal with? I made another suggestion.

'While you keep his head pinned, take his tail in your other hand and lift it as high as you can. I'll hold the bucket in the bath and have the towel ready. Then, quickly, and at the same time, release his head and lift him. I'll get the bucket underneath as you drop him and I'll throw the towel on top.'

It took a few minutes of confidence building, then the gentle hand was once again laid on my shoulder and his quiet voice said, 'You know, Enid. I *am* frightened.'

With a grin, I assured him that if he were bitten, I would get him to hospital quickly, having first done all the necessary snakebite things ... and he had better be ready to do the same for me.

Well, he did it! The snake was in the bucket, the towel was on top and my brave friend made a hasty dash through the house, out the back door, down into the bush and heaved the bucket.

A rough release for my snake—but he didn't come back to complain.

Next time, I'll do it myself.

YARNS!
Didja Hear About...

Chapter 1

DOING IT TOUGH

WHEN I was an anklebiter back in the fifties, Australia still felt very much British—and kept reminding itself of the fact. In our corner of the bush just west of Melbourne, it was a carefree time, full of rabbiting, wagging school and rambling around the bush. Nights were taken up with crouching around the old Astor Mickey radio, listening to radio serials, starting with 'Hop Harrigan' from 3AW in Melbourne about 6.00 pm, then thundering on to 'Captain Silver and the Sea Hound', or 'Tom Corbet, Space Cadet', 'Superman', 'Tarzan' and, at 7.00, 'Gunsmoke', featuring the adventures of Marshal Matt Morgan. When the television version of 'Gunsmoke' first hit Australian screens in the late fifties, we were amused to see the Marshal's American name was originally Matt Dillon. The radio version had obviously been tailored for antipodean audiences. A name like Dill-on and the connotations associated with it would have had no credibility with the millions of little bush kids who tuned in—so, sensibly, they changed it to Morgan. There were home-grown heroes, too, like Smoky Dawson and his partner Jingles and a rash of great comedies like 'Life With Dexter' and 'Laugh Till You Cry'.

The nearest cinema was about 20 kilometres away in Bacchus Marsh, but occasionally travelling picture shows came around. Every few weeks we could crowd into the local hall and watch the ancient adventures of Charlie Chaplin, the Marx Brothers or the Three Stooges.

But the most common films were propaganda things shot during the recent war, constantly delivering to us heroic scenes from the Battle of Britain or the Western Desert. Occasionally we'd get a glimpse of Aussies spraying the kunai grass of New Guinea with Owen guns or struggling through the mud of the Kokoda trail, but generally, it was just lashings of how Mother England had battled through, alone and unaided.

A memorable scene which came up time and time again was an old girl being dragged out of the rubble of a bombed house who cackled at the camera, 'You've got to laugh, or you'd go mad.'

For years impressionable Australians accepted that the old stiff upper lip was the exclusive property of the Poms. Technically, it was—at least the stiff lip part. What we did wrong was confuse it with the ability to laugh at your troubles. There's some common ground, but physically, you can't laugh satisfactorily with a stiff upper lip. It comes out 'Urrgh! Urgh! Urgh!' instead of 'Ha! Ha! Ha!'

That old girl in the rubble definitely didn't have one. In fact, if I remember rightly, she'd lost her dentures somewhere in the mess and physically couldn't keep her upper lip stiff. But, by crikey, she could laugh. I wouldn't be surprised if she eventually scraped together the 10 quid, migrated out here and added to the ranks of Aussies who've perfected the art of making hard times into one big giggle.

It's only relatively recently that we've come to realise that our ability to bypass the SUL and go straight to not taking our predicament seriously is an important part of the true Australian character. As times have become harder in the bush through droughts, floods, financial shenanigans and vanishing markets, it's a resource more and more people have had to draw on. Thankfully, the traditional whingeing cocky is slowly becoming a threatened species. 'You've got to laugh, or you'd go mad' is probably as close to a national philosophy as we've got.

Going back to those halcyon days in the fifties, I remember a string of battling dairy cockies on smallholdings along the road between our place and Bacchus Marsh. They all did it hard, but they were a cheerful lot. Not long ago I caught up with one family, with whom I boarded for a few months during one of our own family crises.

'God, we used to laugh,' reminisced my former landlady. 'I remember one time we were getting the cows in for milking in the freezing cold and pouring rain. We were both knee deep in mud and manure. I was trying to push this cranky old Friesian into the milking bail, when one of me gumboots come off and started filling with mud. When I tried to get it back, the other one came off. As far as I know, they're still there.' And she laughed a deep, satisfied chuckle.

'The old man was so tickled he couldn't stop laughing. In fact, he laughed so much, his false teeth flew out across the yard and landed plop in a freshly done pile of cow dung. We were both hysterical and the cows nearly didn't get milked. God, they were good times.'

They weren't good times. They were hard, harsh and unrelenting. To my knowledge, none of those families ever had two bob to rub together—until things got too much and they finally sold up. It's heartening to know that the number of Australians who manage to find humour during hard times still greatly exceeds the number who go mad. It's a characteristic that goes back a long way, as this simple reminiscence from Mrs ME Liddievat on Tomakin, NSW shows.

The Debil Debil

This is a story of an episode in the life of my grandmother, dating back about the 1870s. My grandparents at that time lived a little way out of Kempsey in the bush. One day my grandfather took the dray into town, some miles away, to replenish stores. After he left, my grandmother saw a group of Aborigines coming towards the house. They were carrying spears and looking very threatening.

Quick-thinking grandmother wound up the alarm clock. The unwelcome visitors demanded food and 'baccy' (tobacco). They raised their spears, looking like they were ready to attack. Suddenly the alarm clock rang. The visitors got such a fright, they ran around crying, 'Debil! Debil!' and then ran away.

Grandmother had saved the day and wasn't troubled again. I think it was very courageous of her.

I'm always pleased to include yarns from the Kempsey area in these books, because that's where the Hayes family now makes its home. Since we moved there in 1994, everyone's been telling us about the big floods that used to trouble the Macleay Valley. Other areas might have their bushfires, droughts or duststorms, but we have our river. 'You couldn't imagine what it was like during the big flood of . . . ' is a great conversation starter for any local interested in letting a new chum know at least what things *used* to be like. These days, dry times and an over-commitment of the Macleay's water have contributed to reducing its mighty flow to a relative trickle, or so the old timers assure me.

Neil Fisher of Port Macquarie has been able to give us a clearer view of just what the Macleay could come up with. He covers his own backside by attributing this yarn to his great uncle Harry. Ah, Neil, it's funny how there are so many great uncle Harrys around the place prepared to deal with the truth so lightly. I will admit, though, that in full cry, the Macleay carries some sort of official title like, 'the second fastest flowing river in the southern hemisphere'.

The Mighty Macleay River

Harry Penrith was an Aboriginal bloke from Greenhill near Kempsey. He was well known as an athlete and a strong swimmer. During one of the many floods on the Macleay, Harry wandered down to the riverbank to gather some melons and pumpkins that were floating down from the farms on the upper river flats. Harry dived in to gather one particularly large pumpkin. However, before he could get back to the riverbank, a wall of water surged down the Macleay and took him with it. He'd not travelled far when he was hit by a large, solid object and was winded. Despite having the breath knocked out of him, Harry managed to crawl onto the mystery object and take a firm grip.

On and on he went with the current, down the river past the quarry, Hennessy's sawmill, the Stones, the great wood traffic bridge at Kempsey and Glenrock Plains, before it swept in towards the Frederickton wharf. Whatever Harry had ridden down the river hit the wharf with a great crash and sank. Harry managed to crawl up and along the decking to safety.

After sheltering in a shed for the night, Harry found the water had receded sufficiently for him to return to the river. He dug in the mud to investigate what it might have been that saved his life. Once he'd cleaned most of the mud away, he found it to be a very large piece of metal. It looked somehow familiar. With the aid of some water, he rinsed it a bit more and found the initials 'J.C.' stamped into the top of it. Yes, he was right. He had seen it before. It was Jack Carroll's blacksmith's anvil from Greenhill.

Some weeks prior to the flood, Jack Carroll had obtained the services of Jack Hudson and his bullock team to haul the anvil from the blacksmith's shop down to the wharf at Greenhill so he could carry out repairs on a riverboat. It was lucky he had. The anvil, washed into the water by the flood, had saved Harry Penrith's life.

Some say it took Jack Hudson and his team of bullocks another two days to haul the anvil back to Greenhill from Fredo.

It would be grossly improper, after discussing floods, to drop the subject of natural disasters without balancing the ledger and considering the ultimate Australian adversity—drought. Even when the rain's failed to turn up, the creeks are dry, the dam's empty and cracked and the grass long gone, the raw Australian sense of self-deprecating humour survives. At least it did with Bill Young from Broken Hill.

If Only ...

Things were crook on Tiger Smith's run, west of Cunnamulla. The drought had ruined poor old Tiger. About half the sheep had perished, and when the rain finally came with a vengeance, most of those left in the plains paddock near the river had floated away down the Balonne. Some mongrel had rustled a truckload of his cattle on agistment in the mulga country further south. The bank had issued an eviction notice, giving Tiger 90 days to clear out. The stockie from the DPI [Department of Primary Industry] had quarantined what remained of his sheep for lice and his cattle for brucellosis. He couldn't even get credit from the stock and station agent for a drum of Clout to dip his sheep.

Out in the paddock, Tiger had time to think about ways of saving money. When he came back to the homestead that night, he gave his wife a peck on the cheek and gently touched her breast.

'Ah, darling,' he said softly, 'If only we could get milk out of these, we could sell the cow and wouldn't have to buy any more feed. Think of the money we'd save.'

The next night when he came home, he found his good lady bending over the stove taking an emaciated leg of mutton out of the oven. He gently patted her bum.

'Ah, darling, if only we could get eggs from there, we could sell the chooks and wouldn't have to buy them feed. Think of the money we'd save.'

The following night, when he came home, his wife met him at the door, gave him a kiss and undid his fly.

'Ah, darling, if we could only get this to stand up, we could

sack the jackeroo ... and *then* think of the money we'd save.'

--------◆--------

Of course, adversity doesn't always have to occur on a scale as grand as a Macleay Valley flood or a Queensland drought. Personal crisis is just that—a very personal thing. As Lenny Lower is quoted as saying, 'What is happiness to a man who's been bitten by a bullant?'

While yarns tend to focus on tall tales and true from the bush, it's obvious that a little judicious editing could place many of them in the city or suburbia. Harry Collins's yarn was submitted from the dry, dusty wilderness of Glebe in Sydney.

Grandpa's Stroke

This is a true story that a woman told me. It concerns her great grandfather, who had quite a reputation for making wine from the local blackberries. Unfortunately, he had a habit of over-indulging. On this particular occasion, the whole family was celebrating a big wedding for her auntie and everybody was enjoying a great time on the wine, including Grandpa. At one stage he decided to go to the loo, which, in those days, was a little tin shed way up the back of the yard. He was away for some time and Grandma started to worry. Finally, she decided to go and look for him. Not long afterwards, she came running back to the house, calling, 'Quick! Quick! Something has happened to Grandpa.'

Everybody rushed out to help. They found Grandpa inside the loo, leaning against the wall wailing, 'Get some help. Get some help. I've had a stroke! I'm paralysed.'

By then, Grandma was in tears and everyone else was screaming in dismay. In the end, someone headed off to the nearest phonebox, which was some distance away. In the meantime, the women were crying and the men were saying, 'Don't move him.' Eventually an ambulance arrived. The ambulancemen found Grandpa still leaning against the tin wall, still apparently paralysed down one side. They brought him out and laid him on a stretcher.

'Hang on! The silly bugger hasn't had a stroke.'

What *had* happened was largely due to the skinful of blackberry wine Grandpa had indulged in. In those days, men wore no zippers on their flies, just buttons and button holes. Finished with his business in the loo, Grandpa had buttoned his shirt cuff button to his fly buttonhole. No wonder he couldn't move down one side!

From that time on, every time those ambulance blokes went into the pub and told the story, there were drinks shouted all round.

Another mini crisis, ignored and unrecorded by more conventional historians, was passed on to me by one Peter Ryle. He swears it's fair dinkum. 'I wouldn't want anyone to think it was made up or anything.'

Pawing the Poor Pawpaw

There was this bloke living in a bush town who had to go to Cairns for a bit of medical treatment. It wasn't real serious and he didn't have to stay in hospital, so he moved into a friend's house.

It seems that on the Sunday morning, this bloke from the bush looked out of his window and spotted a big ripe pawpaw on a tree in his friend's yard. His salivary glands went into top gear and he decided to enjoy an early fruit brekkie before anyone else woke up.

The tree was quite tall and the fruit well out of reach but, being from the bush and, like all real bushies, adept at improvisation, he looked around and found a petrol drum. When he climbed onto it, he found he was still a bit short of reach. Further search brought to light a four gallon drum (a 20 litre one for youngsters who don't remember real measurements). He placed the smaller drum on top of the larger one.

Once again he climbed to the top. By reaching to his full height,

he could just grip the pawpaw. Slowly, he turned the fruit to break it off.

Now this bloke was no spring chicken and he'd developed quite a gut. Anyone who's studied these things will know that when a man reaches up with his hand—especially a man with a belly—the bulge tends to travel upwards too. When you add that effect to the laws of gravity, you can understand what's apt to happen to a pair of shorty pyjamas.

As the pawpaw broke off in his hand, his shorts slid gracefully down to his knees. By locking his knees tightly together, he managed to keep what must have seemed to him a bit of decorum. His efforts to balance on the drums while trying to keep hold of the fruit made it impossible to retrieve his shorts—which became only too clear when he tried to do just that. As he attempted to bend his body to grip the offending article of clothing, his knees parted and the said article slid slowly to his ankles. To add insult to injury, when he tried to descend, his tangled legs refused to cooperate. He did manage to keep hold of the pawpaw, though, as he rolled on the ground.

Keeping hold of his dignity proved difficult, however, owing to his friend's neighbour's wife hanging over the fence laughing herself silly as he fled back to the kitchen with his shorts still around his ankles and the pawpaw still in his hands.

It's said he wears braces with his pyjamas now. And he goes a real pasty colour when anyone mentions using a drum instead of a ladder.

Sometimes you get the feeling that the participants in these disasters don't see the humour in the situation until afterwards. Hilarity definitely increases with hindsight. David Thompson's yarn from Vincent in Queensland, his favourite and originally told by his brother-in-law's uncle Jack, is at first glance pretty horrifying.

The Only Decent Thing He Could Do

This story is about Jack's two brothers, Joe and Ron, who used to ride a horse to school through the scrub. Joe was the eldest, so he rode in front, with Ron behind. They had to travel a fair way to the schoolhouse and were often in strife for being late.

One morning, they were galloping through the bush, endeavouring to make it on time, when Joe saw a low-hanging branch up ahead. He ducked, but forgot to warn Ron.

'Whack!' His brother was knocked from the horse and lay on the ground unconscious.

Nevertheless, Joe still managed to make it to school on time and eventually got round to telling the teacher what had happened.

'Goodness. What did you do?' she asked—a fair enough question under the circumstances.

'I just put my coat over his face, so the crows wouldn't peck his eyes out.'

Poor old Ron didn't regain consciousness for three days!

These days, that poor teacher would be snowed under with official forms, insurance claims, legal disclaimers and other assorted bumfodder. We often tend to forget the difficulties today's chalkies face in their line of work. Instead of sympathy, we shower them with accusations of having more holidays than the rest of us or conveniently being able to arrange pupil-free days immediately after long weekends.

Some great yarns have come from the experiences of teachers—especially new chums—confronting the realities of battling the bush for the first time. It's a toss-up whether the travails of old time chalkies were more or less traumatic than the bureaucratic nightmares teachers face today.

Terry Hennessy of Mt Surprise in Queensland seems to have strong views on the subject.

Urandangie Uproar—or A Pedagogue's Penance

When I was a boy in Sydney during the 1940s, my father gave me two pieces of advice regarding future employment. First, always earn your living with your coat on and, second, become a teacher and you'll never be out of work.

I suppose they were wise words in those days, and I started following his advice. After teaching down South for 11 years, I headed for Tennant Creek in the Northern Territory on a one year working holiday ... or so I thought. My initial impression was that Tennant Creek was at the end of the earth.

After two very enjoyable years there, I transferred to Santa Teresa Mission on the edge of the Simpson Desert, 100 kilometres south-east of Alice Springs.

Now *that* was definitely the end of the earth.

Two and a half years later, I went to Papunya, an Aboriginal settlement, 250 kilometres west of the Alice, on the edge of the great Western Desert. Surely if I'd have gone any further, I would have fallen off the edge of the world. I lasted two and a half years there before transferring to Lake Nash—peace after Papunya! And *definitely* the world's end. The regional office was in Tennant Creek, 500 kilometres away, and my nearest Territory school, at Utopia, only 200 kilometres closer.

I had come, seen and conquered. I had experienced everything and could tackle anything. However, nothing could have prepared me for Urandangie.

For those good souls asking, 'Where?' I should explain that if you look at a Territory or Queensland map and locate where the Georgina River crosses the border, you'll find Lake Nash. It's two kilometres on the NT side, and Urandangie is 14 kilometres on the Queensland side ... but 100 kilometres further south. Not too far? Well, it took three hours to get there.

Urandangie had seen better days and, at that stage, only two dwellings were occupied—the pub and the store-cum-post office-cum-weather station. The store was owned and operated by Frank and Beth Austin. Although I had reservations about their sanity *before* I went to Urandangie, now I have none. But I do understand why.

After piteous pleading from Frank about the need for Beth to have a holiday, I agreed to spend my school vacation as an unpaid postmaster, weather observer and storekeeper—a piece of cake for anyone as experienced as I. The welfare of two dogs, six cats and 48 goats was also thrown in there somewhere, but still, they'd be no problem.

I was issued with the following instructions:

1. The weather: take the weather observations at 3.00 am, 6.00 am, 6.00 pm and 9.00 pm. Record them in the book and encode them to send the details to Brisbane by telegram.

2. The telephone: it's one of the old party line type. The station people have cooperatively agreed not to ring out of hours.

3. The store: well, anybody can run a small store.

4. Dogs and cats: just feed them.

5. The goats: let them out in the morning, make them go through the yard quickly so they won't eat the fruit trees. Pen them at night. Again, no problem.

And for the first week or so, everything went well. Then it happened. After doing the 9.00 pm weather check, I crawled into bed, tired but satisfied. At 10.00 pm the phone rang—an urgent call to one of the stations—out of hours, but, oh well, it *was* an emergency. Back to bed.

Loud knocking and yelling suddenly awoke me from a deep sleep about an hour later. One of the camp's young babies was having difficulty breathing and seemed rather sick. I contacted the flying doctor base in Mt Isa. I was told the baby could have pneumonia.

'Give it an injection of Byacyllin.'

'Hang on, they never taught me how to give injections at teachers' college.'

'Oh, it's easy. Just give it in the upper quadrant of the buttocks. If you don't, the child will have to be brought to Mt Isa, and that's a 240 kilometre drive from where you are.'

As my vehicle was the only reliable one around, I became more than willing to become the medico.

It took two adults to hold that baby down. Obviously it wasn't keen on getting that injection and bucked furiously. The needles went in and out of its buttocks many times, only making the situation worse. It didn't help that the dogs decided the invaders inside had to be driven out and continued barking loudly. Eventually, I succeeded in hitting the right spot with the needle. 'Thanks, Terry.' The grateful parents took the baby back to camp and I retired back to bed and blissful slumber.

'Hiss! Scream! Thump!' The bunyip had me. My throat had been cut. I arose like the Man from Ironbark. Thump! I was knocked down again. Two tom cats had been fighting in the rafters and had fallen onto the bed. It was about 1.30 am and shock was starting to set in. Luckily I managed to find that rum I was sure Frank kept around the place. Another attempt at sleep. Then, the alarm again. To hell with the 3.00 am weather check. I was on strike.

Ah, there's the phone.

'Mt Isa here, Terry. Where's the weather? Thought you must have slept in.'

Everyone was out to get me. I took the readings and sent them off. Back to bed ... nothing on the agenda until 6.00 am and the weather again.

Then it was time to let the goats out. They must have sensed I wasn't quite with it and made a beeline for the fruit trees.

'Better get dem goats out, Terry. Missus'll get proper cranky.'

It took many naughty words, sticks and stones, but eventually they left, after stripping the orchard almost bare.

The water had boiled for coffee and breakfast when a Toyota pulled up outside. The ringers were heading out and wanted a few goodies. That meant the store was officially open, so all the camp children decided they wanted goodies, too. By 7.00 am the patience of the station folk had ended and they started ringing out. Between the store, the weather and the phone, it was full on until 9.00 pm.

The phone rang one last time. It was Frank and Beth. They were in Mt Isa and would be home tomorrow. The locals couldn't understand why Terry, who, until then had been proper cranky, was now laughing hysterically.

At last Frank and Beth returned, refreshed from their holiday and happily chatting about the fishing at Karumba. I, too, was at peace with the world. Happiness was Urandangie in the rear vision mirror. I was heading back to Lake Nash—the end of the world. But at least it was on the earth. Urandangie was positively unearthly.

As for my father's advice, I did indeed have a coat, but the moths ate it. And I'm still a teacher, but, along with 10 000 others in Queensland, I'm not in full-time employment.

Thank goodness.

Is it possible to go too far, laughing at our troubles? I suppose there's a certain slapstick element in getting knocked unconscious from your horse, or getting an injection from a stumblebum amateur. What about dentistry? Is there anyone so inhuman that they can recount, with affection, the sort of yarn that makes the old flesh positively crawl?

Of course there is. Sam Scott from Hall in the ACT is one of them.

Say 'Arrrggggh!'

Back in the late sixties, I was managing a station called 'Yarrum' in the Gulf Country. Though it sounded like the Aboriginal name for horses, 'yarrowan', it was really Murray spelled backwards: the name of the man who first took up the land. The station's northern boundary was the Albert River and on the north-west it was Beam's Brook, a freshwater stream. There was a tree on Yarrum that had been marked by the Burke and Wills expedition, which had included an ancestor of the man after whom Beam's Brook had been named. The Albert River divided the station from the township of Burketown, only seven kilometres away.

Burketown, named after Robert O'Hara Burke, had a mixed population—descendants of Chinese gold miners and Japanese pearlers, as well as Aborigines and some whites. Because Burketown was close by, I was happy for the Aboriginal stockmen I employed, with whom I got on well, to go to town at night once or twice a week. They were reliable and would always be waiting for me when I went back to pick them up.

One of the stockmen on Yarrum was Homet Hoosan. His father was one of the Afghan camel drivers who delivered supplies to the inland settlements after collecting them from the ship *Cora* which brought freight from Bundaberg via Thursday island. Homet's mother was an Aboriginal woman and he was renowned as a tracker and a stockman. In the early fifties he had been employed continuously by exploration companies searching among the copper and tin lodes for uranium. Homet's sister, Alice, had married a hard-rock miner who owned the Pandanus mine, which he left to Alice on his death. For five months of the year, it mined copper, yielding 80 per cent to the ton. Homet told me he could show me how to collect tin lying on the ground, without having to dig for it. He was amazed that the exploration companies weren't interested in tin or copper, only uranium. Homet told me he was 16 when the Albert River bridge was built, so, in 1968, he was 56 years old.

One night, I drove to Burketown to collect Maurice Shadforth, a part Scot, part Aboriginal stockman, and two or three others who had been visiting the town. Maurice told me that Homet had been hurt, and we went to look for him. We found him behind the hotel, a sorry sight. He had obviously been in a fight and was still partly drunk. Two of his side bottom teeth were hanging out, the roots still connected, and two front teeth were sticking straight out, their roots free at the back and only held in place by the other front teeth.

I asked him what had happened but he wasn't interested in answering. What concerned him, to the exclusion of everything else, was that he wasn't going to eat rib beef any more. That was a terrible blow to any Aboriginal stockman. When a beast is killed, the rib cage is thrown on the fire and is regarded as a great delicacy. People in those parts thought it might have been the origin of the saying, 'The nearer the bone, the sweeter the meat.'

So I took Homet to the bush hospital and saw the matron, Marion. She told us, 'This is self-inflicted damage. There's no way the flying doctor will come out for this,' She added that she had no experience in dentistry. Nor, for that matter, did Dr Tim O'Leary, the flying doctor. 'There's a dental surgery out back that hasn't been used for several years but it's still equipped with implements like forceps.'

'Let's go and have a look,' I suggested.

'But you don't know anything about dentistry, either.'

'I bloody know enough to put those teeth back in.'

Twenty years earlier I had been on Augustus Downs Station and I'd had the same lower side teeth removed by a flying doctor, without anaesthetic, while I sat on a water canister carried by a pack horse.

Now Homet wasn't exactly known for his courage. Sometimes the stockmen would do some wild driving across the claypans when they were covered by a few centimetres of water. Some of the wilder drivers would drive at top speed then slam on the brakes and see how many times the car whirled around. Once Homet had been a passenger and registered his extreme panic by screaming 'No! No! No!' throughout the whole ordeal. After that, he stayed a spectator.

Homet had been listening to the conversation between matron and myself but had obviously decided his desire to get his teeth fixed for rib beef had overcome his lack of courage. Matron and I got him into the dentist's room, where there seemed to be enough tools for the job. While Homet was in the chair, I picked up the forceps. He held me by my left arm and I can still feel the pressure of his grasp. He could have got out of the chair, but he didn't. Marion cleaned up all the blood and supplied warm, salty water for the gargle and wash.

I could have taken the teeth out in about 60 seconds, but there would have been no more rib beef for Homet, so I set to and swivelled the front teeth until I got their rather short roots back into their sockets ... more or less. Next, using cotton wool, I pushed the teeth up until their bottoms were level with the others. Then I straightened up the two side back teeth until they fitted into the rest of the row. We packed both front and back with cylindrical cotton wool pieces soaked in a sterile solution and told Homet to keep his jaw clenched till further notice.

Matron made him some soup and stews for several days until he was able to eat again.

When I left Yarrum in 1970, Homet still had all his teeth intact.

———————

While we're in the business of flesh crawlers ... We might as well get this next one over and done with. I have a personal affinity for it. As kids we were sometimes reduced to having little else to eat than rabbits and yabbies. To this day, the smell of either one cooking can make the old stomach churn—and we never experienced anything like the nightmare suffered by Lockie Beauzeville of Lake Cargellico, NSW.

Curried Rabbit and Rice

In 1937 my brother Joe and I went with our cousin Dud out to a property on the Peak Hill Road, about 14 miles (that's a bit over 20 kilometres) from the small town of Trundle in the central west of New South Wales, where we lived. I was 13 and my brother was fifteen. Dud was probably about 10 or 12 years older than me.

Our means of transport was an old grey horse pulling a spring cart. We were there to trap rabbits for their skins. Our camp was set up in a 300 acre (about 120 hectares in current parlance) paddock overgrown with tea-tree, just too high to look over and too low to look under. There were hundreds of rabbits in that scrub patch, nothing like the post-war plagues, but there were plenty for our purpose. We built a rough camp with a few sheets of iron we had taken with us and an old tarpaulin. We'd also taken our camp stretchers with us, so all in all, it wasn't a bad

camp. We finished erecting it by mid-afternoon and were ready to set out our 120 traps.

We boys hadn't had much experience with that type of trapping, but Dud had been at it for years. It was decided we'd make three runs each day—one an hour after dark, another about midnight and the last one at daybreak, after which we'd have a bit of breakfast. Then we'd skin and peg out the hides before moving or re-setting the traps. We'd prepared hurricane lanterns for the night run.

Apart from getting lost a few times in the tea-tree, things went along fairly well. We were getting plenty of good quality skins.

During our time there, we practically lived on nothing but rabbit stew, rice and bread, with a few spuds and stinging nettles for greens. The bread was delivered every second day by the mailman, who left it in the fork of a tree opposite our camp site. One day, after we'd been in camp about a week, I made up a curry of rabbit and rice. I dished some out for the evening meal and put the rest back in the metal meat safe that was hanging under a shady tree. I thought at the time it would be great on toast for supper after we'd finished our first run later that night.

So after the run, we returned to camp and I had a really good wash up, peeled some spuds and placed them in a spare billy can. I put it on the coals next to the tea billy, then brought over the billy of left-over curry from the safe and stirred it up well, before putting it on the fire to heat up. I remarked at the time how good it smelled. Stew, soup or curry is always better the second time around. We had a slap-up feed of curry and rice with mashed potatoes and big mugs of piping hot tea. Dud declared it a great meal and announced I was a better cook than I was a trapper.

While we were cleaning up by the light of a hurricane lamp, Dud decided to empty out the remains of the curry and rice so he could wash up the billy. He looked inside to see how much was left, intending to feed it to the greyhound dog tied up away from the camp. To everyone's horror, he found that what he'd thought was rice in the billy was really a host of well cooked maggots!

After a while, we recovered sufficiently to take the lantern and inspect the meat safe. Sure enough, there was a hole about as big as the end of a little finger rusted in the corner of the mesh— Open Sesame! for the blowies.

It was many years before I could even look at curry or stew. In fact, it wasn't until I joined the army in 1942 that I ate stew again. There, I had no choice, it was eat it or starve!

Just one more ...

This yarn originated from Len Pump of Callignee, Victoria.

Bernie's Home-grown Pasture

Bernie, a neighbour and friend of mine, had been a bullock driver in his heyday. He was as tough as they come. Being a bachelor without a car, he would order his supplies via the mailman. One day the PMG boys, on arriving for work, found the order he'd put in for three pounds (about 1½ kilograms) of sausages from the local butcher. Deciding to play a joke on Bernie, they added a nought, making the order for 30 pounds (for those no good at sums, that's about 15 kilograms).

When the meat was delivered, Bernie wasn't at all perturbed. He just slung the huge string of sausages over a tree limb and used them as required. It worked all right for the first few days, but eventually the sausages started to appear slightly limp and green, and finally the flies moved in. But old Bernie, being a thrifty man, used them all.

It was not long after this that Bernie became conscious of a severe irritation at the rear of his heel. He knew he'd had a blister there for some time, but decided he'd better investigate. He wasn't accustomed to removing his boots—even to sleep—so he hadn't taken them off for about four months.

To his great surprise, he found the blister had become infected. A grass seed had found its way into the wound and had started growing. The blades of grass were more than two inches (a good 5 centimetres or so) long!

Bernie calmly pulled out the offending plant and put his boots back on.

———————

Of all the disasters that can befall Australians, bushfires are probably the most shocking. They can come out of nowhere, and if conditions are right, nothing can stop them. They used to be just a bush phenomenon, but now, as our cities start sprawling, it's usually outer suburbia that's most at risk. Some cynics have suggested that the devastating New South Wales bushfires of 1993 might have gone unnoticed had they not threatened the trendy outer Sydney suburbs favoured by certain media identities. I've written before about a somewhat twisted hobby-farm wife who described bushfire brigades as 'male Tupperware parties'. She hit the nail right on the head. Despite the vital service they provide, all the brigades I've been involved with have been mini-circuses. Or maybe it's just me.

A Peach of a Fire

It had been one of those typical western Victoria summers. Just as we started stripping the crops, the temperature climbed and the north wind set in. Every eye was constantly being drawn back to the dazzling blue horizon for the telltale sign of smoke.

It wasn't long before a ripper of a bushfire started out further west, way over the other side of the Grampians. Local legend has it that some silly coot had ignored the total fire ban imposed by the CFA (the Country Fire Authority, for those who don't know) and had been stripping his oats crop. Somewhere in the guts of his ancient harvester, two metal edges had rubbed together, generating a bit of heat, a spark or two and, suddenly, the whole countryside was ablaze.

The cruel January winds were expected to carry the blaze through the dense eucalypts of the Grampians in a relatively short time. On our side of the national park, there were dozens of farms and one or two towns, some of them nestled under the very lip of the rugged ranges.

Our lot were sent off with other similar Dad's Army style fire units to a small farm area right in the path of the fire. God knows what they expected us to do. A thin, rusty line of ancient blitz wagons equipped with grossly unreliable pumps and leaky water tanks didn't stand a chance against the ruthless monster laughing its maniacal way towards us.

We parked our pathetic conglomeration of vehicles in an untidy line at the bottom of a large bluff. Overhead, the afternoon sky was one black mass of smoke. Its underbelly rippled with the reflected red of the flames slashing their way through the thick forests on the other side of the bluff.

A handful of pretty cottages lay scattered along the valley we were supposed to protect. We thought of the poor people who'd been evacuated by the police earlier in the day. They must be worried sick. It was early in the most recent drift away from the cities to the bush. People had bought the small mixed properties to get out of the rat race. They'd done them up to chocolate box perfection, all of them with freshly painted green roofs and heritage colours and surrounded by carefully nurtured gardens and orchards.

It was stone fruit country and all the fruit trees were groaning under festoons of plump, ripe peaches.

'Y'know, it'd be a shame if this fire destroyed all that fruit,' muttered George, my brother-in-law-at-the-time. No one else said anything for a while.

'Yeah, it'd be a damn shame. My kids love peaches,' someone else said from the back of the fire truck.

Another short period of silence.

'Y'know, it's all going to be destroyed anyway. We're not going to be able to stop that fire. It'd be a *crime* to let that fruit waste.'

It was unanimous. We fossicked through one of the sheds, found one full of fruit crates and proceeded to save the crop from the merciless red steer we were sure would come roaring over the bluff any tick of the clock.

'Someone just keep an eye on the fire, in case it gets here early,'

George called from the top of the tree he was harvesting.

The fire didn't interrupt our fruit harvest. We had crates haphazardly stowed aboard every fire unit in the valley, and still the crimson angel of death hadn't arrived.

Nor had he fronted an hour or so later.

Come night-time, there was still no appearance, your worship.

In fact, the fire didn't turn up at all. Somewhere over the other side, the wind changed, some rain fell, or it ran out of fuel—anyway, it fizzled.

Volunteer fire units do a great job. Often, against the odds, they perform miracles. But that afternoon, we found it bloody impossible to screw stolen peaches back onto their branches before being sprung by their rightful owners.

Thankfully, the Search for the Great Aussie Yarn proved that it wasn't just me or the bushfire brigades I'd been involved with that tended to resemble a Mack Sennet comedy. Merrick Webb of Table Top, near Albury, had similar misadventures.

A Sticky End

Having spent most of my early days in the hilly and timbered country on the western slopes of the Blue Mountains, I had experienced a good number of bushfires. We fire-fighting farmers usually gained a victory over them, even though the fire-fighting equipment back then was less than basic when compared with the mobile tanks, pumps, sprays and hoses now available. Those 50 or 60 years ago, our efforts were organised by the local Agricultural Bureau.

In 1943 we moved with our young family to a spot in the hills district about 12 miles (or 20 kilometres) from Parramatta. The area was then given over to citrus fruit and poultry. There were still many areas under native bush—towering eucalypts, with an understorey of extremely thick and menacing vines and undergrowth.

As Christmas approached and the hot summer steamed in, my

education in fire fighting was considerably upgraded by the most terrifying fire one could imagine. It swept suddenly from the west, heading towards our little village, where the general store and petrol pump were just across the road from our place.

Clouds of thick smoke surged from the fire, driven uphill by a strong westerly wind through a thickly timbered valley. It produced flames the like of which I'd never seen before or, fortunately, have ever seen since. As though by magic, people appeared, running in all directions, but full of purpose. They managed to surround the most threatened buildings and saved many of them.

Most houses suffered a blackout as the thick underscrub threw up savage flames that burned through the powerlines. Two dwellings, two vineyards, various chook sheds and orchards fell to the scourge. Then the fire moved down into a gorge where a supply of creek water and bare roads made it controllable.

Amid all the drama, a moment of respite occurred in Mrs Moody's busy little store across the road from our cottage. Mrs M was a good manager and stocked her store to advantage. Some time previously, she'd bought up a supply of canned golden syrup, which was stacked in rows in her cool cellar under the main shop. There was plenty of room in the cellar and that's where the fire fighters stored much of their equipment. When a fire broke out, they had to rush in and extract their gear from among the stored goods. On this occasion, they had to clamber over various stacks of tinned goods, crates, boxes and drums.

Dear Mrs Moody, in accepting her bulk order of golden syrup, hadn't been told that because of wartime restrictions, the familiar round dark golden syrup containers were now being made of cardboard, except for the lid and bottom of each one.

There's no need to elaborate on the state of the cellar after all those heavy boots had tramped over the stack. And there's no way a six inch (that's 15 centimetres) stack of golden syrup can be restored to a saleable state.

It turned out to be one Christmas that didn't satisfy dear Mrs Moody's somewhat obvious economic leanings—it was one that, for the moment at least, was simply all gummed up.

Of course, these uniquely Australian mishaps do actually get the better of some of us, and the worst does indeed sometimes come to the worst. But even funerals aren't sacred to the dedicated yarn spinner, as Dale Johnston of Buninyong, Victoria proves.

The Burial

I'll never forget the day of old McPhee's funeral. Bloody hell it was hot! Even the lizards were tiptoeing across the bitumen, and while we were waiting for the service to start, we toasted sandwiches on the bonnet of the car. Inside the church, you could hardly breathe. The preacher looked a bit like a boiled yabby. His sermon went off pretty well, though, and didn't last too long. He did go on a bit about how much old McPhee had done around town. I could have added a few more things, but I reckon it's best not to speak ill of the dead. Old McPhee's widow never shed a tear, either—a strong woman.

It wasn't until we were on the way out to the cemetery that things started to go wrong. Big Charlie Segal stopped his car in the middle of the road and held up the whole procession. On the side of the road, he'd spotted a dead kangaroo that had been knocked a few days before. Charlie had a heap of dogs and not much money, so he was always on the lookout for free meat. He threw the kangaroo into the back of his station wagon. You should have seen the blowies following that car!

When we got to the cemetery, Charlie decided he didn't want to walk far in the heat. He found himself a parking spot really close to proceedings. The trouble was, it was upwind. When they brought the coffin round, the preacher got the wrong idea and went mad at the funeral parlour blokes for not keeping the lid on properly. Everybody got in a bit of a flap. Then someone found a hammer and some nails and started slogging away at the coffin.

By the time we realised it was only Charlie's kangaroo, Mrs McPhee was real upset. She grabbed the hammer and went after

Charlie like a turkey at Christmas. They did a few laps around the grave until Charlie started running out of puff. In the end, he got desperate and tried to take a short cut over the top. Somehow he didn't quite make it. All 23 stone (that's a hefty 145 kilograms) of him ended up in McPhee's grave. It wouldn't have been so bad, except the grave had been dug for someone skinny. It wasn't anywhere near wide enough for Big Charlie. He got well and truly wedged about halfway down, with just his head and shoulders sticking out.

McPhee's widow had him right where she wanted him and went absolutely berserk. It was lucky some of the relatives dragged her out before she actually killed him or she might have been charged with murder.

The doctor said afterwards that Charlie died of heat exhaustion from struggling so much. We'd all had a go at getting him out, but he was so heavy, no one could lift him. All of a sudden, he'd gone real red in the face, and that was it. Poor old Charlie.

No one seemed to know what to do, then someone suggested, 'Why don't you just make the grave a bit bigger and leave him where he is?'

In the end, that's what we did. Charlie didn't have any relatives that anyone knew about and it just didn't seem right to bring in a forklift to get him out. We'd only have had to put him back again later. We just widened out the hole a bit and let him slip down to the bottom.

The preacher said a prayer and that was it.

Later that night, they towed Charlie's car away and dug another hole for old McPhee. After that, we had a cool change. Next day, everybody turned up again and did the job right by giving old McPhee a proper burial.

Sounds far-fetched? Well, after a lifetime of yarn spinning and broadcasting, the only time I felt duty bound to exercise a bit of self restraint, self censorship and common decency was when the coffin of a late neighbour of ours stuck in the top of his grave, necessitating some heavy footwork from his mourners. At my own dear old Mum's burial, which we were given official approval to carry out ourselves on the home property, the greatest worry was that some of her over-enthusiastic and overprimed well-wishers might fall into the grave while filling it up. A wheelbarrow full of dirt is a cumbersome thing if you're not careful. On both occasions, it occurred to me that the dear departed would have thoroughly enjoyed the humour of the situation.

A final say on the matter of funerals goes to WH Dunn of Taree, NSW.

The Hypochondriac

This doctor was getting sick and tired of being constantly revisited by the same hypochondriac.

'Doc, I think I've got gout. Isn't there something you can give me?' Knowing it was useless to argue, the doctor would write out a script and send the nuisance off.

Two days later, he'd be back. 'Look, Doc, I think I've got the measles this time.'

After a quick examination, 'No mate, you're OK. It's just a heat rash. Take this tube of calamine lotion.'

'Beauty, Doc. I wonder what I'm going to get next.'

Two days later, the same story. 'I think it's ulcers, Doc.' This time, it'd be a bottle of Mucaine and a curt goodbye.

But the bloke would persist. 'It's me heart, I reckon, Doc. There must be *something* you can give me for it.'

'Look, you're fine. There's nothing wrong with you. Get out!' This time, the doctor instructed his receptionist not to let the offending patient back into the surgery.

About a week later, the doctor arrived at work to be greeted by the receptionist brandishing the local paper. 'Oh dear, Doctor, it says here that that hypochondriac suffered a heart attack and died.'

The doctor ordered her to cancel all his appointments that afternoon. 'I'm going to the funeral. I want to make sure he's *really* dead and gone.'

After the service, the elated doctor dropped into a pub for a celebratory drink. The barman noticed his good mood and struck up a conversation. The doctor explained why he felt so happy and won himself a couple of extra drinks on the house. Eventually he staggered from the bar and walked straight under a fast-moving semi.

Two days later, it was the doctor's turn to be buried. They laid him to rest in the town cemetery, right next to the hypochondriac. When all the mourners had left and the grave had been filled in, the doctor heard a rapping on the lid of his coffin.

'Hey, Doc, you wouldn't have anything for worms, would you?'

Chapter 2

OFF THE STRAIGHT
AND NARROW

THERE'S no doubt about it, all Australians respond to that unique character, the larrikin. I'd like to think a minority of us respond negatively, like certain stern Rotarians I've occasionally encountered who firmly believe Crocodile Dundee would have more effectively served Australia's cause if he'd been portrayed as a diligent, responsible time and motion expert.

I suppose a government department somewhere should have appointed a team of consultants to report back to a working party on the findings of a select committee appointed to look specifically into implementing a strategic plan arising from a white paper discussing the most desirable feminine term to match the word 'larrikin'. I've got a sneaking suspicion they'd come up with that grand old word 'sheila'. As a result, female yarn spinners contributing to these hallowed pages will also be regarded as larrikins—the terms larrikinesses or larrikinettes not only maintaining sexist overtones but being almost impossible to pronounce after too many doses of certain easily obtained proprietary cough mixtures.

Similarly, people who seem to find the concept of a multicultural Australia such a chore may be anxious to argue that a term like 'larrikin' doesn't take into account the diverse ethnic groups which contribute so much to our nation.

As an immigrant my good self, from a culture that couldn't be further removed from what's recognised as truly Australian, may I suggest that, deep down, it was the very spirit conjured up by that cheeky word that drew so many of us here in the first place. 'Larrikin' is synonymous with 'freedom' in its most basic form. There aren't any larrikins back in Sri Lanka where a lot of our mob originated, but there are a few of us here who've never had much trouble fitting the description. There aren't any in Bosnia, China or the Middle East. But there's quite a few larrikins called Branko, Quong and Mahomet.

One characteristic of a true larrikin is the ability to never quite be capable of 'doing the right thing'. The opposite action, which they have no trouble carrying out, is, of course, 'doing the wrong thing'. It's not quite the same as committing a crime or performing an atrocity. It's a relatively harmless, often unintentional mischief which, more by accident than design, really doesn't hurt anyone . . . or at least, anyone else.

A typical example is this yarn from 'A concerned mother of 4' from 'somewhere in the southern hemisphere'. It must be true. Ms X especially asked for no names to be used in case the local railway authorities got shirty.

A Bit of a Spin

Two blokes were working at a local silo on a Saturday afternoon. The silo yards were deserted, as were the remains of a once busy railway siding. In an old corrugated iron lean-to, they found a trike padlocked to a side line. Escapades and challenges were all part of these fellows' lives and the sight of that old trike and miles of empty railway line stretching to the horizon was just a little too tempting to leave.

They put a battery into the trike motor, fixed a 40 watt globe in the light socket, and whistled up two accomplices and a dog, proudly announcing, ' We're taking her for a spin.'

'Where'll we go?'

'Better not take the main line. Might hit a train.'

Off they chugged on a spur line, with a good 15 miles (25 kilometres or so) of narrow gauge track ahead of then. It was a line only used by trains during the grain harvest, so they were unlikely to get any nasty surprises coming the other way. They soon got the hang of driving, and negotiating bends wasn't a problem.

They picked up speed and confidence and drove along happily until they came across the first of several cyclone fences strung across the line and hung with a bag as a warning to any rail traffic. Quite a few local farmers grazed their sheep along the line. At each such temporary stop, the travellers carefully opened every apology for a gate in the fence, manoeuvred through, then pulled it shut again behind them. At one stage they realised their dog had disappeared into the scrub and spent a frantic 10 minutes calling and searching until he reappeared, looking very wet and bedraggled, but quite pleased with himself.

Their next major obstacle was a road crossing. Mud had built up over winter and had covered the line. One of the intrepid locomotive enginemen walked across the paddock to a farmhouse. There wasn't anyone home, but he used the phone to call the nextdoor neighbour. He wasn't there, either, but his wife was.

'Shirl, bring a towrope, a camera and a six pack.' She did . . . and used the rope to pull the trike over the crossing. They then continued to the end of the line, where across the paddock, a local footy match had just ended. The travellers joined the teams and supporters in a beer. All four were in fact from an opposing team and there was quite a bit of interest in how they'd got to the match.

'Came by rail.'

'Oh yeah, sure.'

'Come and see.'

Everyone was suitably impressed. The trip home, fuelled by several more beers, was faster than the journey out. The little bulb lit their way through the mallee–and *all* the cyclone fences.

Arriving happily at the station, they locked the trike back onto its own line, removed their battery and light bulb and sought sanctuary in their own footy club. They couldn't keep their adventure secret. Even the local policeman was terribly impressed by their escapade.

And they *did* have the decency to phone all the farmers along the line the next day to suggest they check their sheep and be prepared to do a bit of drafting.

Squaring up after doing the wrong thing might recover a few lost Brownie points, but some faux pas go beyond forgiveness. Such is the case with this yarn from Geoff Dean of Mt Sturt, Tasmania.

Bert Morley's Killing

Bert Morley was a travelling salesman who'd been making seasonal trips to the district for nearly 20 years. His lines ran to needles, threads, balls of wool, pins, soft fabrics, sewing boxes, clothing and sometimes–when he could talk one of the wives into believing that her sewing machine was on the blink–he could even conjure up the very latest, foot-controlled, 'do everything but sit up and bark' electric model.

In his late fifties, Bert was a lugubrious man, whose expression rarely changed. His speaking voice was flat, without any inflection whatsoever. Consequently, when he spoke, he seemed always to be complaining about something, even if he wasn't. His slight figure, clothed in a dark blue double-breasted pinstripe suit, with a plain red tie to match, was permanently stooped, as if he carried the woes of the world on his narrow shoulders.

Phyllis Barnes from the bakery always reckoned that Bert's personality was more suited to the undertaking profession than the sales game. 'Even when he tells a joke, it comes out more as a lament,' she said, 'Whenever he comes into my shop to buy his meat pies, I feel depressed for the rest of the day.'

Bert drove an old Ford bus that he'd had converted into a combination caravan and mobile showroom. All the seats had been removed and lines of cupboards built along each side of a central aisle. The cupboards were hinged so that they opened up and out in steps, for easy access.

At the bottom of one row of cupboards he had a bed, which he could wheel in and out with the minimum of fuss. Just to the side of the front exit door, there was a small kitchen space which, during business hours, converted to a counter for charging and wrapping. Bert's customers entered the bus from the back end and made their way through his lines of goods to the front door. All in all, it was a very efficient self-serve system that suited Bert and his customers alike.

Because his overhead costs were lower than the local shopkeepers', his prices were very competitive. Business was brisk from the moment he arrived and set up his bus in the main street until the time he packed up ready to move on to the next town. The local shopkeepers didn't much like Bert taking their business away. Whenever he was in town, they were always grumbling about money leaving the district. But there wasn't much else they could do about it, because Bert always made sure his current hawker's licence was prominently displayed in the front window of his bus.

However, in spite of running a profitable little business, Bert was often heard to confess that he got a bit sick of always being on the move and one day he intended to retire with his long-suffering wife to a little cottage by the sea he'd had his eye on for quite a while. 'I'd do nothing then but grow vegetables out the back, read the papers and stare out the window at the sea. All I need is a couple of thousand more of these ... ' he told his customers repeatedly, as he shoved their banknotes into his ancient metal till. Whenever he mentioned the subject of his retirement, Bert was inclined to go off into a thoughtful reverie, as if, at that very moment, he was looking out of his dream cottage window. Then he'd give a big sigh, followed by a wistful smile and continue wrapping the packages of goods he had before him.

For all the enthusiasm displayed by the local ladies towards his wares, though, retirement still seemed a long way off. The cold, hard facts were his profit margin was low and his costs were rising every year. What Bert really longed for was something special to sell—something that he could really get his teeth into—a sale line with such potential he could make a quick killing and finally realise his dream of retirement. What it could be, he had no idea!

That was until on one trip to the district, he found a letter waiting for him at the town's post office. It was from an acquaintance who worked in a clothing warehouse, offering him the chance of a lifetime—500 ladies' frocks at less than half cost price!

'The frocks are excellent quality,' wrote his acquaintance. 'The only problem is they're last year's fashion, something I thought wouldn't particularly worry your country clientele. All sizes are available.'

Back in his bus that night, Bert re-read the letter for the umpteenth time and, with his pencil, began jotting down a reasonably optimistic estimate of how much profit he could make if he sold all the frocks at slightly above wholesale rates, a price most of his customers wouldn't be able to resist. The total he came to was considerable. It certainly seemed as though his ship had come in. If he could sell the majority of the frocks at such a price, that little cottage by the sea would be within easy reach. First thing in the morning he would ring his acquaintance and accept his offer. In anticipation, he wrote out his cheque and put it in an envelope, ready for mailing.

He was so excited by the prospect of his fortuitous windfall that he didn't get to sleep until almost morning. When he did, his dreams were crowded with images of rows and rows of green vegetables, trailing vines, garden gnomes, the soft humming of bees and the gentle thudding of surf on sand (which was in fact the bakery's machinery across the road, kneading the dough for the early morning loaves). If anyone could have seen Bert's sleeping face that morning, they would have been surprised by his broad and contented smile.

On his return to the district a week later, Bert picked up the consignment of frocks from the railway station. Later, in his bus, he unpacked the boxes with trembling fingers. Would his windfall be as good as he expected? Sure enough, as his acquaintance had promised, the frocks were of excellent style and quality. Opening the first carton revealed a rich collection of blue with white polka dots. He opened the second carton: another 20 blue and white frocks. A slow realisation began to dawn. In rising panic, he began to rip open all the cartons, and his terrible suspicion was finally confirmed. Each carton load was duplicate of the first—500 blue frocks with white polka dots!

'The bastard!' he moaned over and over. 'The bastard's sold me a factory job lot.'

As he drove back to the caravan park, Bert pondered the calamity. How in the blazes was he going to sell 500 identical frocks in a close-knit community at any price? Even if he toured the entire countryside, he'd be unlikely to sell more than half a dozen in any town. He broke out in a sweat just thinking about it. Gone was his chance for early retirement. When his wife found out what he'd done, she'd most likely kill him. His pleasant dreams of the previous week were already turning into nightmares.

That night, for the first time the locals could recall, the frugal hawker turned up at Connolly's public bar and set about getting roaring drunk. He lined up six beers and steadily worked his way through them. When he got to the last beer, it had hardly had time to go flat.

One of the locals, who was even more intoxicated than Bert, sidled up to him and offered to shake his hand. 'Good on yer,' the man said, 'Yer a real boozer after all. Have a drink on me to celebrate.'

Already suffering the beginnings of a hangover, Bert waved the suggestion away with weary hand. 'Not me, mate. I've got nothing to celebrate. I've got to be up early in the morning. There's a lot of ground to cover to make up for what I've lost this week.'

The man, who introduced himself as Kev Parker, looked a little disappointed. 'It's a real shame. We boozers got to schtick together, y'know. There ain't many of us left. Will yer be back for the races, then? I could put yer onto a couple of real good starters next Friday night.'

Bert stared back at the man for several seconds. In the turmoil of his recent disaster, he'd forgotten about the district races. Apart from show day and the footy finals, it was the biggest event on the local calendar. Even in his hazy and inebriated state, he thought he could see a faint glimmer of hope.

'The races, eh?' he said finally. Then, with more enthusiasm than he'd shown all week, he reached out, grabbed the man's hand and shook it vigorously. 'Too bloody right I'll be here. I wouldn't miss it for quids. I'll see you right here next Friday night.' With one vague wave in his new friend's direction, Bert staggered out of the pub and into the night, a diabolic plan already beginning to form in his addled mind.

Come race day, the weather was perfect. A record crowd showed up. The only thing that marred proceedings was the embarrassment and suppressed wrath of several hundred or so of the local ladies—of all shapes and sizes—each sporting what was, according to Bert Morley, who'd shown up on their individual doorsteps during the previous week, the very latest, top quality, blue and white fashion frock of exclusive design that he'd kept especially for them, his favourite customer.

One of the unfortunates hiding in the ladies' retiring room that afternoon was heard to express the general sentiments of her fellow sufferers. 'No wonder the miserable little bugger suggested I keep it a secret. "What a surprise you'll be on race day," he said. I promise if he ever shows his face in this district again, *he'll* be the one who gets the surprise. I'll have his nuts for a necklace.'

That was something that wasn't likely to happen. The word went about that a week or two after race day, Bert sold up his business and disappeared, probably to that little cottage by the sea he'd had his eye on for so long. What with the price he got for his business, the six quid profit he'd made on each of those frocks, and the doubles' winnings his new-found mate Kev Parker had placed for him that day, he could afford to.

———————————

It's amazing how often the demon drink rears its frothy head in the informal world of larrikins ... and yarn spinners. Some may see fit to purse their lips in dour disapproval and mutter gravely about promoting substance abuse, antisocial behaviour and human disintegration. However, the fact remains, the so-called foaming article has often provided the final impetus to transform an otherwise unremarkable quantity surveyor or bean counter into a fully fledged larrikin. Our continuing ability to maintain that delicate balance between colourful character and pathetic relic will undoubtably decide our future as a nation.

A perfect example of how to do that is here demonstrated by Mr John Alexander Sherrington, a former Brisbane union official, who happened to drop in at our place about the time Jupiter was being bombarded by asteroids, for a dose of larrikinism. What might have been a rather shameful affair was saved when Mr Sherrington saw fit to translate his experiences into an astronomical thesis. The fact that he expressed himself in doggerel verse remains a major blot on his copybook, and I'm sure he apologises accordingly.

The Deep Creek Dive

I'll tell you a story that simply amazes
Of a tilting floor at the Deep Creek Hayes's.
It happened to me, this enigmatic riddle,
Early one morn as I went for a piddle.

One couldn't quite say that I was all that drunk
But many's the glass of fine vino I'd sunk.
I'd risen erect from my bed on the floor,
Seeking to find out which way was the door.

But so dark was the night, as I seem to recall,
That I put out my hand to steady the wall,
When up came the floor with an almighty rush
And my wrist and my rib cage it tried hard to crush.

I wrestled quite strongly against the attack
And hip-threw that floor fair square on its back.
It settled down quickly with nary a moan,
The both of us left in a position called prone.

Why did it happen, causing so much confusion?
I can only arrive at one final conclusion—
When Jupiter was struck with remarkable might,
The poor bloody floor just jumped up in fright.

It's hard to believe the strength of that hit.
But that's my story, and I'm sticking to it.

Get the idea? So let's enjoy some yarns which aren't so much a glorification of the lunatic soup as a remembrance of a time when a drunk was someone who could still manage to walk their bicycle home sideways.

On the other hand, the one encountered by Don Smith of Leederville, WA was one of those blokes whose wit and charm undoubtedly only developed with hindsight.

Sorry Boys

Some blokes get really serious when they're playing pool, and that's what it was like in this bayside pub. The atmosphere was tense. The room was full of smoke. The loudest noise was the 'tock' of cues hitting balls, or now and then, the sound of a ball falling into a pocket, the clink of a glass or the hissing of the tap behind the bar. All eyes were on the pool—not so much on the game itself, but the way people played—how they took the cue from the last person, how they approached the table, how they sussed out the balls and, most importantly, how they held their left hand—the one the cue slid through. It was like a dance ritual, leading step-by-step to that climactic point where the ball was actually hit. Then the focus moved to the player's face—would he smile, grimace, pout, pucker or leer—anything? No! No emotion. Not even the clumsiest, stupidest shot sparked any show of feelings. That would have been just too uncool.

I wondered what might happen if, say, one of the legs on the pool table collapsed . . . or the cue broke in half . . . or the ceiling fan dropped and smashed in the middle of the table. Would the player crack and finally show some sign of emotion, or would he casually glance back at his mates, pause, and say, 'Two shots'?

On this particular night, the atmosphere *was* shattered. Just at the moment when the room was really full and the coins were piled high on the tables, a middle-aged bloke came into the room. He'd been in the front bar. He was drunk, *very* drunk. He moved like drunks do, searching for balance, over correcting and swaying like an elephant made of jelly. He wasn't a no-hoper, though. He had a bit of style, a dark coat, a pork pie hat and a tie. He looked like he might have just stepped out of the Christmas party at the local cop shop.

Most people were trying hard not to look at him. They were there for the pool game. But I was entranced. There was something about him—a look of irony, a sardonic leer that said, 'I might be old and drunk, but, hey, who cares?'

The drunk smiled a big smile that went right around the room and seemed to embrace the entire place. He started to move among the players. They snarled and snorted as he passed. Then the drunk knocked someone's cue as he shot for the eight ball. The player turned quickly, sneered and pushed. The drunk lurched away to another table. Then he just drifted out the front door and into the night.

Half an hour later, Steve and I had managed to swallow our beers and had contemplated the pool tables and decided the Twilight Zone would be more interesting. We stood outside in Eric Street for a while, hitching for a lift, but it was too early. People weren't in a party mood. A bunch of blokes in a Mini roared along the curb and screamed something at us. We decided to wait a bit longer before walking to the highway. Then, out of the carpark came an old Valiant. It was moving . . . but only just. It stopped about five metres past us. We whooped with joy and ran over to it. Steve opened the door and we both looked in.

It was the drunk. He still had his hat on, but by then it had moved down to his ear and made him look like an old monkey. 'G'day, boys, where y'going?'

'Up the highway.' It seemed possible at the time.

'Sure, hop in.'

We both clambered in the back and watched him move the automatic shifter into drive. It took a lot of concentration. The Eric Street hill is one of those coastal hills that slopes gradually on the ocean side but drops down steeply on the other . . . *really* steeply.

The drunk cruised the Valiant to the top of the hill. I had that intense feeling of anticipation you get when you climb the first rise of a roller coaster. Steve turned to me. His eyes had that 'Oh well, here we go' look about them.

Down we went. The old bloke just seemed to plant his foot and aim at something in the distance. About 50 metres from the bottom of the hill, the car mounted the curb and careered along the grass. Steve and I said nothing. We didn't want to upset the driver's judgment. Then the car sideswiped a box tree. Steve and I yelled. The drunk took no notice. We scraped *another* box tree. Still nothing from the driver. Finally, he managed to steer the car *between* the third and fourth trees and ran straight into a brick wall. It was one of those single-layer walls people build to keep the noise out.

Fortunately, we'd dived for the floor, so we were OK. We dragged ourselves onto the backseat and looked out the window. Bits of brick and greenery spread across the car. The Valiant was well and truly wedged in. We didn't know what to do. Outside, lights were going on and dogs barking.

We peered over the seat at the driver. We weren't sure whether he was conscious or not. Then he moved, groaned and finally peeled his face off the steering wheel. He sat staring straight out through the windscreen.

The drunk then turned, looked at Steve ... then at me and, in the most casual and carefree way, said, 'Sorry, boys, this is as far as I'm going.'

You don't have to be Politically Correct with a capital P and a Capital C to recognise that behind the wheel of a car is no place for a drunk—colourful or otherwise. However, there was indeed a time when the constabulary looked upon a bit of self-induced euphoria with a less stringent eye. We still hear calls for a return to the old-fashioned copper who'd 'give you a kick up the bum and warn you not to be so bloody stupid again'. And, by crikey, it worked! It has yet to be put to the test by a royal commission.

David Geddes of Uki, NSW obviously knows about such times.

Good Old Sarge

In the late 1940s–early 50s, I was a young man living on my father's property about 25 miles (that's 40 kilometres) north-west of Manilla, NSW. We had a twice-weekly mail service, Monday and Friday, run by a young man by the name of Bobby Grant. There were three more boys in the family and, with their father, all had country mail runs using horses and sulkies. They were all partial to a drink, normally sweet sherry. Driving a mail sulky in all weather would make anybody drink!

As it transpired, one Friday's mail day fell on Christmas Eve. Bob didn't turn up until the following day, Christmas Day, and in a *taxi*. I saw him in town a few days later and asked what had happened on Christmas Eve. He explained that he'd gone into town with his older brother Darky and collected bread, groceries and mail from the post office. They also bought half a dozen

bottles of wine each. Back at home, they knocked over a couple of the bottles and Darky invited Bob to join him on *his* mail run, which went up the Namoi River and almost to Uralla in New England.

According to Bob, every place they came to, they had to have a Christmas drink. Coming back that night, the road took them right past the Manilla cemetery. In those days, it had a high railing fence around the Catholic section.

Bob didn't know how it happened, but he'd ended up on one side of the fence and Darky on the other, passing the bottle of wine to each other through the bars. At that time, the sergeant of police at Manilla was a Sergeant Rollinson, who had a reputation for being very tough. From his side of the cemetery fence, Darky remarked to Bob, 'They can say what they like about old Rollo, but he's OK by me.'

'Why?' asked Bob.

'Well, look at us. He's run us in, but he's put us in cells next to each other and even let us bring the grog in with us.'

Jack Goldsmith of Millthorpe, NSW also had a brush with ad hoc bush justice back in his larrikin days, and confronted disapproval from another source.

For Whom the Bell Tolls

Jack and a mate were drinking in the top pub at Normanton, up in the gulf country of Queensland back in 1958. They'd been at it nearly all night and were starting to get a little rowdy (in a friendly sort of way). The local police sergeant pulled the price of a dozen 26 oz (that's 750mL, these days) bottles of Fosters out of the money they had sitting on the bar, put the carton on his shoulder and ordered, 'Follow me, you two.'

He took Jack and his mate to the edge of town, telling them, 'Now you can fight, yell and argue all you like.' Then he left.

They found themselves sitting under an old tower, part of the ruins of what had obviously once been an old church. A big brass bell was still up in the tower, with a rope still attached. Seeing it was the early hours of the morning, Jack and his mate considerately decided the place needed a bit of livening up. So they started ringing the bell—quite a din at two o'clock in the morning.

Up on the hill, Normanton's only preacher was wakened by the noise. Poor bloke, even with his family swelling the number of people in the pews, he could only struggle to attract a dozen or so converts to his church from the local community, and that was on a *good* Sunday. On hearing the ringing of the bell, he surmised something was up and marched out of town to the old ruined church to ascertain exactly what.

'G'day, pastor, have a beer,' offered Jack.

The reverend gentleman gave him a long lecture on the evils of drink, then added, 'Don't you know that the church bell is only rung to summon sinners to the church?'

'Is that a fact?' replied Jack with interest.

'Yes, it is.'

'Well, pastor, this Normanton must surely be a righteous town.'

'Why's that?'

'Because you're the only one who's turned up.'

Speaking of the clergy ...

I have it on very good authority that the church is a hot bed of yarn spinning. The picture I've had painted for me is one of priests, deacons, archdeacons and bishops rushing their way through the parish or diocesan agendas whenever they get together for business, tapping the keg of dry sherry and swapping yarns. There've been many contributions to these books from members of the cloth. Some of them have requested anonymity and I feel it only right to grant it. There must be some similarity between a yarn-spinning session and confession—but I'm blowed if I can put my finger on it at the moment. Those who haven't requested anonymity have been granted it out of the kindness of my heart. I'd hate to be the cause of a defrocking for a yarn like this next one, passed on by a respected country minister.

The Miracle

A devout country clergyman had been summoned to Sydney to discuss parish affairs. He was making good time along the Hume Highway, when he noticed a semi-trailer pulled off crookedly to the side of the road. The driver had the cabin hoisted up and was obviously toiling away deep in the bowels of the engine. With a bit of time up his sleeve and an amateur's interest in heavy vehicles, the clergyman pulled up behind the semi and strolled over.

'What seems to be the trouble?' he asked the driver's rear end.

'This bloody bastard of a thing's well and truly rooted!' came the muffled, but passionate, reply.

Ignoring the language, the minister pressed on. 'Is there anything I can do to help?'

'Help? Bloody hell. The prick of a thing's absolutely buggered. I've tried every bastard of a thing I can think of and the bloody bastard still won't go.'

'Everything?' asked the clergyman cryptically. 'Have you tried prayer?'

The driver scrambled down from the motor, wiping his oily hands on his shorts. 'Shit. That's the one bloody thing I haven't tried. But I'm buggered and I'm willing to give any bloody thing a go.'

So, together, they knelt in the hard gravel besides the Hume Highway, ignoring the roar of passing vehicles and the derisive hoots and shouts from other drivers. And they prayed long and hard to the Lord to get the big truck going again.

No sooner had the 'Amen' been carried away by the slipstream of a passing Greyhound bus than the truckie climbed into his cab and tried the starter.

The big rig roared to life first go. The truckie fell on his knees, raised his hands above his head and cried to heaven, 'Praise the Lord! Hallelujia!'

'Well, I'll be fucked,' said the priest.

And he thought he was doing the right thing. Most priests do.

But have you noticed that often their attitude isn't entirely selfless? For generations, church-going families have always reserved the most comfortable chair, the biggest chicken leg or the last slice of cake for Father Thingummybob, or Reverend Whatchamacallit. And don't the good God botherers respond with gusto? All donations gratefully accepted, indeed. And it appears family ties don't always count, either.

Marjan Moyses of Cleve in South Australia says this yarn was passed on by a faithful Catholic who'd heard it from a missionary nun. So there!

A Surfeit of Priests

A widowed mother lived on a farm with her four sons, Tony, Peter, Laurence and John. All three younger sons entered the priesthood. Of course, they often called back to visit their mother and older brother Tony, who simply wanted to be a farmer. One time, all three priests decided to be at home at the same time, and their mother and brother were of course pretty excited. It was mid-winter and Mum made sure there'd always be a fire roaring in the large dining room. That first night, they all stayed up late chatting. Next morning, Mum arose early and got the fire going. The first to come down from his bedroom was Fr Peter.

'How did you sleep last night?' asked his mother.

'Wonderful,' he replied. 'I dreamed I was in Heaven.'

The next one down was Fr Laurence, who said almost the same thing as he came into the room. 'I dreamed I was in Heaven.'

Then down came John and . . . guess what? He'd had a beaut sleep, too, and . . . yes . . . he'd dreamed he was in Heaven.

They all sat around in front of the fire, still chatting amiably. Finally, poor old Tony, who'd been outside in the cold doing his farm chores, stumped in to find the only chair available was way across the room from the fire.

'And what did *you* dream about last night, dear?' asked his mother.

'I dreamed I was in Hell,' he muttered.

Poor old Mum was rather taken aback. 'Oh dear, what was it like?'

'Dunno. I still couldn't get near the fire for *priests*.'

Still on priests, this next yarn is not so much a tribute to larrikins as one of the oldest stories told ad nauseam by perhaps the most outrageous of larrikins, Australian musicians. Related by Lloyd Graham of Dunedoo, NSW, it's an oldie but goodie and, in this form, I suspect it may well be the original version of what's become something of a chestnut. Still, it does have a priest in it.

Bum Notes

It was during the 1930s depression and a swaggie was walking into town late one Saturday arvo. He was down to his last two bob, when he passed a nice little country church. He stopped, admired it and walked on. However, a sign on the front fence of the house next to the church caught his eye. 'Organist wanted. Apply within.'

The swaggie stopped, thought for a minute and said to himself, 'I've never played the organ before, but at school I used to play the piano. It can't be that different and I've nothing to lose.'

So in he went and knocked on the front door. A priest answered. 'May I help you?'

'Yes. I'd like to apply for the job as organist, please. I've never actually played an organ, but I have played the piano.' The priest thought for a while. 'I've had that sign up all week and got no replies. There's a service at eight tomorrow morning, so I'd better give him the job.'

Next morning, at 7.45 on the dot, the swaggie arrived at the church and the priest showed him the organ. 'Just sit down, and as soon as I nod, start playing.'

There were quite a few sniggers from the congregation when they entered and saw the bedraggled swaggie seated up at the organ.

The priest was at the back of the church ready to announce the first hymn, when he suddenly cleared his throat. 'Ahem! Ahem!' The swaggie looked up. Urgently, the priest whispered, 'Do you know you have no socks on and I can see your bottom through the cane seat?'

The swaggie thought for a couple of seconds. 'No, but if you hum a few bars, I'm sure I'll be able to pick up the tune.'

And so to yarns about bottoms—another subject not discussed in polite circles.

Dale Johnston has already shared a yarn with us about funerals. Here's his bottom-of-the-barrel view of tennis. Yes, it does involve the drink.

The Grand Final

No one expected Foxhow to make the grand final. They were always short of players and hadn't been in the running since 1928. They even had to call on old Maudy McSloth ... and she'd been dropped from the Cressy number three side 25 years ago.

Bert Bilgeful was the Foxhow captain, and a pretty good player too. It was just that he was always sneaking out the back for a drink, and by late afternoon, he'd start losing his legs. The main reason Foxhow got into the finals was Myrtle Yardfast. Myrtle had never had any training in tennis, but she carried a really heavy racquet and had the muscles to use it. Some of the locals even reckoned it was lucky for the Turks she never got sent to Anzac Cove.

Anyway, they were up against the Cressy number one side and Percy Perrot was their captain. Percy was always wearing tight shorts and was a bit of a smart arse, really. His partner in the mixed was Penny Weatherall. Penny was about as toffee nosed as they come and was always covered in make-up. In fact, it was so thick, no one had ever really seen what she looked like. Percy was pretty keen on Penny and some reckoned he had an eye on the Weatherall homestead as well.

There was quite a crowd by the time the game was ready to start, with cars lining both sides of the court. The Weatherall's Roller pulled in last (as usual) and Percy ran over to make a fuss as Penny got out. He ended up trotting over to the clubhouse with Penny's afternoon tea, while she checked out her nose in the mirror.

The match finally got started and the first few sets were pretty close—which was just as well, because the standard of the play was hopeless. Myrtle missed one smash after another and even put a few balls out into old McPherson's fallow paddock. Percy was trying his guts out and making heaps of mistakes. He'd put on a bit of weight this year and had never got round to buying new shorts. It didn't help his game when Penny said, 'You'll either have to lose weight, Percy, or buy a bigger size.'

They finally got through to the last mixed doubles, with both sides exactly even. Whoever won the last event would take home the trophy ... and both sides knew it. Percy and Penny arrived on court first, looking really confident. Myrtle had gone off looking for Bert and some of the locals guessed she'd found him when they heard: 'Get out o'that, you bloody old soak. We have to win this.'

The gate was flung wide open and Myrtle strode onto the court, Bert trotted along behind, his head and shoulders dripping wet from having been put under the tap. The umpire climbed into his chair and the players had a practice hit, eyeing each other off as they did. Then they tossed a coin and the last and deciding mixed doubles in the Cressy and District Tennis Association final began.

For a while it went all Percy and Penny's way, and Percy's confidence got as bloated as his shorts. But the game wasn't over. Myrtle and Bert gave each other a bit of a blast and then Bert started throwing himself at the ball like his life depended on it. Myrtle attacked the net and smashed winners that hurtled over the back fence and bounced off the clubhouse roof.

In the end it came down to the last game, with Penny to serve. She looked pretty tired and the make-up was running down her neck. For the first time ever, her mum and dad actually got out of the Roller and tried to look supportive. She served a double fault and Percy's shorts started to split. The next ball went in. It was a lollipop and bounced high. Myrtle went for it like a Sherman tank. The ball turned into a yellow blur as it left her racquet. The umpire was really only guessing when he called it in.

Penny served another fault and Bert was relieved. He wasn't seeing too good and his legs felt like rubber. She served again. It was so short that even if he had been able to get his legs to work, he wouldn't have made it.

'Fifteen thirty!' called the umpire.

The Weatheralls looked pleased and even clapped. Myrtle yelled in Bert's ear, 'Bloody 'ell, Bert!'

Percy looked more hopeful. He went over to Penny. 'Good on yer, sweetie! Now just keep yer mind on the job.' It didn't help, though. She served another double fault.

'Fifteen forty!' the umpire called.

Percy's buttocks lost their tone. Things looked bad. All Bert and Myrtle had to do was keep the ball in play and let the others make a mistake.

Penny concentrated and threw the ball high. Bert moved forward, but his rubbery legs let him down. As he fell, he took a pathetic swipe at the ball. It turned out to be the best lob he played all day and landed right in the back corner.

It was really on Penny's side, but Percy panicked. 'Out of the way, yer silly bitch!' he yelled. He tried a lob like Bert's, but it wasn't as good. It was short and Myrtle had it covered.

Percy sprinted across the court. He reckoned he knew where she'd put it. But Myrtle covered six yards (that's metres, these days) in three strides, leaping so high she blotted out the sun. Percy looked up and saw the look on her face. Then, as Myrtle swung the racquet, he chickened out and turned his back.

Once again Myrtle reduced the ball to a yellow blur. The umpire leaned forward, trying to see it. Myrtle, still three feet (about a metre) off the ground, crashed into his stand. He went down like a rotten pumpkin, rolled a couple of times, then, showing real guts, jumped to his feet.

'You'll have to play it again,' he yelled, 'I didn't see it.'

Just then, Percy made a noise like an old cow makes when you kick it in the guts. A yellow ball dropped from where it was buried between his clenched buttocks ... and fell—inside the line.

'Wait!' yelled the umpire. 'It was right! Game, set and match to Foxhow!'

––––––•–•–––––

Of course, you don't *have* to hold up the Eugowra gold coach or swim across Lake Amadeus to uphold the larrikin tradition. Sometimes the slightest sidestep off the straight and narrow is enough to keep the tradition alive. Ann Tappenden of Yarwun, Queensland knows what I mean.

Country Hospitality

I was a city kid but I always thought I knew something about country hospitality. Mum's a country girl whom people always seemed to be drawn to. But I never really appreciated what the term meant until I moved to central Queensland and met my parents-in-law. Frank and Cele are country born and bred and are known far and wide for their unstinting hospitality. I've always been greatly impressed by the quality of their generosity, but a sunny September Sunday is one occasion that stands out in my mind.

Not long after my husband and I were married and living on a small farm, my father and younger brother and sister paid us a visit. Naturally, we were all invited to my parents-in-laws' place for Sunday dinner.

Sunday came and we travelled up to the farm for lunch. We found Frank standing on the front verandah with a man who, on such a fine spring day, was, to my mind, somewhat overdressed. He was wearing grey moleskin trousers, a checked flannelette shirt and a large overcoat with a woollen collar. He was introduced to all of us as Mr Ferguson.

In true country style, we all sat down and concentrated on Cele's magnificent meal. Mr Ferguson, still in his coat, sat at the head of the table and did great justice to the food. Conversation flowed easily around the table and the day was going well. After lunch, the men disappeared to inspect the livestock and gaze over the paddocks. Mr Ferguson (coat and all) gave Frank some advice on controlling burr grass and other pests. By then it was getting warmer—time for another cuppa. We all indulged in afternoon tea with hot scones and the works. Mr Ferguson told a few yarns and joined in the family banter. Presently, he asked Frank if he could trouble him for a lift into town.

'No worries, mate!' and off they went.

On Frank's return, as one voice, we all asked the burning question, 'Where do you know that fella from?'

'I never saw him before in my life. I thought he was a friend of Cele's.'

Cele looked blank. We all started to laugh.

And, to this day, we have never seen Mr Ferguson again—but I bet he enjoyed his visit and the country hospitality.

———————

My favourite yarn about one of the little people shouting in the face of convention has been claimed by quite a few acquaintances as being a story about them. Knowing them as I do, it wouldn't surprise me.

Beyond Your Means

A bloke in terrible nick lurched into a pub and slumped over the bar. 'Quick,' he gurgled to the barman, give us a schooner of Drambuie and, for a chaser, a middy of Courvoisier. The barman raised an eyebrow, but was too experienced to argue. He deftly poured each drink and the customer guzzled them down without taking a breath.

'God!' he muttered, 'With what I've got, I shouldn't be drinking like that.'

The barman raised the other eyebrow. 'Crikey, sir! What have you got?'

'Twenty cents.'

Of course it's our publicans who probably see the Aussie larrikin at his or her best ... and his or her worst. In other cultures, keeping a pub is often seen as a soft and fuzzy way of making a living. I've never met an Australian publican who thinks so. In fact, some of the best, most colourful pubs are run by the sourest, most miserable bastards who ever drew breath. Ernie Sharman of Traralgon, Victoria met up with one in Queensland.

Shot of It

Anyone who comes from the soft southern states sometimes finds things a bit less civilised as they move north. This incident occurred in a little pub up the Peninsula Development Road.

You could have anything you liked there for lunch—as long as it was a stubby of NQ Lager, steak and chips. Being a fair way from the nearest butcher's shop, the publican wasn't averse to knocking over the odd scrub bull to supplement his 'restaurant's' meat supply. The quality of his rumps and T-bones, therefore, tended to be somewhat shaky. While most travellers suffered in silence, there were a few who spoke up about the rough tucker.

On the day in question—which happened to be a Sunday following a fairly heavy Saturday night—the publican's reserves of patience were at a low ebb after a mob of tourists had given his steak and onions a bad time. One had even refused to pay.

Anyway, a Victorian bloke and his wife arrived at the pub that Sunday in their Range Rover. Lunch was ordered. The visitor took one bite of the steak and spat it out onto the plate. He called the publican over.

'Hey, you!' he said, 'This damn meat is bad.'

The publican walked over and looked down at the plate with narrowed eyes.

'Bad? Bad, is it?'

He walked over to the bar and reached under the counter. He pulled out a battered old .45 automatic pistol souvenired off the

Yanks in Cairns in World War II and walked back to the table. The Victorians sat frozen to their chairs, pushed halfway from the table.

'Bad, is it?' repeated mine host. He cocked the .45, put the barrel a couple of inches from the piece of steak and pulled the trigger.

In the silence that followed the shot, the visitors sat covered with bits of chips, onion, gravy and shards of china, staring at the hole in the steak ... and the table.

'Let me know if it gives you any more trouble,' said the publican.

Apparently it was the last time anyone complained about the food.

It can indeed be a battle running a country pub—never mind if yours is the only one in town. In the larger bush communities, there are additional problems, like competition from the blood house down the road. Bob Carveth, of Bredbo, NSW is a talented stills and movie cameraman. He also collects yarns like this one, for which he is entitled to no forgiveness ...

The Moulamein Cocktail Lounge

I don't know how many pubs there are in Moulamein these days, but back when I was last up there, there were a couple. People sometimes puzzled how such a small town, with such fine, upstanding citizens, could support two pubs. It was one of those times when Australians were drinking less than they used to, and business was generally down a bit in the hotel game. Like true professionals, both the publicans in Moulamein decided not to throw in the towel, but to try to outdo each other in order to attract customers.

One pub put on live music on Saturday afternoons—so all the locals flocked there at weekends. The other retaliated by having Friday and Saturday night discos—so everyone's unswerving loyalty immediately swung there. The first pub hired topless barmaids. The second one fought back by hiring nude barmaids. The custom flowed back and forth like the tides of the ocean. Then one publican decided the way to go was to bung on something more sophisticated than his missus wandering around the bar with no knickers. He got a loan from the bank and converted an old parlour into a trendy little cocktail bar. He sent away to some magazine for a free cocktail recipe book and tried to set up shop as a sophisticated rendezvous for yuppies.

Not only weren't there many yuppies around Moulamein at the time, but he had the devil's own job making sense of the bloody cocktail recipes. Everything he and his missus brewed up turned out a sort of grey syrup, with ugly things floating in it and great greasy bubbles popping occasionally on the surface. He needed a professional cocktail barman. So he advertised in the local rag. He'd have been better off saving the money. For weeks, no one responded, which was hardly surprising for Moulamein.

The old publican was just about to give up, sell up and shoot through, when a hot afternoon northerly blew a godsend into town. His name was Richard and he was from the Big Smoke. Sick and tired with the city, he'd thrown in his job at a swank pub and decided to seek his fortune out bush. He'd been wandering around for about a year, trying his hand at anything he could pick up, which wasn't much. Richard's true vocation was as a cocktail barman. When he hit Moulamein, he was just about ready to chuck the towel in himself and return to the city to pick up where he'd left off.

Then he saw the publican's ad and instantly applied for the job. The publican gave him a try and found him remarkable. Richard (Dick to his mates) could whip up the most exotic drinks in a flash, making great display of shaking them up and pouring them grandly into the cocktail glasses they'd had especially freighted in from Sydney.

Dick's Den became *the* place to be in Moulamein ... for about a month. Then business fell off. Because the publican had had to fire a couple of other bartenders to employ Dick, he kept the new bloke on, but Dick was slowly becoming disillusioned with not being able to demonstrate his art adequately. For an artiste like him, there was no skill or job satisfaction involved in drawing endless schooners of Old, or Middies of New, with the occasional Light or rum 'n' raspberry thrown in.

Then one day, a dusty ute pulled up outside. It had a strange sign on the door. The driver lurched in and ordered a beer. Seeing there was no one else in the bar, Dick engaged him in conversation. The bloke turned out to be a CSIRO research scientist, working on a new, more effective strain of myxomatosis way out in the saltbush country. He came into town only once every few weeks.

'I suppose you appreciate a cold beer when you come into town, eh, Doc?' asked Dick.

'Bloody oath, but you know what I crave most of all? You'll think I'm a wanker ... '

'No, Doc, not at all.'

'Well, when I'm working out there in the heat and dust and flies, I think back to when I was living in Melbourne and used to nick up to the Menzies or Scott's for some of those really elaborate cocktails.'

'Really? You like cocktails?'

'Bloody oath—Greasy Nipples, Flaming Flamingos, Bubbling Bowels ... I love 'em. But do you know what I liked best of all? It's a weird one ... '

'Go ahead and surprise me, Doc,' smiled Dick, sure he'd finally found someone who'd really appreciate his particular talents.

'I used to love almond daiquiris ... you know, in the special glass with the nuts and everything.'

'Well, say no more, Doc,' and Dick whipped out to the kitchen, grabbed a packet of slivered almonds from the shelf, came back to the bar and whipped his new mate up a state of the art almond daiquiri.

It was the start of a beautiful friendship. Doc didn't manage to get into town often, but when he did, he made straight for the pub, where Dick would have the daiquiri ingredients—complete with the nuts—all ready to go. Like I said, it didn't happen often, but it did keep them both sane in that quiet little town.

The scientist had been out bush for a while longer than usual, but he sent in a message to Moulamein with the mailman that he'd be in to the pub the following Thursday. On the morning in question, Dick made sure he had all the ingredients for Doc's almond daiquiri. They were all there, bar the nuts.

Unperturbed, he strolled down to the local supermarket in his lunch hour. Crikey! They were out of almonds. He tried the corner store back from the main street. No luck. None of the milk bars had any almonds, either. Dick realised he was in trouble. His mate would be in any tick of the clock, and he still didn't have any almonds. Then, a brilliant idea struck him. Out the back of the pub was an old nut tree. It wasn't a almond, it was a hickory tree. It had been planted about 100 years earlier, when the old pub was built. It was huge, but at that time of the year, except during a bad drought, it always produced a small crop of nuts. Hickory nuts weren't the same as almonds, but scrape them off and slice them up, and they'd probably do.

Dick had no sooner prepared a small bowl of chopped hickory nuts than he heard the familiar growl of the scientist's old ute outside. Doc bounced into the bar, covered in dust and obviously in need of a bit of refreshment.

'The usual, thanks, Dick,' he called from the door.

'No worries, Doc.'

Like a stage magician, Dick poured the liquid ingredients of the almond daiquiri into a shaker, gave it the old treatment and, with a flourish, poured it over a sprinkling of nuts into the daiquiri glass.

The scientist held the cocktail glass to the light and smacked his lips in anticipation. After turning it slowly to admire Dick's handiwork, he lowered it to his lips and took a long sip. A puzzled look came over his face.

'Are you sure this is an almond daiquiri, Dick?' he asked.

'No, it's a hickory daiquiri, Doc.'

(Try saying it fast!)

Margaret Card from Ballan, Victoria was able to observe the great boozy passing parade from the publican's point of view.

The Blokes from Boundary Bend

This yarn doesn't involve anybody rich and famous, but believe me—it happened. Like a lot of strange things, it happened in Kyalite, on the NSW side of the Murray, south of Balranald. An earlier prime minister, Bob (with woolly eyebrows), was on the throne at the time, Aborigines were still considered non-people, blokes were blueing in Vietnam and the run of bush life hadn't changed since they invented it.

Our dad, Leo Murphy, was the publican of the Kyalite Hotel. 'It's always daylight at Kyalite' was our pub's motto, and although I grew up in a hotel, I didn't know until I was 14 that there were such things as official closing hours. Dad's personal reputation was huge as an obliging bloke who would do anything for anybody. The pub was famous for being open all the time (although that wasn't exactly true). Dad served people after hours. We had many night callers who left carrying dozens of beer, flagons of port or sherry and cartons of smokes. Half the time they booked it all up, and half the time again, they didn't pay . . . which Mum thought was a bit much!

Dad died when he was 54, leaving Mum to run the place. It took him nine years to succumb to cancer. He reckoned he was pickled in alcohol. He had been pronounced dead by the district countless times. On one occasion a bloke rang the pub and asked Dad when Leo Murphy's funeral was. Dad gave the bloke a date and time and hung up. We never knew if he turned up. When he finally *did* die, they had to produce notices from the paper, signed by Mum, to prove it.

When she took over the pub, Mum had a very different view of after hours service. She went to bed and stayed there. I heard some local one night ask her for 'A dozen bottles and a couple of packets of smokes.'

'No! The pub's shut.'

'Awwwwww, go on, Mrs Murph.'

'The pub's *shut*,' said Mum, 'Go and get your grog where you got full.'

Those people, I recall, were from Moulamein and had driven

38 miles (that's over 60 kilometres) of dirt road to get to our place. Not surprisingly, they went wild with Mum. Dad had only been dead a few weeks and there could have been no way they wouldn't have known about it. I suppose they thought they could appeal to Mum's sentiment for the old man. Even though Mum was a non-drinker, they'd been great mates.

'Go on, Mrs Murph,' pleaded the travellers, 'Leo always got grog for us.'

'Yes,' agreed Mum, 'And look where Leo is now.'

What I want to tell you about is a time when Leo was still alive—but not well.

That particular night was freezing, wet and windy. A mob from Boundary Bend turned up at Kyalite about 2.00 am and asked the old man for grog. The pub was one of those rambling old joints with seven separate buildings on the place. Mum and Dad's room, with the kids' room next-door, was separated from the kitchen; the kitchen was separated from the pub; the pub was separated from the coolroom ... and so on.

These late night visitors weren't particularly well mannered about their request. One version of this story insists they referred to Mum as 'Marie'—a capital crime in Dad's books (but not Mum's). To everyone, she was Mrs Murphy, or, more familiarly, Mrs Murph.

Dad was savage on bad manners and decided they could go without on this occasion.

'Go to buggery, you ignorant bastards!' he told them. There was a further entreaty, then a threat.

'Piss off!' bellowed Dad.

'Don't tell us to piss off, you crabby old bastard.' A car door slammed and one of the Boundary Bend blokes, famous for his serious bad manners when he was full, got out of the car and approached the wire door where Dad stood in his flannelette 'jamies.

'Listen, sport,' said Dad, who was always game, 'get back in the car or you'll be sorry.'

'What are you going to do, you useless old prick?' The man continued to approach the bedroom door, menacing in the dark.

'I got a bit windy,' Mum admitted later.

'I've got a pot full of piss here,' said Dad, 'And you're going to cop it.' The poor silly bastard continued to approach. As my Nan used to say, 'When the wine's in, the wit's out.'

Dad opened the wire door and let the bloke have it. It was a seriously full pot of what he'd said it was full of.

'You dirty bastard.' said the man from Boundary Bend.

'Have a look at yourself, mate,' said Dad. The bloke took a few steps backwards then continued to move threateningly towards the wire door—now shut.

'Steady on, old man,' said Dad, 'You better get going. I've got the old lady loading up another one.'

According to Margaret, although the yarn only used to be told late at night and in safe company, and didn't do much for Mrs Murph's dignity, her Mum used to laugh herself sick about it. Immediately after the incident, she and Leo laughed till daylight.

Margaret's yarn covers a time before we were aware of the dreadful toll smoking was taking. Those packets of smokes went with the beer and the flagons as readily as bacon with eggs. Ross Leak of Tintinara, South Australia was 83 when he passed on this next yarn. It ended up being the South Australian state winner in the Search for the Great Aussie Yarn.

Clearing the Tubes

One of the big cigarette companies wanted to organise a major advertising campaign to celebrate a quarter century of operations in Australia. Someone came up with the idea of offering a $2000 prize to the first smoker who could prove they'd used the company's brand exclusively all that time.

The way things are with smoking, the response was nil. Facing a public relations disaster, the company took to sending its executives out into the streets to search for likely candidates.

They'd corner anyone over 40 they saw smoking and quiz them about their brand and how long they'd been smoking it. The response was still disappointing.

One afternoon, a bright young executive was walking across a park back to his office after lunch, when he spied an ancient old bloke sitting on a park bench, puffing away. He went over and started talking to the man. Eventually he asked him about his smoking habits.

Yes, the old bloke was smoking the company's brand. Yes, he'd smoked it for years—since it first went on the market in Australia, in fact. The young executive got pretty excited.

How old was the feller? Ninety-seven! And he still got up every day, on the dot at 5.30 in the morning.

It seemed too good to be true, a smoker loyal to the company who'd lived to be nearly 100 years old.

Would the old bloke be prepared to accept the $2000 prize and take part in the company's 25th anniversary advertising campaign?

The smoker thought for a while. No, the $2000 wouldn't be any good to him. It'd interfere with his pension.

The disappointed young executive went back to his office and consulted his superiors. They agreed the old bloke was too good to just ignore. They authorised bumping up the prize money to $5000 in cash, so the pension mob wouldn't know anything about it.

They contacted the 97-year-old again and he accepted their proposition. They delivered the cash and told him all he'd have to do was go on the 'Midday Show' and be interviewed by Ray Martin.

The old bloke agreed.

'Great, we'll pick you up about 10 o'clock so you can be at the studio nice and early.'

'No, that's no good. It's too early.'

'Why? Don't you always get up at 5.30 every morning?' they asked.

'Sure,' said the old bloke. 'But I don't stop coughing until half past one.'

You don't have to be a 'flash young cove' to be a larrikin, eh?
WH Dunn of Taree, NSW has it down pat.

Longevity

An insurance agent was having a beer with a mate, who suddenly
asked, 'Would you give me a life insurance policy?'

'How old are you?' asked the agent.

'I've just turned 60, but don't let that worry you. I come from
a family of long livers.'

The agent shook his head. 'I'll have to check with the company.'
He made a quick phone call and was given the go ahead. 'But
you'll have to undergo a medical examination. We'll pay for it.
I've made an appointment for you to visit the company doctor
at 5.00 pm on Wednesday.'

'Crikey!' muttered his mate, 'I can't go at five o'clock on
Wednesday. I have to play squash with my father.'

The agent was taken aback. 'Your father? How old's he?'

'He's seventy-eight.'

'And still playing squash?'

'Sure. I told you we were all long livers.'

The agent made a couple more phone calls to change the
appointment. 'I've managed to move it to 5.00 pm on Saturday.'
he told his prospective client.

'That's no good, either. My grandfather's getting married again
and I'm best man at his wedding.'

The agent shook his head. 'And how old's your bloody
grandfather?'

'He's ninety-six.'

'Good God! Ninety-six? Why on earth does he want to get
married?'

His mate grinned. 'He doesn't *want* to get married. He *has* to.'

Chapter 3

THEY BROKE THE MOULD

THE yarns people seem to enjoy telling most of all are those about wonderful characters they've encountered. One of the nicest things about yarn spinning is it's seldom malicious. Even the most atrocious mongrels become elevated to the status of 'great characters'. The most boring of individuals are transformed, with the passing of the years, into scintillating personalities. It's the hindsight thing again. Time is a great healer. It's a feature of yarns about colourful identities, so for a storyteller to intimate that 'we shall never see their like again,' it could be true—at least until our anklebiters start telling yarns about us.

Reg Della Bosca of Orange NSW drew from colonial times for

one of his many yarns unearthed in the Search for the Great
Aussie Yarn.

The Do-gooder

Where would our world be without the 'do-gooders', those
enigmatic people who earnestly believe they have a right and a
duty to seek better things for others? In some churches, people
who spend a heroic amount of time and effort trying to adjust
the scales of justice are called saints. But there is a little bit of
the 'do-gooder' in most of us.

We've had many heroic people in Australia who've worked
energetically to help the down and out: the saintly nun Mary
McKillop; Mrs Caroline Chisholm; the controversial JT Lang;
even one of our earliest governors, Lachlan Macquarie. All rate
fairly highly, in my book, as people who've helped make Oz a
fairer place.

This yarn is about a young man who arrived in the colony of
New South Wales before Blaxland, Wentworth and Lawson had
crossed the Blue Mountains. Edward Smith-Hall had a family of
five daughters. He was very respectable. He had worked with
Wilberforce against the slave trade in England and was obviously
acceptable to the local establishment, as he was granted a personal
pew in the Anglican Church and had letters of introduction to
Governor Macquarie.

One of the early problems of the colony had been a shortage
of women. The ratio of men to women among the first settlers
in Sydney Town was nine to one. Many of the early settlers took
as their partners the handsome Aboriginal women. That crossing
of cultures didn't always work out. Forty per cent of the town's
children were Aboriginal. Many were deserted and were foundlings.

There was obviously much scope in the penal colony for the
new crusader, Edward Smith-Hall. He approached Macquarie to
commence a charitable organisation, eventually to be called the
Benevolent Society of New South Wales. It was to become one
of Australia's leading organisations, boasting every governor since

Macquarie as patron. Over 170 years its network came to include institutions such as the Royal Hospital for Women, child welfare homes and villages for the aged.

Smith-Hall started his society of do-gooders in 1813. Not everyone in the colony was appreciative. Who did this upstart think he was? Charitable activity was the job of the established churches. If he was granted land for his work, it could cut into the Anglican Glebe Trust. Was this new arrival some sort of heretic? He had to be shown how many beans made five.

Such was the talk around Sydney Town that even Governor Macquarie hesitated about giving Smith-Hall further approval. After all, people like Sam Marsden weren't only pretty good with the lash in punishing convicts, they were also politically formidable. The establishment decided to teach Smith-Hall a lesson. The personal pew that he and his daughters occupied in church each Sunday morning was boarded up to indicate the depth of his indiscretions.

Next Sunday, the minister came out filled with self satisfaction. Consternation! There, perched on the boarded-up pew like a rooster with a clutch of hens, were Mr Edward Smith-Hall and his five daughters, proving his belief that a little conflict never hurt any good cause.

––––––––––

Another of Reg's yarns refers to more recent times and someone closer to him, his father.

The Long Train Journey

My father was usually a quiet sort of man. As I remember, from when I was a lad, he could have been described as someone with sober habits, very kind to his children and wife, hard-working during the depression and, I suppose, what you could call 'multi-skilled', in that he used a range of abilities to work at part-time jobs and activities, which ensured we were always well fed and cleanly clothed.

Yet, Joe Della Bosca was a local legend among the friends of his youth, like Tony Luchetti, Jerry Waters (one-time flyweight champion) and one of his best mates, Izzy Basser. He'd also won the respect of the local Chinese gardeners, one of whom he'd saved from being robbed by a racist Ocker. He gave the would-be sneak thief a good hiding for his trouble. I heard enough stories from these mates from his early days in Lithgow to wonder sometimes if they were true or somewhat exaggerated to suit local folklore.

I overheard stories, when I was small, of his fighting and sporting skills and his capacity to handle both the drink *and* himself before he married. But my image of him remains as a man concerned about his children, delighted when we did well at school or sport and a father that never hit any of us—even when he was teaching us to box.

Joe Della Bosca, as the name implies, came from a group that the *Sydney Morning Herald* once headlined, 'Lithgow's appalling Italians'. Along with Pellegrinis, Buttas, Luchettis, Cappelinos, Tempones etc, they were in the mould of Garibaldi's Red Shirts and were not easily intimidated by the coal and iron barons who thought, along with the Fairfaxes, that Lithgow should be ruled like the English mining and iron towns—'With a rod of iron made out of greed,' as my grandfather would have put it. They were socialists, dubbed, of course, by the *Herald* as 'communists'. As my father grew older, he became more talkative and left me a locker of stories about his Australia and his mates. They make Zane Grey's wild west seem like a playground for sissies. (Excuse the chauvinism, please.)

My father's reputation for talking had really taken off around Lithgow. Another well-known conversationalist who loved an audience was Wolfie Carp. According to local legend, it was arranged for the two big talkers to have a storytelling contest. They were booked into a dog box carriage on the old steam train from Lithgow to go to Sydney for a football Test and return and were confined to each other's company for a whole day.

The local bookmaker took bets on who would fare best.

The steam train shunted into Lithgow about 11 o'clock that

night. Then the ambulance was heard, siren blaring, racing to the station, and then to the local hospital.

According to my informant, Mr Carp was discharged one week later. The diagnosis? A new and troublesome complaint: word shock!

Huge bets were settled the following Saturday morning and Joe Della Bosca waited hopefully on the railway station corner for the next contestant.

———————

Colonel George McLean of Guyra, NSW also passed on some family anecdotes dating from times long gone—even more long gone than Reg's. I suppose people like his grandfather might seem particularly hard by today's standards, but remember they were indeed products of *their* times.

The first yarn has a familiar ring to it, but it's a genuine event from the McLean family history. What say we change the setting to New Zealand, bring in a couple of American actors to boost the box office and tee up this talented female director called Jane Something to whip it into shape and ... ?

The Piano

My grandmother had died in 1900, and after the 1902 drought, grandfather was living at Collymongle—now part of the Collie Farms cotton area—with my aunts Isabella and Christina keeping house. Grandfather George McLean loved the bagpipes but hated the piano. My youngest aunt, Christina, was musically talented and loved the piano, but, at grandfather's behest, was forbidden one at home.

Christina was a resourceful young woman and determined to get more piano playing, somehow. She organised a piano to be delivered to Collymongle without grandfather's knowledge. After a lengthy journey by ship, rail and bullock wagon, it duly arrived. In the fortunate absence of grandfather, the piano was installed in a little-used storeroom at the end of a long verandah, facing

Collymongle Lagoon. Grandfather was a healthy, active 65-year-old, but, like many of his age and circumstance in those days, he regularly snoozed for about two hours after lunch.

Christina had enjoyed her clandestine playing for over two months, when the inevitable happened. Waking early, grandfather demanded of Aunt Isabella, 'Where's that damned tinkling coming from?' Brushing aside Bella's protestations and attempts at diversion, he stalked the full length of the verandah and threw open the storeroom door. Shouting to Christina, 'Disobedient hussy, we must be rid of that abomination!' and ignoring the tearful pleas of the two girls, he called over two station hands passing in a dray, loaded the piano and tipped it into the lagoon.

It was still there when Collymongle was sold, years later, to Sinclair Brothers.

Day of Reckoning

Grandfather had had a bad morning. Nothing was right—the rabbit plague, drought and lazy station hands. He summoned the bookkeeper.

'Mr Brown, I'm fed up with the useless lot working here. I'm going to sack everyone. Go to it and make out the cheques.'

When Mr Brown returned with the cheques, grandfather skipped quickly through them.

'They're not all here.'

'Oh, yes, Mr McLean, all eleven of them, even the cook's.'

'Well, they're not. There should be twelve. Yours is missing.'

Not every legendary character was as hard as old Macka. Most of the old timers we choose to remember are the quiet, gentle old types, slightly out of kilter with the modern world, who seem simply to bumble through life with little more than a quiet to-the-point remark or two to keep them going.

Bob Musgrave of Murrurundi, NSW shared two yarns with us about a couple of those strictly local identities, the likes of which pop up all over the bush whenever the stories start getting told.

Old Bill Fenton

Bill and his brother settled on land which after the first war was broken up for settlers. I think the year was around 1920. Bill's father worked there as a shepherd. His burial site can still be found in the upper reaches of Timor Creek, a major tributary of the Isis River in the Upper Hunter Valley.

My forebears settled close by around the 1880s and we're still there now, four generations later, on what was selected and known as Allston.

This particular incident involving Bill also involved my grandmother, who, at the time, was only recently married. Old Bill, on passing by Allston, asked my grandfather if he needed anything in town. He didn't, but my grandmother asked Bill if he'd mind picking up some material from the local store. She gave him a penny to cover the cost.

Eight days passed before old Bill returned with what could only be described as a real surprise. The fact he returned at all was probably surprise enough.

'Did you pick up my material for me, Bill?' my grandmother asked expectantly.

Being essentially shy and sheepish, Bill eventually replied, 'Errrr, no, Missus.'

'How come?'

Bill reached into his pocket and presented grandmother with two pennies. 'I didn't know which penny was yours, Missus, and I didn't want to spend the wrong one, so I couldn't get your material.'

Jim Ponder

Jimmy Ponder ran approximately 2000 acres (somewhere around 800 hectares) in the far reaches of the Upper Hunter Valley. We were well and truly in the grip of that drought in the early 1980s. Around Christmas time, someone asked Jimmy how the feed was holding out.

'Pretty short,' he replied.

The young blokes he was talking to commented that, even so, what feed was about was very sweet.

'Ahhhhh! That explains it,' sighed Jim. 'I wondered why all me sheep were dying. I thought it was from starvation, but all the time it was sugar diabetes.'

Every district has characters like that. For nearly 10 years, we lived near Crookwell in southern NSW, between Goulburn and Bathurst. The main character to feature in most of the local yarns there was the late Billy Mills, once head of a large family that still lives in the relatively isolated Peelwood district, first selected by Major Thomas Mitchell when he was surveyor general. The first Mills originally went there straight from the old country, as an overseer on Mitchell's holding, the Big Meadow.

Typical of the Billy Mills yarns is the one in which he went to Sydney by train for the wool sales. In those days, the leading hotels used to send cars to the station to pick up wealthy squatters and offer them a free lift to their accommodation.

As Billy walked out into the sunlight outside Central Station, the drivers started calling out their hotel names—'Prince of Wales!', 'Duke of Edinburgh!', 'Empress of India!'

'No,' replied Billy to all and sundry, 'Just Billy Mills of Peelwood.'

And then there was the time, again at Central, when he went to retrieve his cases from the luggage counter.

'What's your name?' asked the bloke behind the counter.

'All that writing on the side of me suitcase,' replied our Bill.

This yarn isn't about Bill, but Kevin McCormack of Crookwell is a prodigious storyteller about local characters and events.

Rooney

It was 50 years ago, if it was a day, that Rooney came to our farm on the Redgrounds. In those days, Uncle Albert had an old racehorse that he used to take around to bush race meetings. On

their way back from Binda, he and his friends used to break the journey at our place. They arrived one dark evening in a horse and sulky, leading the old racer, called Skipereen.

Mum, Dad and Bill met them at the gate and hands were shaken all round. Uncle Albert, not a man to waste words, simply said, 'This is Rooney' as a sad-eyed, middle-aged man solemnly stepped down from the sulky.

My father was a most logical, sensible, level-headed man in every way, with just one exception—he was a fanatic when it came to card playing. Normally placid, he could fly into a terrible rage over a hand of cards. His wide circle of card-playing friends, such as Uncle Albert, took no notice because they knew his temper was very short lived and when the game was over, all was forgiven and forgotten.

After tea that night, Dad announced to Rooney, 'You and I will play Bill and Albert at Five Hundred.'

It was an evenly matched contest and about 11.30 they were two games each, with both sides confident of winning the rubber. It was after midnight when fate took a hand. Dad and Rooney each picked up slam hands at the same time. Rooney called Spades and Dad called No Trumps. Rooney went seven Spades, Dad, seven No-Trumps. The others dropped out and Rooney went slam Spades. That would have put them out and won the game, but Dad always liked to pick up Kitty. He had nine straight No Trump tricks in his hand and the King of Spades. He knew Rooney *must* have the Ace of Spades, so Dad slammed No Trumps.

He took the nine tricks and smiled as he leaned back and played the King of Spades for Rooney. But, alas, Rooney had 10 spades in his hand—but *not* the Ace. Uncle Albert had it. In his day, Dad had been known to order several of his partners from the table, but in Rooney's case, he ordered him to bed as well. Ten minutes later, as Mum poured the tea for supper and Dad was back to his old self, he said to Uncle Albert, 'Go and bring Rooney back for some supper.'

Uncle Albert came back a few minutes later and said, 'Rooney's sulking and won't come back.'

He was sure everything would be forgotten by morning. Dad and Uncle Albert drank tea and yarned for another hour or so before going to bed.

Next morning, they were late up. Mum made them some breakfast and Dad took Uncle Albert on a sightseeing tour—first the milking cow and calf, then a young bull Dad had bought a week or two before and finally, over to the pigsty. On the way to the pigs, Dad mentioned the couple of acres of new potatoes he had growing between the house and the road. Uncle Albert looked up the road and said, 'I see someone digging a few now.'

'What?' Dad cried. 'Surely not again? There was a mongrel at them last week and he got away with a bagful before I could catch him.'

With that, Dad roared at the top of his voice, 'Get out of that paddock this minute or I'll sool the dogs on you.'

'He's a cheeky fellow,' observed Uncle Albert. 'He's digging all the harder.' Dad shouted and roared again and still the thief kept digging.

'There's only one way,' Uncle Albert said. 'I've had much the same trouble at Taralga with fellows pinching my turnips. Get me your rifle will and I'll show you what to do.'

Dad rushed inside and came out with the old rifle. Uncle Albert fired a couple of bullets high over the thief's head. With that, the thief slung the bag of potatoes over his shoulder and started across the paddock.

'He's a cool customer,' Uncle Albert said. 'But I'll stop him yet.' With that, he whistled a couple of shots a few feet (that's about a metre) above the fugitive's head, which made the thief throw himself down on the ground and wave a white handkerchief.

'Good on you, Albert,' Dad said. 'We've got the coot now.'

Just then, Mum appeared and asked, 'What's all the shooting about?'

'A damned thief's in the potatoes, that's what it's about.'

'My God! Stop!' Mum cried. 'That's Rooney. He was up early this morning and asked if he could do anything. I sent him to dig some new potatoes for dinner.'

Poor Rooney! He was in a state. Uncle Albert brushed him

down while Dad carried the bag of potatoes. They got him back to the house and Mum gave him a nip of brandy to calm him down. She cooked a big dinner that day, but Rooney only picked at his and I noticed he didn't eat any potatoes at all.

Then it was time to depart. There were handshakes all round again. As Dad wrung Rooney's hand, he said, 'Be sure and come back next year and we'll have another card night.'

It was a shaken Rooney who climbed gingerly into the sulky. As they trotted up the road, Uncle Albert, who had a dry sense of humour, asked him, 'What's the chance of you coming back next year?'

Rooney replied, 'About the same as a snowflake in Hell.'

Dawn Murray of Bunbury, WA provided a yarn that requires little comment.

Services Rendered

In a small country town which was the centre for a rich farming area, a bloke named Bob Dicks ran a livery stable around the corner from the largest pub. The livery stable gave Bob a comfortable living without him having to overwork. Farmers and their wives, in town for a day's shopping, or to do some business, would leave their horses and buggies there to be fed, watered and sheltered. Local shopkeepers were happy to send a delivery boy to the stable and leave their customers' purchases with Bob.

Bob's mate, Cobber Clarke, had a barber shop next-door to the stable. When Bob wasn't busy, he could usually be found in the barber's, exchanging yarns and gossip with Cobber and his customers. Most people were only too happy to wander in and rest for a few minutes before going about their business. They'd amble in with a 'G'day, Cobber. How's it going, Bob?' and chat for a while.

There were always exceptions. One of those was a cow cocky from five miles (around eight kilometres) out. He was noted for his abrupt ways and for always being in a hurry. One day, he strode into the barber shop and demanded peremptorily, 'Bob Dicks here?'

Cobber Clarke glanced up from the customer he was shaving and drawled, 'Nah, only haircut and shave.'

Before retirement, Keith Welsh of Sandy Bay, Tasmania had a long career as a newspaperman. Like all good journos, he'd notched up a stack of yarns about his days as a member of the Fourth Estate—especially the early days.

Woolly Aphids

Back in the early 1920s, I worked on an afternoon daily newspaper in a large provincial NSW town. Those were the days when linotype and hot molten lead were considered the height of perfection and visual display terminals and automation weren't even a dream.

At that time, most inland rural centres had organisations dealing with the man on the land. There were the Wheatgrowers' Association, the Graziers' Association, the Poultry Breeders' Association, and so on.

My town had its Agricultural Bureau and it was customary for members to meet once monthly and be addressed by a leader of his or her particular line of primary production. On one occasion, the bureau was addressed by a German migrant who'd established a very successful vineyard. He chose to speak on woolly aphids. A colleague of mine, whom I'll call Alf, was assigned to cover the meeting. He arrived just as the president was resuming his seat after having introduced the vigneron.

The German, with deep guttural speech but a cheery, racy personality, was quickly in his stride. But Alf found him difficult to understand. He noted that the speaker was referring to his notes frequently, so he decided to risk not taking any himself, but to see the guest of honour when the meeting ended.

When the gathering dispersed, Alf approached the speaker. 'Mr Schmidt, I was wondering if you would lend me your notes.'

Mr Schmidt was most cooperative. 'Chertainly, my phoy,' he said and handed Alf an envelope containing the notes. Alf rushed back to the office, sat himself in front of his typewriter and prepared to write his report.

He unfolded the notes. Disaster! They were all in German. Alf remained motionless at his seat. He couldn't approach the editor, because then he'd have to admit that he hadn't taken a note. Fear enveloped him, so much so that he was unable to take other colleagues into his confidence and seek their assistance.

Then a light appeared at the end of the tunnel. He quickly left the office and made his way to the Mechanics' Institute, where the town library was housed. He asked for a copy of the *Encyclopaedia Brittanica*, received it, and quickly scanned the pages. Sure enough, there was an item on woolly aphids.

Alf wrote an introduction and opened the second paragraph with: 'Mr Schmidt said ... ', after which he copied details word by word from the encyclopaedia. That completed, he rushed back to the office, handed in his report and subsided, happy in the knowledge that his work had just been in time for publication.

Next morning, Alf was seated in the reporters' room, which was separated by a small wooden partition from the main office.

'Where is dat phoy?' rang out a guttural voice.

'Why, is there something wrong, Mr Schmidt?' the attendant inquired.

'Wrong?' replied Mr Schmidt. 'No, no. But vot a smart young man you haf. Dat report of his is the best I haf ever read.'

Keith won the Tasmanian state prize in the Search for the Great Aussie Yarn with a succinct little piece from his days as an inexperienced pressman. He was supposed to be cobbling together a funeral notice for a local lady, but somehow the type got scrambled and there was a bit of an overlap with some of the sporting copy.

As a result, his paper's next issue announced, 'Friends of Mr William John Smith are respectfully invited to attend the funeral today of his late beloved wife, Mary Anne. The old hurdler fell and broke her leg while schooling at Wodonga yesterday.'

But he didn't stop there.

The Engagement

Back in my early days as a country newspaper reporter, we were always encouraged to give a local twist to events which may have happened elsewhere. In my circle of friends was a very attractive blonde kindergarten teacher. One day, the state minister for education visited the school and met the teacher. Each fell for the other and in a matter of a few weeks, she was transferred to a Sydney school.

One day, I was reading the *Sydney Morning Herald* and noted a news item recording the engagement of the minister to the teacher. I lifted the item and, to give the local angle, added, 'Miss X was formerly kindergarten teacher at Blanktown.'

Once again, one of those unfortunate things that used to go wrong with country newspapers occurred—the type got mixed, and again it got caught up with a racing item.

Next day, the paragraph detailing the engagement was printed, but when it came to the addition, instead of 'Miss X was formerly a kindergarten teacher at Blanktown,' the item read, 'Miss X was a full sister by Snowden out of Lady Anzac.'

And so, in keeping with that romantic snippet, to matters of the heart. They, too, have changed over the years, as suggested by Elizabeth Goos of Coorparoo in Queensland.

On line

When I received my new telephone directory, this took me back to my telephone operator days during the war. Barely out of my teens, I sat for the entry exam. It was followed by a medical, a declaration of secrecy and six weeks' training. The going was rugged. Delays of four hours in connecting the southern states weren't uncommon. A memory for telephone numbers and names was essential. There were no computers then.

I still remember a Mr Harrison who explained at length that you spelled his name with 'a haitch, a hay, two hars, a hi, a hess, a ho and a hen'.

Somehow I feel automation can never provide the same kind of service, care or involvement. Sweet talking was a way of life; I met my late husband on the other end of a line. But today, conversations between courting couples cost caboodles of cash. When I visit the Post Office museum with its display of relics from those days, I still find myself damp eyed. It was a fascinating era.

Perhaps it isn't so much matters of the heart themselves that have changed, but the way in which they're handled. The mould might have been broken, but it's certainly been replaced by a newer model. Or do things still develop as in Mr GC Bradley's yarn from Bowraville, NSW?

Love within Reason

When Amy Weeks was seen in the company of Andy Smith, eyebrows were raised and tongues began to wag. It was unexpected. The match was out of character. Amy was given credit for having more sense. She was the daughter of Reverend Weeks, whose dignity and piety were above reproach. His daughter was expected to live up to the example set by her parents and the exalted rank of her birthright.

Andy fell far short of being her equal. He was a hot-tempered lout, a foul-mouthed pugilist, anything but a suitor for a girl with the excellent upbringing of Amy—one who knew her responsibilities and had always behaved so sensibly. She was an attractive brunette, punctual and of a courteous disposition—the perfect hostess, who seemed always to be on hand to serve and offer assistance when appropriate.

At first it was only on odd occasions they would be seen together at football matches, where Andy was rather a hero. He was the captain and highest try scorer in the first grade and he was big, strong and athletic, with blond, curly hair and a daredevil smile, which fluttered the hearts of the young female football fans.

Gossip really slipped into top gear when Amy and Andy were seen together at dances and the theatre. Disapproval was expressed as well as disappointment in her judgment. The popular opinion was that it was all an infatuation that couldn't last. Reverend Weeks and his amiable wife, Sarah, being of good Christian character, accepted the match as being the will of God and had enough faith in their daughter to be convinced that Amy would reform the wayward lad.

To the surprise of all, at least temporarily, that was proving a reality—Andy *had* modified his behaviour. He was even attending church and was respectful to all those who chose to judge him harshly. Swearing, at least in public, was no longer part of his repertoire. In the eyes of the elite, that was miracle enough in itself. Love had no boundaries and some of the dignitaries were heard to remark, 'The Lord moves in strange ways.'

In fact, Andy's manner had improved to the extent that he had gone a long way to winning acceptance, even among those who chose to condemn and disapprove. Even so, it came as a shock when wedding plans were announced. Amy and Andy were to be married. Invitations were sent out to a select group of parishioners who were both church regulars and friends of the family, many of whom had been the most critical of the match.

Disapproval was still in their hearts, but their respect for Reverend Weeks assured a full acceptance. There was still some disquiet expressed at the inclusion on the invitation list of Andy's mates, whose reputation in the town was anything but respectable.

The wedding itself went off smoothly. There was enough champagne to make even the most dignified a little tipsy. All the speakers were complimentary, full of goodwill and best wishes. It was a wedding that would be remembered.

The problem began when the newlyweds were ready to set out on their honeymoon, just on dusk. Andy's mates had done a specialist job on demolishing his car. Boots and tins were tied to the bumper bar, paint was splattered all over the duco, the tyres

were deflated and the engine was mechanically disabled. It was seen as an act of vandalism by the church group. 'I told you so' was widely whispered around.

It meant that the first night of their honeymoon had to be spent at Reverend Weeks's abode, and the spare room was prepared with assiduous care.

The celebrations had been tiring, and the two newlyweds excused themselves and retired at a reasonable hour. They found the blue sheets on the double bed turned back, waiting for their embrace. They undressed rather shyly, as newlyweds often do, but when Andy hopped into bed, his bride expressed disapproval. He hadn't said his bedtime prayers. Andy explained, rather taken aback, that he had never said them in his life.

But he had mended his ways considerably for Amy, and their wedding night was no time for rebellion. Under Amy's supervision, he knelt and said his prayers and, what's more, promised to say them every night of their married life.

The next morning, Amy came tripping down the stairs, her cheeks rosy, her grey eyes alight with happiness. Breakfast was not yet served but she found her father sitting in his usual position at the end of the table, his head buried in the paper.

'Father,' she crooned.

Her father grunted.

'Andy did something last night,' she gushed, 'that he had never done before ... and what's more, he's promised to do it every night of our married life.'

The Reverend Weeks let the paper drop into his lap, looked at his daughter with much scepticism and snorted, 'Sheer impossibility'.

Did such innocence really once exist? Or was the reality of young love more along the lines related by WL Schmidt (no relation to the woolly aphid man) of Bowen, Queensland?

I Suppose a Duck's Entirely Out of the Question?

During the war years, I was posted to various places to carry out essential duties of all kinds. One such was Bowen. On my discharge after the war, I decided to start up a business here in my profession in the building and plumbing trades. After a very short time, I was approached by a chap called Happy Jack to help with the formation of an amateur vaudeville show in aid of a charity called Diggers' Follies. He told me he'd heard quite a lot about my entertaining ability, so I agreed to help. He didn't need singers, so I agreed to do my comedy sketches.

About three days later, he was back to tell me that we could rehearse in the local church hall. After three or four rehearsals, the minister announced that next Saturday they were having a church fete. He asked if I'd go along and meet some of the churchgoers. I agreed, and during the fete, a lass of about 18 asked me if I'd buy a ticket in the raffle. I did ... and I won the prize—two live ducks.

I was walking home with a duck under each arm, when I met the same girl who'd sold me the tickets. I asked her, seeing we were walking in the same direction, if she'd mind if I walked with her.

'No!' she replied. 'You might try to take advantage of me.'

'Come off it,' I said. 'How it would be possible under the circumstances?'

'Well,' she said, 'I could hold the ducks, couldn't I?'

And the course of true love has never run smooth. Geoff Dean of Tassie, who told us about Bert Morley's little indiscretions in a previous chapter, is also an expert on what happens when even an apparently long-surviving matter of the heart gets a puncture.

The Amazing Resurrection of Grandma Pike

In her mid-70s, Grandma Pike was known in the district as a tough old bird. In spite of a touch of arthritis in her hands brought on by more years of milking cows than she cared to remember, she still persisted in going about her work without complaint. It was therefore a surprise to everyone when word got around that she had suddenly fallen ill. The story was that poor Grandma Pike had taken to her bed to die. When her many relatives heard the news, they came from far and wide to pay their last respects to the grand old lady.

One of her relatives was a granddaughter called Sharon who was an experienced beautician in the city. When Sharon arrived, Grandma Pike asked to see her immediately and, from her bed, explained to Sharon what she wanted.

'I want to look as radiantly beautiful as I looked when I was a bride,' she told her.

In fact, Grandma Pike had never been the radiantly beautiful type. Her attributes were more of the functional kind. She had been a fine, strong girl in her youth, with a complexion more ruddy than radiant and a body more suited to digging spuds and wrestling recalcitrant poddies into their drinking bays than tripping the light fantastic. Nevertheless, Sharon took to her task with some enthusiasm. If that was what her favourite grandmother wanted, then she was determined to bring all her skills to bear to accomplish her final wish.

It took all the morning and half the afternoon to satisfy Grandma Pike eventually, and only then did the old lady consent to see the remainder of her relatives. They trooped through her room one by one, some bravely hiding their tears and others openly weeping.

Grandma Pike lay back on her pink pillows with apricot-coloured lace edging, wearing a wan and fatalistic smile on her heavily made-up face. 'Don't be sad,' she told each one of them. 'I'd rather go now while I still have my good looks than when

I'm old and ugly.' She smiled, feebly and bravely, as she grasped each hand and puckered her ruby lips for the final kiss. 'I've had a good life ... I'm happy with my family around me ... that's all that counts.'

'Poor Grandma Pike, what a wonderful old lady,' a daughter-in-law remarked tearfully when she had emerged from the bedroom. It was a sentiment that, judging by the tearful expressions and general serious nodding of heads, all agreed with.

Finally, it was Grandpa Pike's turn to pay his final respects. He made his way sadly into her room. He sat in the bedside chair and took hold of his wife's hand. In Grandpa Pike's eyes, his partner of 45 years was indeed beautiful—as beautiful as the day they'd been married. Tears streamed down his cheeks as he sat there gazing soulfully into her eyes.

Grandma Pike squeezed his hand and told him what she told all the others. Only to Grandpa Pike, she quietly mentioned one regret about her life—and that was his possible infidelity all those years ago with the red-haired dairymaid who'd come to work for them briefly when Grandma Pike had gone off to hospital to give birth to their youngest son.

'It's always troubled me,' the old lady confessed. 'Not so much that you'd been unfaithful. I could have lived with that. It's the not knowing that makes me so sad. I think I could go to my grave quite happy, even if it were true, but I couldn't rest if I thought you'd lied to me.'

Grandpa Pike was so moved by his partner's plea that he broke down into unrestrained grief. His whole body shook with his sobbing. His tears, which had been trickling down his face, ran freely. His wife offered him a weak smile and gave his hand another squeeze. Only, this time, Grandpa Pike thought he detected a slight fading of her strength. He looked anxiously into his wife's face and saw her eyelids begin to flutter. She was trying to speak. He lent forward to hear the words that came with small puffs of breath into his ear.

'Please ... tell me the truth, dearest ... for the sake of your soul ... as well as mine.'

Grandpa Pike could control himself no longer. All those years he'd managed to keep his guilty secret safe. But now, in these special circumstances ... ? It just didn't seem right to deny his lifetime mate the truth.

'Yes,' he confessed suddenly, 'it *is* true—but only once ... and I didn't really like it at all.'

As he gazed into Grandma Pike's eyes, with the relieved, wet-eyed expression of a man who'd finally made restitution, he was surprised to see, rather than the peace she had promised, a very definite look of triumph. He was even more surprised when he saw her suddenly throw back the covers and begin struggling out of bed and into her slippers.

'You skinny little blackguard,' she shouted.

She grabbed the old dogwood walking stick she kept by her bed and, grasping it tightly in her gnarled old hand, took a vicious swing at her startled mate. There was nothing left for Grandpa Pike to do but run towards the bedroom door—which he did with some alacrity. But Grandma Pike wasn't satisfied with just one swipe at her mate. She was after his blood. Still swinging the walking stick around her head, she staggered after him.

Relatives and friends scattered in all directions as Grandpa Pike charged into the living room, at such speed that he collapsed right across the afternoon tea table, sending plates of scones and cakes in all directions. Hot on his tail, Grandma Pike managed to get one good thwack across his buttocks before he recovered his balance enough to scramble across the wrecked table to the french windows leading out onto the verandah.

Neither, it seemed, was one good hit going to satisfy Grandma Pike's lust for revenge. Without hesitation, and with an agility that belied both her years and her poor state of health, she scrambled after her fleeing husband, thwacking furiously and threateningly at the air between them.

Thus the pursuer and the pursued lumbered their way down the garden path, until they eventually disappeared from sight into the high grass and scrub that grew alongside the creek. The sounds of the chase and the periodic thwacks and cries of Grandpa Pike floated up to the startled relatives who clustered around the open french windows trying to get a better look at the amazing resurrection of Grandma Pike.

Eventually it was up to Sharon—who everyone said came from the more practical side of the family—to organise the remainder of the Pike clan. 'Well,' she said brightly, 'it seems as though Gran's taken a turn for the better. Perhaps we should clear up this mess and go home. There doesn't seem to be much else we can do at this point, don't you agree?'

Except for the three great-grandchildren, who'd entered into the spirit of proceedings by conducting their own game of chasy around the pile of broken plates and scattered cakes, no one else had any objections to such a sensible suggestion.

Whether it was Grandpa Pike's final confession that gave new life to Grandma Pike, or whether she had set the whole thing up in the first place, was never revealed. All everyone close to her knew for sure was that Grandma Pike's amazing resurrection lasted for another nine years. She survived her wayward husband by only a few months. And it was always said that except when she was asleep, she rarely, if ever, in those nine long years, allowed Grandpa Pike out of her sight.

Finally, a yarn about shearers. They've been the heroes of many a tall tale. In fact, yarn spinners have given these sheep barbers a far nobler profile than they perhaps deserve. They're always made out to be such strong, athletic types. In fact, they're usually skinny little blokes with crippled hands, stuffed backs and yolk boils. The mould of the typical Ryebuck shearer was broken long ago.

This yarn came from Leo Davis of the Eventide Home in Canowindra, NSW.

Life's Motorway to Heaven

The three shearers who worked for us, Bluey, Tom and Jack, always shore together, travelling from shed to shed. One day, Bluey's wife died. They decided to send her off in style. They drank solidly for nearly a week, without eating. Sure enough, all three became very sick and weak. The next week, they continued their boozing.

Bluey died that Friday, Tom the next day and Jack on Sunday. All three were buried on the Monday, and naturally, they all reached the Pearly Gates at the same time.

St Peter ran through the rules with them. 'It's a big joint up here and you'll need vehicles to get around. You'll get something appropriate to the way you lived your life Down There.'

He turned to Tom. 'I hope you were good to your wife—looked after her, stayed faithful and all that?'

Tom shrugged. 'I was OK at the start, but things sort of dropped off, so I had a blonde on the side.'

'Hmmmm,' mused St Peter. 'Well, I think you'd better make do with that old '48 Holden over there.' Tom thanked him and went to try to get the old car started.

'Now, Jack,' continued St Peter. 'How did you go with your missus?'

'No worries,' beamed Jack sanctimoniously. 'I looked after her real good. Never even looked at another woman.'

'Good man. You take the keys to that new Camry over there.'

Finally, he turned to Blue. 'I did my best,' said the honest shearer. 'Often, when my missus was out late with her girlfriends, I cooked her a late supper and made her a cup of coffee when she came home. I reckoned nothing was too good for the woman I loved.'

St Peter clapped him on the back. 'You go to the top of the class,' he told Blue. 'See that brand new Mercedes over there? That's yours.' Blue drove off, elated.

However, next day when St Peter was doing his rounds, he found Blue sitting down in the Heavenly gutter looking perfectly miserable. 'What's up, Blue? Why so sad? Your fidelity to your wife has been justly rewarded with that new Mercedes.'

'It's not the car,' wailed the glum old shearer. 'It's just that I've bumped into me missus again—and she was riding around on a rusty old tricycle.'

Chapter 4

GETTING ABOUT

A SURE way to spark a passionate discussion is to list the latest atrocities being subjected to your wallet by your vehicle. In the best yarn-spinning tradition, everyone else present will try to outdo your catalogue of misery and disaster. It's a tradition that dates back well before the horseless carriage. When we relied on four-legged transport rather than four-wheeled, our parents and grandparents would obviously have done the same thing.

The getting from point A to point B with a minimum of fuss has always been a major concern. It's never been just a matter of making your journey on time and in comfort. The affairs of transportation have long been tied up with the greater affairs of humankind. We've all heard the old rhyme: 'For want of a nail, a shoe was lost; for want of a shoe, a horse was lost; for want of a horse, a man was lost; for want of a man, a battle was lost etc.'

More recently, it was said that the Six Days War in the Middle East was lost by the Egyptians so quickly because that's as long as it took for them to run out of juice for their vehicles. The virtual disintegration of what was once the Soviet Bloc has been blamed on the lack of a USSR—wide transport infrastructure. These yarns aren't just amusing stories, you know, they're parables of great importance to humanity. The whole fate of our planet depends on being able to get about.

———————

I can remember in my own youth, a few bush families still relying on horses for transportation. The Kirbys used to travel in to school from far off Yalloak Vale, where their Dad trapped rabbits for a living, in a battered old sulky. Our primary school still had horseyards in one corner, and the Kirby's solitary horse would spend the day there. Travel around the farm was still mostly done on an old sled pulled by an ancient draughthorse. Cars were by no means universal. Many of them were still stately old A-model Fords with canvas tops and wooden-spoked wheels. Crikey! And it wasn't all that long ago, really.

Why Drubb Lost the Election

One local family who couldn't afford a motor vehicle was the Gormleys. Their pride and joy was an old piebald clumper—half draughthorse, half God knows what—strong enough to do the heavy farmwork, drag the family sulky to town and back and keep the kids amused riding about the paddocks sitting like willy wagtails in a row down his long back.

It was quite a tragedy when the old horse got crook. He went right off his feed and bloated up like a balloon. With the horse in obvious discomfort, the Gormleys had no way of getting anywhere to seek professional help. None of us had phones back then. The only course of action was to send one of the kids off to seek advice from a neighbour. The kid scampered across the paddocks, hurdling any fences like an Olympic champion. He appeared a couple of hours later, driven by Fred Gillespie, the neighbour, who owned a wooden-sided Willy's station wagon. The kid had obviously explained in detail what was wrong because Fred had brought with him an old black Gladstone bag weighted down with what the Gormleys could only assume were emergency supplies. Fred had a reputation up the valley as something of a horse doctor, so he must have brought some of his home-brewed medicines with him. From the way the gladstone bag was sagging, it was obvious that he wouldn't have hurdled many fences on the trip back to the Gormley's if he'd had to walk.

The old horse was still in the yard. By then he'd gone down and was lying on his side, whinnying in pain from his bloated gut. Fred gave him the once over. He didn't say much, but started fossicking in the gladstone bag. Eventually he'd lined up a row of paperbags containing a variety of powders on the ground in front of him. He sent Ma Gormley inside for a large dixie of lukewarm water and a few empty jam jars. Ma supplied everything and Fred mixed up a variety of potions in the jars. 'While I'm doing this, Mrs G, why don't you fire up the wood stove? I'll need a medium oven for a while.'

Eventually he mixed everything together in one big jar. The resulting brown mixture wasn't so much a liquid as a gritty mud. Finally, Fred took the mud out and started kneading it like dough. Once he'd squeezed more moisture from it, he rolled it into a ball, slightly smaller than a pingpong ball, and gave it to Mrs Gormley with instructions to bake it in the oven for an hour.

It's lucky it didn't take longer than that because by the time the hour was up, the poor old horse looked ready to turn up his toes. Ma Gormley came out of the kitchen holding Fred's masterpiece in her oven mitt.

'Now,' said Fred, looking around expectantly. 'Do you have anything like a tube or a funnel?' Everyone looked puzzled.

'Hang on, I'll explain. What's wrong with your old horse is a build up of half-digested rich feed in his gut. That's why he's bloated like that. The blockage is fermenting and producing gas and the poor old bloke's just blowing up inside. What we've got to do is dissolve the blockage and let the gas out. That pill I'll give him can dissolve concrete. But we've got to find some way of getting it up his arse.'

Everyone rushed round to help. One of the kids turned up with a short length of downpipe, but Fred shook his head. 'No, it's too smooth. The pill might take some time to work. What we need is something with a little lip at one end so it won't slip out before the job's done.'

Mr Gormley had a brain wave. Going inside, he grabbed an old post horn that had hung over the fireplace ever since the Gormleys first selected their block. An original Gormley had been a mail coach driver back in the old country. When he migrated to Australia, he brought the horn with him as a memento of his former life. The horn was really just a straight bugle, about five feet (not far short of 2 metres) long, flared at one end, as bugles are, and with a little lip around the other end for a mouthpiece. The old-time mail coach drivers used to blow the post horn to warn communities of their imminent arrival or departure.

The old coach horn was just what Fred Gillespie needed. He slid the mouthpiece into the sick horse's anus and wriggled it gently. 'There, if he moves suddenly, it won't fall out,' he declared. Then, holding the post horn at a bit of an angle, he rolled his ball of horse medicine in from the flared end. It actually rumbled as it went down.

Talk about an instant cure. The old horse's eyes suddenly opened wide. He neighed loudly. You could actually see the distended sides of his stomach start to ripple. Before anyone knew it, the old nag had leaped to its feet.

'Crikey! I hope the horn stays there,' someone shouted.

It sure did. In fact, it remained up the horse's posterior as if it were part of him. Of course, it clanged loudly on the ground when the nag stood up. The unexpected noise startled the horse even more. He whinnied and took off, with the post horn still banging the ground behind him, prompting even more panic. By then, Fred's medicine was really starting to work, because the horse started farting loudly. With each internal explosion, the post horn bounced out horizontally and, naturally enough, sounded a loud, clear bugle call.

That, of course, spooked the old horse even more and he doubled his speed, making much better time across the paddocks, and over the fences, than any of the Gormley kids had ever done.

In minutes he was well out of sight. In fact, once clear of Gillespie's place, there was nothing to stop him for about 20 miles (and that's over 30 kilometres). The last anyone in the valley saw of the horse he'd galloped onto the back road over the ranges and was following it in the general direction of Ballan.

Unaware of the drama unfolding so many miles away, Trevor Drubb was reading a three-day-old newspaper in his little shed beside the Great Western railway line. Trevor lived in a little cottage behind the shed. He had an important job. Twice each day he was responsible for swinging shut the railway crossing gates over the back road, when the Overlander zoomed past on its way either to or from Adelaide. Trevor took his job seriously, cognisant of the fact that he was personally responsible for the safety of scores of train travellers and the occasional local road traveller. In fact, he took it so seriously that he'd nominated for a seat on the local shire council. He believed a man on whom so many people's lives depended was the ideal person to steer the shire into the 1950s.

Trevor was shaken awake from his slow perusal of the *Sun Pictorial* by the loud blaring of an approaching horn. What on earth was it? The east-bound Overlander wasn't due for another four hours. Nevertheless, the speed with which the noise was coming indicated the need for fast action. With characteristic flourish, he folded his paper and strode out to the crossing gates. He briskly swung them shut and awaited the approaching ... whatever it was. Imagine his surprise when instead of a thundering express train on the main line, he was greeted by a knocked-up, lathered old horse with a trumpet sticking out of its bum, which staggered up the back road and leaned on the shut crossing gates as though to say, 'Thank Christ, someone's finally stopped me.'

So, in the end, it mostly worked out well. The Gormleys got their horse back and could still go into town whenever they wanted to, and the horse had managed to blow out all the stuff

that had caused it to bloat and was as fit and happy as it had
ever been. The only person who wasn't happy was Trevor.

Three weeks later, when we went to the polls, he didn't score a
single vote (apart from his own). People in the valley agreed that
anyone who couldn't tell a horse's arse from the Overlander
wasn't worth voting for.

Horses and their funny little quirks also concerned the family of
Janet Kinsey of Nevertire, NSW.

Behind Bluey

My father tells me from time to time of his early life in the
depression years. It was a constant battle trying to find enough
work, to buy or acquire food and to feed a large family. But there
were also some amusing incidents.

This one took place along the banks of the Namoi River, near
Wee Waa. Dad, his mother, stepfather and three brothers were
living in one tent, his sister and her husband in another. The
families would move around in search of work, but they'd been
at that one spot for quite some time. Dad's sister had an old
horse, Bluey, who used to pull the sulky. He was a giant of a
horse and had the most placid nature. He was the family's sole
means of transport and would pull two adults and a couple of
children easily. The kids used to love travelling into Wee Waa
to get the meagre rations, flour being the mainstay.

Bread making was a daily event, and while other food may have
been lacking, there was always some bread to eat. As work was in
short supply, this meant food was too. That included food for
the horse. Rather than let the poor beast go hungry, the family
fed him on bread. Bluey seemed to enjoy it and consumed quite
a quantity.

All went well until one afternoon when Bluey was harnessed up
and started his walk into town. The family were sitting enjoying
their journey, when Bluey lifted his tail. Every step he took, he
broke wind—and sent a shower of breadcrumbs over the passengers.

The whole scene turned into total uproar—kids laughing, adults chuckling, poor old Bluey still breaking wind, and breadcrumbs flying everywhere.

The trip that day was abandoned and Bluey's rations more closely monitored from then on!

Never mind the farters and the duds. Of course, a decent horse was worth its weight in prune juice. Transport was all very well, but their recreational value was also well appreciated. A horse might do well behind a plough or a jinker, but if you had one that could race or jump ... well he could always bring in a few extra bob. But, like humans, a flash, athletic type of horse mightn't necessarily be too cluey upstairs. Arthur Collins spun this yarn from Melville, WA.

Coulda Been a Champion

In the shearing shed one smoko, the talk turned to horses. One of the blokes was skiting about a good jumper he'd had. Peter, the old wool roller, reckoned his dad once had a Clydesdale teamhorse that could have beaten any flash showjumper. He waited for the laughter to die away, leaned back in the wool and told his tale.

'He was a cunning old bugger, too. He developed this habit of jumping into Dad's lucerne patch, which was next to the horse paddock. To stop him, we first put a barbed wire along the top of the posts. But old Diamond still jumped over. Dad nailed a batten to each fence post and strung *another* barb about a foot (around 30 centimetres) higher. By then, the top wire was a good five feet (around 160 centimetres) above ground—but still the old horse got over.

'I reckoned I knew how to fix him, so I tied a heavy trace chain, about 30 foot (over 9 metres) long, to his neck. With that draggin' behind him, he'd never be able to jump the fence.

'I thought I had him beat when, for nearly a week, he stayed in the horse paddock. Then, one morning, as I went to milk, there he was, chain and all, in the middle of the lucerne paddock.

'I was determined to beat him, so I found a couple of old cast-iron plough journals in the scrap heap—about 50 pounds (almost 25 kilograms) weight each—and tied them to the end of his chain. I had him grounded *this* time. But sure, lo and behold!, next morning, there he was again. With what he'd eaten and the damage caused by the dragging chain, the lucerne patch was indeed a sorry sight. Dad was ropable and went to get his gun, but I said, 'Let's find out how he does it.'

'There was a fairly good moon that night, so I hid in the cow shed and watched through a crack in the slabs.

'I must have dozed off in the warm hay, because, about midnight, I woke with a start to the thunder of hoofs. Looking out, I saw Diamond at a flat gallop towards the fence, the chain streaming out behind him like a ribbon. As he reached the fence, he swerved and propped. The weighted chain, still in the air, swung right out over the fence. Just at the right moment, Diamond jumped and followed that chain over the fence into the paddock.

'The old man reckoned the horse was too smart for us, so he sent him off to the saleyards, a pity really. With the hair off his legs and a bit of schooling, I reckon he might have done all right on the show circuit.'

Anyone who's experienced a knuckle-dragging teenager lurching in asking to be granted their L plates so they can start learning how to become a menace on the roads will know what a feeling of warmth and wellbeing it promotes. Of course, there's an automatic assumption that Mum or Dad should be the driving instructor. As we all now know, the first rule of survival, both for you and for other road users, is never to teach your own kids to drive. It was no different in the horse and buggy days. Ask Betty Ferguson of Leadville, NSW.

Do the Right Thing

In the early 1930s, we lived in a small country town in Victoria. My brother and I went to school, driving our own sulky. Naturally, we did as our mother told us, always staying on the right side of the road. Unfortunately, our mother had such a poor road sense that when granting her a car licence, the local policeman made her promise that she'd never drive the car to Melbourne.

After a few weeks into the first term, our father was talking to the local agent, who asked if he knew who the young kids were who came from out his way and drove to school each day in a sulky, always on the wrong side of the road.

'Oh, my gosh!' said Dad. 'Those boys belong to us. Maybe their mother should have told them to stay on the *left* side of the road.'

Also from up Betty's way is Hilton Bennetts of Dunedoo, who proves that even Way Back Then, road accidents were a concern for everyone—even if some people did tend to get hold of the wrong end of the stick.

Shock! Horror!

When I was a small lad, my dad used to lease a property near Gillinghall, between Wellington and Dunedoo. Most of the farming was done by horses in those days and my dad used to sow a small area to wheat each year. This particular year, he had a good crop and he needed a man to help with the harvest and cart the wheat to the Wellington flour mill. All us kids were too small to be of any use.

He decided to drive into Wellington in the horse and sulky to see if he could get a suitable man. When he arrived in town, he went to one of the stock and station agents to see if they knew anyone requiring that particular kind of work. The agent said there'd been a man in that morning inquiring about work. He was camped down near the bridge on the Macquarie River. Dad

went down and interviewed the bloke, whose name was Joe. Yes, he'd done plenty of harvest work and had driven a horse team. Dad decided to engage him and said he'd go back to town, do the shopping and pick him up on his way home that afternoon.

When they arrived home, it was just about teatime and Mother had cooked a leg of mutton plus enough roast potatoes and pumpkin to feed all of us—including us five children and the new hand.

Joe must have been without a good feed for some time, because when Mum put the big oval dish down at the end of the table for Dad to carve the meat, the new hand just sat down and started eating. He did finally admit, 'I think I've got a wee bit too much meat here, missus.'

A couple of days later, Dad went down to the mailbox and picked up the mail. When he arrived back, he emptied the mailbag out and announced that the latest papers were in if Joe cared to look at them while waiting for dinner to be served.

At that stage, we didn't realise Joe could neither read nor write and was obviously a bit too embarrassed to admit it. He just took one of the papers and opened it up—upside down. Back then, instead of the nice car ads you see these days, it was all horses, buggies and sulkies. Businesses would advertise with fine pictures of their horse teams and coaches, with their names advertised on the side.

Pretending to read, Joe came to the first horse and buggy ad and declared, 'By cripes, Roy, there's been a nasty accident here.'

When Dad looked, he had the buggy on its hood and the horses' legs in the air. Joe thought it had turned over.

It might seem that the old horse and buggy days were a lot more laid-back than now, but people still had their hairy moments, as related in one of the many yarns spun by Dawn Murray of Bunbury, WA.

The Bomb on Wheels

In the days before everything was so highly regulated, supplies of blasting dynamite that were used in a small country town were ordered by a shopkeeper and kept in a cellar below his shop. The dynamite would arrive by goods train. It was always an exciting time for the town. The shopkeeper would notify the local businesses that he'd ordered a new consignment. The stationmaster would announce the day and time of arrival. Then the local carrier, Pooler Paice, would be alerted that his services were needed. On the day the consignment was due, there'd be an air of expectancy in the main street. Pooler Paice would arrive at the station early, his flat-top dray well cushioned with stooks of hay covered with chaff bags. While he waited for train, he would wrap his horses' hoofs in old bags, adjust its blinkers so it couldn't be startled from the side, and carefully check all buckles and straps. When satisfied, he'd hang red warning flags on each side of the dray.

When the train carrying the explosives arrived, there'd be none of the usual bumping, jarring and jangling as it came to a stop. It'd arrive with a gentle glide and a delicate hiss as the driver eased it to a stop. Watched carefully by the stationmaster, the guard and a porter would transfer the boxes to the platform and then to the dray. While that was going on, two boys, puffed with self importance for the occasion, would be sent along the streets to tell all the shopkeepers that the explosives were coming. Customers were shepherded to the back to shops, the doors were closed and the blinds pulled down, in case of a mishap.

The town would literally hold its breath as Pooler, slowly walking at his horse's head, led the dray up the slight slope to the shop at the top of the town. The only sound would be the horse's hoofs clopping, the dray creaking and crunching over the coarse gravel road and Pooler's quietly soothing voice making horrendous threats to the horse, should it stumble. Eventually, the dray would be unloaded, the explosives stacked in the cellar of the store and everyone would breathe freely again. Pooler would repair to the pub and be treated to a few settling beers after his valiant efforts.

On one particular occasion, everything went as usual, except for a slight hitch when the train was unloaded. The consignment note with the explosives said there were supposed to be six boxes, but there were only five in the guard's van. Deciding there must have been a mistake in the paperwork, they loaded the five boxes and Pooler took off on his slow trip. He was in the middle of town, halfway up the slope to the top end, when he heard a commotion behind him.

'Mr Paice! Hey, Mr Paice! Wait on!' a young voice was yelling. There was also the sound of iron wheels approaching rapidly. Pooler looked behind and stood with his mouth open. The junior porter was struggling up the road towards him, pushing a two-wheeled luggage trolley with a box on it.

'Mr Paice! Wait, Mr Paice!' he yelled as he panted up beside the dray. 'There *were* six of them. The other one was covered by a blanket. I've got it here.'

'God in Heaven, boy!' said Pooler, his face white. 'You could have blown yourself and the whole town to smithereens, bouncing it around like that.'

'Yes, but if the stationmaster found I'd left a box of explosives behind, he'd have sacked me,' said the boy.

Naturally, horse teams were as prized at today's ritziest BMW, and the passion of old-time chaff heads (as opposed to today's petrol heads) was often the stuff of which family rifts were forged.

Heirlooms

The old man was getting on in years, likewise his two horses, which pulled the night cart in the small country town they lived in. The horses were past their prime, to say the least. They looked so decrepit, people wondered how they could pull themselves along, much less the wagon. But any sort of a horse team was an asset in those hard times of the great depression.

The old man's two boys, Dave and Bill, made a living wherever they could, labouring on the surrounding stations and in the sheds. They both coveted the old man's team.

When their father died, Dave asked the owner of one of the few motor vehicles in the town if he could run him out to the Twelve Mile, where his brother was ringbarking. Once he knew the sad news he wanted to convey, the driver was only too willing to help.

It was quite a trip out to the Twelve Mile, but eventually brother Bill could be seen through the scrub, about 100 yards (metres, these days) away.

'Whoa! Stop!' Dave called. 'This is near enough.' Whereupon he put both hands to his mouth and bellowed, 'Dad's dead and the horses are mine!'

Of course, you can't discuss Australian transport without referring to our railways. And what's the common tie than links all our state networks, irrespective of inconsequential details like the diverse gauges of our lines or the excellence and efficiency of the service provided? Railway food, of course. Allan Shaw of Tuncurry, NSW put it in a nutshell (or perhaps a stained paperbag).

The Railway Pie

In the 1960s, when the Cooma mail train was running from Sydney and extending to Bombala on Mondays, Wednesdays, Fridays and Saturdays, a family dispatched a dog from Sydney one Sunday night for what was to be an epic journey. The poor old dog first travelled all the way to Bombala and then *back* to Cooma on the Monday afternoon. Just before the train was due to return to Sydney, a whimpering sound was heard from the dog compartment of the guard's van. The station staff found the dog still there. Because there wasn't another train from Cooma to Bombala until Wednesday, the dog was unloaded and tied up on the platform at Cooma to wait for it.

You wouldn't want to know, but two days later, the same thing happened. Once again, they forgot to unload the poor dog at Bombala and it landed back at Cooma, where it was dutifully

unloaded again and tied up to await Friday's train. But the same thing happened a third time. Seeing another train was scheduled the next day, the odds seemed to be improving. But alas, the same thing occurred again. By then, the dog was becoming pretty emaciated. Surely the train to Bombala on Monday morning would put everything right?

Sadly, when the train arrived from Sydney on the Monday morning, the unfortunate dog had already gone to that Great Kennel in the Sky.

Understandably, the family who owned the dog claimed compensation for its loss. Head office sent an inspector down to the Monaro to get to the bottom of it all. Accordingly, he confronted the guard who'd been in charge of the train at Bombala and who should have unloaded it.

'Why didn't you put it off?'

'I forgot.'

'Then why didn't you care for the blessed thing?'

'I did. By Sunday I was feeling pretty sorry for it, so I fed it a railway pie. And it died.'

The arrival of the car took some time to win acceptance from a few bush people. Bung Harris was one of the Snowy Mountains' legendary horsemen and bushmen. But as skilled as Bung was on the back of a horse, he had an awful lot of trouble adjusting to petrol-fed transport. Alan Reid of Canberra tells of Bung being cajoled into trying to drive an old ex-army jeep across Little Peppercorn plain some time in the fifties. Bung stuck to the bucking vehicle across the tussocks and wombat holes, until it finally threw him and rolled into a bit of a creek. 'Bloody thing!' cursed Bung as he staggered back to camp. 'It's never been mouthed properly.' Another Bung Harris confrontation with transport was related to me on separate occasions by state MP Peter Cochrane and mountain identity Tom Barry. So it *must* be true.

Plum Pudding

It took the police in Tumut some time to grant Bung Harris his driver's licence. In the end, they took to teaching the old bushman to drive themselves. Eventually it worked. Bung coincided the granting of his licence with the purchase of an old World War II surplus jeep. It may well have been the same one that bucked him off on the Little Peppercorn plain. Bung had ridden his horse into Tumut for his final driving test. Now that he was declared fit to drive a car, the question arose about how best to get both the horse and vehicle back up to Coolamine, where he lived and worked.

Someone suggested he try a local handyman who'd knocked up a single horse float and was offering it for sale. It was a narrow-gutted, unstable sort of float, but good enough for a single trip back up Talbingo Hill to the mountains old Bung loved so much.

Bung left Tumut in the jeep, with his horse safely on the float and his dog and a few boxes of supplies in the back of the jeep. A few locals shook their heads and wondered to themselves if the old bloke'd actually make it to his destination. The licence only proved that he'd managed to stick to the rules of the road while he was in the company of his mates from the police station.

Bung was expected to call in at Yarrongibilly on his way home. When it became late and he still hadn't fronted, another legendary mountain identity, Tom Taylor, became a bit worried and decided to drive back down towards Tumut to see if Bung had suffered some mishap.

His worst fears were realised. There on Talbingo Hill, he found Bung's jeep on its side. The float had also rolled and lay smashed in a gully. Bung's dog lay dead beside the jeep. There was no sign of the old mountain man or his horse.

Tom returned to Yarrongibilly and did a quick ring around. His heart leaped when he buzzed Coolamine and Bung picked up the phone. Yes, the old bloke had survived the crash. So had his horse. Disgusted with the handling of the jeep and the capricious, narrow-gutted horse float, he'd saddled up his trusty steed and ridden home.

Tom was glad old Bung was OK, but expressed commiserations that his dog had died in the accident.

'Dawg? He didn't die in the accident,' snarled Bung. 'While he was riding along in the back of the bloody jeep, the mongrel ate the plum pudding me sister had made for me, so I throttled the bastard.'

They bred 'em tough in the Snowy Mountains.

As depressing as the road toll is, people relish stories about accidents. Luckily there's enough minor scrapes to keep yarn spinners and their victims amused for centuries. My old ex-Crookwell, almost neighbour, Kevin McCormack, strikes a chord with an almost—motoring yarn a lot of us can identify with.

Ned

The year 1940 marked the end of an era for the little bush school on the Redgrounds and its last teacher, Mr Leonard W Rambley. Mr Rambley was a little man, about four foot ten (a bit under 150 centimetres) tall, with a shiny bald head, who wore tortoiseshell glasses on the point of his nose. He was a good old teacher—when he was in control. However, he was easily sidetracked and at such times could be susceptible to all sorts of mad hatter ideas. To sum up—he was fine with orderly pupils but was in constant trouble if there was a rogue pupil in the class. I suppose it was sad that Redgrounds was his last school and he happened to encounter the greatest rogue pupil of all times, my close friend and classmate, Ned.

It was a tense time for all when the school inspector visited the area on his annual visit. From the time it was known he was about, we practised and studied at a rate undreamed of for the rest of the year. Every morning, Mr Rambley would blow a whistle and the dozen or so pupils would form into lines in front of the school. At another blast of the whistle, we'd march in single file into the one-room school.

We were just assembling into lines on this particular morning, when we heard a car coming over the hill. When it turned into the school lane, we realised it was 'the inspector'. The car was an A-model touring Ford, and the way it swerved into the drive and bumped viciously over the stones gave us our first insight into the personality of the inspector. It put us on guard early.

The school was on the side of a fairly steep hill and we watched in awe as the car raced around the back of the building and skidded to a stop alongside the building, facing down the hill. We continued to watch as the driver pushed the gear lever into low gear and dragged on the handbrake. Then he jumped out and went across to the wood heap, where he grabbed a log of wood to push under the front wheel. He snatched his briefcase from the backseat and bounded up the steps and stood alongside Mr Rambley.

You never saw such a contrast. The inspector was twice as big as Mr Rambley and as red in the face as Mr Rambley was white. Mr Rambley timidly extended his hand, which the inspector ignored. Instead, with a powerful voice, he introduced himself to all and sundry as Mr Thunderbolt. He completely took over and marched us into the classroom.

It turned out to be a disaster from the word 'Go!' The inspector started asking questions on general knowledge. I still remember my first question. 'Where are the Blue Mountains?' I pointed out the window and said, 'Over there!' Mr Thunderbolt then moved on to history, which was worse. By then, he was prancing backwards and forwards across the classroom, while Mr Rambley shrank even further into the background, wringing his hands. You would have thought the situation couldn't have got any worse. But it did!

Mr Thunderbolt developed the hiccups. As terrified of him as we were, some of the kids began to titter. The inspector's face started to get redder and redder, until I thought he'd burst into flame. His condition deteriorated to the state where he would hiccup in the middle of a question. That would bring a roar of laughter from the school. It was a desperate situation and one which called for drastic action. Realising the seriousness of the matter, Mr Rambley acted on the spur of the moment and made a decision he'd live to regret to his dying day.

He beckoned Ned. They popped behind the open door, the only spot in the room that offered any privacy, and he and Ned held a hurried whispered conversation. Mr Rambley told Ned the only sure cure he knew for hiccups was a fright. Could Ned arrange one?

Poor Mr Rambley. He knew Ned was the only one with the ingenuity to come up with something to frighten Mr Thunderbolt's hiccups. He also knew that if you gave Ned an inch, he'd take ten miles, but under the circumstances, he had no option. In those few moments, he appealed to the spark of decency within Ned and begged him not to go too far.

Ned scurried unseen out the door like a shadow and Mr Rambley waited with bated breath for the stone on the roof ... or the big knock on the door. He should have known better!

It was a chance of a lifetime for Ned to show his real style. He raced around the school like a spear through the air, leaped into the inspector's car, knocked it out of gear, let the handbrake off, kicked the log from under the front wheel and gave the Ford a sudden push, sending in it on its way. Then he let out a bloodcurdling yell at the window. 'The car's bolted!'

In the lunch hour next day, as we sat on a log and ate our jam sandwiches, we held a debate as to the merits or otherwise of a fright in curing hiccups. Jimmy argued against it. He recalled the events of the previous day, particularly the scene of the accident. He claimed that as the bigger pupils pulled as one to drag the car off the stringy bark tree and the smaller ones collected the broken glass and bits and pieces into a bucket, he distinctly heard Mr Thunderbolt hiccup.

But Ned said no! He remembered it clearly. It wasn't a hiccup—it was a sob!

Chapter 5

THE LAIR OF THE BEAST

ONE of the most successful publishing ideas of recent years has been the beaut ABC books by Angela Goode, like *Great Working Dog Stories*, volumes 1–354, and *Great Working Horse Stories*. Whether Angela plans to get into *Great Working Chooks*, *Great Working Mice* or *Great Working Budgies*, I'm not sure, but our Aussie yarn spinners came up with enough stories to suggest it mightn't be a bad idea.

Let's start with their own version of dog stories, like this one from Ken Dodd of Fernmount, NSW.

Bikini Babes

Some of us are old enough to remember the introduction of bikinis to our beaches. It was said that they were like barbed wired fences—enough to protect the property but not to spoil the view. But there were risks involved in wearing the early bikinis.

One beautiful young lady walked from the surf, proud to be seen in the latest gear. She found she was the centre of attraction for dozens of beachgoers but, on glancing down, discovered the top section of her new bikini was gone. Blushing with embarrassment, she wrapped her arms across her chest and turned to dash back into the surf.

Of course, the inevitable Ginger Meggs type was playing in the smaller waves. As the lady ran by, he called, 'Hey, miss!'

She stopped in the hope of a solution to her problem.

'If you're gunna drown them pups, can I have the one with the red nose?'

Dogs are, as we all know, pretty smart. But they're a bit like anklebiters—you can never trust them entirely. Somewhere in their pointy little heads is a doggy agenda that doesn't always match ours. There's absolutely no logic behind what happened to Diane MacMaster of Cowra. It doesn't matter how smart (or stupid) your dog seems, sometimes you just wish they could talk and explain exactly what they were thinking at the time.

Sheer Shelfishness

Really heavy rain had fallen during the night. My husband arose to discover a small flood in the laundry, kitchen and dining room. We had to move all the furniture and lift all the drenched carpet and other floor coverings to try and dry everything out. As we had a very large pantry, we unloaded the sideboard and packed all our crockery on a couple of shelves. We also had a small son, so we carefully put all the good stuff out of the reach of little fingers. After the clean up, we went into town for a bit of R and

R, but first we chained our dog to its usual place at the side of the house.

After a couple of pleasant hours with friends, we arrived home to see only the dog chain stretched into the house through the pantry window.

Oh no! The dog must have jumped in through the small window. It was something he'd never even tried before. We rushed in, expecting to see him hung at the end of his chain. What a sight—smashed crockery, food tins all over the floor and one large border collie, still with his chain on, lying stretched out on the middle shelf. He'd somehow managed to scramble up there to avoid being strangled—but in the process had pulled everything off to make room for himself. He just sat there with his big eyes innocent and an expression that said, 'I didn't really do this.'

I didn't know whether to laugh or cry. I unclipped the dog, who made one hasty retreat, and started to clean up again. One small relief was our precious Royal Doulton teaset sitting on the next shelf untouched and undamaged.

Of course, if dogs can't explain their little foibles, there's sometimes some discerning human around who knows exactly what they're trying to get across, like Graeme Denholme's dad in Devonport, Tasmania.

Life is Butter Melancholy Flower

I was just a lad when World War II ended but I remember well how coupons were required for the purchase of many everyday commodities, such as sugar, tea and butter. We children were taught to use sugar and butter sparingly. Honey often replaced sugar on our breakfast cereals and dripping, more often than not, was used in place of butter on our toast. Just about every Christmas holiday, we used to go and stay with my grandmother (on my father's side) for a few weeks at her really old farmhouse way back in the country in north-eastern Tasmania. Living in a city during the year, the holiday was something I really looked forward to with great excitement. In fact, all the family loved to go for our holiday on the farm. Mum and Dad would make a special effort to save up a few coupons in the weeks before we left, so that we could take along a few pounds of sugar, tea and butter as a special offering to Grandma.

Grandma was a great provider in her own right. She always had a pantry full of preserved fruit and jam, a large can full of honey, kerosene tins full of farm eggs (preserved in Kee-Peg), homemade chutney ... and so on. There was always raspberry vinegar to mix with water from the well, or plenty of milk to drink. It was really great to sit down to her meals, which were almost exclusively home-grown. My favourite was baked seasoned rabbit and gravy, with new potatoes and green peas fresh from the garden, followed by blackberry pie and cream.

The only drawback was Grandmas's homemade butter. Dad, in particular, always complained that it was far too salty. I guess we all agreed with him, although I must admit that I always thought it was better than the dripping we usually got on our toast at home. Dad always made sure that we took along enough factory made butter bought from the shop with our coupons to last us for our stay ... plus a bit extra.

One of my indelible and early recollections in life goes back to one of our arrivals at the farm. After all the usual hellos, kisses and unpacking of gifts and goodies, Dad proceeded to unwrap and cut off a section of shop-bought butter with his usual pride and authority. The butter dish for the table was kept in an airy old safe in the cool of the back verandah. The dish contained a fair dollop of Grandma's homemade butter, which Dad replaced with his shop brand. In his haste to put the homemade portion back into the butter crock, he dropped in on the verandah floor. I was the only witness to his accident and, quick as a flash, he scooped it up and threw it off the back verandah. Typically, the fowls came running and flapping from all directions to gather up whatever scraps were on offer from the house.

No sooner had the great gathering of poultry surrounded the

lump of butter than the old farm dog swooped in from nowhere, skittled all the chooks and scoffed down the butter in one swift gulp.

The old dog stood motionless. Then his tongue slowly circled his top and bottom lips two or three times. Suddenly, he started going round and round, licking the spot underneath where his tail joined his body.

I was bewildered by the dog's behaviour, and as he continued to go around vigorously licking his posterior, I asked Dad why.

Without so much as a slight smile, Dad simply explained that the poor dog was trying to get the taste of Grandma's butter out of his mouth.

You couldn't expect a yarn spinner like Kevin McCormack of Crookwell to forgo the chance to tell a dog yarn. By the same token, you'd also expect his old chalkie, Mr Rambley, to whom we were introduced in a previous chapter, to have fallen foul of the odd pupil's mutt in his long-suffering days at the Redgrounds school. And you'd be right.

Sam

Our little bush school, of about fifteen pupils, was awaiting, yet again, with apprehension and a certain amount of fear, the annual visit of the inspector. Our fearsome visitor would report not only on the pupils but the teacher as well, so it was a vicious circle. The teacher knew our performance would fall back on him. We were a pretty dull lot in those days, about 50 years ago, so there wasn't much Mr Rambley could do. However, one area in which we *could* shine was attendance. If the inspector could glance back two or three weeks through the roll book and see a good attendance record, it gave a good first impression that might help him overlook some of the later disasters.

So Mr Rambley appealed for 100 per cent attendance until the inspector was due to arrive. We knew he was in the district and would soon call. Mr Rambley begged us not to miss a day, no matter what happened. He promised us a day off if we could achieve our goal. It sounded good, so we accepted the challenge with enthusiasm. Now, Mr Rambley, a little old man at the end of his career, was less than five feet (that's less than 150 centimetres) tall, bald, with thick glasses. He could easily be fooled.

When little Bertha Haystack came to school looking very pale and seedy, her older sister Gertie announced she wouldn't bring her the next day unless she was better. We were all worried. At lunchtime, little Bertha seemed worse. Gertie said they'd been over at their cousins' a week or so before and everyone there had had the measles. It was logical to assume that little Bertha would go down with them. Goodbye 100 per cent attendance. Goodbye day off.

Everyone talked at once and all sorts of suggestions were made. Martin said it was no use, Bertha couldn't possibly come to school if she had the measles, so we may as well accept our fate. At least we'd tried. Ned, however, could usually be relied on to come up with an idea. After some deep thought, he formulated another of his brilliant little schemes.

The Haystacks had an old collie named Sam who was almost human. He'd been trained as a pup to do all sorts of tricks. He could walk around on his hind legs, shake hands, sit up on chairs and do many other clever things. Ned suggested Sam be dressed up in some of Bertha's clothes and take her place at school. Bertha was a shy, stupid little girl who Mr Rambley had long ago given up trying to teach. She had a soft little voice that he couldn't hear, so he rarely took any notice of her.

Gertie didn't like Ned's idea, but we finally talked her into it. We couldn't believe our eyes the next morning when she arrived at school with Sam instead of Bertha. In fact, Ned, who exaggerated a little at times, said he had great difficulty telling the difference.

Things went fairly smoothly for the next two or three days, although there were some worrying moments. One problem was Sam's bladder. He needed to pass water once or twice each class. That wasn't really a problem in itself, as Bertha's toilet program was much the same. But, of course, Bertha would always put her hand up when she wanted to go. Now we had Gertie putting her hand up for Sam. Mr Rambley didn't seem to notice on the first day, but the next morning, he was pretty grouchy and asked, 'Why can't Bertha put her own hand up if she wants to be excused?'

That caused us to call an urgent meeting at lunchtime and Joe, whose dad was quite a handyman and had passed his ability on to his son, was given a rushed job. Joe found a suitable stick, fashioned a little hand onto the end of it and, with the help of an old glove and a few pieces of clothing, produced a fake arm—a true work of art. When Sam needed to be excused, Gertie could raise the little hand alongside him. Mr Rambley only needed to see it and he'd give his nodded permission. He well remembered an earlier time when, in a cantankerous mood, he'd refused Bertha permission to go—with disastrous results.

Gertie would order Sam, 'Stand up and go!' and Sam would walk out on his hind legs and relieve himself. Perhaps the most worrying part of it all was agonising over the possibility that Sam might decide to go home instead of coming back in.

We finally survived through to Friday. Gertie said she was sure Bertha would be fit for school on Monday. It had been a long week, but we were starting to relax.

Then fate dealt a cruel blow. It was mental arithmetic time for the whole school. Mr Rambley would stand out the front and ask different levels of question for each class. Who knows what got Sam so excited, but suddenly, he barked, 'Woof!'

'My God!' Mr Rambley stopped in his tracks. 'Who barked?'

No one answered. Mr Rambley glared and there was complete silence. After a pause he resumed the questions.

'Woof! Woof!' There was no mistaking the direction from which the barks came. Mr Rambley pushed his glasses off the point of his nose and glared towards Sam. Quick as lightning, Ned, who was across the other side of the room, went 'Woof! Woof!' The teacher swung his glance across to Ned.

'Woof! Woof!' went Sam.

'Woof! Woof! *Woof*!' went Ned.

Bedlam broke out as the whole school started barking. It was like being in the middle of a dog show. Mr Rambley turned and

ran to the bookcase behind the door, where he kept the cane. As he turned his back, Gertie lugged Sam out the back window with a cry of 'Get home, you old mongrel!'

Mickey Shearer called at home the next day in his T-model Ford. He told Dad he thought he would have a spell off the hard drink until his nerves settled.

'I had a very nasty experience yesterday afternoon, Will,' he said. 'I was coming home from town and halfway down Winstone Hill, that young Haystack girl ran straight out in front of me on her way home from school. I'll never know how I missed her. It must have given her a terrible fright, too, because she jumped clean over the barbed wire fence. The terrible part of it all was that as she cleared the fence, I could have sworn she had a long bushy tail.'

Who knows where it came from, but that great Aussie word for poultry, fowls, chickens etc is a beauty, isn't it? Chook! And chooks produce googs. Fair dinkum—it's more Australian than saying . . . 'Fair dinkum!'

Chook breeders are a unique species. Forget about all the bitching and backbiting that the yuppies go on with at a cat or dog show. Your average chook show, invariably held in a dark room below the showground pavilion of any country town, is as full of intrigue and in-fighting as any suburban ALP branch meeting. Oh what passions simmer beneath the brown acrylic cardigan of a chook fancier. Of course, there's more to chooks than questioning the marital status of the judges at your local chook show. It's died off a bit now, but there was a time, not all that long ago, when a penful of chooks was as much part of the family as a Burmese cat or a Rottweiler. Really rugged individuals branched out into exotica like turkeys, ducks, geese or pigeons. Protecting such important family members was a crusade as honourable as recapturing Jerusalem from Saladin's Saracen hordes—as Glenys Leckie of Ungarie, NSW well knows.

You Wouldn't Believe It

Times were tough back in the thirties. I was just 15 and I lived with my six brothers and sisters on a soldier settlement block which my Dad, a returned soldier from World War I, had drawn. Eight hundred acres (around 320 hectares) of virgin land, it was, with no house, no shed ... no nothing. It certainly wasn't conducive to living like a millionaire.

My brother Ken and I each slept in a hammock in a tree near the caravan where the rest of the family slept. It was all right in the summertime, if you could keep the mossies at bay, but, I tell you what, we grabbed all we could to keep warm in winter.

We spent long days helping Dad to clear the land so we could run more sheep and plough more country to grow enough wheat to make enough money to feed and clothe everyone. Our only means of transport was a horse and sulky. Otherwise, we went by foot. I often wondered whether I'd ever make enough money to have a car of my own. Surely there must be a way to make a few extra bob? Ken used to make his extra cash raising turkeys—rearing them until they were large enough to kill, pluck, clean and sell.

One day, Mum said I could set an old black chook that had gone clucky and keep whatever chickens hatched. What a lucky break! Mum had shown me how to set a clucky hen. You just made a nest in an old box or cut-down tin and put in a dozen hand-picked eggs. Just on dark, you went to the fowlyard, picked up the very docile clucky hen and placed her gently in the nest.

That evening, with all that done, I ran back to the house feeling great. I was already planning what I'd do with my 12 chickens when they were fully grown.

'Don't count your chickens before they hatch,' cautioned Dad, who never seemed to share in my excitement.

I went to bed feeling on top of the world. Before breakfast, I raced down to see if Sootie—the clucky hen—was still sitting on the eggs. There she was, just like a queen on her throne. I decided I'd mark off each day on the calendar so I'd be sure to be there when the chickens hatched. That first day was Saturday,

October 3. That meant the chickens should be due on Friday 23, just one day before my birthday.

Every day I went to check Sootie in the morning and late afternoon. She seemed just as excited as I was. Soon I could think of nothing else apart from 12 healthy chooks hatching out on Friday, October 23, by then only three days away.

As I raced down after a tiring day of helping Dad with some fencing, I saw Sootie in the yard rather than on her nest. She seemed pretty agitated. Something was wrong! Oh, no! There were no eggs in the nest—no chickens, no shells, no nothing! What had happened?

What was that rustling in the leaves?

It turned out to be the biggest goanna I'd ever seen. 'Mum! Dad! Help!'

I just knew that goanna had taken all my eggs. In my anger, I picked up a stone and threw it at the goanna. With what looked like a sly grin, he slowly but surely clawed his way up a nearby ironbark tree. What could I do? I would never have believed such a thing could happen to me. But then I had an idea.

I galloped back to the camp, told Mum the devastating news and outlined my plan to her. We often went rabbiting and Dad kept the .22 rifle outside, so I grabbed it, and a packet of bullets.

The goanna was still up the tree. 'Bang!' The big lizard flinched and then came slowly sliding down, clawing at the bark. With a thump, he landed on the ground, dead. Quickly, I pulled out my pocketknife and slashed open the skin of his belly. Was there still hope, or was I just being silly? I couldn't believe my eyes. There were one ... two ... three ... four ... 12 eggs. Two were cracked, but the others were still complete and all were warm.

I took my hat off, carefully placed each egg into it, carried them and placed them just as carefully back in the nest. I didn't have to catch Sootie. As soon as she saw the eggs back, she popped on top of them as if nothing had happened.

Three days later, 10 black, fluffy chickens were 'cheep! cheep! cheeping!' around their very proud mum.

That was the best birthday present I ever had.

Did that sound far-fetched? It's nothing compared with the chook yarn from Ellis Campbell of Dubbo NSW.

Fowl Elocution

I thought I might as well shut the pub and have an early night. My only customer was old Ern Harris, the dingo trapper, and he was broke. Right then he was slumped on a stool in the corner near the doorway, snoring loudly. His white-bearded chin sagged forward onto his chest. His battered old hat hung askew on his head, but his short black pipe still stayed firm in his mouth and his little fox terrier remained asleep on the sugarbag near his feet. The terrier snored, but not as loudly as Ern.

Nothing much happened in Razorback most of the time. When there was something going on, I sometimes kept the pub open all night, but when it was quiet, like it was this night, I'd take the chance to catch up on some sleep.

I heard a car pull up and five shearers on their way home after the cut out at Warragloaming Station came in. They seemed to have plenty of time and money and were in a frolicsome mood, so I forgot my plans for an early night.

After a while, old Ern opened his bleary eyes and grinned, showing the hideous yellow stumps that served as teeth. A look familiar to me crossed his face.

I don't quite know how, but the conversation got around to the merits of talking parrots, and each of the shearers had a yarn to tell about some eloquent bird or other. Ern eased himself off the stool and shuffled quietly across to the bar.

'Reminds me of a talkin' rooster I had one time,' he said. The five men turned to stare at him.

'Chooks can't talk,' one of them said flatly.

'Yeah. Well, maybe you're right at that,' Ern conceded. 'But this was no ordinary chook. He was so large that he could have had a dash of emu in him ... and talk about run!'

'That wouldn't help him much. Emus can't talk, either.'

I was just refilling the glasses and Ern stared hard at the man who was ordering. The shearer took the hint and nodded, so I poured a glass of port, old Ern's favourite beverage. He grasped the glass longingly and drank half the contents in one gulp.

'Come to think of it, he could fly pretty well, too, y'know,' he said reflectively. 'Maybe he had a cross of eaglehawk in him somewhere.'

'What the bloody hell would that have to do with him talking?' asked another shearer.

Ern thoughtfully puffed his short black pipe. 'Certainly was an unusual breed of fowl. I got them from a bloke who bred 'em specially for cock fighting. He sold them to me when the law got on his tail.'

'I think you've got a little mixed up, mate,' one of the visitors jeered. 'It's not cock fighting you're talkin' about—it's cock and bull yarntelling.'

They all laughed, except Ernie.

'They weren't a very domesticated type of fowl at all,' he said, rubbing his chin. 'Flew around like birds and lived in trees.'

'They might have lived in trees and flown to the moon, but I'm buggered if fowls can talk,' a dark man with a scar on his chin argued.

Ern shuffled slowly out through the parlour and made his way towards the men's toilet, down the backyard. The terrier rose to its feet, shook itself and trotted after him. The shearers looked after his retreating form with knowing looks and laughter. I smothered a smile as I turned and poured him a nip of rum. In all probability, the old trapper had deliberately given them this opportunity to talk about him behind his back. Ern returned in time to push his glass across for a refill when another member of the shearing party shouted.

'Oh, they couldn't all talk,' he renewed the conversation, 'only Charlie. He got caught in a rabbit trap when he was a chicken. He had his leg broke, so I had to take him into my hut and nurse him till it got right.'

The blond, curly-headed man struck a match and touched it to his cigarette. 'So that's when you taught him to talk?' he asked. 'Did you use a textbook or dictionary or something?'

A loud howl of laughter went up from all of them, but Ern ignored them.

'A man gets pretty lonely when he's camped hundreds of miles from nowhere with no one to talk to,' he said sadly. 'I found meself talkin' to the chicken and couldn't believe me ears one day, when he began to answer back.'

Ern wandered off again, taking his drink with him and talking to himself. Taking off his old felt hat, he ran a drop of water into it from a tap on the corner of the verandah. Then he set the hat on the ground and the little dog lapped noisily at the water. Ern leaned on the verandah rail and stuffed tobacco into his pipe with a teak-like black thumb. He stared into space, puffing away at the rank old pipe as if he'd forgotten the men inside.

He returned in time to pick up his fourth glass of port, again paid for by someone else. A tall, dark man with a mole on his temple took a threatening step towards the old dingo trapper. He appeared more intoxicated and belligerent than his companions.

'I still think it's all bull,' he persisted. 'This raving about a talking rooster.'

'Kept me from goin' mad,' continued Ern. 'Havin' someone to talk to.' The others arched their eyebrows, exchanged sly looks and tapped their foreheads.

'Missed him badly when he died,' Ern added sadly.

'What happened? Did he talk himself to death?' They all laughed boisterously.

Ernie's face was glowing and his eyes sparkling with the effects of the wine. He knew that one more of the shearing party would shout and then they'd expect him to dig into his own pocket and buy a round. He knew he must time his yarn to end during the consumption of the fifth glass of port and walk quietly out. He had a faraway look on his face as he said sombrely, 'Sure had a tragic ending, all right, old Charlie. I was camped out to buggery, trappin' dingoes, when I got word that the station owner was callin' in. Never had a bit of meat in the camp, so the only thing to do was kill a chook. Of course, I couldn't catch one and wring its neck or chop its head off, because they all ran so fast. The only thing to do was shoot one ... and that was no easy task, seeing they was so fast on the wing, too. Anyway, I loaded up my rifle and took aim at a flock flyin' swiftly overhead. One plummeted from the sky and I walked across to pick it up. It was poor old Charlie. There he lay with an accusin' eye, fading fast. With his last breath, he croaked, 'What the bloody hell are you doin', Ern? I never thought you'd shoot *me*.'

Chooks mightn't talk, of course, but cockies certainly do. Ask Io Dominick of Broadbeach Waters, Queensland.

A Cockie and Bull Story

My father-in-law, Jack, was born in Cobar, NSW around the 1840s. By the time I knew him, he was a man in his seventies. He'd lived in the bush all his life and told a wealth of stories. He always swore they were true.

When Jack was a young man, he and his brother used to visit a pub in the small central western New South Wales town of Nevertire. That pub was a rambling old timber building, the only hotel for many miles around. It was owned and run by George and his wife. She didn't work in the bar, but looked after the accommodation side of things.

George owned a pet sulphur-crested cockatoo, which was a great favourite with all the customers. At the end of the day, when the men would crowd in for their beer, Cocky would run up and down the bar, keeping George company.

The men would all want to be served at once, and as he was rushing up and down, George would repeat over and over again, 'One at a time, please boys, don't rush me.' Cocky used to copy him. The blokes loved to give Cocky a drink of their beer, too. The bird was a real attraction.

One day, there was a loud explosion in the pub—something to

do with the changing over of the beer barrels. Cocky got such a fright he took off and flew out the door. George wasn't unduly worried, as he felt sure the bird would soon return. But after 48 hours, when there was still no sign of him, the regulars started getting upset. They decided to band together into a search party. They went on horseback and on foot. Eventually, the loud baying of dogs could be heard, so they rushed towards the noise.

There was Cocky, backed up against a large gum tree by three dogs, screaming, 'One at a time, please boys, don't rush me!'

Finally, while we're discussing matters ornithological, here's what Peter Ryle of Manunda, Queensland has to offer.

Pigeon

There was this bloke and his wife in the old days who used to bag a few pigeons to supplement their meat supply. The pigeons would come in to drink at the waterholes before sundown. The idea was to sneak quietly through the low scrub and get in a few shots before the birds could figure out where the noise was coming from.

One particular day, old Tom and his missus were down on their hands and knees squirreling their way through the scratchies. Tom was leading the way with his trusty .22. Mum was bringing up the rear with a bag for the pigeons.

All of a sudden, she let out a hoarse whisper. 'Tom!'

Without looking around, Tom waved her to silence. He gave a loud 'shhhh!' and kept crawling. Soon afterwards, she was at it again. 'Tom!'

He kept going, giving her another wave and another shoosh to warn her to be silent. A couple of minutes later, and she gave another burst—louder this time. 'Tommy!'

He gave up and dropped back onto his haunches. He let her catch up.

'You'll frighten the bloody pigeons with all your racket. What the hell's the matter with you?'

She was just about out of breath, but she managed to gasp, 'We forgot the bullets.'

Tom looked at her for a minute, then shook his head. 'Yeah. But the bloody pigeons don't know that, do they?'

And so to cattle. In many philosophies and cultures, they're supposed to represent calm and serenity. However, in Aussie yarns, they tend to be associated more with mayhem and chaos. Perhaps it's something to do with the fact that we're in the southern hemisphere and the water goes down the toilet a different direction than it does above the equator.

Rodger Swan of Utungan, NSW swears this particular yarn is native to his district, but it's surprising how many other places also claim it as their own. Not that I'm casting aspersions on Rodger's veracity. Perhaps it's just a common occurrence and happens everywhere. Anyway, it is undoubtedly the definitive Australian cattle story.

Not Guilty

In cattle country, duffing or poddy dodging is a way of life. In our particular district, it's become an art form. It's no new experience to find a calf with your neighbour's brand sucking one of your cows.

Some years ago, a well-known exponent of the art was apprehended by the stock squad. They caught him red-handed, with the cattle in his possession. Charges were duly laid and the matter was set for hearing by the local court. As the community was small and close knit, the sheriff had considerable trouble empanelling jury members who were neither related to nor in some other way known to the defendant. Nevertheless, after much examination and rejection of prospective jurors, the matter finally came to trial.

After five days of evidence, the judge instructed the jury and invited them to retire to consider their verdict.

Within ten minutes, the jury returned and announced, 'Not guilty—but he has to give back the cattle.'

The judge showed admirable restraint and patiently explained that that sort of verdict wasn't acceptable under law. He directed the jury to retire and reconsider.

They returned within five minutes and announced their decision. 'Not guilty and he can keep the cattle.'

The relationship we humans have with cattle obviously goes back a long way. After all, those prehistoric cave paintings in France show plenty of long-horned beasties that these days you see only occasionally in the wilds of northern Tasmania. Our own house cow, Alice, although in her dotage, still provides plenty of inspiration, fun and manure. Pity about the milk! We've had her since she was about six weeks old, blinking prettily from the boot of a mate's car. Les Squires of Werris Creek, NSW is well aware of the near human qualities some cattle adopt.

The Pram

Back in the fifties, a family called the Browns arrived in Werris Creek. They'd once had their own farm and, having moved to town, missed a lot of things—particularly having a house cow. Although they lived on a small block of land in town, they eventually bought Daisy. She was mainly Jersey, a kind and friendly animal and a wonderful milker. Daisy was well accepted by all the neighbours. She was usually tethered along the street or in a vacant house block, acting as a lawnmower. Wherever she was, Daisy was milked on the spot.

I came into the story because my daughter Leslie was friendly with the Browns' daughter.

After 18 months of being regularly milked, Daisy was two or three months off calving again and due for a spell. Leslie asked, 'Dad, can Daisy spend a month or two with our cattle until she calves?'

I was glad to help out. The next day, Daisy was proudly led by halter through one end of the town, past the sportsground, over the railway line, across the street, alongside the silo, over the railway line, and back again, and onto the black soil plains of our place, Robynville.

The feed was good and Daisy enjoyed her holiday. She grew round and contented. One day, without any fuss, she produced a light brown baldy-faced calf. You could imagine the joy and excitement in the Brown household. Of course, Daisy was supposed to make the long trip back there with the calf, but I assured them they were right at our place for as long as necessary.

Imagine my surprise when, next day, while I was on the verandah having a quiet smoke, I saw a couple coming towards the house, pushing a big high-wheeled perambulator over all the bumps, holes and cracks in the track. Henry and Liddie Brown had come to collect Daisy. The pram was for the new calf. Now, Daisy was so quiet and at home with her owners, she submitted surprisingly well to seeing her calf dropped into the pram and lightly strapped in.

Off they went again, thank you very much, without even time for a cuppa. We watched them bumping their way with Mum, sturdy and wearing her apron, pushing the pram and Daisy, led by Henry, close behind. Periodically, they'd stop and let Daisy come right up to the pram, sniff her precious calf until she was quite satisfied, then continue on their way again. Occasionally, Dad would take turns in negotiating the cracks and potholes. It should have gone well. The pram stood up to it and Daisy and her calf were perfectly behaved. We only became aware of their problem when we decided to go for a walk and almost caught up with them.

It was a quiet Sunday afternoon and Werris Creek was playing football against their arch rivals. Unfortunately, we weren't doing too well. The Browns had hoped to be well clear of the football ground before the final whistle, but their timing couldn't have been worse. The local team was well and truly beaten. No one wanted to hang around after the match and chat about the result—it was too painful. So quite a crowd was coming out of the

ground—just in time to encounter Liddie, Henry, Daisy and the calf, still in the pram.

Suddenly confronted with adults, kids ... and prams of all kinds, Daisy panicked. Some of those prams were exactly like the one the Browns had. Where was her precious little bundle?

Breaking into a canter and snorting like mad, she began a tour of inspection of each and every pram and pusher. Imagine a toddler's reaction when Daisy's hot breath and wild eyes suddenly appeared from nowhere. On top of that, women screamed and men shouted and waved their arms. Even those who knew Daisy weren't much better. It was pandemonium. We were watching from the ridge at the railway line, too far away to be of any help.

No one was hurt and the crowd dispersed in record time. Soon there was only one pram left. Daisy, hot, puffing and concerned, poured her relief in large sniffs and dribbles all over the innocent cause of her maternal panic, the warm, brown, furry calf.

Luckily, there wasn't much further to go to the Browns' place ... and weren't they all glad to get back there again!

Yes indeed, as old Banjo Paterson so eloquently put it, 'The drover's life has pleasures that the townsfolk never know.' WJ Pike of Bunbury, WA has a swag of yarns about his stock-moving escapades half a century ago.

No Arrangements Made

During the 1939–45 war, my parents had a butchering business in the town of Collie, in the south-west of Western Australia. As a 16-year-old, it was part of my job to drive stock from the railway stock ramp, through town to our country abattoir, about four kilometres away. Usually, it involved moving about 12 cattle, maybe 200 sheep and about 40 pigs at any one time. My father always bought large beef cattle which weren't able to run very fast or far, particularly in hot weather. Collie *is* hot in summer, when temperatures average over 25°C and sometimes soar to over 38°C.

One hot day, I unloaded 12 large Hereford steers and proceeded to drive them to our slaughter yard. There was no one to help me but my very good horse and dog. Those particular cattle insisted on running, and we'd gone almost three kilometres due west on the main road before I was able to turn them north again ... in the direction I wanted them to go. I caught them at the picket fence around the local cemetery. Unfortunately, two of them went through the open gate. I ran one out, but the second was beyond turning. They get that way under stress.

In the cemetery, two fresh graves had just been dug, about 35 metres apart. One of them was ready for a funeral that very day—in about an hour's time, in fact. The other was about three-quarters dug—obviously for a funeral the next day.

The wayward beast suddenly tumbled into the 75 per cent completed grave, upside down with its feet protruding into the air. From the tank provided to water the flowers, I fetched a bucket of water and poured it on the animal's head. It promptly died.

I was faced with quite a situation, with that dead steer stuck upside down in a grave and a funeral due to take place only 35 metres away. Although my horse was considerably exhausted, I urged it to its limits and rode into town to arrange for the local carrier, with his truck and chain, to remove the dead beast.

As all three of us, the carrier, the Hereford and myself, departed the cemetery and headed across the road into the seclusion of the adjacent bush, the hearse and following vehicles came slowly into sight over a slight rise.

We'd made it by about 60 seconds.

Mrs J Carr of Malanda, north Queensland also had trouble with her family's cows—not to mention the pigs.

Without Missing a Trick

This happened on our old farm when I was about 10. In those days, we were shepherding our cows around the railway yards in search of grass. On this particular night we were running late and were still working after dark. After we'd milked, Mum asked me to help her feed the pigs. Our old sow also grazed out with the cows and had to be brought in for the night. Mum asked me to stay at our corner and block the sow if she came that way. She'd pour out some milk in the hope that it'd coax her over.

Mum came around the corner with a hurricane lantern in one hand and a tin of milk in the other. It was dark and Mum was wearing a new navy dress, which made her pretty hard to see. The old sow came running, went straight between Mum's legs and carried her off, riding back to front, all the way to the dam— still holding the hurricane lamp and the milk. I waited nearly half an hour for Mum to come back. When she did, she proudly showed us how she'd not spilled a drop of the milk.

This next yarn appeared in a completely different form in an earlier volume of this fine collection. Back then, it had nothing to do with cattle. Once again, the fact that the story comes in a different form from another source is pure coincidence; Neil Fisher of Port Macquarie couldn't possibly be stretching the truth, eh?

Scrub Cattle at Carrai

Ben and Bill Supple were brothers living on a cattle run, part of a squatting station on the Upper Macleay Valley. They were sons of early settlers who'd moved to the new river from the Port Macquarie settlement. They were noted horsemen, with great tracking ability, learned from the Wabbra-Cunderung-Dangee group of Aborigines from the Danggadi tribe. Squatters in the area often employed them to muster stray cattle that often spread far and wide on the unfenced runs.

On one occasion, they decided to track down a mob that was said to be at the top of Stockyard Creek, up on the Carrai Plateau. By early afternoon, they'd had some success and were moving a small mob along a cattle pad through the scrub. Suddenly, a wild bull charged Ben, causing him to spur his horse into the bush to dodge out of the way. He narrowly missed a stringy-bark tree, but a wait-a-while vine that was entwined around it caught his waist coat and ripped it, leaving a few scratches down his side.

Ben eventually caught up with Bill and, as the cattle were now moving quietly down the valley, suggested it was time to boil the billy. Ben looked for his fob watch to check the time and discovered, to his dismay, that it was lost, probably as a result of his encounter with the scrub bull and the lawyer vine. It was a valuable watch that his father had given him and had kept perfect time.

The next time Bill journeyed to Kempsey for essential supplies, he bought another watch from John Simpson, the storekeeper. It proved a good buy, as it too kept excellent time.

It was some five years before the brothers returned to the Carrai for another muster. This time, after following a well-marked cattle pad, Bill remarked that they were very near to the spot where Ben had had his encounter with the wild bull. Further into the scrub, Ben noticed a well-grown stringy-bark and rode towards it. He was joined by Bill. They spelled their horses under the tree. Suddenly, Ben heard a faint 'Tick! Tick! Tick!' up above them. He looked up and about 20 feet (a good 6 metres) above them was an object shining in the sunlight. Ben shinnied up the tree and found, to his surprise, that it was his lost watch, hanging from a wait-a-while that clung onto the trunk. He checked out the time with Bill and was further amazed to find that his watch had kept perfect time over the years—probably being wound as the breeze rubbed it against the stringy-bark.

Of course, to really capture people's attention, a true yarn spinner pulls all stops out and combines a couple of tried and true topics. In Andrea Stevenson's case, it's cattle *and* snakes ... a sure-fire winner.

Being Prepared

Now, here's a bit of advice which has helped me throughout my life and may do the same for you. *Never go anywhere without a soup spoon.* You just can't tell when it may come in handy.

A few years ago, I was driving up past Emerald and stopped to pick some mushrooms. Naturally, I locked my car. You always should. But try not to leave the keys inside. That's what I did.

I didn't realise what I'd done until I got back with the mushrooms. There were my keys safely inside, and I, outside. I went through all my pockets, but all I could find was a soup spoon. I've no idea why I'd put it there, but anyway ...

It turned out to be a lucky break, but at the time, all I could worry about was my keys. The obvious thing to do was find a bit of wire to pick the car lock. There was bound to be a fence somewhere around, so I went for a look.

Sure enough, I found one, made entirely of rusty old wire, except for one shiny new strand. Hanging off that newer line was exactly what I needed—a loose twist of wire. I grabbed it. Instantly, I found out it was electrified. By then, so was I.

I'd been quite gymnastic at school and it turned out I hadn't lost my touch. I jumped backwards off the fence ... but had the misfortune to land on a neatly coiled red-bellied black snake. The snake was quite astonished. So was I. The only thing I could think to do was leap forward again. I did the best sort of scissor jump you could imagine and found myself in the mud on the other side of the fence, some distance from the snake. He appeared as pleased about the arrangement as I was.

I decided to walk along the fence. At the very least I might find a wire of a lesser voltage than that first one. I might also find a more dignified way of getting back over.

I hadn't walked very far before I found out why the fence had been electrified. There was a jersey bull in the paddock. He came to investigate me at quite a considerable trot. Perhaps I should have repeated my scissor jump then and there, but this time the attack wasn't coming so much from below me as from straight ahead. So I ran straight the other way.

I well might have once been gymnastic, but after three kids and a hysterectomy, my staying power wasn't rated very high. I saw a low concrete wall up ahead. On the grounds that the concrete would handle the caress of the bull's horns a lot better than I would, I finally attempted that scissor jump again.

The concrete wall did indeed stop the bull. It should have, it was already stopping about three hundred gallons of water—and several kilos of green slime, as I discovered when I landed.

It got quite chilly sitting in the trough waiting for the bull to lose interest. Once he'd wandered off, I counted to fifty and emerged from my fortress. On checking to ascertain I was still in one piece, I rediscovered the soup spoon in my back pocket. But I still didn't recognise its worth. I just put it back and, my head full of thoughts of home, hot showers and hair that wasn't green, started towards the car. Back at the electric fence, I realised that being wet and rather stiff, the scissor jump wasn't likely to work a third time. I didn't even have the snake handy to give me inspiration. It was then that enlightenment, in the form of the mysterious soup spoon, overcame me. I'd use it to dig my way *under* the fence.

It took a little time and there *was* a tree root or two in the way but I eventually got quite a way underground. Suddenly, I heard the sound of a car pulling up. Help was at hand. Quite excited, I started digging faster. As I broke through the other side, I surprised two young hoons breaking into the car. They'd had the foresight to bring their own piece of wire.

In a moment, they had the door open. Wasting no time on social niceties, I leaped towards them, covered in mud, plastered with green slime and brandishing... my soup spoon. They took one look and fled.

The car was open, the keys were still in the ignition, so I drove home quite happily. The only consequence of my adventure was a rumour going around the hills of a giant wombat on the rampage.

But the lesson's clear. *Never go anywhere without a soup spoon.*

I know whenever city people visit our place, they comment not on the quiet, as you'd expect, but on how *noisy* the bush is. I suppose the soothing rumble of Sydney's Cahill Expressway pales to insignificance compared with the throaty roar of a night-calling willy wagtail or the hideous cackles of rabid chooks settling down for the night. No semi-trailer crashing through its gears can strike terror into a sleeper like the barking of a dog half a mile away.

Nina Henderson of Coolah, NSW, expressed it eloquently in the yarns she shared with us.

Noises in the Night

Night-time in the bush is usually extremely beautiful. Night noises can be calming and restful, tranquil and peaceful. But the bush can also distort noises. A browsing wombat can sound like a marauding elephant; a surfacing dugong, like a drowning man.

We were at Boggy Hole in the Finke River Gorge in Central Australia. The hole was serene in the early evening. As we approached, the sheer cliff wall towering over the water made it a natural amphitheatre. We set up camp on the sandy beach at the waterhole, arranging our sleeping gear near the fire.

Although Boggy Hole is in a national park, many feral horses came to drink and graze around the water that night. It was very beautiful, the stuff that geographic magazines thrive on. Our day had been long, hot and dry, with many hours of driving. We'd spent the hottest part of the day in the middle of the dry Palmer River, trying to unbog a city off-road driver. He'd been equipped with everything except common sense.

We'd just drifted off to sleep when the rumbling woke us both— a distant scrub bull! Sleeping under the stars with our kids is very romantic, but not when an angry bull's in the vicinity. He was getting closer and getting angrier. By the time he'd reached the far end of the lagoon, his rumblings were ending up with a bellow. It's not a pleasant sound at any time. In the crystal clear night air of Central Australia, it was quite unnerving. Our unease increased dramatically when an answering bellow sounded from the other end of the waterhole, perhaps two or three kilometres

away. It enraged the first bull even further. His next challenge was astounding–'Rumble! Rumble!', then a dozen or so 'Huffs!' and grumbles, followed by an enormous roar that even the most hardened football commentator would have been proud of. We waited in the silence and, sure enough, a distant bellow answered from down the lagoon.

The age-old male territorial battle began. Bellowing furiously, our old feral bull ponderously lumbered down the lagoon, while his adversary, sounding off right on cue, also approached. We were camped right between them, feeling extremely vulnerable. A sleeping bag isn't a lot of protection in a bullfight!

My husband stoked the fire to a blazing inferno. In its light we could see the bull plod past not ten metres away, rumbling ominously before stopping to bellow. He was a huge, horny Hereford, looking even more terrifying in the flickering light.

Just then, one of the kids sat up, muttered something about his father making a noise and went back to sleep. They slept all night, oblivious to the drama. We lay in wait for the encounter between the two old ferals, but as our bull moved further away, so did the answering challenge. By then, most of our fear had evaporated and we could afford to be analytical. The answering call was an exact replica of the challenge—every groan, huff, puff and rumble was the same. It had been an echo, carried down the cliff face with a four or five second gap.

Our poor old king never found his challenger . . . although he bellowed throughout the night. About five the next morning, we heard him scrunch past on the river gravel, still rumbling. Not far from our camp, he turned into the scrub and ambled off.

Darkness had made him a terrifying defender of his waterhole. Daylight transformed him into a shambling, cumbersome, wormy, senile old fool.

Our prolific yarn spinner Geoffrey Dean of Mt Stuart, Tasmania has had a story for every other occasion—so why not one about cattle?

Willum and the Tax Men

Rolly Hills dropped in to Nola Prate's farm one day about afternoon tea time and, over a cuppa, complained to her that he thought old Willum was going around the bend.

'I was up at his place, this mornin',' Rolly explained, 'An' you know what the silly old duffer's done this time? He's gone and shut his ten best heifers in his loadin' yard. When I asked if he was goin' to sell 'em, he told me he wasn't. Would you believe, he says the reason they was in the yard was because he's teachin' them a lesson?'

Nola Prate smiled a bit. 'So what, Rolly? That don't make him crazy.'

Rolly wasn't convinced. 'Don't it now? What if I told you they was there because they kept breakin' out of their paddock and, in old Willum's words, he'd given 'em a fair trial, found 'em guilty and sent 'em to gaol for a few days?'

Nola didn't seem impressed or surprised. Old Willum had been baling her hay for the past 20 years and she'd witnessed many such eccentricities. 'If old Willum's got his heifers shut up, you can be sure there's a good reason for it,' she said. 'Though, for most, the reason might be a little hard to fathom, that don't make him crazy. I reckon you just won't see it because you're still smartin' over the time he did you over.'

The incident Nola referred to was the time when Rolly had bought six Jersey heifers from old Willum that might or might not have been in calf. Rolly had cast a lightning quick eye over them. They were so huge gutted they literally waddled into the loading yard. It had been Rolly's estimation they were all very heavily in calf. Therefore, the price Willum was asking seemed very reasonable.

Unfortunately for Rolly, by the time he'd run them down to the coast, where he knew of a farmer willing to pay premium prices for pregnant heifers, their respective guts had subsided rather dramatically. It was a very forlorn bunch of bony hipped poddies that he'd unloaded into the farmer's yard—and a very dirty truck they'd left behind. Its floor and sides ran with the smelliest, runniest manure this side of the abattoir. The farmer had suggested there was enough to fertilise a four acre (that's more than 1½ hectares) spud paddock—if it hadn't of looked so bloody poisonous.

Naturally enough, Rolly wasn't very amused. He'd had to accept a price much lower than he'd expected. He worked out that what with the hire of the truck and the petrol, he didn't make a cracker out of the deal, and that was without honouring his promise to return the truck in the pristine condition he'd hired it.

To put it bluntly, Rolly had been pretty pissed off that day ... and even more so when he found out later that Willum had been running the heifers on strawberry clover all the week. They'd been in gas rather than in calf. The trip to the coast had simply shaken the gas out of them, one way or another. It was an incident a smart operator like Rolly didn't need to be reminded of.

But he still remained unconvinced about Willum's condition. 'I reckon the real reason those pods nearly blew up was more to do with stupidity than cunning,' he told Nola. 'I bet the old bastard di'n't even know what he was doin'. I reckon he was dead surprised I gave him his price without arguin'.'

Nola smiled. 'I reckon you're wrong, Rolly. He set you up. Who better to take down than a smart operator, like yourself, eh? If you want further proof, what about the time he done over them two city tax men?'

Rolly supped his tea a little resentfully. He hadn't dropped in just to hear how smart old Willum was when he knew damn well he was as crazy as a headless snake. But any info he could get on how to win out over the tax department could be valuable. 'OK. Prove me wrong.'

'Well,' said Nola. 'It was a couple of years back, when these two tax men turned up at his farm and wanted to see his books. You know old Willum's bartering system—he never buys or sells anything for money, certainly not by bank cheque, like that truckload of spuds he charged me for my three heifers ... and which later he swapped for Albie Jones's stump jump plough. And what about the time he swapped me one of his heifers for a litter of weaner pigs? Old Willum never does anythin' ordinary.' Nola filled Rolly's cup again and pushed the plate of scones closer. 'Anyway, by the time old Willum had dragged out six sugarbags of rough scribbled notes and receipts, dating back, I might add, to the horse and buggy era, them tax men must have known they was in for a long stay. When one of them suggested it was all a bit of a mess, Willum simply pleaded lack of schoolin'.

'According to Willum, the tax men had suggested that maybe he could get some help from an accountant, or someone he could trust who knew about figures.

'Old Willum scoffed at the suggestion. He couldn't afford an accountant an' there was no one in the district he *could* trust. He wasn't goin' to let some stranger poke into his business, either.

'It took them tax men three whole days to do a stocktake of old Willum's machinery. As you know, he's got stuff up there datin' back to the pioneers—an' he stows it in heaps. Them tax men must have thought they was on an archy-logical expedition. It took 'em nearly a full day just to find his potato plough. They was nearly frantic by the fourth day. It seemed like they was goin' to have to spend the rest of the year doin' old Willum over. Even he must have taken pity on them, because eventually, he arranged with Mrs Haas to get them a good hot meal that day.

'As you know, the Haases was never too particular. My info was that the meal consisted of a bowl of over-stewed turnips mixed with what looked like a heap of wholegrain barley an' a lump of greasy mutton. The meat was so full of maggots, it looked in danger of crawlin' off the table and right out the door. Willum reckons them tax men took one look at it and turned pea green. That's when they decided to do the rest of old Willum's tax back in the city.

'As they were leavin', I believe one of them suggested to him that they'd write when they finally got his bits and pieces sorted out. Old Willum told them that wouldn't do no good, because he couldn't read or write. The other geezer reckoned they could ring him. Old Willum told them his phone line was down and he couldn't afford the wire to fix it.'

Nola Prate smiled as she poured Rolly a third cup of tea. 'Of course, when them two tax men were gone, Willum took that hot meal out and dumped it back in the pig bin. That's where it had come from in the first place. No, Rolly, you can't kid me that old Willum's crazy.'

She stood up and offered a wan smile. 'Now, Rolly, seein' you're here an' so nicely warmed by my tea and scones, how'd you like to come out to the bull yard and offer a woman on her own a bit of advice on de-hornin' a bull?'

Apart from a starring role in jokes about New Zealand, sheep don't seem to have much of a sense of humour. But a few of them have turned up in yarns (no woolly pun intended). Doris Edmundsen of Port Macquarie, NSW came up with her version of the definitive sheep story.

Watch the Road

The sheep were enjoying a beautiful spring day, feeding on the lush green grass along the roadside. Along came a ram, making a nuisance of himself. He wouldn't leave the ewes in peace. 'I'll fix you,' thought one dear little ewe. And off she trotted into the middle of a nearby road, making sure the ram saw her. He took up the chase. The faster she ran, the faster he chased. Suddenly, the ewe ran out of sight. The ram was going so fast he didn't realise he was almost off the road and into a gully. Over he went, before he knew what was happening. 'Help!' he cried as he disappeared from sight. 'I didn't see that ewe turn.'

Of course, sheep mean shearers, and we've all enjoyed plenty of yarns about them and by them. Forget all those 'faster and better' yarns about shearing. Celia Sexton of Dangarsleigh, NSW is a shearer of a different ilk.

The Gun

I was sitting on the ground, my sun hat on and the radio playing away beside me. Before me was a rug and on the rug was a sheep, lying on its side with three of its legs tied together, immobilising it. Clipping away with hand shears, I had shorn almost that one whole side of the fleece and had peeled it back onto the rug, free from the grit and litter on the ground. It was nearly the time to roll the sheep over and start inching away with the clippers on the other side. However, a noise behind me made me turn down the radio and look around.

Now this was very rough country. 'Timbered granite' was how it had been described in the 'For Sale' ad I'd read a few months earlier. There was a thousand acres (which is a good 400 hectares) of it—huge trees and acres of rock. My three high school sons had fenced off a tiny corner and put up a round timbered yard for me against the boundary fence. We ran a handful of coloured sheep. Our round timber and bark cookhouse was close by with our two tents. At the front was an established grazing property, but down this side, the block next-door was as spectacularly wild and rough as ours and probably bigger, but no one lived there.

Down our boundary fence, though, came a man on a horse—stepping slowly, and both of them a mile high. He pulled the horse up, pushed his hat back a couple of inches and introduced himself as the owner of the block, looking for his wethers to bring them in for shearing.

We both stayed put—him in the saddle and me sitting on the ground with my shears in hand. We chatted across the fence about things like how dry it was. After a relaxed couple of minutes, he pushed his hat forward again, bid me good day and continued his amble down the boundary. I went back to snipping away at my patient sheep and turned Margaret Throsby back up again.

A while later, I was in town at the one and only pub. I went there for an occasional shower and perhaps a lemonade and a chat with a townsperson called Ned. Because I was the only newcomer in the district and had to be told things that everyone else knew, I'd been warned about what a wag Ned was and what a keen wit he had. On previous occasions, I'd listened with interest to the build-up to each of his yarns, complete with actions and gestures—and hadn't been able to work out what he was talking about at all. I'd come to regard him on pretty much the same plane as we lesser mortals. So there we were, engaged in the most ordinary of conversations, when Ned, without a change of pace or flicker of any sort, remarked, 'They tell me you hold the shearing record round here.'

Goats, on the other hand, are a laugh a minute. People don't give them the credit they deserve. You'd think that all goats did was eat garbage and smell. Even Peter Ryle, another of our stalwart yarn spinners, can't avoid their olfactory presence in his two goat yarns.

A Stinking Thing to Do

Back in the old days, before refrigerators and electricity and all that sort of stuff, most people in the bush kept a few goats to provide milk and meat. Of course, the majority of the goats were of the feral variety—a mixture of most breeds known to humanity. Right up in north Queensland, a bloke living in a small railway town called Mt Surprise decided to send for a well-bred Saanen billy to upgrade his herd. This bloke wasn't averse to putting on a bit of dog, and soon he was promising those friends he favoured a free service for their nannies by his new billy. By the same token, he lost no time telling the people who weren't in his affections that there'd be no such favour for them.

By the time his new goat was due to arrive, the town was evenly divided between the Haves and the Have Nots—or more appropriately, the Will Haves and Won't Haves. Everyone was at the railway station to witness the arrival of the famous goat. The train pulled up and the proud owner rushed to the dog box to claim his animal. He opened the door ... and out straggled the rankest feral billy anyone had ever seen. Obviously someone further down

the track had seen the noble goat and swapped it for their old one. No more was ever heard about improving the goat herd at Mt Surprise.

The Stinker's Revenge

We lived in a small country town when we were kids. When I say 'small', I mean it didn't even have water or electricity. That didn't stop my old man being progressive-minded. He was the first in town to install a septic toilet, back about 1946. The concrete tank had to be railed up from Cairns and installed entirely by hand. A whole gang of men used ropes to lower the heavy tank into the hole.

There were obstacles to overcome before the grand loo became a reality. Dad had sent for all the information and had a hard time convincing Mum that the effluent wouldn't come to the surface and make us all sick—or worse. He made a bold statement. 'By the time the water comes to the end of the trench, it's pure enough to drink.' Luckily, he didn't believe it enough to put it to the test. The thing I remember best about the whole episode is the reason we got a septic in the first place. Dad maintained it was for health reasons—but that was a blind.

Like most other families in the area, we had quite a few goats. They supplied fresh milk daily and an assured supply of fresh meat. Any goat kid unlucky enough to be born a male soon lost his family jewels. When those wethers were fat enough, they were killed and eaten. The goats had the run of the town by day and the whole backyard was fenced in for their night accommodation. Right in the middle of their yard was the dunny, with its pan toilet.

Dad never kept a billy for the herd. He'd borrow one from a friend when he needed the females serviced. He had the billy locked in the yard one Sunday, when I felt a great need to visit the loo. Halfway between the gate and the dunny, the billy saw me. I just beat him to the door.

My screams soon brought Dad out to see what was going on.

He picked up a piece of four b' two and tried to 'teach the bloody goat a lesson'. The timber broke over the goat's horns and the billy fairly revved it up Dad. Suddenly, there were two of us in the loo.

Of course, the billy was a bit upset and started to attack the building. I soon knew how Ned Kelly felt when all those bullets were hitting his armour—noisy inside ... with imminent death waiting outside.

I screamed my lungs out while Dad braced his feet against one wall and held the opposite one with his hands to stop the building toppling over. The old dunny wasn't exactly built to sustain that sort of punishment and soon it was showing distinct signs of instability. The billy rocked it on its stumps every time he butted the wall. In the end, having proved to his lady friends that he was indeed brave, the billy returned to his admiring harem. We sneaked out of the yard in great shame.

The billy disappeared soon afterwards—and so did the old loo. It was replaced by a new structure fixed firmly on its stumps. It was close to the house, for safety, and even boasted a real electric light (a torch bulb fixed to the ceiling, wired to two batteries on a shelf). It was a long sight better than sitting in the dark with the spectre of a horned devil waiting outside.

Chapter 6

STILL MORE BEASTS IN STILL MORE LAIRS

The old show business axiom of never working with children or animals certainly doesn't apply to yarn spinning—just as animal yarns don't just apply to the obvious ones, like dogs and horses. Pigs also feature strongly in the bush storytellers' repertoire. This next yarn from R Johnson of Bendemeer, NSW is, like some of the yarns on other subjects in other chapters, the well tried and tested yardstick for all pig stories.

The Three-legged Pig

There wasn't too much money around for the purchase of new farm machinery and the salesmen were doing it hard. One rep had been travelling and spruiking for months, trying to drum up business. One day, he arrived at one of the local places and was invited to have a cup of tea on the front verandah. While he and the owner were sitting discussing tractors and other things, the salesman noticed a big pig out in the front garden. What drew his attention the most was the fact that the pig had three wooden legs.

'Hey, what's with that pig out there? It looks as though it's got three wooden legs.'

'Nothin' to do with you' came the reply. After another couple of cuppas, curiosity still got the better of the salesman. 'Come on, why has your pig got three wooden legs?'

'Nothin' to do with you.'

And so it went on, until, in exasperation, the farmer spluttered, 'OK, I'll tell you ... and then you can bugger off. That pig is a wonder. About two years ago, the youngest kid wandered off down to the dam and fell in. He couldn't swim and would have drowned if that pig hadn't seen what was going on, raced down, jumped in, grabbed the kid by the scruff of the neck and dragged him out.'

Said the salesman, 'That sounds great, but what about the three wooden legs?'

'Hang on,' said the farmer. 'I haven't finished. Last year, we were all asleep in the old house, when a spark from the fire set light to a curtain. Being old, the place went up just like that! We probably would have burned to death or suffocated if that pig hadn't smelled the smoke, raced up to the house, smashed its way into the kitchen and woken us up in time.'

'Yes, but ... '

'Wait a minute. I still haven't finished. This winter just past, I was out riding the fences and the horse shied at something. It took me by surprise and threw me. My leg was broken in three places and I couldn't move. The horse shot through and I probably would have died before they found me, it was so cold. But the pig saw the horse come back to the sheds without me and realised something was wrong. It backtracked the horse and, when it found me, returned to the house and tugged at them until a couple of the men followed him and rescued me.'

'OK, OK! A great pig ... but why does the bloody animal have three wooden legs?'

'Well, if you had a pig as good as that one, would you want to eat him all at once?'

Just as goats are labelled as smelly and omnivorous, pigs have become stereotyped as gluttons hell-bent on avoiding the dinner table. Jim Brooks of Broken Hill, NSW has probably the most sensible advice of all to anyone contemplating going into the pork business.

Never give Christmas Dinner a Name

Amaroo Station is about 200 kilometres north-west of Julia Creek in central Queensland. Although not far in terms of mileage, it takes about five hours in a four-wheel drive to traverse the winding road over hot, arid plains, dry riverbeds that can flood without warning and rocky outcrops of ironstone that can tear a tyre and leave you stuck in 590° heat with no option but to change it as soon as possible.

It's an area with simple pleasures. People commonly drive for an hour or so to sit under a great ghost gum in a dry riverbed, enjoying the slight breeze, a cold beer or a cup of billy tea and watching the birds flit through the trees. There are finches, parrots (including millions of budgerigars) and the beautiful azure kingfisher. There are emus on the plains, big red kangaroos grazing next to them and beautiful pink dancing brolgas.

But there are also feral animals—dogs that can tear a sheep to pieces in no time at all, cats that devastate native birds and smaller mammals, and pigs that root and tear at the dry riverbanks to get to the roots of trees for their food. It's not uncommon for pigs to trap a person up a tree for hours, waiting to tear them limb from limb should they venture down. That's never much fun ... but it's where this yarn begins.

A few of the ringers at Amaroo Station decided to celebrate the success of the previous week's muster with a trip to a favourite waterhole for a swim and to enjoy a few XXXX beers—or yellow cans, as they're known locally. That Sunday, four of them left on the 70 kilometre drive, with their carton of yellow cans, a small rifle, some bully beef and a damper that Jenny, back at the homestead, had made for them. Once there, they stripped off (except for their hats) and went for a swim. No one noticed the pigs wandering up the riverbed, coming closer to their camp.

The men skylarked and enjoyed themselves, until one of them spotted the first of the pigs between them and their dilapidated old Toyota ute. That's where they'd left the rifle ... and the Esky of beer ... and the bag of food. The food was on top of the Esky, much to the pigs' delight. All the ringers could do was watch them enjoy the beef and damper. Then one pig accidentally knocked over the Esky. Ice and beer cans spilled onto the dusty ground. Another pig trod on a can and split the seam. The beer mixed with the dust. One very game pig sniffed and decided to lick the beer. It actually liked it—and the others soon joined in.

One by one, the pigs stomped on other cans to break their seals and drink the contents. A sow with a couple of piglets in tow joined the party. In fact, one piglet liked the taste of the beer so much, he got more than his fair share.

And the ringers? Well, they were still stuck in the water, unable to do anything but yell at the pigs. Of course, the pigs took no notice, but eventually they finished and ambled slowly away—all bar the piglet, small and possibly the runt of the litter, who seemed a little drunk, but still wanted more beer. The danger seemed to have passed, so the ringers elected to kill it for dinner the next day. They crept from the waterhole and surrounded the piglet, who was concentrating more on gaining entry to the remaining beer cans than what the ringers were up to.

But when someone jumped and grabbed the pig, it bit him on the leg, let out a screech and bolted. The chase continued fruitlessly until the pig blundered into the hessian bag they'd carried the damper and bully beef in and became trapped.

There those ringers were, in the middle of nowhere, standing around a wriggling, squealing hessian bag, wearing only their hats—but they could still raise a grin. It'd be a good night for pig on a spit.

Back at the homestead, Jenny refused to have anything to do with killing and dressing such a small pig—and none of the ringers could do it, either. It was decided to fatten it up and dress it for Christmas dinner. It'd be the best Christmas ever at Amaroo.

The Boss said the pig had to be kept in a proper pen, so the four ringers built a small sty . . . and, although it was a sow, gave the pig the name Bartholomew. They had yet to learn the unwritten rule—never give Christmas dinner a name.

Three months later, it was time to start thinking about dressing Bartholomew for Christmas. During the fattening up period, they'd taught her a few tricks. She could bow on her front legs and, if taken out of the pen, would follow them around like a dog. However, she still had that one vice. She loved beer and the ringers would gladly share some of theirs with her on a Sunday. On more than one occasion, after a night on the turps, she'd ransack Jenny's kitchen. One time, Bartholomew even smashed her way into the coolroom, trying to get at the beer and chips. Of course, the ringers had to clean up the mess. It was after just such an episode that the Boss and Jenny renewed the death sentence on Bartholomew. With tears in their eyes, the ringers drew straws and one was selected to 'do the deed'.

Bartholomew was taken to the knocking pen, where all the cattle were killed and dressed. The ringer put the rifle to her head and closed his eyes. Bartholomew had grown to trust those blokes and didn't realise what was up. The ringer's finger slowly squeezed the trigger. 'Click!' The rifle didn't fire. The bullet was a dud.

That was enough for the ringer. With tears still welling, he had to tell his mates and the Boss that he couldn't go through with it. They didn't laugh. The station owner even agreed they could keep the pig, as long as it didn't escape again and ransack the kitchen.

After another year, Bartholomew grew into a very friendly pig indeed. But one balmy November Sunday, she blotted her copybook again. By then, Bartholomew was so big she didn't miss knocking a single thing over. Cooking oil was mixed with other foodstuff on the floor. The harder the pig tried to get out, the more she slipped and the more mess she made.

Drawn by the din, Jenny was aghast at what she found when she turned on the light. Somehow, she was unable to see the humour in a pig covered in flour, oil, butter, salt and hundreds and thousands.

Bartholomew had to go. Because no one at Amaroo had the heart to kill her, she was put in a crate and sent by ute to the butcher in Julia Creek. Sure they were seeing her for the last time, everyone came out to pay their last respects as the ute bounced off down the dry dusty road.

Every week, the Boss would ring to see if Christmas dinner had been prepared. The butcher always replied, 'I'm too busy with my other work. I'll do it next week.'

Christmas came and went, and to everyone's secret relief, they didn't have pork for lunch. Then, in early February, the station coolroom broke down and a refrigeration mechanic had to be called in from Mt Isa to fix it.

That's how I came into the story. I was working with the refrigeration mechanic. As is normal practice, before the long drive, I picked up some fresh bread, the last week's papers and some meat. Some station people like to eat someone else's meat occasionally. When I called at the butcher, and mentioned I was going to Amaroo, he said he'd had to dress a pig for the station and could I take it? Naturally, I could.

Five bumpy, dusty, tedious, dry, hot hours later, I arrived. It must still have been 40°C at nine o'clock at night. I parked in the shed and, amidst the barking of blue cattle dogs, walked to the homestead. I handed over the papers and other stuff and added a note which the butcher had given me. The Boss called up Jenny and the ringers to help unload the ute. When we walked into the shed, everyone laughed and cheered. Bartholomew was home. She stood there in the back of my ute, inside the very same crate she'd gone to town in.

The note from the butcher explained. 'Every week, for months,

I tried to kill this bloody pig, and every time, it bowed on its front knees in prayer. Kill your own bloody pets and don't let someone else do your dirty work.'

Bartholomew was built a sturdy new sty. From then on, she was always given plenty of fresh water and good food—but never any beer. Three months after returning from the butcher, she gave birth to 16 piglets. She must have had an extra good time in Julia Creek.

From then on, there was always pork at Amaroo at Christmas—but none of those piglets ever had a name.

It's funny that, Amaroo Station aside, people normally associate pork as a meal with luxury and wealth. But you don't see many pork producers driving around in Rolls Royces, eh? Nevertheless, quite a few punters elect to give the pigs a go as a way of making a fast buck. Our WA yarn spinner, WL Pike, knew just such a bloke.

Money in Pork

Tommy Dillon lived in a coal mining town in the south-west of Western Australia. He was a small man, a coal miner, and an expert horseman and bushman, with a wonderful and well-earned reputation for his veterinary knowledge and expertise—despite not being able to read or write. He also loved a drink and a bet on the horses. His favourite hobby was catching bush brumbies, breaking them in and selling them. Anyone who knew him always associated him with livestock.

Late in his working life, he approached the local mine manager and stated his intention of leaving the industry. He was giving his compulsory notice and intended going to Queensland. The manager, appreciating Tommy's limitations, suggested that he had only a short time to go with the mine and he'd be able to retire on a good pension.

However, Tommy was quite adamant. The manager asked if he was going to work on a cattle station, or something like that.

'No,' Tommy replied. 'I'm going to go in for pigs.'

The manager had a slight knowledge of the pig industry and explained to Tommy the pitfalls, particularly that there wasn't really a lot of money to be made, considering the price fluctuations.

'I'm sorry,' Tommy said, 'but there *is* lots of money in the pig industry. Why, one of the men read out of the paper during the crib break where a person in Queensland had paid $250 000 for an artesian bore. There *must* be money in pigs, and I'm off up there to get some of it.'

In all our years of funny farming, we've never actually been tempted to go in for pigs on the Prickle Farm. We've tried just about everything else. It's not as though people haven't tried to rope us in. Now we're living on the Upper Macleay in New South Wales, we're in *real* pig territory, but we're still not tempted. Fred Chapman of nearby West Kempsey can give as good a reason as any for our reluctance to diversify into pigs.

Lantana Pork

Back in the 1920s, dairy farming was the popular occupation on the Upper Macleay. The Toorooka butter and bacon factories were operating, so pig raising also occurred on a large scale. It meant that farmers needed improved pastures to boost the cream production from their dairy herds and corn crops to feed their pigs.

Green Point used to be a dairy farm miles up the other side of the river from the Toorooka factory. It had been established by Arthur Harrigan, who, on one particular year, put in a large acreage of corn. When it was ripe enough, he turned his pigs into it to graze. Lantana bush was already a pest and quite out of control on Green Point. On the headlands of the cultivated areas, many large clumps of lantana had also become mixed in with the corn crop.

A pig buyer called Frank Turner was travelling the Upper Macleay buying pigs direct from the farms. Word reached him on the grapevine that Arthur's pigs, grazing on the corn, were particularly good, so Frank became very interested. You couldn't drive to Green Point, so Frank made the trip across the river from Toorooka on horseback.

Arthur had a large assortment of dogs on his place, from greyhounds to cattle dogs. When Frank arrived, he was told they'd go down into the corn and use the dogs to round up the pigs. According to Frank, Arthur would send the dogs into the corn ... and the pigs would duck straight into the lantana. 'Did you see that lot, Frank?' Arthur would ask. They'd move on and the next mob would see them and dart into the lantana. 'Did you see that lot, Frank?'

The routine was repeated many times without any sale being made. When poor old Frank called in at the Willawarrin hotel on his way back to Kempsey, someone asked him, 'Did you buy Arthur's pigs?'

Frank replied, 'You might as well try to buy bloody lightning.'

Although we've established that the pig market's never been the most reliable way of making a few bob, not everyone in the game misses out. Dang Donaldson of Finley, NSW remembers a local pig farmer from the fifties who managed to manipulate the market very nicely, thank you!

Selling the Boars

Joe was a second generation Italian living with his parents and younger brother on a mixed farm in the south-west Riverina. It was traditional for the Italian farmers to raise pigs for their own salami, bacon and ham. In his early days, Joe had been involved in a Junior Farmer pig-raising project and, as time went by, came to be considered locally as an expert on pigs. Many farmers around here raised them as a sideline and as production increased, market prices dropped. In that slump, Joe hung on to his pigs until the farm was over-run with them. There were fatteners in the sties, the old stables, the hayshed and the sheep yards, and breeding sows and boars free ranging in the paddocks. Joe's parents and brothers became angry and declared that either Joe or a large number of pigs would have to go.

Joe organised a carrier to come out and, with relatives and neighbours mustering, first loaded up his boars, then the backward sows and choppers, with fat pigs and slips finally filling the double-decker transport to capacity. Early next morning, the pigs were driven to a large provincial market. Joe supervised the unloading and drafting of the pigs at the saleyards. There were 15 boars and he allocated each of the six operating agents a share of pen lots. The first four agents, in order of draw, were given two boars each to sell; the fifth was given three medium-sized boars and the last one, the four youngest hogs. Before the auction, Joe learned the average price of boars at the previous market had been down to about four pounds ten each. He remarked at the time that he might end up having a couple of boars knocked down to himself, in which case the driver could jump them off a couple of miles from home. When the pigs found their way back there, the old people might believe they'd missed the muster.

The auction started. There were seven regular buyers present, who moved along elbow to elbow with the auctioneer and staff on a catwalk above the pens. Joe, dressed in his farm clothes, complete with gumboots and old felt hat, kept to the back, behind the buyers, other sellers and spectators.

When it came to the auction of the boars, the first buyer started with a bid of two pounds. As was the custom, the other buyers, in turn, raised the bidding 10 shillings a time. Again, as was usual, the final bid would come from whoever had started. However, part of the way through the bidding, Joe, up the back, put in a 'Yeah!' in a high-pitched voice. The bidding continued, with the starter being declared the buyer and allowed the customary discount for the last bid. Each of the seven buyers took turns in offering the starting bid ... and being successful on the fall of the hammer. And, each time, Joe put in his additional 'Yeah!', which bumped up the price an extra 10 bob.

After a while, the buyers decided to have a little joke among themselves and started increasing their opening bids. Joe was undaunted. On the last open, he even managed two extra 'Yeahs!'

As a result, that last boar was knocked down for fifteen pounds. The successful buyer closed his book and turned to Joe. 'You can have him. You've been trying all day. You book him up.'

'But I don't want him,' responded Joe.

'Come on,' said the buyer, used to Italian farmers seeking boars to make their salami, 'You've been after one of these boars for the entire sale. You take him. I've had a good day.'

'Look,' Joe replied. 'Keep him. I've had a good day, too. I've been selling those boars.'

———◆———

In my previous yarns masterpiece, *Tell Us Anotheree*. I related some of the snake tales people seem to love so much. There's probably some deep, dark, disturbing reason Australians seem so fascinated with snakes. Second place in the list of oddball animals we love to yarn about must go to rodents, mainly mice and rats. I guess anyone who's experienced an inland mouse plague will probably understand that those long-tailed little whiskery devils, by sheer weight of numbers, can indeed capture one's attention. Liz Hall of Mintaro, SA knows exactly what I mean.

A Tiger in Your Tank

It was an ideal spraying day: bright, crisp and clear, with hardly a breath of wind to cause any drift. A perfect day—the first for the week—with the crops at just the right stage. But with the forecast promising more rain and accompanying gale-force winds, Greg was itching to get out and spray. As with all farmers, the sense of urgency was strong. When conditions are right, they just have to go, go, go!

The spray unit on the back of the old ute was in perfect working order. It had just been returned after a stint down at Blyth, at my brother's farm, and everything had been checked out. They'd even filled the ute with petrol so Greg could get spraying straight away. It was all systems go!

Now, we knew about the mouse plague. Out on the plains in the warmer areas of the state, the stories of mouse plagues weren't considered funny any more. Every farmer had a litany of woes: shrinking haystacks; mice dripping from trees, so deep you needed a four-wheel drive to get across the yard; chooks and piglets eaten alive; thousands of acres to re-sow; hundreds of bags of feed lost; wiring in vehicles, farm machinery and household appliances eaten through; curtains ruined—the cost was incredible.

Here in Mintaro, where it was cooler and wetter, we'd been lucky up until then. Our fox terrier had kept the mice away from the backdoor and the old-fashioned trap—a bottle and stocking hanging over a bucket of water—caught only one or two a night.

But the gloom mongers assured us the mice were there—they'd just gone underground, built S-bends in their nests to keep the water out and stored away enough food to last until spring. Then they'd be ready to climb the stalks of the crops and break off the heads. The only hope, I was told, was that their first onslaught might thin the crops out enough so the mice wouldn't be able to climb up to the heads. Apparently, they climbed by straddling *two* stalks . . .

Anyhow, back to Greg and the spraying . . . You remember that fuel company slogan, telling us we needed a tiger in our tank? Well, if they'd realised the problems one mouse was about to cause, they'd have got a new advertising agency.

Greg hadn't even completed his first lap around the paddock when the ageing ute chugged and lurched to a half-hearted stop—and just wouldn't start again. The UHF radio was working, but I was picking up the children from school and out of range. Greg's only course was to walk home. Of course, that particular paddock was at the extreme end of the farm.

He eventually had the spray unit going again. The problem had obviously been a fuel blockage, so it had been easy enough to replace the filter with a spare. But what was that furry stuff coating the pores of the old filter? With the problem solved, why worry? There was still enough light left to finish the paddock—if he were quick—and, anyway, wasn't spray supposed to work better after dark?

By teatime, the steam was fairly rising from his head. The same thing had happened. A second spare filter was found—and so was some more of that felty stuff in the one it was replacing. What on earth could it be? Perhaps the fuel cap had been misplaced one time and a bit of cloth someone may have stuffed in the hole had fallen in. We hadn't discounted the possibility of it being a mouse—but there just didn't seem to be any way one could have got in.

We looked forward to the next day, which, according to the weatherman, would be even better for spraying, because the predicted change looked like slipping away to the south.

But the next morning did *not* start well. First, the sheep were in the crop for the fourth day in a row and had to be returned to their paddock before breakfast. A morning frost had frozen the LPG in the car, so the children had to be taken to school in our other little ute. By the time I'd returned home, Greg was back too—and not very happy. The spray unit had stopped again, and we were flat out of spare filters. It was time we called a mechanic to try for a more permanent solution.

After some more fuel filters and a bit of creative mechanical work, all systems seemed go again by lunchtime. It hadn't helped that the shape of that particular fuel tank made it almost impossible to get at. The best solution had been to bypass the problem with a length of tubing. Hopefully it'd last until the spraying was completed. After that, the ute could be taken to the garage and fixed properly. By then it was also clear from the assorted bits recovered from the filters that a mouse was indeed the problem.

It turned out that when the ute had been filled with petrol prior to its return from Blyth, a new hose had been fitted to my brother's overhead fuel tank. Although, as a precaution, it had been blown out, the offending mouse must have held on tightly, or perhaps it was already dead and stuck to the side of the pipe.

Whatever, there wasn't much doubt that that was how it had come to be in the tank.

Thankfully, the spraying of that paddock was completed before the weather changed and the ute was delivered to be completely cleaned out. When it was returned a week later, the mechanic was confident the problem had been solved.

How wrong could you be? As soon as Greg started spraying again, mouse fur was again sucked into the engine and he had to limp to a friend's place to send out a distress call. It was patched up again, the spraying completed and the ute returned to the mechanic.

For two days, the lumps of mouse fur and entrails were syphoned, scraped, sucked and blown from places they had no right to be. The carburettor and fuel pump were inspected and cleaned. More fuel filters had be ordered when the garage's supply ran out. Eventually, it was time for the test drive. It never even made it back to the workshop. Finally, the whole fuel tank was removed, flushed and replaced. With fading confidence, and rising anger, the mechanic tried another test run. This time the lines remained clear.

The gruesome piles of mouse remains established the body count at 10: two adult mice and eight babies. The labour charge was for sixteen hours! The parts required included *ten* fuel filters— that's without taking into consideration down time and general frustration. If only 10 mice could cause that much damage, the tally statewide from a mouse plague must be phenomenal. And what would a tiger in the tank have cost?

———

Who was it who said, 'Build a better mousetrap and the world will beat a path to your door'? Whoever it was, his theory mustn't have ever been properly tested, because I don't know that anyone has been able to build a better mousetrap than the old rectangle of softwood and wire contraptions we've always seemed to use. My own brother insists that the best way to do mice in is to offer them a bowl of flour mixed with cement and another one of water. 'Once they drink, that really binds them up,' he assures me. But his joint is still over-run with rodents. There've been attempts to flog electronic devices allegedly sounding a note too high for the human ear to discern—but they don't work either. It's the old 'Nibble, Nibble, Zap!' models that seem to get the result every time. Yet I've seen recently that the Aussie makers of those most successful mousetraps are having to go out of business, too. Apparently, even in their allegedly lucrative business, the world eventually beats a path away from the old door. But, whether it's better mousetraps, other devices or poison baits, as CM Barker of Cairns, Queensland assures us, not all people have given up.

Marinated Mouse

Cyril walked into the bar and climbed onto a stool. Ralph, the publican, had been restacking glasses in the fridge.

'The usual, Cyril?'

'Yeah, mate. Not too much lemonade, though. You've been a bit heavy-handed with the dash lately.'

'Well, try yer thirst on this one.' Cyril picked up the beer and poured it down his long throat. He licked his lips.

'That's better, Ralph.'

A loud snap sounded.

'Struth! What's that?' asked a surprised Cyril.

'Just me mousetrap going off. Wonder if I've caught anything this time.' Ralph looked behind the fridge. 'Bloody mice! They're getting that cunning. They take the pumpkin seeds outa the trap now without getting caught. I'll have to glue the bait on next.'

'Thought yer had a cat,' stated Cyril.

'Yeah, we did, but I think Fang's on holidays.'

'Gone to Surfer's, has he?'

'No, he's just lost interest in catching bloody mice.'

'Only one thing for it mate,' declared Cyril. 'You'll have to try me secret bait.'

'What've I go to do?'

'Just give us another beer, a piece of paper and a pen,' Cyril ordered. The publican put another beer on the bar and rummaged around, before producing a piece of dirty paper and a pen that had seen better days.

'Where did yer get the bait idea from?' he asked as Cyril started to write.

'The missus come up with it, when she was cooking this stir fry chicken one night. She cooks beaut Chinese, the missus does.' Cyril scratched away on the piece of paper as Ralph watched. Fang mooched in and jumped on a stool next to Cyril as he finished. 'There, that's it. They'll love it.'

Ralph read the list aloud. 'Half a cup of soy sauce ... wine ... a teaspoon of sugar ... but this won't kill those mice,' he complained.

'Not meant to,' answered Cyril. But it worked on our Fluff, good as gold.'

'But she's a cat. Just a minute ... this isn't going to hurt old Fang, is it? I've grown quite attached to the old bastard, even if he can't catch mice no more.'

'No worries. He'll think it's the greatest thing since sliced mice. In fact, if you use this bait, you'll end up with a better cat than ever.'

'Better cat? But what bloody good is it if it don't kill mice?'

'Look, yer put the soy sauce in a shallow tray, mix in the rest of the stuff, make sure the sugar's dissolved and grate the ginger on top. If you haven't got ginger, garlic seems to work just as good. And that's it. You just put it down outside the miceholes.'

'Oh, I get it,' nodded Ralph. 'The mice drown in the stuff.'

'No, mate you don't get it at all,' Cyril said, exasperated. 'It's for Fang's benefit.'

'Well, Fang's not likely to drown in *that*. Even if he did, I'd still have mice.'

'Look, mate, it's like this ... when my missus made up that chicken stir fry I was telling you about, there was some sauce and chicken left over, so she put it in a saucer for Fluff. Are you with me so far?'

'Yeah,' said Ralph doubtfully.

'Well, Fluff only ate the chicken that had sauce on it, right?

She didn't go much on the onion and broccoli. And she left the chicken that didn't have sauce on it.'

'And ... ?'

'Geezus, mate! You put the bait outside the mousehole. The mice come out to see what's for tea and walk through the marinade. Fang here won't be able to resist them, will you, mate?' Cyril scratched the cat under the chin.

'I don't believe it,' declared Ralph.

'Look, mate, did the camembert cheese trick work with the cockroaches?'

'Yes, but ... '

'Well, trust me. This argument's giving me a thirst. How about another beer with a *small* dash?'

The woes of AB Longland of Redlynch, Queensland were not confined to mice as such, but the other creepy crawlies their shared environment fostered.

Sleep Strategies

We live where the cane paddock comes up to the scrub. It only takes 15 minutes to walk to the pub and the shop. The road's good, so we usually go barefoot when we go shopping. If the creek comes up in the Wet, we get cut off for a few days. No one's game to swim it, because if the crocs don't get you, the current will wash you away.

The reason for writing is, we've had some noises in the night that disturbed our sleep. It's important you know the solutions to those problems—in case you're similarly afflicted.

The first noise was caused by an accountant—and the cold winter nights, when the temperature plummets to 15°C. The accountant told us a man in the government wanted us to keep all our dockets and things if we bought or sold anything. My wife kept one of the big cardboard boxes that the supplies came in and put it in the corner of the bedroom. Quite soon it was half full of papers. The system worked well. Then, for some nights, we heard scratching and paper shuffling noises coming from the box. I told my wife to stop fussing with the papers and stay in bed. She said she'd never been up in the night.

Next morning, I told Peter, who lives down the hill, what had happened. He said mice had come in from the cold and were breeding in the papers we'd put aside for the government man. The only way around the problem was to throw them away and pay cash for everything. So we carried the box out onto the verandah. As we did, the bottom fell out—with all the papers and the mice. There were so many mice that Ben, the cattle dog, walked off and didn't come back until dark. My wife screamed so loudly that Pete from down the hill even came up to see if we were having another fight. Things settled down afterwards. We haven't had mice again and we just pay cash all the time.

The next trouble was the white-tailed rats who came and did the same thing as the mice, only in our roof. The cane was being burned. Those things had to find a new home, so they just moved into our place. They were as big as Peter from down the hill— well, as big as his feet, anyway. And that's *big*. They'd run around the ceiling all night and keep us awake. When we told Pete, he reckoned we should put some OP rum in the sarsaparilla we always took at bedtime to keep us regular. It turned out to be a very successful double blessing.

Then, as often happens, the fire got away from the cane paddock and burned the scrub as well. The rats had to find new tucker, so they came and ate the coconuts outside our bedroom window. They had good teeth, but it took all night to gnaw through the husk and hard shell of each coconut. The noise was like a grinder going non-stop. We tried shooting and trapping them, but they soon got wise to all that. Now we just stick to the sarsaparilla and OP rum.

All seemed to be going fine. Then we nearly reached the last straw. A new noise started in the roof. It had three parts to it. One sounded like dropping a half full sugar bag on the floor. The next was like dragging a thick, hairy rope through a hole at different speeds. The last noise was a frightened screech. That

was the worst one. It could come at any time and got right up my wife's nose.

Pete from down the hill had absolutely no doubt we had an enormous scrub python chasing the white-tailed rats. He reckoned our sarsaparilla and OP rum had Buckley's. The python had to be twice the size of the dozey old carpet snakes in the roof outside the dunny. In fact, it might have been the one that took three chooks in one sitting. He also warned it could be as big as the one he'd seen eating 13 flying foxes at one time. It appeared the only thing Pete didn't know was how to get rid of the bloody thing.

We began to get black rings under our eyes. My wife found she even had to yawn while she talked—which was highly unusual. The lack of sleep was taking a heavy toll. After a particularly bad night, just on daybreak, my wife leaped out of bed, grabbed the radio and ran into the bathroom. She put the radio on the top of the cupboard, right up against the ceiling, going full bore, and turned to the early morning ABC program. The usual old scratchy records were playing, with Judith Langridge and David Howard jawing away, to each other. From, that day hence, we've never had any more white-tailed rats or scrub python noises. But we still put some OP rum in our sarsaparilla—just to be on the safe side.

What an opportunity for ABC marketing! You know what we said earlier about a better mousetrap ...

Of course, our fear of joe blakes is a self-generating thing. In reality, they're nowhere near as dangerous as folklore and yarns would have us believe. Stephen Lanskey of Edmonton, SA knows about a far nastier customer altogether.

The Leaking Radiator

One Sunday, we were going on a picnic and had decided to visit a couple of places about one and a half hours' drive from home. Not many people went there. We left earlier in our old car. My sister, her husband and their kids followed later, with Mum. The arrangements were for us to go first to Bruce Weir. If they didn't catch up with us there, we'd meet up at Leadingham Creek, a few miles further on.

Sis's husband, Harry, lived in Canberra and worked to the beat of the government stroke, so when he came to us on holidays, he loved to go barefoot. When they finally got to Bruce Weir, we'd moved on. It was a pretty bare place, with a lot of long, dead grass about.

While Sis and Harry organised getting the kids out of the car, Mum took the opportunity to jump out and dash behind it for a quick wee. She was up and back by the time the others got themselves organised. Harry alighted, stretched out and walked around to the back of the vehicle himself.

'They've been here before us,' he announced, referring to us.

Mum was quite astonished at Harry's perception. 'How d'you know?'

'Because their radiator's leaked where they must have pulled up.'

Mum was about to let on to Harry what the 'leak' was when he put his bare foot back into the wet patch and noted with the expertise of the true bush tracker, 'And it wasn't long ago, either. It's still warm.'

Harry took some convincing that behind the car had been a lot safer than in the long grass with the snakes.

The animals which have loomed largest in my own life—and therefore my writing—have been possums. We've had them slide down chimneys and take up residence in our slow combustion heaters. We've had them die in the ceiling and we've been piddled on from a great height while we slept. One possum was even instrumental in causing so much damage to part of our house that we were forced to demolish it and start an expensive rebuilding and restoration program (which we never quite finished).

Once, when I was a crime reporter in Melbourne, I heard a call come over the police radio saying D24 had received a call from a man in Moonee Ponds complaining that a koala had climbed into his baby's bed. It sounded a great story. We jumped in the office car and headed out to the address, just minutes behind the police car sent to investigate.

Outside a two storey Victorian house, still largely in darkness, we waited while the wallopers went up to investigate. A couple of minutes later a young copper beckoned to us to follow him. Up we went and there, fast asleep in a cot, snuggled right up against a sleeping baby aged about nine months, was an old man possum. We wanted to take pictures, but the mother of the house was frightened we'd wake the baby. In those days, reporters were highly ethical (when sober) and, rather than disturb family peace, we retired. We were sitting in the car radioing details of the story to our late-night copytaker, when the same young copper rapped on the passenger-side front window. I wound down the window and he shouted, 'Here, grab this!' and threw the possum into the car.

Crikey! he cut up rough.

After what seemed like hours of mayhem, my photographer managed to throw a coat over the crazed phalanger and we subdued him and released him in a big gum tree outside the Moonee Ponds courthouse.

Yes, I *love* possums. But not quite in the same way as Joyce Shiner, of Albany, WA.

Great and Small

Some years ago the family got involved in the development of a virgin block in the south-eastern wheatbelt of Western Australia. We were camped in a lean-to humpy attached to the rear of a superphosphate shed in a patch of mallee and gimlet. We knew nothing about pygmy possums until one sunny morning at seeding time, when I was going about the business that usually seems to become the lot of the new land-farmer's wife—tidying the yard after the men. There'd been a shower overnight and I was busy picking up and hanging bags on the fence to dry. A small heap of damp bags on the loading ramp were left until last.

As I bent down to pick up the very last one, there on the bare jarrah sleepers were what appeared to be a couple of sleeping mice. I raised a foot to crush them, but stopped when I noticed their very long tails were curled at the end. These were no ordinary mice. I picked one up. Its crumpled appearance made it look for all the world like something newborn. It felt very cold, but the incredible softness and density of the fur, the rounded ears, four little hands and a little black face set me wondering.

We were in the middle of a mouse plague. Baits were laid everywhere. Thinking they'd died from eating a bait, I dropped them both into the large pocket of my sugarbag apron and went on working. The men had taken lunch out with them, so it was nearly sundown when they came in.

I lost no time showing my find. I had hung the apron on a nail behind the kitchen door and checked them several times during the afternoon. Imagine my surprise when I put my hand in my pocket to find the little corpses beginning to move. They seemed plumper and softer since I'd last looked at them, half an hour earlier. Although we were familiar with the dunnart, those courageous little pouched mice that stopped the tractors at night as they reared up in the headlights to defend their nests, these little creatures were different.

They started becoming quite lively. We found a wooden box which had once held welding rods, put them inside with some straw, then covered the box with a heavy piece of plate glass from the side window of an old utility. Soon they were leaping from end to end with such energy that I put a brick on top, just in case.

Later that evening, a young neighbour, Allan, came over for an after-tea chat. He was so fascinated with the little strangers that he offered to leave for the city a day earlier than usual to take them to the museum for identification. He arrived at daylight next morning to collect them and carried them off, having tied the glass firmly to the box with rope.

When he returned from the weekend in the city, he told us the little creatures had been identified as pygmy possums. However, there was only one in the box when it was opened at the museum.

We were naturally disappointed and mystified.

Presently, we received a letter from the curator of the museum:

'We were delighted to receive the live female pygmy possum from you and regret that its mate must have escaped in transit. This little animal is also known as the dormouse possum and has a fairly wide range in Western Australia. But most of the specimens we receive are caught by cats. They are seldom seen, as they are nocturnal and feed on a mixed diet of insects and nectar when they emerge from their retreats at night. Your little specimen is being kept alive for study and when it ultimately dies, it will be preserved in the spirit collection.'

Then followed details for feeding them in captivity should we find the escapee. The writer also mentioned that, should it be a male, the museum would be delighted to have it.

About a week later, I was searching in the ragbag behind the kitchen door for a piece of soft cloth, when I felt something cold at the bottom of the bag. Expecting it to be something like a half-eaten apple or even a snake, I was surprised when it turned out to be the cold crumpled form of a pygmy possum. After holding it for a while, I gently put it back in the ragbag, deep in thought. Then it dawned on me that this could be the explanation for the disturbed nights we'd suffered ever since the box had gone to Perth. Every night, as soon as we put out the light, there'd be a miniature commotion as something came flying in through the glass louvres at the head of our bed and over the top of us, heading to the kitchen ... and then out again. It was repeated many times during the night and often we would get up to investigate, even setting mouse traps, but never setting eyes on the culprit. We'd even failed to connect the sudden appearance of a large number of insect wings on the windowsills and the tracks in the sugar bowl with the missing possum.

This one turned out to be a pouched female, too, but we had no worries deciding what to do with it. The wide-eyed little beauty managed its own diet at night and spent the days dozing in the ragbag behind the kitchen door.

One day, our little friend was gone. As I walked to our primitive 'one holer' with a torch that night, there they were—pygmy possums galore, leaping in the gimlet branches like shooting stars, to and fro in the torchlight, high above my head.

Things that go 'Bump!' in the night ... Mrs HJ Cox of Malanda, Queensland reminisced about her grandfather.

Grubby Little Buggers

My grandfather, who lived around Murwillumbah in New South Wales, was sick and tired of flying foxes eating his peaches, especially at night. He decided to install a light in the peach trees to scare them off. Once the light was up, he went to bed expecting a good night's sleep. However, he was wakened by an even noisier racket than usual coming from the peach trees. He quickly jumped out of bed and ran outside to see what was causing such a commotion. He couldn't believe his eyes.

'The flaming flying foxes were fighting over the light to see if there were any grubs in the peaches before eating them!'

Strictly speaking, this next couple of yarns might have been better placed back in the last chapter, along with the rest of the more conventional livestock. But I suppose camels, like the one Merle Lumis of Orange, NSW told us about, are among the more unusual subjects of animal stories.

Shipwreck of the Desert

My sister Margaret lives in an outback town in Queensland. She's the devoted owner of a young camel. At first she kept it in the backyard, but it eventually needed more space and was transferred to a property about 20 kilometres away. One day a friend reported that he'd noticed the camel with some fencing wire caught around one of its legs. He said it looked fairly distressed, so Margaret

and her husband, Jack, drove out in their four-wheel drive truck to investigate.

They found the camel without difficulty. Margaret put a rope around its neck to hold it while they tried to untangle the fencing wire. Jack and the camel had never enjoyed a particularly close relationship, so when he tried to help, it bit him under the arm. It also took off, wire and all, across the paddock, dragging Margaret with it. Weighing all of 40 kilos, she'd never moved so fast. Jack suggested she let go, which she did and ended in a heap on the ground. They jumped into the truck and took off after the camel, with Margaret hanging out the door swinging a noosed rope. She actually managed to lasso it. Jack stopped the truck and tied the rope to the rear bumper. The camel immediately sat down and refused to get up again. Prodding, poking, cajoling and one or two firmer suggestions didn't work, so they jumped back into the truck and drove very slowly towards a pole in the ground some distance away, dragging the still-squatting camel behind them. They tethered the beast to the pole, but it maintained its policy of non-cooperation.

Margaret and Jack decided to drive back to town and fetch some food and water. Perhaps, after a little refreshment, the camel would improve its mood.

By the time they returned to the property with some feed, a large empty drum and some disused gas cylinders full of water, the camel had managed to further entangle himself in the rope around the pole. When Jack tried again to free it, he was bitten on the top of his head.

After some comments about the camel's ancestry and habits, Jack began to fill the drum with water. Unfortunately, just as he was finishing, he dropped the cylinder onto the drum and all the water ran away. There was nothing else they could do but return to town, get Jack's wounds treated and go back out to the property with another drum and some more water.

This time, it worked and the camel was finally released from the fencing wire. Although that all happened a year ago, since then I haven't been game to ask Margaret and Jack how the camel's getting on.

Our other camel yarn, from Bill Crane of Wauchope, NSW, may well help solve one of the world's great mysteries.

The Laurieton Monster

When I was a lad, there were lots of stories going around about the famous monster in Scotland's Loch Ness. From what I recall, it was supposed to have a long neck and a hump or two along its back. The funny thing is there doesn't seem to have been any sightings of Nessie recently—and I think I've solved the mystery.

Years ago, there was a golf course along the bank of Loch Ness. It was eventually abandoned because of the cost of maintaining it. The funny thing is its closure seemed to coincide with the decision by Nessie to retire from public view. My personal view is that some canny Scot had found a spot in the loch where there were plenty of lost golf balls and chose those misty, dark nights to do a bit of secret diving to collect them. A naked Scotsman wallowing and snorting in the water on a dark night would deter anybody.

Or else there's my other theory ... In the early twenties, there were quite a few circuses travelling throughout the Australian countryside. Some even had their own trains. One such circus came to Kendall on the New South Wales mid-north coast. I can just remember being taken to see the animals in their cages in the railyard. Apparently some mystery ailment had broken out among them and they were put under quarantine for safety's sake. The circus camels, however, seemed healthy enough and showed no sign of illness. Their keeper was given permission to take them to the sandhills at Laurieton beach to break their monotony, and they became quite happy.

One night, two fishermen arrived at the beach, unaware that the camels were there. As was common practice among beach fishermen, they split up and went in different directions, looking for a good fishing spot. Imagine the shock handed out to one of them wandering along the beach, when he came across not one, but several monsters, uncannily like the famous Loch Ness monster.

On being disturbed, the camels rose and snorted—pretty frightening indeed. Panic and fear lends wings to one's feet and that fishermen fled back to his mate, speechless, out of breath and wild-eyed. His mate shared his jitters, but agreed to return with him to further investigate the monsters.

On being disturbed again, the camels became even more indignant and protested even more loudly. Imaginations ran riot. Nessie had indeed arrived at Laurieton. Abandoning their gear, the fishermen fled to the local police station, where the copper on duty, who knew them as sober citizens, realised something was seriously amiss. When he returned with them to confront the monsters, he made sure he had a firm grip on his powerful torch—and a .303 rifle.

The rest of the story's left to your imagination ... but it sure went the rounds of the village.

———————————

Min min lights, yowies and bunyips aside, Australia's most tantalising mystery animal captures everyone's imagination because, until recently, it definitely *did* exist. It also stands as a reminder of how precious our wildlife—in fact, our whole environment—really is and how easily we can muck it up. So the question remains—in the depths of the bush somewhere, does the thylacine (or Tasmanian tiger) still exist? Vilia Flemming of Harvey, WA, thinks it does.

A Tall Story
(Which just happens to be true)

January 1970 is etched in my memory as if it were yesterday. One morning, as was the norm, I went down the back to feed the geese and chooks, only to discover there'd been wholesale slaughter. Everything lay there minus their heads. The only ones left alive seemed to be some of the geese, and they'd flown the coop. The coop in question was surrounded by a high wire fence supported by saplings. At first, I blamed the carnage on a fox.

A couple of days later, just on dusk, I was watering the garden. The geese started making a heck of a racket. Quickly, I turned off the tap and walked down the back towards the pen. I found our kelpie bitch had 'the fox' bailed up in a tea-tree thicket which grew at the back of the pen and along a drain bank. I could hear a furious battle going on. I followed the noise past the pen and into a grove of fruit trees.

When I stopped, an animal suddenly burst out of the undergrowth and ran straight towards me ... followed by the erstwhile Jessie. The strange animal looked up at me, circled my feet and trotted off back the way it had come. I realised I'd never seen anything like it before. It was about the same size as the kelpie, light beige, with white stripes and pointed, pricked ears. It had dark, dark eyes. As it slipped under the fence along the drain bank, it turned, and there was the marsupial tail, thick at the base and tapering to a point.

I'd had an encounter with a Tasmanian tiger. I could have pounced on it and become a celebrity!

When I told my two sons, who'd been away, conveniently, in Perth, they laughed and said, 'Mum's seen a mangy fox.'

Ah, but I know differently, don't I?

Years ago, a dodgy-looking photograph started appearing in many publications, claiming to be a shot of a Tasmanian tiger taken near Ozenkadnook in western Victoria. Somewhere I still have an original print, which isn't surprising, because a crafty old mate actually set the shot up. The thing is, that hoax picture has been published without question by literally scores of books and magazines dabbling in the (shudder!) Unknown. But you can't blame a bloke for trying. Andrea Stevenson's yarn comes from that same tradition.

Stripes

Some people expect you to believe anything. Some of them are politicians. Most of them are men. But none beat the time Matt Garret brought his Tasmanian tiger round to Auntie Win's place. He walked straight in with this pale sort of dog on a lead. Auntie Win looked up and yelled, 'Matthew, what are you doing with that dog in my house?'

By then, Matt and the dog were on the lounge-room carpet. Auntie Win and I stopped to have a good look. It seemed to be a kind of kelpie—except it had stripes.

Matt looked at us with a grin from ear to ear. 'Winifred,' he said to auntie. 'This beast is going to make my fame and fortune. How'd yer like some shares in her?'

Auntie Win looked thoughtful, so Matt developed his theme. 'I've got a bloke from the telly coming round tomorrow,' he said. 'They're rushing over to get footage of the first-known cross between a Tasmanian tiger and a dog.'

I choked on my cuppa. Matt looked pleased that he'd impressed me. 'Ladies,' he said grandly, 'this is a great moment in your life. As you look on this here dog, you're seeing history in the making.'

What I thought I was seeing was a dozen or so fleas being scratched onto Auntie Win's bone carpet. Auntie Win wasn't looking. She was putting her mind to Matt's concept.

'What are you going to call it? A Tasmanian dog? You'll need something catchy.'

I thought the fleas looked pretty catchy myself, but Matt accepted it as a good question.

'I did think of the "tog",' he said. 'But I wanted something grander. So now it's a toss up between "tasma-dog" or "hound-iger"—unless you can think of something good.'

'You could call it "Spot",' I suggested. For some reason, he seemed to think I wasn't taking it too seriously.

'Are you questioning the integrity of that there dog?'

'You bet!'

The dog looked a bit worried at the tone of our voices, so I gave her a rub on the tummy. She rolled onto her back, waving

her paws in the air and looking much happier. But Matt didn't look happy at all.

'No offence,' I assured him. 'I like your idea and I like the dog. But I've got a few problems believing you.'

'Name them,' he challenged. 'You tell me what they are, me girl, and I'll put you straight.'

'Glad to,' I said, sitting up. 'Problem number one: a cross between a marsupial and a dog isn't biologically possible.'

Matt didn't bat an eyelid. He just pointed at the dog. 'Wrong! Here you have the living proof.'

He'd handled that pretty well, so I didn't argue the point. 'Problem number two: the last Tasmanian tiger died about 60 years ago. This dog doesn't look more than five.'

Matt nodded gravely and leaned towards me. 'Just between the two of us—and *you*, Win, too—a mate of mine in Launceston's got a couple of Tassie tigers hidden in his garage. We're keeping it quiet, but. Don't want no bloody zookeepers coming round.' He straightened up again. 'Well, are you convinced, now?'

I sighed. 'Matt, I've still got another problem—and it's a bit of a clincher.'

'You're nothing but a bloody doubter. Just you tell me what's worrying you about this here tasma—dog of mine and I'll put it right.'

'Someone's going to have to put it right,' I agreed. 'It's like this, Matt—at this very moment, your tasma-dog's stripes are rubbing off all over Auntie Win's bone carpet.'

'Matt!' yelled Auntie Win. 'Get that dog out of here!'

What Matt said doesn't bear repeating. But I've since heard he's been feeding vitamin pills to the neighbour's pet emu—so I guess the moa's next on his revival list.